D0217606

SUFFRAGE AT 100

SUFFRAGE AT 100

Women in American Politics since 1920

EDITED BY
STACIE TARANTO AND
LEANDRA ZARNOW

Johns Hopkins University Press
Baltimore

© 2020 Johns Hopkins University Press
All rights reserved. Published 2020
Printed in the United States of America on acid-free paper
9 8 7 6 5 4 3 2

Johns Hopkins University Press
2715 North Charles Street
Baltimore, Maryland 21218-4363
www.press.jhu.edu

Library of Congress Cataloging-in-Publication Data

Names: Taranto, Stacie, editor. | Zarnow, Leandra Ruth, 1979– editor.
Title: Suffrage at 100 : women in American politics since 1920 / edited by Stacie Taranto
    and Leandra Zarnow.
Description: Baltimore, Maryland : Johns Hopkins University Press, 2020. |
    Includes bibliographical references and index.
Identifiers: LCCN 2019055938 | ISBN 9781421438689 (paperback) |
    ISBN 9781421438696 (ebook)
Subjects: LCSH: Women—Political activity—United States—History. |
    Women—Suffrage—United States—History. | Women politicians—United
    States. | Women political activists—United States. | United States—Politics and
    government.
Classification: LCC HQ1236.5.U6 S83 2020 | DDC 320.082/0973—dc23
LC record available at https://lccn.loc.gov/2019055938

A catalog record for this book is available from the British Library.

*Special discounts are available for bulk purchases of this book. For more information,
please contact Special Sales at specialsales@press.jhu.edu.*

Johns Hopkins University Press uses environmentally friendly book materials, including
recycled text paper that is composed of at least 30 percent post-consumer waste, whenever
possible.

To the goal of women's full representation and equality—in every sense—in American politics, and to the women continuing this fight

CONTENTS

· PART III ·

LOOKING TOWARD A NEW CENTURY
Women in Politics, 1990s–2010s

SUFFRAGE AT 100

From Voting Power to Political Power

STACIE TARANTO *and* LEANDRA ZARNOW

"INTEND TO take the cause of women—America's oppressed major-ity—to the halls of Congress." Antiwar grassroots organizer Bella Abzug delivered this promise in 1970 as a Democratic congressional candidate from New York City. Abzug had spent much of the last de-cade "chasing down the halls and buttonholing Congressmen" as a lob-byist for Women Strike for Peace.[1] No more. As her campaign slogan made clear, "A Woman's Place Is in the House—the House of Repre-sentatives." Embodying the progressive wing of the Democratic Party, she declared that women must fight "against the discrimination that condemns most working women to low-paying jobs, gives women wel-fare instead of income, keeps them out of the professions, denies them day care facilities and mis-educates their children, gives third-rate health care to Black, Puerto Rican and poor women, and forces them to risk their lives by submitting to illegal abortions." These issues, Abzug con-tended, had to be addressed but would gain little ground politically if women did not move past the ballot to substantial representation in government. The change would only come if women, sanctioned to the "back room where the telephones and typewriters and the file cards are located," got "out front." Now, she encouraged, we need to "share in the political power that [we] create."[2]

Halfway across the country in southern Illinois, Phyllis Schlafly—a longtime conservative Republican activist who would become the face of antifeminism in the coming years—was also mounting a bid for the US House of Representatives in 1970. She too emphasized the need for more women in politics. But rather than link that desire to liberal and increasingly feminist policy proposals, as Abzug did, Schlafly argued that greater female political representation could boost conservative Republican priorities, such as reducing federal social spending and expanding defense. As the economy strained from global market shocks and domestic deindustrialization, Schlafly declared, "Women do the family spending. They are more careful with other people's money and better at getting a dollar's value for every dollar spent."[3]

At a time when the two major parties were gravitating away from the center and becoming more polarized, female activists on both the grassroots Left and Right tried to justify women's place in the overwhelmingly male political world by leaning into that growing partisan divide—claiming new space for women in the process. In a few years, Abzug and Schlafly would be squaring off against each other to debate the proposed Equal Rights Amendment to the US Constitution and the merits of feminism more broadly. Yet they agreed in one respect: politics had long been a male pursuit sorely in need of more women, particularly those who shared their respective policy priorities.

It is telling that both Abzug and Schlafly made women's limited representation in public office part of their congressional campaigns in 1970—the year that marked the fiftieth anniversary of women's suffrage. The issue of gender parity in politics remains unresolved as we mark the one hundred–year anniversary in 2020. Women have remained outsiders in American politics and American political history since achieving the constitutional right to vote with the ratification of the Nineteenth Amendment in 1920. Looking at the US Congress, the increase in women elected in most campaign cycles since women got the vote has been one or two percentage points, and before 1981, the total number of women serving in Congress in any given session never extended beyond twenty.[4] While Schlafly did not win her House bid in 1970, Abzug did as one of fifteen women in Congress. This bipartisan cohort tried to break through the "old boys' club" on Capitol Hill but found the resistance to their structural challenge palpable. Congresswomen experienced difficulty convincing male legislators to take their expertise seriously in areas not related to women and children. Congresswomen's internal reform and policy proposals were buoyed by a mass feminist movement that ushered forth new legal rights for women in the late 1960s and early 1970s. Yet, feminist organizing focused on the political arena did not ultimately translate into equal female representation in politics at any level.

Women made the most progress in Congress in 1992. Dubbed the Year of the Woman, their numbers went from thirty-two to fifty-four women across both chambers, an increase of four percentage points. That cycle, women translated their outrage into electoral gains in response to the way the all-male Senate Judiciary Committee handled law professor Anita Hill's sexual harassment claims against Clarence Thomas during his Supreme Court nomination hearings in 1991. The midterms that followed in 1992 ushered the first woman of color into the US Senate, when Democrat Carol Moseley Braun of Illinois was elected. Before 1992, only eleven women of color had served in the House of Representatives, and since, five have served in the Senate and sixty-two in the House.[5]

Similarly, women candidates in 2018 built on Secretary of State Hillary Rodham Clinton's narrow loss to Donald J. Trump in 2016—the closest a woman had ever come to the presidency up to that point—and the momentum generated from the Women's March in 2017 and the #BlackLivesMatter and #MeToo movements. Translating grassroots mobilization into electoral action, women organized voting drives, fundraised and trained candidates, and ran for offices from the local school board to the US Senate. This outpouring of political engagement was unprecedented and achieved historic results during the 2018 midterms. American voters elected the largest, in absolute numbers, and most diverse, by every metric, group of women to Congress; the total number of congresswomen grew from 110 to 127, or from 20.5 to 23.7 percent. While for much of the 1970s the Senate remained all men, this threshold shifted by the twenty-first century to include ten women senators in 2000. By 2019, women comprised a quarter of the United States' most powerful legislative body. This is a huge accomplishment. Still, it is sobering to consider that nearly half of all women who have won a seat in Congress have been elected in the years since 1998. And it appears unlikely that women will achieve 50–50 parity in Congress in 2020, which was a founding goal set forth by the feminist-led National Women's Political Caucus in 1971.[6]

Looking at these congressional markers helps gauge the gendered imbalance of power in the United States, but the story of women in politics since 1920 should not be limited to the arena of federal lawmaking or winnowed down to a numbers game. This collection challenges those tendencies and encourages historians to widen their definition and expectations of women in politics at this centennial moment. It may come as a surprise that no full history of women in politics since suffrage has been written, but this absence reflects how narrow the definition of politics continues to be. Indeed, historians, like many Americans, continue to assess political power and time through a gendered lens. The central focus of political history remains the presidency. Political worth is measured by electoral wins and losses, and political time undulates at the pace of campaign cycles. By these standards, women, who have only in recent decades hit greater strides in winning federal office and have not inhabited the Oval Office, are seen as minor players in political history.[7]

Political historians have largely treated women's limited presence in electoral office as a sign of disinterest or disqualification. We know this is not the case. We, the editors of this collection, met over a decade ago in the Special Collections library of Columbia University, where we looked at the papers of Representative Bella Abzug—a collection of more than one thousand boxes that documents very clearly the range of women's political interests. We came to this collection from different angles, considering intersectional feminist politicking and the backlash that it engendered on the Right. We found ideologically opposed women, working in their communities and inside the halls of Congress, traversing the same informal and formal political spaces. Some engaged in organizing in the name of family, home, and country, and others described their work as achieving justice, liberation, and equality. All intentionally sought to augment their political citizenship past voting power to its next level: the pursuit of political power.

Women's presence in politics is everywhere if one looks closely. This collection does not offer a comprehensive mapping of women's political action but, rather, illuminates a few points on a wide constellation that we hope will be connected as more research is completed. Archives should be built, more oral histories conducted, and data need to be mined to bring women's "back room" and "out front" political labor as organizers, canvassers, delegates, analysts, lobbyists, campaigners, aides, appointees, and office holders into the historical record. Women have been the backbone of political movements and campaigns before and since the ratification of the Nineteenth Amendment. Bringing women's individual and collective work into view, expanding the place of politics to include "kitchens, hallways, and living rooms," and analyzing how women approach political leadership distinctly is necessary historical work.[8] The result will present unquestionable evidence that women's sustained, diverse political engagement warrants more than its current sporadic, tokenistic, and peripheral attention. At the same time, this scholarship will reveal the endemic difficulties women have faced when attempting to participate as leading actors in US democracy, for the nation was founded as and continues to be a patriarchal state.

The collection begins by making this case. The immediate verdict delivered after a united women's voting bloc did not form in 1921 was that suffrage was a failure, and women lacked the capacity to be serious political actors. In chapter 1, we complicate this simplistic narrative with a synthetic overview of women in American politics that spans the final stage of the suffrage struggle through the century that followed the ratification of the Nineteenth Amendment. We show that women's diverse political interests made universalist goals untenable, discriminatory practices thwarted all women from voting, and men who supported women's enfranchisement did not equally accept them as political counterparts. This wide and long overview provides the foundation for the twenty essays in this collection that follow, each one complementing and at times purposefully complicating our overview. We have selected these accompanying essays to offer a snapshot of scholarship underway featuring lesser-known political activists, organizations, issues, regions, events, and ideas. In the case of women and the rise of the New Right, for example, in chapter 15 contributor Bianca Rowlett discusses Ambassador to the United Nations Jeane J. Kirkpatrick, who served on the National Security Council under President Ronald Reagan. Rather than focus on abortion or the Equal Rights Amendment, Rowlett instead discusses the intersection of conservative politics, feminism, and foreign policy. Drawing attention to queer history before World War II, in chapter 6 Dean Kotlowski explores the political leadership of lesbian Mary Elizabeth Switzer. And responding to the transnational turn in history, Judy Tzu-Chun Wu in chapter 13 considers Representative Patsy Takemoto Mink's articulation of Pacific feminism. Taken as a whole, these essays weave together a vibrant tapestry depicting women's broad political engagement, but they also leave loose threads for historians to shape with future scholarship.

This expansive collection is divided into three sections, with Part I, entitled "Voting Rights Real and Imagined: Women's Political Engagement in the Decades after Suffrage, 1920s–1950s," examining the impact of the Nineteenth Amendment from the 1920s to midcentury. Essays in this section by authors Melissa Estes Blair, Claire Delahaye, Liette Gidlow, Holly Miowak Guise, Dean Kotlowski, Johanna Neuman, Katherine Parkin, and Nancy Beck Young assess the amendment as both a rallying point and symbol, as well as a measure that had the potential to open up new political and policy opportunities for women. Opening this section with a chapter looking at former white suffragists' efforts to commemorate the century-long struggle that led to the vote draws focus on women's public history. This preservation work—forming a suffrage imaginary—is juxtaposed with the realities facing diverse women as new voters. Women may have gained the right to vote, but the face of political power was still white and male. This meant that white women often had to align with men in office or position their politics in familial and gendered terms if they wanted to participate politically beyond the ballot box. Indeed, in this period, being a widow of a man who had held office was the surest path for women to be elected.

Women used their vote to achieve greater political clout, especially as political parties became increasingly preoccupied with attracting women as "swing voters." Much of women's political influence, however, remained indirect as letter writers, lobbyists, and campaign volunteers, in supportive roles as political aides, or in government agency positions pertaining to "women's issues." Women of color participated in politics extensively during these years, but had narrow access to the ballot box. This section highlights African American women's immediate, organized challenge to disenfranchisement under Jim Crow and reminds us that the Nineteenth Amendment was largely a win for white women until the Voting Rights Act of 1965. Indigenous women similarly exercised considerable democratic imagination to advocate for rights, as they challenged the very underpinnings of the United States as a colonial state.

Part II of the collection, "Women's Political Leadership Takes Shape: Reform and Reaction, 1960s–1980s," highlights the groundswell of women's political activity that occurred in these three decades as women engaged in liberation, ethnic nationalist, civil rights, environmental, consumer, antipoverty, antiwar, and education-centered movements. As a mass feminist movement coalesced in the late 1960s, so too did a conservative women's movement set on maintaining traditional values, with both groups effectively engaging the political arena. Essays by Kathleen Banks Nutter, Bianca Rowlett, Sarah B. Rowley, Ana Stevenson, Judy Tzu-Chun Wu, and Barbara Winslow illustrate that even as new doors opened for women across the ideological spectrum, male-centered political institutions and patronage systems remained durable. Together, the articles demonstrate how women politicians won office by capitalizing on diminishing public confidence in male leaders during the Vietnam War and after the Watergate scandal. Feminists maximized their political clout at the grassroots and in Congress to achieve landmark legal gains for women. Yet women of color and queer women still faced the steepest political barriers, for the American leadership ideal remained white, male, and heterosexual. As conservative Republicans gained power, an achievement marked by the election of President Ronald Reagan in 1980, white women within the party carved out new political opportunities for themselves. Four of these essays use biography to trace individual approaches to women's political leadership, focusing attention on Louise Day Hicks, Shirley Chisholm, Patsy Takemoto Mink, and Jeane J. Kirkpatrick. This grouping begs the question: Are there distinct features of women's approach to politics despite differences based on race, class, and partisan ideology? Likewise, as more women enter politics, what should we make of "political husbands," and how does the masculine political ideal change as a result? Finally, continuing with the theme of public history, this section explores the evolution and importance of feminist political reporting and the political project of women's history during this period.

Finally, Part III of the collection, "Looking Toward a New Century: Women in Politics, 1990s–2010s," evaluates the place of women in politics in the twenty-first century. This section—featuring the work of Eileen Boris, Marisela R. Chávez, Nicole Eaton, Emily Suzanne Johnson, Monica L. Mercado, and Ellen Rafshoon—offers essays that are among the first to historically contextualize the consequential 2008, 2016, and 2018 elections. Focusing on grassroots engagement alongside the quest to shatter the highest political glass ceiling that has barred women from the Oval Office, these articles define distinct features of women's political leadership and intersectional feminist engagement in electoral politics. Some of these essays draw on recently completed oral histories and freshly available records, while others make the case for why scholarship on women's political engagement remains underdeveloped. Together, they demonstrate how much recovery work is needed before we can fully see and understand the diverse political traditions out of which activist-politicians such as Alexandria Ocasio-Cortez or Stacey Abrams come. Returning at the close to the theme of commemoration, this section considers how American women have attached diverse meanings to the centennial of women's suffrage, while using this occasion to newly demand greater political representation and power. All told, the essays in this collection demonstrate that the march continues along the uneven road toward full equality for women in American politics.

Notes

1. "A Message to the Second Congress to Unite Women from Bella Abzug, Candidate for Congress, 19th C.D.," undated, Administrative Files–Campaign–1970–General, box 64, Bella Abzug Papers, Rare Book and Manuscript Library, Columbia University.

2. "A Message," Bella Abzug Papers.

3. Donald T. Critchlow, *Phyllis Schlafly and Grassroots Conservatism: A Woman's Crusade* (Princeton, NJ: Princeton University Press, 2005), 199.

4. "History of Women in the U.S. Congress," Center for American Women and Politics, Rutgers University, 2019, https://www.cawp.rutgers.edu/history-women-us-congress.

5. "The Year of the Woman, 1992," History, Art & Archives, US House of Representatives, accessed May 15, 2019, https://history.house.gov/Exhibitions-and-Publications/WIC/Historical-Essays/Assembling-Amplifying-Ascending/Women-Decade/; "History of Women of Color in U.S. Politics," Center for American Women and Politics, Rutgers University, 2019, https://www.cawp.rutgers.edu/history-women-color-us-politics.

6. "Program of Goals and Action," with notation, undated, Personal–NWPC–Background Information," box 990, BSA. See also "History of Women in the U.S. Congress" and Congressional Research Service, *Women in Congress: Statistics and Brief Overview*, updated April 9, 2019, https://www.everycrsreport.com/reports/R43244.html#_Toc5717364.

7. This trend is shifting, with Meg Jacobs and Julian E. Zelizer leading the call for a more expansive "new political history" that extends the theater of politics and influential political figures. Meg Jacobs and Julian E. Zelizer, "The Democratic Experiment: New Directions in American Political History," in *The Democratic Experiment: New Directions in American Political History*, ed. Meg Jacobs, William J. Novak, and Julian E. Zelizer (Princeton, NJ: Princeton University Press, 2003), 1–19, 2. Political scientists have more fully explored women in politics than political historians. Recent historical works include Catherine E. Rymph, *Republican Women: Feminism and Conservatism from Suffrage through the Rise of the New Right* (Chapel Hill: University of North Carolina Press, 2006); Jane M. Martin, *The Presidency and Women: Promise, Performance, and Illusion* (College Station: Texas A&M University Press, 2003); and Ellen Fitzpatrick, *The Highest Glass Ceiling: Women's Quest for the American Presidency* (Cambridge, MA: Harvard University Press, 2016).

8. Instructive here is Dionne Espinoza, María Eugenia Cotera, and Maylei Blackwell's notion of alternatively "mapping *movidas*" of Chicanas' political engagement, "Introduction," in *Chicana Movidas: New Narratives of Activism and Feminism in the Movement Era*, ed. Espinoza, Cotera, and Blackwell (Austin: University of Texas Press, 2018), 1–30, 11.

A year after the Anita Hill–Clarence Thomas Supreme Court nomination hearings, Senator Barbara Mikulski (D-MD) stands with women senatorial candidates at the 1992 Democratic National Convention. Remembered as the "year of the woman," this election cycle brought the largest increase in the percentage of women in Congress since 1920. Photography by Laura Patterson; photo courtesy of the Library of Congress.

Congresswoman Patsy Takemoto Mink (D-HI, *back row, fourth from left*) and the women of the Eighty-Ninth US Congress in 1965. Mink was sworn into office that year on the precipice of modern feminist movements, at a time when widows and other female placeholders still composed a majority of women in Congress. Photograph courtesy of the National Archives and Records Administration.

CHAPTER 1

A History of Women in American Politics and the Enduring Male Political Citizenship Ideal

STACIE TARANTO *and* LEANDRA ZARNOW

IN MARCH 1965, Representative Patsy Takemoto Mink—a third-generation Japanese-American woman from Hawaii, and the first woman of color elected to the US House of Representatives—sat down with Jack Anderson of *Parade* magazine to discuss the state of women in politics. Mink had arrived on Capitol Hill two months earlier, at a time when only twelve women served in Congress, making up just 2 percent of both chambers, and women only held 3 percent of the top federal jobs. Mink underscored the need for more qualified women to join her in Washington. "It is folly," she asserted, "to exclude a brilliant woman from the top policy-making councils simply because she is a woman and men are accustomed to running the show." Mink spoke of women's responsibility to participate as political decision makers just as she highlighted the cultural and systemic barriers they faced to gain office and high-level appointments. Her intersectional approach to women's rights embodied the mass feminist movement coming to form. Casting her vote for the Voting Rights Act of 1965, she helped deliver a lasting blow to the Jim Crow system of legal segregation and political disenfranchisement. Still, after calling out men for "running the show," she argued that it was "for the sake of the home that women should play a more active role in politics and go after top government jobs."[1] In other words, more women should join her at the seat of American political power because their different perspective as mothers was needed to make politics more responsive to family needs.

Mink's appeal highlights the main predicament women have faced since they received the constitutional right to vote. The underlying assumption that historically barred women from voting—the notion that they belong in the home—persisted after women's suffrage was enshrined in the Constitution in 1920. The majority of Americans still believed that men's temperament and skill made them better suited and more inclined to serve in government than women. How then could women interested in entering the political arena overcome this cultural viewpoint and assuage male public officials' fears about being replaced? While some women called for equal rights alone, many political women espoused a commitment to family, children, and community as a means to achieve fuller integration into electoral politics. Yet this maternalist approach, or arguing for women's equal representation in politics because of women's difference, is tricky. On one hand, women have directed more attention toward family care, women's health, and intimacy, gradually shifting what topics are debated and valued as political issues. On the other hand, women have had difficulty breaking into male-dominated political spaces, in part, because these "women's issues" are coded as separate from "real" (male) politics. The gendering of political issues must therefore be considered alongside women's inability to achieve gender parity in politics.

In this overview essay, as well as those that follow, we explore this great dilemma that American women have faced since the ratification of the Nineteenth Amendment in 1920. Drawing attention rhetorically and tangibly to women's difference because of motherhood has proven to be the surest way for women, especially those who are white, to enter traditionally male political channels of influence. Yet, when looking at suffrage at one hundred, it is important to ask: What have been the benefits and costs of this long-used tactic?

After women gained the constitutional right to vote, much like before, they continued to use their moral authority as mothers to seek political influence and frame their policy demands. Historian Paula Baker has traced this "domestication of politics" back to the nineteenth century. Women's political actions conducted in the name of motherhood, Baker has shown, were persuasive because they "did not violate the canons of domesticity to which many men and women held," but instead left them largely intact.[2] After 1920, women, heterosexual and queer alike, found it beneficial to reference their special qualities as mothers to gain access to the political arena. Whether a woman was actually a mother did not matter; by virtue of being a woman, she possessed maternal qualities.

As whiteness and wealth were measures of ideal womanhood and motherhood, it was more difficult for women of color and poorer women to be recognized as mothers in politics, let alone to be able to vote though they tried. Women of color who referenced motherhood did so at considerable risk in order to seek recognition in this role and call for greater civil rights and social betterment. Historian Eileen Boris observed, for example, black suffragists "demand[ed] voting on the basis of their *work* as—rather than their mere being—mothers." This "maintenance of difference as distinction within the search for equal rights before the law and in social practice" continued as women of color challenged disenfranchisement through the time Representative Mink gained office.[3]

For most of the twentieth century, women who ran for office without using a mantle of widowhood, motherhood, or political family connections were exceptional. In the immediate decades after 1920, the ideal political citizen largely remained one who was white, male, heterosexual, and economically secure enough to support his wife and children on a single income. As a result, maternalist campaigns gained more traction than asking outright for equal rights for the female sex.[4] Presidents in the twentieth and early twenty-first centuries catered to this form of political citizenship, highlighting, for instance, the need to protect the "forgotten man" and a male "silent majority."[5] Women of color, queer women, and poorer women have been persistently reminded that their position in society is the farthest from this ideal. As this collection makes clear, these women have consistently advocated for voting rights and engaged in the political arena despite disenfranchisement and limited political representation. To see this range of activism, it is essential to define politics broadly to encompass grassroots, issue-based activism. It is also important to acknowledge that there is a shifting scale of opportunity in politics based on ideology, location, class, race, ethnicity, and sexuality. Indeed, because of voter intimidation and racist, classist voter registration restrictions, such as poll taxes, residency requirements, and literacy tests, access to the ballot box has been extremely unequal among women since 1920, as has the opportunity to run for elected office. For at least the first fifty years after winning suffrage, the "woman's vote" was mostly an affluent, white women's vote, and even these privileged voters faced difficulty being recognized as capable or preferable political actors and elected leaders.

Suffrage activists, chiefly women, had worked for nearly seventy-five years to win the vote, and the next one hundred years continued to be a "century of struggle," in which they learned that their political citizenship was qualified.[6] For this reason, women have used a range of strategies at their disposal, including using motherhood as an entry point into the political arena. How women tried to make the leap from the backroom of politics into the halls of power is an important story to tell. Women may no longer be complete outsiders in US politics, but in many ways, the original white, male, heterosexual, breadwinner political ideal was never fully uprooted. While the culture of politics is changing in the early twenty-first century, the preference for the imagined male political leader in the United States stubbornly persists in the American psyche.

The Road to 1920

With politics historically reserved for men, women continuously petitioned for suffrage rights. The first sustained effort occurred in 1848, when roughly three hundred women and thirty men gathered to discuss women's rights in Seneca Falls, New York.[7] The "woman suffrage" plank of the "Declaration of Sentiments" that they signed in Seneca was the only one that drew controversy, reflecting how hard it was to imagine women as part of the political sphere. Suffragists' earliest victories occurred out West, with Wyoming leading the way in 1869. These feats, however, typically featured male politicians using suffrage as a means to achieve goals unrelated to women's rights. Mormon legislators, for example, backed women's suffrage in the Utah territory in 1870 to help dispel the commonly held assertion that their faith, which then sanctioned polygamy, was overly oppressive to women. This concession, while prompted by rights-focused Mormon women, did little to overturn the dominant white male model of political citizenship.[8]

Suffragists faced a quandary that led to the creation of a fictionalized women's voting bloc. As outsiders lacking basic suffrage in most states, let alone political capital, how could women compel male lawmakers to listen to them? One strategy suffragists used was to promise male lawmakers that newly enfranchised women, voting together, could be powerful backers ensuring men's electoral prospects. Of course, men had never voted as a gender bloc, nor had women out West ever done so. Nonetheless, these specious claims—resting on the notion that women would behave differently than typical political actors—gained currency.[9]

Women also linked the goal of suffrage to other policy goals that were tied to the "private sphere" of the home, not the male "public sphere" of politics and economics. By the 1890s, for example, the Woman's Christian Temperance Union—the largest women's political group in that era—argued that women needed suffrage to vote for "home protection" measures, such as outlawing alcohol so that inebriated husbands would not be abusive or drink away family wages. By the early twentieth century, Progressive Era social reformers advocated "civic housekeeping" along similar lines. As social reformer Jane Addams asked in 1910 in *Ladies' Home Journal*, "May we not fairly say the American women need this implement in order to preserve the home?"[10] This maternalist argument was a shrewd tactic for suffragists to deploy since male legislators were accustomed to seeing women strictly through the lens of domesticity and motherhood. These legislators had little incentive to shed this viewpoint after women gained the vote, and continued to expect women to limit their interests as voters and politicians to the concerns of women and children. In other words, women's wedge into the political arena as "civic housekeepers" made it difficult for them to shed their outsider status.[11]

After women secured the constitutional right to vote with the passage of the Nineteenth Amendment in 1920, the anticipated women's voting bloc never materialized in large part because the suffrage movement had always been racially and ideologically diverse. Many suffragists first got their start as early as the 1830s in the abolitionist movement that sought to end slavery, then the nation's most pressing political concern. After the Civil War, however, tensions developed during negotiations over new constitutional protections that would help integrate freed slaves as full participants in US democracy. The suffrage movement divided because the suffrage of African American men was prioritized over women's suffrage. Longtime ally Frederick Douglass, who had attended the Seneca Falls Convention and supported women's suffrage, argued that it was the "Negro's hour." He and others worried that adding "sex" to the proposed Fifteenth Amendment—which prohibited voting discrimination based on race—might sink the amendment altogether, given that political citizenship was clearly gendered male. Though very disappointed, some former abolitionists, led by Lucy Stone, prioritized giving black men the vote before women and formed the American Woman Suffrage Association (AWSA); they tied the pursuit of women's suffrage to a broader agenda of equal rights. Others pushed for universal suffrage, seeing this concession as unacceptable. These advocates, led by Elizabeth Cady Stanton and Susan B. Anthony, created the National Woman Suffrage Association (NWSA) to exclusively focus on women's suffrage. Still others challenged women's suffrage altogether, with antisuffrage clubs forming to defend women's position as moral guardians, an entitlement only open to elite white women like themselves, which they claimed would be sullied by entering the corrupt male world of politics.[12]

NWSA unsuccessfully worked on a variety of fronts to achieve women's suffrage. One campaign, dubbed "the New Departure," deployed radical tactics like leading hundreds of women to the polls to be turned away, an action that was the basis of a Supreme Court case, *Minor v. Happersett*, which failed to achieve women's suffrage in 1874.[13] NWSA leaders tried to expand the group's ranks, but their exclusionary practices reflected the white segregationist and nativist prejudices of their time. Playing to the biases of male legislators was pragmatic, but many white suffragists also shared these views. In an 1868 issue of *The Revolution*, Stanton argued: "Think of Patrick and Sambo and Hans and Yung Tang who do not know the difference between a monarchy and a republic, who never read the Declaration of Independence or Webster's spelling book, making laws for Lydia Maria Child, Lucretia Mott, or Fanny Kemble."[14] It was an injustice, she believed, for less educated new immigrants and men of color to have the vote, while most women, including educated white ones like her, did not. White suffragists made a similar argument in 1898 when the enfranchisement of men in the Philippines was debated after the United States won the territory in the Spanish-American War.[15] Such thinking slowed outreach to female immigrants who arrived from Europe in waves at the turn of the century; eventually, cross-class alliances were formed as women reformers sought to clean up sweatshop conditions where many immigrant women labored.[16]

The suffrage movement remained racially divided through the passage of the Nineteenth Amendment in 1920. NWSA—and its later incarnation after it merged with AWSA in 1890, the National American Woman Suffrage Association (NAWSA)—was dominated by the leadership and goals of white women.[17] Mary Church Terrell implored NAWSA to welcome African American women like her into their ranks in an 1898 speech, concluding: "We knock at the bar of justice, asking an equal chance."[18] But more often, NAWSA leaders were conciliatory to white supremacists, such as Mississippian Belle Kearney, who argued that suffrage should be given to white women to "retain the supremacy of the white race."[19] In the South, Jim Crow rule set in through suppressive legal and violent extralegal tactics during the last decades of the nineteenth century. Black women living there necessarily concentrated on broader "racial uplift" to try to end legal discrimination and, in the meantime, deliver quality education and key services presently being denied to African Americans.[20] Still, suffrage remained a constant concern for black women. Antilynching activist Ida B. Wells, for instance, founded the Alpha Suffrage Club in Chicago in 1913, which had two hundred members in three years' time and was not the only club in town.[21] The National Association of Colored Women established a suffrage department, and in 1914, the Baptist Women's Convention convinced their main church organization to endorse suffrage.

Ultimately, it took updated tactics and positioning the suffrage cause differently—as a wartime measure, campaign for modernity, and national cause—to gain the vote. Suffragists refocused their energy away from state-based campaigns to supporting a national constitutional amendment. They used new technologies, from silent movies to lighted billboards, to spread their message. They also capitalized on America's entry into World War I by completing volunteer defense work while wearing a white suffrage sash. By the 1910s, NAWSA, led by Carrie Chapman Catt and Maud Wood Park, delivered a "winning plan" to put pressure on male lawmakers with continuous letter writing and targeted visits to members of Congress and President Woodrow Wilson. Inspired by the more confrontational, successful approach of British suffragists, NAWSA members Alice Paul and Lucy Stone broke ranks and formed the National Woman's Party (NWP) in 1916. NWP members endured jail time when they took up a White House picket and faced arrest because they did not have a permit to do so. Their calculated stunts, such as reading transcripts of Wilson's speeches outside the White House, visually highlighted how empty Wilson's wartime promises were as he rallied Americans to defend democratic freedoms in Europe's war while American women were denied voting power at home. After the press called imprisoned women "iron-jawed angels" for undergoing hunger strikes and forced feedings in jail, Wilson eventually realized that the only way to stop these embarrassing displays was to back women's suffrage.[22]

Both the NWP's more radical tactics and NAWSA's national lobbying network were needed to move the Nineteenth Amendment over the finish line in August 1920. President Wilson parroted NAWSA's wartime rhetoric by thanking women for their home-front service when he announced his support for suffrage, choosing not to acknowledge NWP members who had overstepped proper gender boundaries and forced his hand. NAWSA's deep organizational structure subsequently ensured that the Nineteenth Amendment would make it through Congress with the necessary two-thirds majority and be ratified by three-fourths of the state legislatures. The amendment process came down to the wire, turning on just one vote in the Tennessee legislature and a mother's prodding of her twenty-four-year-old son, Harry Burn, who served in the chamber.[23] Phoebe Ensminger Burn urged in a letter, "Be a good boy and help Mrs. Catt [of NAWSA]." Knowing better than to cross his mother, Burn voted, "yes."[24] This act enshrined women's legal right to vote in the US Constitution, positioning them—particularly those who were white—to exert their place in electoral politics and government.

The 1920s: Women's Politics Forged during a Red Scare

After the Nineteenth Amendment was ratified, the diverse suffrage community no longer had the unifying goal of suffrage to bind it together and mask the very real ideological, racial, and tactical rifts that divided women. The first chance to test the much-exalted women's voting bloc arrived just months later when Americans went to the polls in November 1920. Predictably, women did not vote uniformly in that cycle or in any since.[25] Ironically, antisuffragists, who had long rallied to defend gender traditionalism, were initially the most successful women in the political arena as voters and government employees. Conservative women gained direct access to the administration of President Warren G. Harding, a Republican who promised a "return to normalcy." A Red Scare that began during World War I continued to dampen the political climate afterward, with former suffragists such as Jane Addams and Carrie Chapman Catt targeted especially. Being called a socialist or a communist became a catchall for limiting dissent, which included former suffragists' continued challenge for full political citizenship. Unsurprisingly, it was difficult for women to make inroads in electoral politics in this environment.

Former suffragists from the NWP directly seeking equal rights and greater inclusion in the male body politic were among the least successful women in this political climate. In 1923, the NWP launched a new campaign advocating for the passage of an Equal Rights Amendment (ERA), which would enshrine legal equality for men and women into the Constitution and make laws gender neutral. The NWP viewed this as the natural next step after suffrage. Conservatives strongly challenged the ERA, but it also met opposition among former suffrage allies. Labor feminists, including those who had worked with NAWSA during the suffrage fight, did not support the ERA until the equal rights era of the 1960s because they wanted to preserve their hard-won workplace protections that applied to women workers only. Within Congress, the ERA also gained little support, where it was not voted on until the early 1970s.

Others from NAWSA turned to voter outreach and education. The nonpartisan League of Women Voters (LWV) was formed in 1920, as the Nineteenth Amendment was being ratified, with the goal of registering women to vote and informing them about a range of issues. The LWV faced an uphill battle convincing women to show up to vote and do so independently of their husbands; it took time to acculturate these new voters in an era of low turnout.[26]

NAWSA's former president, Carrie Chapman Catt, led the LWV and encouraged women to enter party politics because, she reasoned, "It is vain to try to get hold of the steering wheel until you get into the boat."[27] Hundreds of women ran for office throughout the 1920s, with 346 elected as state representatives during the decade. Although no women were elected to a full Senate term in the 1920s, nine were currently serving in the US House of Representatives by decade's end, whereas before 1920, only Representative Jeannette Rankin, who won as a Republican from Montana in 1916, had been elected to Congress. Though their numbers were slowly on the rise, women remained outsiders in electoral politics, with widowhood or familial proximity to a male politician still one of the surest entry points. The vast majority of women who answered Catt's call to enter politics did so by joining sex-segregated divisions of the major and third parties, as part of the Republican Party (the National Federation of Republican Women would be founded in 1938), the newly constituted Democratic Party Women's Division, and the National League of Republican Colored Women. Women also initiated "50/50" campaigns at the state and national level in both major parties to press for equal representation on political committees. Although they achieved this commitment from the parties at the national level and in eighteen states by 1929, these efforts were more symbolic than evidence of true leadership sharing for women.[28] Party men continued to make important decisions in isolation, prompting Democratic organizer Emily Newell Blair, who headed the Women's Division, to recall feeling like "stage furniture and nothing more."[29]

Another faction from the old NAWSA coalition formed the Woman's Joint Congressional Committee (WJCC), which relied on maternalist politics to convince Congress for a short time to fund the nation's first taxpayer-funded social welfare measure. The bill, known as the Sheppard-Towner Maternity and Infancy Care Act of 1921, provided federal matching funds for states to educate women about how to combat America's high maternal and infancy mortality rates, particularly in poorer nonwhite and immigrant communities. The WJCC built on maternalist legislative successes at the state level prior to 1920. Male legislators accustomed to believing that motherhood was women's primary concern fell in line in 1921, lest they be voted out of office by their new female constituents. Opponents, including a sizable number of former antisuffragist women, painted Sheppard-Towner as a waste of taxpayer dollars and a dangerous communist encroachment of big government. Pressure continued to build, with Congress failing to reauthorize the law in 1929. The old white suffrage coalition, and women's electoral politics more broadly, had been muted on all fronts. More broadly, this debate shattered the myth that women would cast aside ideology and vote as a unified gender bloc.[30]

The situation continued to be even worse for nonwhite, working-class, and immigrant women in this era of anticommunist conformity and growing racial violence and xenophobia. Outside of the South, black women organized in party clubs and in municipal politics to make what political inroads they could for their sex and race. In states that enacted "white primaries," African American women continuously attempted to register to vote, cast ballots, and procure much-needed protections and services, but measures were put in place to thwart these efforts and systemically deny their enfranchisement. The Ku Klux Klan, a violent, racially motivated organization first formed to target African Americans in the Reconstruction-era South, reemerged nationwide in the 1920s, adding recent immigrants, particularly Catholics and Jews, to their list of enemies. This occurred as Congress, led by Anglo-Saxon white Protestant males, put in place severe immigration quotas in 1924 that disproportionately targeted new immigrants' countries of origin. These quotas were modeled on prior immigration restrictions, notably the Page Act of 1875, which aimed to stop the immigration of Chinese women to America on the basis that they were not sexually chaste, and the broader Chinese Exclusion Act of 1882. In this constrained environment, women's citizenship continued to be linked to their marriage status. From 1907 to 1934, an American citizen married to an immigrant husband, particularly a man from an "undesirable" country or territory like the Philippines, was required to choose: dissolve her marriage and stay in the United States as a citizen or risk deportation alongside her husband and have her citizenship stripped.[31]

Women who came of age in these "roaring twenties" were not old enough to remember suffragists' battles to gain the vote and took this constitutional right for granted as a result. These "new women," or "flappers," as they called themselves, expressed their citizenship by breaking down former gender barriers through consumption—an act that led them to greater personal freedom but did not challenge the political status quo for women. Like men, they began buying pants, wore shorter haircuts, experimented sexually, and frequented Prohibition Era speakeasies (the Woman's Christian Temperance Union had finally succeeded in outlawing alcohol in 1919). But in the absence of widespread legal and economic rights for women beyond suffrage, the flappers of the 1920s eventually had to rely on men, typically husbands, for support. With acceptable sexual practice still tied to marriage, and reproduction a form of racial and national gatekeeping, women's reproductive rights were severely restricted along these lines. The Supreme Court decision *Buck v. Bell* (1927) nationalized a practice already under-way in states where poor women and women of color deemed unfit for motherhood were sterilized without consent or knowledge. Eugenic thinking was similarly deployed by women and their male allies on both sides of debates over whether abortion and birth control should be le-galized. A common thread woven through all of these discussions in the 1920s was that women's primary concern was motherhood and family life and that only white women could be "proper" mothers—ideas that had structured American political life since the nation's founding.[32]

The 1930s through 1950s: Reinforcing a Maternal Political Ideal for Women

When the US stock market crashed in October 1929, inciting the Great Depression as American and global markets spiraled into an economic tailspin, the liberationist spirit that some women had felt after suffrage faded alongside US affluence. In the next three decades, women's politi-cal engagement was shaped by protracted economic depression, global war, and the reemergence of anticommunism during the Cold War. In the midst of crisis and economic rebuilding, the long-standing white, male, breadwinner model of political citizenship became even more pro-nounced. During the Great Depression, the government focused on how to get men back to work, and this national effort cost many women their jobs; indeed, the 1932 Economy Act required women employed by the federal government to give up their jobs if their spouses were government workers, too. When men shifted from being citizen-workers to citizen-soldiers during World War II, women were given greater opportunity to enter the workforce, but this economic service—or womanpower—was expected to be temporary and still cast women as helpmates. In both periods, women's political prospects were limited to support roles in campaigns, midlevel positions in government, and to less than a dozen women serving in Congress. The situation only wors-ened with the onset of the Cold War in the late 1940s, as American citizenship and global security were tethered to the valorization of a traditional American citizenship. With domesticity elevated as a sign of US superiority over the Soviet Union's communist state, women's electoral prospects, legislative impact, and social and economic possibilities were constrained.

The Great Depression had jolted the nation to the point that some Americans questioned the system of capitalism, but this period of social and political experimentation was short-lived. With the male breadwinner economy and political order disrupted, left-liberal women sought greater social equality and opportunities to raise their political voice. They did so as civil libertarians and antiracists, pacifists and Zionists, liberal New Dealers, and members of the Communist Party. They promoted antilynching legislation and sharecroppers' rights in the Jim Crow South. They backed legislation that formed a more inclusive union, the Congress of Industrial Organizations (CIO), and led Unemployed Councils and Housewives Leagues to challenge housing evictions and demand fairer consumer prices.

Women served in student government and ran for elective office, mostly in the Democratic Party and third parties since the economy had crashed under Republican rule. On balance, however, their numbers were not significantly better than in the 1920s. Nonetheless, women harnessed this self-evaluation moment to draw focus to their political demands. The most radical and far-reaching example is a 1936 Communist Party Woman's Charter, in which they outlined the importance of women's equality in all aspects of life.

They theorized about "the woman question" alongside "the Negro question" and "the labor question," seeing the injustices experienced due to gender, race, and class as deeply connected.[33] Many of these ideas were tested out on the fringe of American politics and not widely incorporated into policy, but left-liberal women's increased visibility during the 1930s highlights the range of women's political engagement.

Democratic women gained direct influence in Washington with President Franklin D. Roosevelt's election in 1932—as they helped usher in a brand new form of liberalism predicated on an expanded federal government but interwoven with very old ideas about gender. FDR, prompted by his wife Eleanor Roosevelt, appointed seasoned women social reformers to key posts in his administration, creating a steady channel for women into government. Molly Dewson, who served as head of the Women's Division of the Democratic National Committee from 1932 to 1937, was part of this cohort, as was Frances Perkins, whom FDR appointed as his secretary of labor. Perkins was the first woman to serve in a presidential cabinet, in a role where she regularly drew upon her deep maternalist roots in the National Consumer League and Women's Trade Union League.[34] Yet Dewson noted that women's power in the Roosevelt administration was "pathetically small," where "their looks, their money, or their late husband's service to the party" were prized above "their ability."[35] Women may have been let in the door, but they were clear outsiders whose potential was filtered through a traditional prism. Even the presence of a female secretary of labor could not shift the gendered conceptualization of government aid during economic crisis. FDR's New Deal reforms were crafted around the white male breadwinner ideal that had long been at the center of American politics. Following the dictates of British economist John Maynard Keynes, FDR aspired to put more cash in Americans' pockets by putting them to work on government-funded projects. But there were far fewer, lesser-paid opportunities for women who might, for example, be hired to sew American flags to adorn the post offices that men had built.[36]

The welfare state set up during the New Deal similarly rested on traditional gender norms. Secretary Perkins, who had helped enact mother's pensions on the state level in the 1910s, presided over the Aid for Dependent Children (ADC) provisions of the 1935 Social Security Act. ADC was America's first federal cash assistance program for single mothers living at or below the poverty line. As with mother's pensions, a woman could not work for pay if she received ADC, for this new form of aid was meant to stand in if a male breadwinner was absent to provide care. In creating this type of federal assistance, Perkins and her cohort codified the notion that women, particularly mothers, belonged in the home, an idea that their very presence in national politics should have forcefully challenged.[37] This framing was, in part, a strategic choice made by these insider reformers to get the policy outcome they were after—putting cash in the pockets of struggling Americans—from male legislators who only saw women as economic dependents. As Agnes Leach, a lifelong friend of Perkins once put it, the trailblazing secretary of labor was a "half-loaf girl: take what you can get now and try for more later."[38]

ADC was as racialized as it was gendered. In addition to excluding domestic and agricultural work from the old-age benefits of the Social Security Act—decisions that most adversely impacted African Americans and Mexican Americans, particularly women—female reformers further pacified the solid and powerful Democratic southern segregationist bloc in Congress with provisions that allowed ADC recipients to be targeted by race. Women of color on welfare were routinely subjected to unannounced raids in the middle of the night more than white women in similar circumstances; if an adult male was present in their homes, women could lose their benefits. This coercive surveillance laid the groundwork for the racialized "welfare queen" trope that would later become prevalent in the 1980s. Despite FDR allowing women to influence policy and appointing a so-called black cabinet of advisors, including reformer Mary McLeod Bethune, the New Deal did very little to disrupt traditional ideas about race, gender, and political citizenship.[39]

America's entry into World War II created new opportunities for women to move temporarily into the workforce and challenge the white male breadwinner ideal. With younger men off to war, the demographic most readily hired into heavy manufacturing, there was a dearth of workers to build the needed tanks, airplanes, and other armaments for war. The US government leaned on corporations to hire women for lower-paid "light manufacturing" to fill this void. Women's trade unions—which had grown as a result of the 1935 Wagner Act that Secretary Frances Perkins had presided over—helped win higher pay for women in these wartime roles and even temporary government-subsidized nursery schools and childcare centers funded by the Lanham Act. But the iconic image of Rosie the Riveter, the fictive, white female defense factory worker the government created to help recruit women into wartime employment, presented a clear message: they should maintain their femininity on the job and keep womanpower out of politics. Predictably, when the war ended, women were fired from these well-paid jobs to make room for men returning home.[40] Yet, women did not leave the workforce, though white middle-class women largely shifted to part-time work. Female trade unions actively advocated for equal pay for equal work, laying the groundwork for the passage of America's first Equal Pay Act in 1963.[41]

At war's end, America's capitalist economy soared as US tensions with the Soviet Union escalated; the government responded in part by promoting traditional notions of gender and family as a Cold War imperative. The biggest political objective at home and abroad was to highlight how the United States, the self-proclaimed leader of the free world, differed from its archenemy, the communist Soviet Union. One tangible way to highlight the two countries' differences was to describe them through the familiar lenses of domesticity and family. At the American National Exhibition in Moscow in 1959, Vice President Richard Nixon debated these differences with Soviet Premier Nikita Khrushchev as the two men stood in model kitchens from their respective countries. Nixon underscored how business competition in a capitalist country leads to more innovative products like those on display in the American kitchen. Most Soviet families, by contrast, lived in state-sponsored apartments, where it was more cost-effective for the state to provide only basic amenities and place extended families, from children to grandparents, together in one housing unit.

Conversely, the US government promoted single-family white home-ownership inhabited by a "nuclear family"—a fitting new name for the atomic age—that consisted of two heterosexual parents, dad as a wage earner, mom as a housewife, and their children. The Servicemen's Readjustment Act (the GI Bill), which effectively only white men, including recent European immigrants qualified for, made attaining this national ideal more feasible by offering free college education and heavily subsidized home mortgages. Both major parties backed the legislation as good for domestic stability and national security. In effect, as the

United States sought to contain the spread of communism in the realm of foreign policy, the government also promoted a form of "domestic containment" at home that limited the spectrum of acceptable private lifestyles and political behavior.[42]

Women challenged the Cold War status quo, but doing so carried great risk, so they often did so under the veil of maternalism. Women were highly engaged in social reform and party club organizing during the late 1940s and 1950s, but it was most acceptable for women working across a range of causes to tie this work to home and family. Mamie Till Bradley, for instance, the Chicago mother of fourteen-year-old Emmett Till, who was brutally killed by white supremacists in 1955 while visiting family in Mississippi, famously insisted that her son's casket remain open at his funeral. She couched this act of political defiance in tragic maternal terms, remarking: "Let the people see what they did to my boy."[43] Bradley's activism also highlights how black women—inspired, in part, by the sexual violence they continued to endure with no legal recourse whatsoever—led the fight for civil rights during the 1950s. Meanwhile, white suburban housewives were highly engaged in political organizing through voluntary associations and political clubs, but typically entered the political arena under the guise of protecting their children. Anticommunist women, for instance, led a campaign to remove fluoridation from public water supplies, which they framed as a big government, quasi-communist attempt to wrestle the health care of children from mothers.[44]

Women seemed to be everywhere and nowhere at the same time in the 1950s—in the room, but without substantive decision-making authority and true political power. They continued to put pressure on the male body politic for causes they believed in across the political spectrum, to run for office, and to work for presidential administrations and the two major parties. Yet, the Democratic Party's decision to end its Women's Division in 1953, and the persistence of sex-segregated women's clubs and committees in the Republican and Democratic parties, underscored how peripheral women remained in party politics.[45] The NWP unsuccessfully kept trying to pass the ERA and other measures promising political and legal equality for the sexes.[46] Women's political engagement was largely depoliticized as mere women's work, supposedly driven by biological impulses, not political ones. White middle-class women with flexible schedules and resources had the most time and money to devote to the political arena, where their representation remained mostly unchanged from prior decades. In this period where women's political identity was tied to the homemaker ideal, women of color faced the steepest barriers—from continued political disenfranchisement to discriminatory laws and practices that marginalized them as low-wage earners working outside the home. In this environment, women's politics at all levels operated in the shadows in the 1950s, severely limited by the strict parameters of the Cold War and the dominant form of political citizenship.

1960s Turning Point: From Womanpower to Women Power in Politics

In the early 1960s, women continued to draw on the mantle of domesticity and motherhood when framing their political activism. While loyalty programs and blacklisting waned, civil defense remained a preoccupation of Americans as US-Soviet tensions revived during the Cuban Missile Crisis in October 1962. In this climate, women in conservative groups such as the John Birch Society and Minute Women of the U.S.A. defended nuclear arms buildup as a national security interest. Whereas, women in disarmament groups such as Women Strike for Peace, Mothers for Peace, and the longer-running Women's International League for Peace and Freedom, actively lobbied for greater nuclear controls. WSP affiliates in a choreographed uniform of tailored suits and heels visited more than half of the congressmen on Capitol Hill during their "Mothers Lobby for a Test Ban" in May 1963, which helped pressure President John F. Kennedy to sign a partial test ban treaty.[47] Women peace activists boycotted potentially radioactive milk and duck-and-cover drills in schools, just as they promoted peace candidates often in the Democratic Party.

Using similar tactics for different purposes, conservative women promoting strong national defense and anticommunist ideas actively participated in political campaigns. In California, for instance, Parents for Rafferty sent out 3 million fliers to elect Max Rafferty as state superintendent in 1962, who promised to counter suspected communist teachers' "red psychological warfare." Housewife Patricia Gilbert, a participant of this group, recalled, "We sat around the table just like we were planning a senior prom or something."[48] Meanwhile, mothers throughout the South in the mid-1950s and 1960s resisted school integration, which some suggested was a communist conspiracy.[49] Conservative women proved to be such capable grassroots organizers they helped secure the nomination of anticommunist, anti–civil rights presidential candidate Arizona Senator Barry Goldwater in 1964.

Women clearly divided over how to approach issues from education to national security, the role of government in providing health, welfare, and social services, and whether women's continued entrance into the workforce since World War II was a good thing. These examples from across the political spectrum illustrate how women blurred formal and informal politics. In this period, women became increasingly aware of and frustrated by being central decision makers in grassroots campaigns and undervalued in electoral politics. As Senator Goldwater acknowledged, Republican women did the "tough political chores" of the party.[50] Political campaigns focused more on attracting women voters and volunteers than recruiting women as paid staff. Women only comprised 24 percent of federal employees in 1961 and were sequestered to clerical and nonpolitical staff.[51] Kennedy's Presidential Commission on the Status of Women (PCSW) was established that same year, and like its corollaries on the state level, it focused in part on how to increase the ranks of women in public office. Commissioners debated whether the best path forward was through the professions, party infrastructure, or a trickle-up effect with women seeking local offices first. The PCSW pressed Kennedy to increase high-level appointments and advocated for 50–50 representation at the Democratic Party convention. Kennedy's PCSW helped refocus legislative attention on the Equal Rights Amendment and advocate for the Equal Pay Act of 1963.[52]

In the early 1960s, women active in the Black Freedom Movement moved national conversations about political representation and voting rights forward. Septima Clark was instrumental in building a network of Citizenship Schools to prepare southern African Americans with the historical knowledge and literacy skills needed to pass registration tests. One Citizenship School graduate, sharecropper Fannie Lou Hamer, addressed the vigilante violence she had faced when attempting to vote in Mississippi in fearless, pointed testimony before the Credentials Committee at the 1964 Democratic National Convention (DNC) in Atlantic City. She did so as a member of a group she helped found, the Mississippi Freedom Democratic Party (MFDP), which protested Mississippi's all-white delegation at the DNC that year and the lack of racial parity in Congress generally. MFDP's women-led actions, alongside better-known mobilizations such as the Selma march, helped shift support toward passage of the Voting Rights Act in August 1965. Only then did the Nineteenth Amendment truly apply to all women. National Council of Negro Women President Dorothy Height underscored that race and gender suffrage were deeply connected, commenting, "Fifty years ago women got suffrage . . . but it took lynching, bombing, the civil rights movement and the Voting Rights Act . . . to get it for Black women and Black people."[53]

The 1964 Civil Rights Act was another important watershed moment for women, not only delivering a final blow to legal segregation but providing women with a powerful tool to challenge sex discrimination at work. American Civil Liberties Union lawyer Pauli Murray argued that Title VII of the act must highlight sex alongside race because "in accordance with the prevailing patterns of employment *both* Negro and white women will share a common fate of discrimination" and "Title VII without the 'sex' amendment would benefit Negro males primarily."[54] As a black bisexual woman, Murray understood how multiple forms of oppression intersected, and her argument influenced feminist attorneys, legislators, and activists going forward. In contrast, the NWP echoed earlier white supremacist calls for women's suffrage in their critique that Title VII without "sex" added "would not even give protection against discrimination because of 'race, color, religion, or national origin,' to a *White Woman*, a *Woman of the Christian Religion*, or a *Woman of United States origin* [original emphasis]."[55] This reasoning appealed to southern segregationist Representative Howard W. Smith (D-VA), who while a supporter of the ERA, introduced this "sex" amendment in an attempt to block the overall passage of the Civil Rights Act. Representative Martha Griffiths (D-MI) found this tactic frustrating and insulting. "If there had been any necessity to have pointed out that women were a second-class sex, the laughter would have proved it," she commented, addressing some legislators' spontaneous chuckles during debate. In the end, Congress passed the Civil Rights Act with Title VII's sex protections intact, and women workers seized this new mechanism to hold employers accountable, filing one-fourth of initial complaints lodged with the Equal Employment Opportunity Commission in 1965.[56]

The National Organization for Women (NOW) was developed in part to oversee this process as an independent watchdog. More forgotten is how NOW directed focus on the political arena too, noting in its founding "Statement of Purpose," "We will strive to ensure that no party, candidate, president, senator, governor, congressman, or any public official who betrays or ignores the principle of full equality between the sexes is elected or appointed to office."[57] NOW's message indicated women's increased determination to translate the womanpower they had long contributed to political campaigns, party organizations, and grassroots politics into greater women power in politics.

Early 1970s: A Groundswell of Women's Political Engagement

This demand for greater political representation of women in party delegates, elected and appointed offices, and leadership roles was sounded by Republicans, Democrats, and third-party affiliates at greater volume in the early 1970s. The nonpartisan emphasis of the National Women's

Political Caucus (NWPC), founded in 1971, reminds that women's rights was not immediately framed as a progressive feminist agenda, though this group ultimately skewed in that direction. Fannie Lou Hamer and other women from the civil rights movement were founders of NWPC alongside leading Congresswomen Patsy Takemoto Mink, Bella Abzug, and Shirley Chisholm, reflecting the political pressure group's intersectional orientation. The NWPC, which topped thirty thousand members in 1973, filled a void in politics, training and backing women candidates to offset a political patronage system that had long favored men.[58]

In part because of NWPC's immediate force, reporters predicted that 1972 might be "a year of the woman" in politics.[59] The group was most successful in augmenting women's delegate strength at party conventions—from 13 to 39 percent at the DNC and from 16 to 30 percent at the Republican National Convention.[60] Increasing women's clout as delegates was more easily accomplished than assuring greater numbers of women in office. Even so, a record number of women ran that year. Most notably, Chisholm and Mink ran for president as intersectional feminist and antiwar change candidates, with Chisholm securing 151.25 delegate votes at the DNC. Five diverse women were also newly elected to Congress, Representatives Yvonne Burke (D-CA), Marjorie Holt (R-MD), Elizabeth Holtzman (D-NY), Barbara Jordan (D-TX), and Patricia Schroeder (D-CO). Women made even more sizable gains in state legislatures, where women's representation increased by 50 percent, or 282 to 437 between 1972 and 1974.[61] This boost led to noticeable changes. Women inside President Richard Nixon's administration successfully pressed for more women appointments and integrated the White House gym.[62] Feminist Democrats capitalized on their party's majority, with help from Republican allies, to pass landmark women's rights legislation, including the Comprehensive Child Development Act in 1971 (which Nixon ultimately vetoed), the Equal Rights Amendment and Title IX of the Educational Amendments Act in 1972, the Equal Credit Opportunity Act in 1974, and $5 million for a federally sponsored National Women's Conference (NWC) in 1975. For this reason, this period is seen as a watershed for legal feminism.

Women in Washington transformed political discourse and modeled a different workplace culture, hiring women-led staffs, showcasing collaborative decision making, and advocating for the use of gender-neutral language in government publications.[63] These corrections irreversibly shifted the language of politics and increased substantive work opportunities for women in government, but the "old boys' culture" was more difficult to crack. Likewise, the window for sizable women's rights legislative reforms closed by the late 1970s. The push for universal childcare did not regain momentum after President Nixon vetoed the 1971 bill, and the ERA stalled during the ratification campaign when the remaining three states needed to ratify the constitutional amendment did not do so by the 1982 deadline.[64]

These setbacks highlight three important elements that continue to impact women's political position in electoral politics. First, while women's influence in the Republican and Democratic Parties expanded during this period, they still faced considerable resistance. It is telling, for instance, that when a Nixon aide characterized an image of NWPC's founding conference as "like a burlesque" show, the president agreed.[65] This exchange reveals how difficult it was for women to shift male perspectives—alongside wider cultural viewpoints—about their political leadership abilities and legitimate presence in politics. Second, women drew heavily on gender difference during the 1974 midterms, when a few thousand candidates ran on the message that they were best suited to clean up political corruption in Washington on display during the Watergate scandal.[66] This argument, predicated on women's limited representation in Congress and their continued casting as the nation's moral guardians, reinforced the idea that women had special qualities and interests in politics. Third, feminists who mobilized to demand women's greater political representation incorrectly assumed that most women leaned progressive and minimized the very real ideological differences apparent since women won the vote in the 1920s. Indeed, the legislative accomplishments prized by feminists were despised by women who sought to defend their traditional values, religious beliefs, and personal liberty against what they saw as government-sanctioned social engineering. Conservative women organized new resistance groups, such as the New York State Right to Life Party and Stop ERA, to reverse feminist gains in the courts and in government. Their purpose, however, was not to launch a wholesale challenge of women's rising presence in elected offices, from which they benefited and to which they contributed.

Many American women engaged in political action outside of the two-party system to challenge the US government while applying pressure on these traditional power centers. For instance, members of the lesbian-feminist Furies Collective advocated the creation of a separate Federation of Feminist States.[67] The Black Panther Party slated Elaine Brown as a candidate for Oakland City Council in 1973 and 1975, and while she did not win, members Audrea Jones and Ericka Huggins gained seats on the Berkeley Community Development Council Board.[68] Chicanas Martha P. Cotera, Ino Alvarez, and Olivia "Evey" Chapa helped form Mujeres Por La Raza within La Raza Unida Party, ensuring that this Texas third-party's first platform in 1971 addressed women's rights and family concerns. The next year they mobilized "100 'very politicized' Chicanas" to attend the NWPC state meeting and influence its direction, while also holding forums on how to make greater political inroads at every level.[69] Chicanas in Texas forged coalitional partnerships with lesbian and antipoverty activists more easily than white feminists, whom, according to Cotera, actively ignored their presence, social problems, and political demands.[70] This tension came to a head at the National Women's Conference in Houston in 1977, an event that highlighted the collaborative potential of women in politics as well as schisms that divided women.

The Late 1970s and 1980s: Women's Civic Engagement during Polarized Times

As the only federally funded women's conference in US history, the National Women's Conference was a considerable feat that involved both President Gerald Ford and President Jimmy Carter's administrations and had bipartisan backing in Congress. Responding to a growing call for global human rights, this conference was the United States' answer to the United Nations International Women's Year gathering in Mexico City in 1975. In the United States, more than one hundred fifty thousand women and some men gathered at meetings in all fifty states and six territories during the spring and summer of 1977 to set the terms of debate for the NWC. Two thousand elected delegates came together at the culminating conference, held over four days in Houston during November 1977, to deliberate over and pass a twenty-six-issue "National Plan of Action." As per law, presidentially appointed commissioners gave President Carter the conference's policy report, *The Spirit of Houston*, in March 1978.[71] The NWC law included a diversity quota for elected delegates, and women of color, queer women, and welfare rights activists held conference organizers accountable, requiring considerable representation. With one-third of delegates to the NWC women of color, this gathering's diversity starkly contrasted with the still overwhelmingly white and male US Congress. Women of color defined this unifying term as they crossed ethnic and racial lines to draft a robust Minority Rights plank. Lesbian women mobilized, with Commissioner Jean O'Leary providing instrumental leadership, and achieved such influence that the full body in Houston considered and passed a Sexual Preference plank well ahead of the American public.[72]

The NWC stands out as a transformative moment that showcased both women's collectivist spirit and the very real ideological differences that continued to complicate the prospect of a united voting bloc. In hotel suites and convention hallways, women animatedly discussed at all hours the impact of federal policies on their lives. For some, attending a NWC state meeting or traveling to Houston was their first political act, and for others it was a point on a continuum of organizing in, around, and beyond electoral politics. NWC served as a meeting place for women of shared backgrounds; for instance, women of the Red Nation used this occasion to connect nationally and discuss indigenous autonomy and rights. The conference highlighted developing movements from disability rights to sexual assault. New organizations, such as the

National Coalition Against Domestic Violence, were formed. The NWC served as a seedbed for emerging politicians such as Representative Maxine Waters (D-CA) and Texas Governor Ann Richards, then in local government. This event also exhibited the effective counterorganizing of antifeminist activists, who believed using tax dollars for "Big Sister government" was dangerous and unfair.[73] Opponents mobilized to achieve a sizable presence in some state delegations sent to Houston, set up a Citizens' Review Committee that monitored meetings, and were highly vocal during floor debates, especially over the topics of abortion and the ERA. In kind, Lottie Beth Hobbs, founder of the antifeminist Women Who Want to Be Women organization, initiated a "pro-family" conference held simultaneously at the Houston Astrodome that attracted around sixteen thousand attendees.[74]

Tensions among feminists and antifeminists were increasingly fraught over issues related to the family, reflecting the lasting resonance of women's politics being interwoven with maternalist concerns. While feminists advocated for benefits for displaced homemakers, antifeminists defended "God, home, and country" against a perceived attack.[75] In this moment, conservative women were most effective in couching their political demands from lower taxes to limiting public spending on social programs as a defense of the nuclear family and challenge of government encroachment on parental rights. This growing contest over who best represented the American family initially played out within each major party, evident from the presidential candidacy of Ellen McCormack, a founder of the New York State Right to Life Party, in the 1976 Democratic primary.[76] Both sides tried to maintain the rhetorical advantage. For instance, Representative Patricia Schroeder, a Democrat and feminist from Colorado, titled her 1989 book *Champion of the Great American Family*.[77] This shifting terrain was one reason that, working one decade prior, President Carter had largely ignored *The Spirit of Houston* report; after sparring with his National Advisory Committee for Women committed to furthering its proposals, he fired its cochair, Bella Abzug.[78]

President Ronald Reagan ran for the nation's highest office in 1980 on a "family values" message, a sign of conservative women's—and especially Christian evangelicals and Catholics—influence in shaping his campaign and subsequent policy agenda. His election hardened a political realignment underway since the early 1970s in which internal Democratic reforms moved the party toward feminist policy goals and so-called identity politics, while the Republican Party became associated with traditionalist concerns. This partisan remapping, however, did not indicate either party's turn away from women. To the contrary, conservative women led the call for traditional "family values," and leaned on President Reagan to embrace faith-centered domestic policies such as school prayer, a constitutional Human Life Amendment to outlaw legal abortion, and abstinence-only sex education. While the former two campaigns were unsuccessful, the antiabortion movement and "culture wars" over education gained considerable traction. Meanwhile, Republican feminists, a dwindling presence in the party, secured Reagan's promise to appoint the first woman to the US Supreme Court at the 1980 Republican National Convention, which led to the successful nomination of Justice Sandra Day O'Connor the following year.[79] Reagan also broke ground in the area of foreign policy, appointing political scientist Jeane J. Kirkpatrick to the cabinet-level position of US ambassador to the United Nations. And so, despite increasing hostility between feminists and antifeminists, the goal of women's representational advancement moved forward.

Yet, more women in high-level appointments did not transform the conditions of all women for the better. The austerity policies and deregulation efforts of the Reagan administration that cut social services and made it difficult to unionize had a devastating effect on poor women, working-class women, and women of color. In a climate where women of color were cast as "welfare queens" and "deadbeat moms," they claimed the power of motherhood as a tool of protest. As Mothers of East Los Angeles, they successfully challenged a prison project slated for the predominantly working-class, Mexican-American neighborhood of Boylan Heights.[80] As the Indigenous Women's Network, they countered deculturalizing practices in tribal schools, engaged in native environmental activism, and challenged sexism in Tribal Councils. "We wanted to talk about organizing, and strategies that are working and challenges that we're facing—and despair and hope and all those pieces," recalled founding member Winona LaDuke, an activist from the White Earth Nation in Minnesota.[81] For women of color still facing rigid barriers, taking up community and family-centered concerns remained the steadiest avenue through which to enter electoral politics. For instance, the majority of Latinas in public office in the mid-1980s—152 of 376, or 12 percent of Hispanic officeholders—served on school boards.[82] Reclaiming a mothering space was not only a reflection of the political circumstances facing women of color but also a defiant, self-affirming act for women historically denied the mantle of maternalism because of their race.

The 1980s through 2020: The Unfinished Campaign of Bringing Women into Politics

From the 1980s forward, candidates have become increasingly fixated on closing a "gender gap" among women voters, though the preoccupation with capturing women as "swing voters" is hardly new. Political scientist Susan Carroll notes, "Democratic women and moderate Republican women alike tended to see the major dividing line among women not as party, but rather as ideology."[83] Even so, political commentators and political scientists located and studied a gender gap in the electorate once 8 percent fewer women favored Reagan in 1980.[84] Women partisans sought to capitalize on this attention by exerting "super pressure"—as a Democratic Women's Presidential Project described—on party leaders for meaningful representation and sharing of leadership.[85] The result: in 1984, Democratic nominee Walter Mondale, Carter's former vice president, selected Queens Representative Geraldine Ferraro as his running mate. Ferraro wore white, as a nod to suffragists, when accepting her nomination at the DNC, but she did not reference gender in her acceptance speech and was seen by party moderates as an unthreatening choice. Blame went around when Mondale lost, with one male advisor calling out feminists for not delivering "their sisters," and prominent feminists criticizing party leaders for "the frantic quest for white male votes, which did not materialize."[86] Meanwhile, the Reagan administration sought to close the gender gap by, as historian Marissa Chappell argued, "adopt[ing] the feminist movement's rhetoric of equal opportunity and choice while denying the need for federal intervention to promote gender equality."[87] The major gap in both parties, however, remained its lack of mentorship and financial support for women candidates.

In the 1980s and 1990s, a multitude of diverse women-centered political action and lobbying groups proliferated to address this imbalance. Leading the way, NWPC veteran and philanthropist Ellen Malcolm hosted the founding meeting of EMILY's List, which stood for Early Money Is Like Yeast (it rises), at her home in 1985. This effort helped elect Barbara Mikulski (D-MD) to the Senate the following year.[88] While EMILY's List limited focus to female candidates supportive of legal abortion, its founding set the stage for parallel political action groups such as the antiabortion Susan B. Anthony List in 1992 and nonpartisan The White House Project in 1998.[89] In these years, long-standing grassroots networks formalized their operations as well. For instance, immigrant rights and domestic violence advocates formed a National Network to End Violence Against Immigrant Women, which effectively applied pressure on local law enforcement and federal lawmakers to expand legal protections to battered immigrants.[90] Similarly, LGBT parental support groups, such as the one started by Jeanne Manford in New York City, joined together in 1981 as the Federation of Parents and Friends of Lesbians and Gays, Inc.[91] These networks were well situated to successfully advocate for legislation such as the 1994 Violence Against Women Act and state and federal level hate crime laws.

President Bill Clinton's election in 1992 provided an opening for feminists in Washington, nurtured by First Lady Hillary Rodham Clinton and widespread interest in realizing a "year of the woman." Her treatment in the press during the campaign underscored how gendered the political terrain remained. An accomplished lawyer, Hillary Clinton was ridiculed after she responded to a reporter's question about her career: "I suppose I could have stayed home and baked cookies and had teas, but what I decided to do was to fulfill my profession."[92] Her apologies ran alongside increasing coverage of the record number of women running for office—218 ran for Congress in the primary, with 109 winning House nominations and 11 for Senate.[93] Many of these candidates credited as a galvanizing act the Senate Judiciary Committee's pointed, highly sexualized questioning of law professor Anita Hill, who accused Justice Clarence Thomas of sexual harassment during his Supreme Court nomination hearings in 1991. Beyond this controversy, divided government, economic downturn, and the Gulf War piqued voters' willingness to consider new faces in politics. And while Gallup Polls administered since the 1970s had shown steady improvement in American voters' willingness to vote for women, an NBC News poll taken in October 1992 revealed that voters saw women as the most likely to create change.[94] Redistricting and retirements also produced an unusually large number of open seats (sixty-five in the House, seven in the Senate), which made incumbency—a long-used excuse not to back new, often untested women candidates—less of an issue.[95] Additionally, women raised more money than men of similar backgrounds due to increased investment by political parties, well-orchestrated fundraising drives by more than forty women's political action committees, and small donation direct mail campaigns spiking after Anita Hill's testimony.[96]

Democratic women were the majority who picked up seats in 1992, but Republican women also gained momentum in the wake of the Hill-Thomas controversy. For example, Texan Kay Bailey Hutchison helped increase the number of women in the Senate to seven. Reflecting on her choice to run for Senate, she mused that her deceased father would have dismissed her ambition, saying, "Kay, there are a lot of wonderful things you can do with your life, but that's probably not one of them."[97] Progressive feminists saw her win as a loss. Calling her a "female impersonator," Gloria Steinem contended, "having someone who looks like us but thinks like them is worse than having no one."[98] Thus, the goal of gender parity became increasingly thorny for feminists, as they rallied for equal representation, but had to face the ideological differences that separated women. The Hill-Thomas controversy galvanized women across the political spectrum. The Independent Women's Forum, a conservative group founded in response, promoted free-market liberalism alongside issues originally championed by feminists, such as paid family leave and domestic violence.[99]

The Monica Lewinsky scandal and President Bill Clinton's impeachment in 1998 further muddied the waters of who represented women's best interests in politics. Characterized by reporters as the "feminists' dilemma," it was difficult to tease out Clinton's abuse of sexual power relations with his White House intern, Monica Lewinsky, from his record of women appointments and support for feminist policy proposals, the strongest of any president to that point.[100] The decision of notable feminists to oppose Clinton's impeachment and not meaningfully defend Lewinsky was later scrutinized in the wake of the 2017 #MeToo movement, which brought renewed attention to the issues of sexual harassment, sexual assault, and gender inequality in the workplace.[101]

Since 1998, women have steadily increased their numbers in public office, with half of the women elected to Congress in US history entering from that point forward. However, Hillary Clinton's difficulty distinguishing herself from her husband, running first for the US Senate from New York in 2000 and for president in 2008 and 2016, underscored the remaining hurdles women face as candidates. In 2008, Clinton's approach was to emulate masculine leadership by downplaying gender, which backfired when the press cast her as unlikable and zeroed in on the tears she shed in New Hampshire.[102] In 2016, she did an about-face, discussing her joy of being a grandmother and how she would crack the nation's highest glass ceiling. Her loss to President Donald Trump, who clinched a victory despite the leak of an *Access Hollywood* tape from 2005, in which he bragged he could "do anything" to women, including "grab 'em by the pussy," shocked many women.[103] So too did the returns that showed that white women, particularly those married and over age forty-five, favored Trump by a small margin—

47 percent to Clinton's 45 percent according to a Pew Research Center study.[104]

Since the 2000s, gauging how women vote has remained an obsession of pollsters, politicians, and the press. While women do not vote together as a bloc, they are assumed to have a directional pull that is shaped by motherhood and womanhood. Democratic Senator Joe Biden remarked in 2002 that since the terrorist attacks of 9/11 the year prior, "soccer moms are security moms now."[105] Biden's characterization was predicated on the still deep-rooted assumption that women swung together as voters; in this case President Bill Clinton's "soccer mom" supporters became President George W. Bush's "security moms."

Close watch of women voters has only grown since the Women's March in January 2017, when an estimated 3 million to 5 million—the largest mobilization of women (and male allies) to date—marched in suburbs and major city centers in the United States and internationally to promote intersectional feminist concerns. Held the day after President Trump's inauguration, this march that began with a Facebook posting by Hawaiian Teresa Shook, provided a cathartic experience for women frustrated by Clinton's loss. According to one commentator, Clinton was "shoved to the side by what a sizable chunk of the nation saw as that classic historical figure: the male chauvinist pig."[106] Women went beyond a onetime mobilization to prepare for office, drawing on recently founded groups such as She Should Run and Raising Our Sisters' Assets (ROSA PAC). Of the 277 candidates for Congress and governor in the 2018 election cycle that followed, 125 won their elections. The Senate was one-quarter women for the first time, and Congress contained more women of color than ever before.[107] This groundswell reflected a historic challenge for gender parity but also fit a pattern in which women historically made their biggest vies for office during times of moral crisis. In this instance, they gained considerably.

Debbie Walsh of the Center for American Women and Politics cautioned before the midterms, "We are not going to see, in one cycle, an end to the underrepresentation of women in American politics that we've seen for 250 years. The concern is, we need this energy and engagement to be here for the long haul. This is a marathon, not a sprint."[108] Indeed, women's struggle to achieve equal political power alongside voting power has stretched beyond the roughly seven decades women spent fighting for the constitutional right to vote. Significantly, the American presidency and vice presidency remains elusive for women, despite both major parties' attempts to the contrary in recent decades. In 2020, six women—Senators Kamala Harris, Elizabeth Warren, Amy Klobuchar, and Kristen Gillibrand, Representative Tulsi Gabbard, and self-help practitioner Marianne Williamson—entered the race to secure the presidential nomination in the Democratic Party. Press coverage of these candidates fluctuated from preoccupation with their likability and role as bosses and parents to highlighting unfair coverage and calling for voters to "make 2020 the real Year of the Woman."[109] This varied treatment suggests a cultural shift underway alongside resistance to this change, for women politicians are increasingly seen as viable candidates for the presidency and yet receive undue scrutiny. Progress has been made, but political citizenship remains historically tied to an imagined male voter and male political leadership ideal.

To be sure, 2020 is not 1920, and perhaps no other recent electoral story makes this clearer than Democrat Stacey Abrams's governor race in Georgia in 2018. A Yale-educated lawyer and graduate of Spelman College, she became the deputy city attorney of Atlanta at twenty-nine years old and went on to serve in the Georgia State Assembly beginning in 2007. Political scientists Jennifer L. Lawless and Richard L. Fox deem women's greatest gender gap to be political ambition, noting a "winnowing effect" still prevalent in how women and men are socialized differently to think about and pursue power.[110] Abrams would agree. "Communities that are not considered normative are often discouraged from not only having ambition, but they're also told that there is something inherently arrogant in wanting more and that we should be satisfied with whatever we get," she noted.[111] Her gubernatorial campaign highlighted the necessity of confronting this cultural bias that allows systemic inequity to persist. She took on the political establishment in her state as an individual but not without a collective force of predominantly women of color behind her.

In Georgia, a state marred by a history of slavery and segregation, Abrams came close to winning. Her opponent, Republican Brian Kemp, subsequently faced investigation for potential voter suppression since he served as Georgia's secretary of state during the race, when erroneous polling site closures, voter roll purges, and unfilled voter registration applications in districts with high voters of color and Democrats raised concerns.[112] Abrams's very narrow loss—48.8 percent to Kemp's 50.2 percent—suggests that this voter tampering may have made the difference. As Abrams noted, "Georgia citizens tried to exercise their constitutional rights . . . democracy failed Georgians of every political party, every race, every region. Again."[113] This disenfranchisement was not isolated. In North Dakota, Native American groups were caught off guard by a new voter ID law that required verification of residents' street addresses instead of post office boxes, which many people living on reservations used.[114] This kind of tactic was much easier to implement after the Supreme Court no longer required states to preclear new voter laws or regulations before an election in the ruling *Shelby v. Holder* (2013), undercutting the 1965 Voting Rights Act.[115]

And so it was that Rosanell Eaton, who died a month after Abrams lost her race, would have to lodge two major fights to vote as an African American woman in her lifetime. In 1942, at age twenty-one, she rode two miles by wagon to the Franklin County Courthouse in Louisburg, North Carolina, to cast her first ballot. There, three white men told her she could vote only if she could recite the Preamble to the Constitution, and as her high school valedictorian, she did so effortlessly, outmaneuvering this disenfranchisement tactic. In 2013, at ninety-three years old, she was tested again. This time, the name on her voter registration card—Rosanell Eaton—did not match her driver's license—Rosa Johnson Eaton. Getting the ID cards corrected took eleven trips to banks and government offices, a grueling process that required traveling a few hundred miles and many hours. After the ordeal, Eaton was furious.

"You know, all of this is coming back around before I could get in the ground," she remarked out of frustration.[116] Resisting this outcome, she joined a lawsuit that made its way to the Supreme Court in 2017. Ultimately, the North Carolina law was struck down, with the state reprimanded for its procedural morass meant to "target African-Americans with almost surgical precision." Inspired by Eaton's story, President Barack Obama noted, "She's still fighting to make real the promise of America."[117] Women like Eaton will not tire of this struggle until women can express their full political citizenship as voters and in government.

Notes

1. Jack Anderson, "Congresswoman Patsy Mink of Hawaii Tells: Why Women Are Needed in Government," *Parade,* March 28, 1965; "Women's Issue's, Women in Politics and Government, News Clippings, 1966–1976, undated," folder 4, box 565, Congressional–Legislative File–Central File, Patsy Mink Papers, Library of Congress, Washington, DC.

2. Paula Baker, "The Domestication of Politics: Women and American Political Society, 1780–1920," *American Historical Review* 89, no. 3 (June 1984): 620–647, 625.

3. Italics in the original. Eileen Boris, "The Power of Motherhood: Black and White Activist Women Redefine the 'Political,'" *Yale Journal of Law and Feminism* 2, no. 1 (1989): 25–49, 26, 31.

4. Judith N. Shklar, *American Citizenship: The Quest for Inclusion* (Cambridge, MA: Harvard University Press, 1991).

5. See, for example, Matthew D. Lassiter, *The Silent Majority: Suburban Politics in the Sunbelt South* (Princeton, NJ: Princeton University Press, 2007); Robert O. Self, *All in the Family: The Realignment of American Democracy since the 1960s* (New York: Hill & Wang, 2012).

6. Eleanor Flexner, *Century of Struggle: The Women's Rights Movement,* 3rd ed. (Cambridge, MA: Belknap Press, 1996).

7. For a history that places Seneca Falls in a wider spectrum of organizing, see Nancy A. Hewitt, "From Seneca Falls to Suffrage? Reimagining a 'Master' Narrative in U.S. Women's History," in *No Permanent Waves: Recasting Histories of U.S. Feminism* (New Brunswick, NJ: Rutgers University Press, 2010), 15–38.

8. Beverly Beeton, "How the West Was Won for Woman Suffrage," in *One Woman, One Vote: Rediscovering the Women's Suffrage Movement,* ed. Marjorie Spruill Wheeler (Troutdale, OR: New Sage Press, 1995), 99–116;

Marjorie Spruill Wheeler, "A Short History of the Woman Suffrage Movement in America," in *One Woman, One Vote*, 9–20.

9. See the various essays in Wheeler, *One Woman, One Vote*.

10. Jane Addams, "Why Women Should Vote," *Ladies' Home Journal,* January 1910, http://www.digitalhistory.uh.edu/disp_textbook.cfm?smtid=3&psid=3609.

11. Carolyn DeSwarte Gifford, "Frances Willard and the Woman's Christian Temperance Union's Conversion to Woman Suffrage," in Wheeler, *One Woman, One Vote*, 117–34; Ruth Bordin, *Woman and Temperance: The Quest for Power and Liberty, 1873–1900* (New Brunswick, NJ: Rutgers University Press, 1985); Kathryn Kish Sklar, "Hull House in the 1890s: A Community of Women Reformers," *Signs* 10 (Summer 1985): 658–77.

12. Susan E. Marshall, *Splintered Sisterhood: Gender and Class in the Campaign against Woman Suffrage* (Madison: University of Wisconsin Press, 1997).

13. Ellen Carol DuBois, "Taking the Law into Our Own Hands: *Bradwell, Minor,* and Suffrage Militance in the 1870s," in Wheeler, *One Woman, One Vote*, 81–98.

14. This article is a representative reevaluation of public discourse surrounding this fissure in the suffrage movement and white suffragists' racist ideology. Elizabeth Cady Stanton, as quoted in Ta-Nehisi Coates, "The Great Schism: From Their Onsets, Suffragists and Abolitionists Shared Many of the Same Values, So What Caused the Movements to Split Apart?," *The Atlantic*, October 18, 2011, https://www.theatlantic.com/national/archive/2011/10/the-great-schism/246640/.

15. Kristin Hoganson, "As Badly Off as the Filipinos: U.S. Women's Suffragists and the Imperial Issue at the Turn of the Twentieth Century," *Journal of Women's History* 13, no. 2 (June 2001): 9–33.

16. Ellen Carol DuBois, "Working Women, Class Relations, and Suffrage Militance: Harriet Stanton Blanch and the New York Woman Suffrage Movement, 1894–1909," in Wheeler, *One Woman, One Vote*, 221–244.

17. Wheeler, "A Short History of the Woman Suffrage Movement," 9–20.

18. Mary Church Terrell, *The Progress of Colored Women* (Washington, DC: Smith Brothers, Printers, 1898), Library of Congress, https://loc.gov/item/90898298.

19. Belle Kearney, "The South and Woman Suffrage," *Woman's Journal*, April 4, 1903. Reprinted in *Up from the Pedestal: Selected Writings in the History of American Feminism,* ed. Aileen S. Kraditor (Chicago: Quadrangle Books, 1968), 262–265.

20. Elsa Barkley Brown, "To Catch the Vision of Freedom: Reconstructing Southern Black Women's Political History, 1865–1880," in *African American Women and the Vote 1837–1965*, ed. Ann D. Gordon and Bettye Collier-Thomas

(Amherst: University of Massachusetts Press, 1997), 156–169; Rosalyn Terborg-Penn, "African American Women and the Woman Suffrage Movement," in Wheeler, *One Woman, One Vote*, 135–156.

21. Wanda A. Hendricks, "African American Women as Political Constituents in Chicago, 1913–1915," in *We Have Come to Stay: American Women and Political Parties, 1880–1960,* ed. Melanie Gustafson, Kristie Miller, and Elisabeth Israels Perry (Albuquerque: University of New Mexico Press, 1999), 55–64.

22. Margaret Finnegan, *Selling Suffrage: Consumer Culture and Votes for Women* (New York: Columbia University Press, 1999); Lynn Dumenil, *The Second Line of Defense: American Women and World War I* (Chapel Hill: University of North Carolina Press, 2017); Linda G. Ford, "Alice Paul and the Triumph of Militancy," in Wheeler, *One Woman, One Vote*, 277–294; Robert Booth Fowler, "Carrie Chapman Catt, Strategist," in Wheeler, *One Woman, One Vote*, 295–314.

23. Anastasia Sims, "Armageddon in Tennessee: The Final Battle over the Nineteenth Amendment," in Wheeler, *One Woman, One Vote*, 333–352.

24. Phoebe Ensminger Burn quoted in "90th Anniversary of the 19th Amendment," National Archives, August 12, 2010, https://www.archives.gov/press/press-releases/2010/nr10-134.html.

25. Kristi Anderson, *After Suffrage: Women in Partisan and Electoral Politics before the New Deal* (Chicago: University of Chicago Press, 1996), 49–76.

26. Anderson, *After Suffrage*; Nancy F. Cott, "Women in Politics Before and After 1920," in Wheeler, *One Woman, One Vote*, 353–374; Cott, *The Grounding of Modern Feminism* (New Haven, CT: Yale University Press, 1987).

27. Carrie Chapman Catt quoted in Anderson, *After Suffrage*, 44.

28. Mary Hawkeworth, *Political Worlds of Women: Activism, Advocacy, and Governance in the Twenty-First Century* (New York: Taylor & Francis, 2012); Anderson, *After Suffrage*, 77–109; Doris Weatherford, *Women in American Politics: History and Milestones* (Washington, DC: CQ Press, 2012), 97–99; "History of Women in the U.S. Congress," 2019, Center for American Women and Politics, https://www.cawp.rutgers.edu/history-women-us-congress.

29. Emily Newell Blair quoted in Kathryn Anderson, "Evolution of a Partisan: Emily Newell Blair and the Democratic Party, 1920–1932," in Gustafson et al., *We Have Come to Stay*, 109–119, 115.

30. J. Stanley Lemons, "The Sheppard-Towner Act: Progressivism in the 1920s," *Journal of American History* 55 (March 1969): 781–782; Sonya Michel and Robyn Rosen, "The Paradox of Maternalism: Elizabeth Lowell Putnam and the American Welfare State," *Gender and History* 4 (Autumn 1992): 367–370; Richard A. Meckel, *Save the Babies: American Public Health Reform and the Prevention of Infant Mortality, 1850–1929* (Baltimore: Johns Hopkins University Press, 1989).

31. Evelyn Nakano Glenn, *Unequal Freedom: How Race and Gender Shaped American Citizenship and Labor* (Cambridge, MA: Harvard University Press, 2004); Nancy MacLean, *Behind the Mask of Chivalry: The Making of the Second Ku Klux Klan* (New York: Oxford University Press, 1994); Evelyn Brooks Higginbotham, "In Politics to Stay: Black Women Leaders and Party Politics in the 1920s," in *Women, Politics and Change*, ed. Louise A. Tilly and Patricia Gurin (New York: Russell Sage Foundation, 1990); Mae M. Ngai, *Impossible Subjects: Illegal Aliens and the Making of Modern America* (Princeton, NJ: Princeton University Press, 2004); Candice Lewis Bredbenner, *A Nationality of Her Own: Women, Marriage, and the Law of Citizenship* (Berkeley: University of California Press, 1999).

32. Paula S. Fass, *The Damned and the Beautiful: American Youth in the 1920s* (New York: Oxford University Press, 1977); Linda Gordon, *Woman's Body, Woman's Right: Birth Control in America* (New York: Penguin Books, 1976).

33. Kate Weigand, *Red Feminism: American Communism and the Making of Women's Liberation* (Baltimore: Johns Hopkins University Press, 2001); Daniel Horowitz, *Betty Friedan and the Making of "The Feminine Mystique": The American Left, The Cold War, and Modern Feminism* (Amherst: University of Massachusetts Press, 1998); Landon R. Y. Storrs, *The Second Red Scare and the Unmaking of the New Deal Left* (Princeton, NJ: Princeton University Press, 2013).

34. Susan Ware, *Beyond Suffrage: Women in the New Deal* (Cambridge, MA: Harvard University Press, 1981).

35. Ware, *Beyond Suffrage*, 69.

36. Alan Brinkley, *The End of Reform: New Deal Liberalism in Recession and War* (New York: Alfred A. Knopf, 1995); Self, *All in the Family* (see n. 5).

37. Linda Gordon, *Pitied but Not Entitled: Single Mothers and the History of Welfare 1890–1935* (New York: Free Press, Macmillan, 1994); Robyn Muncy, *Creating a Female Dominion in American Reform, 1890–1935* (New York: Oxford University Press, 1991); Theda Skocpol, *Protecting Soldiers and Mothers: The Political Origins of Social Policy in the United States* (Cambridge, MA: Harvard University Press, 1992).

38. Ware, *Beyond Suffrage*, 100; Cathy Moran Hajo, *Birth Control on Main Street: Organizing Clinics in the United States, 1916–1940* (Urbana: University of Illinois Press, 2010).

39. Ruth Feldstein, *Motherhood in Black and White: Race and Sex in Modern Liberalism, 1930–1965* (Ithaca, NY: Cornell University Press, 2000); Gordon, *Pitied but Not Entitled*.

40. Nancy Gabin, *Feminism in the Labor Movement: Women and the United Auto Workers, 1935–1975* (Ithaca, NY: Cornell University Press, 1990); Alice Kessler-Harris, *Out to Work: A History of Wage-Earning Women in the United States* (New York: Oxford University Press, 1982).

41. Dorothy Sue Cobble, *The Other Women's Movement: Workplace Justice and Social Rights in Modern America* (Princeton, NJ: Princeton University Press, 2004); Ruth Milkman, *Gender at Work: The Dynamics of Job Segregation by Sex during World War II* (Urbana: University of Illinois Press, 1987).

42. Elaine Tyler May, *Homeward Bound: American Families in the Cold War Era* (New York: Basic Books, 1988).

43. Elliott J. Gorn, "Why Emmett Till Still Matters," *Chicago Tribune*, July 20, 2018.

44. Feldstein, *Motherhood in Black and White*; Susan Lynn, *Progressive Women in Conservative Times: Radical Justice, Peace, and Feminism, 1945 to the 1960s* (New Brunswick, NJ: Rutgers University Press, 1992); Danielle McGuire, *At the Dark End of the Street: Black Women, Rape and Resistance—a New History of the Civil Rights Movement from Rosa Parks to the Rise of Black Power* (New York: Knopf, 2010).

45. Jo Freeman, *A Room at a Time: How Women Entered Party Politics* (New York: Rowman & Littlefield, 2000), 93.

46. Weigand, *Red Feminism*.

47. Marjorie Hunter, "Women Besiege Capitol, Demanding a Test Ban," *New York Times*, May 8, 1963, 17.

48. Max Rafferty and Patricia Gilbert quoted in Michelle Nickerson, "Moral Mothers and Goldwater Girls," in *The Conservative Sixties*, ed. David Farber and Jeff Roche (New York: Peter Lange, 2003), 51–62, 54.

49. Elizabeth Gillespie McRae, *Mothers of Massive Resistance: White Women and the Politics of White Supremacy* (Oxford: Oxford University Press, 2018).

50. Barry Goldwater quoted in Catherine Rymph, *Republican Women: Feminism and Conservatism from Suffrage through the Rise of the New Right* (Chapel Hill: University of North Carolina Press, 2006), 162.

51. Janet M. Martin, *The Presidency and Women: Promise, Performance, and Illusion* (College Station: Texas A&M University Press, 2003), 65.

52. Cynthia Harrison, *On Account of Sex: The Politics of Women's Issues, 1945–1968* (Berkeley: University of California Press, 1988); Martin, *The Presidency and Women*, 49–86.

53. Dorothy Height quoted in Sara Evans, *Born for Liberty: A History of Women in America* (New York: Free Press Paperbacks, 1997), 297; Katherine Mellon Charron, *Freedom's Teacher: The Life of Septima Clark* (Chapel Hill: University of North Carolina Press, 2006); Kay Mills, *This Little Light of Mine: The Life of Fannie Lou Hamer* (Louisville: University of Kentucky Press, 2007).

54. Pauli Murray quoted in Serena Mayeri, *Reasoning from Race: Feminism, Law, and the Civil Rights Revolution* (Cambridge, MA: Harvard University Press, 2011), 22.

55. National Woman's Party resolution quoted in Harrison, *On Account of Sex*, 176.

56. Martha Griffiths quoted in Susan M. Hartmann, *From Margin to Mainstream: American Women and Politics since 1960* (New York: Alfred A. Knopf, 1989), 55; Nancy MacLean, "The Hidden History of Affirmative Action: Working Women's Struggles in the 1970s and the Gender of Class," *Feminist Studies* 25, no. 1 (Spring 1999): 42–78.

57. "Statement of Purpose," National Organization for Women, 1966, https://now.org/about/history/statement-of-purpose/.

58. Hartmann, *From Margin to Mainstream,* 77.

59. "Women in Politics," Cover, *Life,* June 9, 1972.

60. "Fact Sheet on Women in the Electorate," undated, box 168, Gloria Steinem Papers, Sophia Smith Collection, Smith College, Northampton, Massachusetts.

61. Susan Tolchin and Martin Tolchin, *Clout: Womanpower and Politics* (New York: Coward, McCann & Geoghegan, 1974), 15; Hartmann, *From Margin to Mainstream,* 85; "Summary of Women Candidates for Selected Offices, 1970–2018," Center for American Women and Politics, December 3, 2018, http://www.cawp.rutgers.edu/sites/default/files/resources/can_histsum.pdf.

62. Martin, *The Presidency and Women,* 123–166; Memorandum, July 18, 1973, "Chron File–July 1973," box 11, Barbara Franklin Papers, Richard M. Nixon Presidential Library, Yorba Linda, California.

63. For wider discussion of these efforts, Leandra Zarnow, *Battling Bella: The Protest Politics of Bella Abzug* (Cambridge, MA: Harvard University Press, 2019); Anastasia Curwood, "Black Feminism on Capitol Hill: Shirley Chisholm and Movement Politics, 1968–1984," *Meridians* 13, no. 1 (2015): 204–232.

64. Mary Frances Berry, *Why ERA Failed: Politics, Women's Rights, and the Amending Process of the Constitution* (Bloomington: Indiana University Press, 1998); Donald G. Mathews and Jane Sherron DeHart, *Sex, Gender, and the Politics of the ERA: A State and a Nation* (New York: Oxford University Press, 1990).

65. William P. Rogers quoted in "Women's Caucus Target of White House Jokes," *New York Times,* July 14, 1971, 17.

66. Jules Witcover, "Women Candidates Capitalizing on Clean Political Image," *Washington Post,* June 16, 1974, L1; Tolchin and Tolchin, *Clout;* John A. Lawrence, *The Class of '74: Congress after Watergate and the Roots of Partisanship* (Baltimore: Johns Hopkins University Press, 2018).

67. Anne Valk, "Living a Feminist Lifestyle: The Intersection of Theory and Action in a Lesbian Feminist Collective," *Feminist Studies* 28, no. 2 (Summer 2002): 303–332.

68. Ashley D. Farmer, *Remaking Black Power: How Black Women Transformed an Era* (Chapel Hill: University of North Carolina Press, 2017), 81.

69. Teresa Palomo Acosto and Ruthe Winegarten, *Las Tejanas: 300 Years of History* (Austin: University of Texas Press, 2003), 240, and generally 236–41;

Cynthia E. Orozco, "Mujeres Por La Raza," *Handbook of Texas Online*, Texas State Historical Association, https://tshaonline.org/handbook/online/articles /vimgh. See also Maylei Blackwell, *¡Chicana Power! Contested Histories of Feminism in the Chicano Movement* (Austin, University of Texas Press, 2011).

70. Martha P. Cotera, "Mujeres Bravas: How Chicana Feminists Championed the Equal Rights Amendment and Feminist Agenda in 1977 at the Texas Women's Meeting and the International Women's Year National Conference," in *Chicana Movidas: New Narratives of Activism and Feminism in the Movement Era*, ed. Dionne Espinoza, María Eugenia Cotera, and Maylei Blackwell (Austin: University of Texas Press, 2018), 51–75.

71. *The Spirit of Houston: An Official Report to the President, the Congress and the People of the United States* (Washington, DC: Government Printing Office, 1978).

72. Doreen J. Mattingly and Jessica L. Nare, "'A Rainbow of Women': Diversity and Unity at the 1977 U.S. International Women's Year Conference," *Journal of Women's History* 26, no. 2 (2014): 89–112, 89; Marjorie J. Spruill, *Divided We Stand: The Battle over Women's Rights and Family Values That Polarized American Politics* (New York: Bloomsbury USA, 2017).

73. "Ford, Congress Increase Funds for Militant Women's Lobby," *Human Events* 36, no. 22, May 29, 1976, 1.

74. Spruill, *Divided We Stand*.

75. Spruill, *Divided We Stand*; Lisa Levenstein, "'Don't Agonize, Organize!': The Displaced Homemakers Campaign and the Contested Goals of Postwar Feminism, *Journal of American History* 100, no. 4 (March 2014): 1114–1138.

76. Stacie Taranto, *Kitchen Table Politics: Conservative Women and Family Values in New York* (Philadelphia: University of Pennsylvania Press, 2017).

77. Patricia Schroeder, *Champion of the Great American Family: A Personal and Political Book* (New York: Random House, 1989).

78. Claire Bond Potter, "Paths to Political Citizenship: Gay Rights, Feminism, and the Carter Presidency," *Journal of Policy History* 24, no. 1 (2012): 95–114, 100.

79. Rymph, *Republican Women*, 228–229.

80. Louis Sahagan, "The Mothers of East L.A. Transform Themselves and Their Neighborhood," *Los Angeles Times*, August 13, 1989; Mary Pardo, "Mexican American Women Grassroots Community Activists: 'Mothers of East Los Angeles,'" *Frontiers* 11, no. 1 (1990): 1–7.

81. Winona LaDuke, "Reclaiming Culture and Land: Motherhood and the Politics of Sustaining Community," in *The Politics of Motherhood: Activist Voices from Left to Right*, ed. Alexis Jetter, Annelise Orleck, and Diana Taylor (Hanover, NH: University Press of New England, 1997), 77–83, 82.

82. *Roster of Hispanic Elected Officials of 1984*, Acosta and Winegarten, *Las Tejanas*, 259; women today hold 44 percent of all school board positions (https://www.nsba.org/about-us/frequently-asked-questions, accessed May 15, 2019).

83. Susan J. Carroll, "Representing Women: Congresswomen's Perceptions of Their Representational Roles," in *Women Transforming Congress*, ed. Cindy Simon Rosenthal (Norman: University of Oklahoma Press, 2002), 50–68, 63.

84. Carol M. Mueller, "The Empowerment of Women: Polling and the Women's Voting Bloc," in *The Politics of the Gender Gap: The Social Construction of Political Influence*, ed. Carol M. Mueller (Newbury Park, CA: Sage Publications, 1988), 16–36, 16.

85. Howell Raines, "Mondale's Tough Choice: His Aids Try to Alleviate 'Super Pressure' to Pick a Woman, and Feminists Are Split," *New York Times,* July 3, 1984, A1.

86. Frank Mankiewicz quoted in David Farrell, "Democrats' Misguided Bows to Feminist Groups," *Boston Globe*, December 3, 1984, 19; Bella Abzug and Mim Kelber, "Despite the Reagan Sweep, a Gender Gap Remains," *New York Times,* November 23, 1984, A35.

87. Marissa Chappell, "Reagan's 'Gender Gap' Strategy and the Limitations of Free-Market Feminism," *Journal of Policy History* 24, no. 1 (2012): 117–134.

88. Ellen Malcolm, with Craig Unger, *When Women Win: EMILY's List and the Rise of Women in American Politics* (New York: Mariner Books, 2017).

89. Garance Franke-Ruta, "The White House Project Shutters Its Doors," *The Atlantic,* January 28, 2013, https://www.theatlantic.com/politics/archive/2013/01/the-white-house-project-shutters-its-doors/272576/; Kate Sheppard, "Susan B. Anthony List Founder: Republicans Hijacked My PAC!," *Mother Jones*, February 22, 2012, https://www.motherjones.com/politics/2012/02/susan-b-anthony-list-sharp-right-turn-rachel-macnair/.

90. Leandra Zarnow, informal conversations with network participants and legal advocates Leslye Orloff and Janice Kaguyutan, 1999 to present.

91. On PFLAG's founding, https://pflag.org/our-story.

92. Hillary Clinton faced lasting ridicule for this comment but tried to reclaim her position during her 2016 election campaign. Clinton as quoted in, Amy Chozick, "Hillary Clinton and the Return of the (Unbaked) Cookies," *New York Times,* November 5, 2016.

93. Clyde Wilcox, "Why Was 1992 the 'Year of the Woman'? Explaining Women's Gains in 1992," in *The Year of the Woman: Myths and Realities*, ed. Elizabeth Adell Cook, Sue Thomas, and Clyde Wilcox (Boulder, CO: Westview Press, 1994), 1–24, 4.

94. Carole Chaney and Barbara Sinclair, "Women and the 1992 House Elections," in Cook et al., *The Year of the Woman*, 123–40, 126; and Robert Biersack and Paul S. Herrnson, "Political Parties and the Year of the Woman," Cook et al., *The Year of the Woman*, 161–180, 164.

95. "Table 2.9. House and Senate Retirements by Party, 1930–2012," *Vital Statistics on Congress,* April 7, 2014, Brookings Institution, https://www.brookings

.edu/wp-content/uploads/2016/06/Vital-Statistics-Chapter-2-Congressional
-Elections.pdf.

96. Chaney and Sinclair, "Women and the 1992 House Elections," in Cook et al., *The Year of the Woman*, 130; and Biersack and Herrnson, "Political Parties and the Year of the Woman." See also Elsa Barkley Brown, "'What Happened Here': The Politics of Difference in Women's History and Feminist Politics," *Feminist Studies* 18, no. 2 (Summer 1992): 295–312.

97. Paraphrased in Stephen Chapman, "Some Women in Politics Still Face Special Hurdles," *Chicago Tribune*, June 10, 1993.

98. Gloria Steinem quoted in Chapman, "Some Women in Politics Still Face Special Hurdles."

99. On the Independent Women's Forum, https://www.iwf.org.

100. Bob Herbert, "In America; The Feminist Dilemma," *New York Times*, January 29, 1998.

101. William H. Chafe, *Hillary and Bill: The Clintons and the Politics of the Personal* (Durham, NC: Duke University Press, 2016); and on Gloria Steinem revisiting her 1998 defense of Bill Clinton, Molly Redden, "Gloria Steinem on Her Bill Clinton Essay: 'I Wouldn't Write the Same Thing Now,'" *The Guardian*, November 30, 2017.

102. Liette Gidlow, ed., *Obama, Clinton, Palin: Making History in Election 2008* (Urbana: University of Illinois Press, 2011).

103. "Transcript: Donald Trump's Taped Comments about Women," *New York Times*, October 8, 2016.

104. "An Examination of the 2016 Electorate, Based on Validated Voters," Pew Research Center, August 9, 2018, https://www.people-press.org/2018/08/09/an-examination-of-the-2016-electorate-based-on-validated-voters/.

105. Joe Biden quoted in Joe Klein, "How Soccer Moms Became Security Moms," *Time*, February 10, 2003; and for analysis, Susan J. Carroll, "Security Moms and Presidential Politics: Women Voters in the 2004 Election," in *Voting the Gender Gap*, ed. Lois Duke Whitaker (Urbana: University of Illinois Press, 2008), 75–90.

106. Amanda Hess, "How a Fractious Women's Movement Came to Lead the Left," *New York Times Magazine*, February 7, 2017.

107. "125 Women Won Their Election Seats," *Washington Post*, November 6, 2018, https://www.washingtonpost.com/graphics/2018/politics/women
-congress-governor/.

108. Debbie Walsh quoted in Kate Zernike and Denise Lu, "A Surge of Women Candidates, but Crowded Primaries and Tough Races Await," *New York Times*, May 12, 2018.

109. For representative supportive coverage, Matthew Yglesias, "The Case for Making 2020 the Real Year of the Woman," March 21, 2019, *Vox*, https://www.vox.com/policy-and-politics/2019/3/21/18273565/women

-president-2020-electability. Tracking negative coverage, Alexander Frandsen and Aleszu Bajak, "Women on the 2020 Campaign Trail Are Being Treated More Negatively by the Media," March 29, 2019 (ongoing update), *Storybench,* Northeastern University School of Journalism, http://www.storybench .org/women-on-the-2020-campaign-trail-are-being-treated-more-negatively-by -the-media/.

110. Jennifer L. Lawless and Richard L. Fox, *It Takes a Candidate: Why Women Don't Run for Office* (Cambridge, UK: Cambridge University Press, 2005).

111. Stacey Abrams quoted in David Marchese, "Why Stacey Abrams Is Still Saying She Won," *New York Times Magazine,* April 28, 2019.

112. Maggie Astor, "Georgia Governor Brian Kemp Faces Investigation by House Panel," *New York Times,* March 6, 2019.

113. Stacey Abrams quoted in Alan Blinder and Richard Fausset, "Stacey Abrams Ends Fight for Georgia Governor with Harsh Words for Her Rival," *New York Times,* November 16, 2018. For return results, see https://ballotpedia .org/Georgia_elections,_2018.

114. Camila Domonoske, "Many Native IDs Won't Be Accepted at North Dakota Polling Places," *NPR,* October 13, 2018, https://www.npr.org/2018/10 /13/657125819/many-native-ids-wont-be-accepted-at-north-dakota-polling -places.

115. Shelby County v. Holder, 570 U.S. 529 (2013). See generally, Allan J. Lichtman, *The Embattled Vote in America: From the Founding to the Present* (Cambridge, MA: Harvard University Press, 2018), 180–251; Carol Anderson, *One Person, No Vote: How Voter Suppression Is Destroying Our Democracy* (New York: Bloomsbury, 2018).

116. Rosanell Eaton quoted in Lichtman, *The Embattled Vote in America,* 196; see generally, 195–197.

117. The Supreme Court determined not to hear North Carolina v. North Carolina State Conference of the NAACP, letting the Fourth Circuit Court of Appeals 2017 decision stand. Appellate Court opinion and Barack Obama quoted in Robert D. McFaddan, "Rosanell Eaton, Fierce Voting Rights Advocate, Dies at 97," *New York Times,* December 9, 2018.

PART ONE

Voting Rights Real and Imagined

*Women's Political Engagement in the Decades
after Suffrage, 1920s–1950s*

Dedication of Women's Pioneer Statue in US Capitol Crypt, February 15, 1921. Records of the
National Woman's Party, Library of Congress; courtesy of the National Woman's Party.

CHAPTER 2

Commemorating the History of the Nineteenth Amendment

The National Woman's Party and the
Politics of Memory in the 1920s

CLAIRE DELAHAYE

IN OCTOBER 1920, sculptor Adelaide Johnson reflected on how monumental it was that her marble rendition of white suffrage leaders Susan B. Anthony, Lucretia Mott, and Elizabeth Cady Stanton would soon be placed in the US Capitol. "No one seems to have arisen to the realization that this is something far more than the simple presentation of three busts. It is the commemoration of an epoch," she wrote.[1] This occasion, Johnson made clear, captured not merely the three leaders she depicted but rather a remarkable period, "an epoch" of struggle for suffrage. The big reveal, a "Memorial Service to Pioneer Suffragists," would take place on February 15, 1921, a date selected by organizers in the National Woman's Party (NWP) because it was the anniversary of Susan B. Anthony's birth. The placement of the monument in the Capitol Rotunda was meant to signal women's growing presence in the seats of power; yet it was quickly taken down to the Crypt. As a result, it became a symbol of women's lack of representation in Congress after the 1920 election.[2]

Gathering over a hundred women's organizations, the unveiling of the monument coincided with the NWP's first postsuffrage national convention in Washington, DC, where participants determined their next campaign would focus on equal rights. Alongside this new policy direction, the group focused on how their past would be documented and represented. Beyond the monument dedication, an exhibition highlighting

NWP's past activities ran throughout the week at the Library of Congress, and the publication of Inez Irwin's *The Story of the Woman's Party* was timed specifically for the convention.[3] These efforts point to the "importance of collective historical memory to the operation of social movements."[4] As historian Lisa Tetrault has demonstrated in her analysis of the making of the "myth" of Seneca Falls in the 1890s, carefully orchestrated representations of the past help "legitimate and unify the messy contingencies of political struggle."[5] Likewise, Julie Des Jardins shows that "organized feminists turned the writing of history into a programmatic act, a political gesture for women's rights in the public sphere."[6]

The NWP undeniably used the commemoration of the suffrage campaign leading up to the Nineteenth Amendment, and their role in this struggle, to craft a narrative of triumph and unity as they sought to quell brewing tensions before their organization's conventions.[7] Indeed, the debates that ensued crystallized the opposition between "social feminists," who "desired equality insofar as it did not infringe upon their demands for protection for women," and "equal rights feminists," who saw protective legislation as incompatible with full equality.[8] Different women's organizations pushed for other agendas, such as reproductive rights or disarmament. Furthermore, African American delegates denounced what could be described as the "whitewashed victory paradigm," which completely ignored the disenfranchisement of many women of color. These convention participants requested that the NWP leadership support a congressional investigation on the matter; yet their request was turned down.[9] While the NWP worked with Puerto Rican suffragists after 1925, the group failed to conduct parallel advocacy of women (and men) of color facing voter suppression.[10] Instead, delegates at this first convention "voted overwhelmingly to accept the majority resolution," which recommended that the "immediate work of the new organization be the removal of the legal disabilities of women." Criticisms soon emerged, highlighting the difficulty facing the NWP to unite women for equal rights "to the degree they had been united for suffrage."[11]

Facing these constraints, the NWP consistently exploited commemorations to justify its political and ideological stance as it transitioned from a suffrage organization to an equal rights for women organization. Known for their White House pickets during the final stage of the suffrage struggle, NWP activists turned to commemoration of these acts as a central part of its postsuffrage communication strategy. As major modes of aesthetic, historical, and spatial expression, women's suffrage commemorations were used to both recall and shape the past, to recruit and galvanize new militants for the future, to legitimize the power of the NWP, and to construct authority within the organization and outside of it, making memory a site of political and ideological struggle.

NWP Commemorations in the Political Climate of the 1920s

After the ratification of the Nineteenth Amendment, many women's rights organizations and individual suffragists focused on preserving, recording, and transmitting the memories of their struggle. Activists consciously worked to shape public memory by publishing memoirs, biographies, and histories and establishing archives, thereby participating in a wide cultural push for commemoration. For instance, Americans were highly preoccupied with memorializing the Great War.[12] The construction of Confederate monuments also peaked in this period, as commemoration became one strategy for upholding white supremacy under Jim Crow.[13] As far as women were concerned, representations of their historical roles were publicized by "feminists, historians of women, corporations, and the advertising industry."[14] Suffragists busily planned pageants and pilgrimages, dedicated memorials, unveiled portraits and statues, and held birthday ceremonies to tell a carefully choreographed story about how women got the vote. This need for public recognition has to be understood in relation to white middle-class women's conviction that they were owed prestige and dignity and faced a long and, at times, violent struggle to gain the vote. For example, many NWP members' speeches referred to what they perceived as selective public memory, which honored those who had fought in World War I but completely ignored white women's struggle for their rights.[15]

Paradoxically, the importance of commemorations suggests a social movement in crisis. In the early 1920s, the NWP was losing membership— the figures in the archives show a steep drop from 30,652 members in November 1920 to 7,243 in October 1923.[16] A lot of activists had decided to retire from politics or had chosen to focus on specific issues, such as pacifism. This loss of membership further reflected widening rifts within feminist ranks due to the group's exclusionary lack of concern for African American women's disenfranchisement and prioritization of the Equal Rights Amendment (ERA), which labor feminists thought would undercut protective legislation.[17] In November 1922, the *New York Times* reported that organizations with an aggregate membership of 10 million had parted company with the NWP over these issues.[18] Antagonism worsened after April 1923, when in *Adkins v. Children's Hospital*, the Supreme Court ruled that a minimum wage law for women violated the Due Process Clause of the Fifth Amendment. Nevertheless, the NWP pursued its policy, and its connected commemoration activities, undaunted. In July 1923, NWP leader Alice Paul presented the ERA at a gathering in Seneca Falls to commemorate the seventy-fifth anniversary of the first Seneca Falls Convention; there, participants also held a pageant and a pilgrimage to Susan B. Anthony's grave.[19] By December, the NWP compelled Senator Charles Curtis of Kansas and Representative Daniel Anthony of Kansas, nephew of Susan B. Anthony, to introduce the ERA in Congress.[20]

The NWP continuously lobbied for equal rights, but it was increasingly isolated politically, as demonstrated by the 1925 congressional hearing on the issue, where the NWP was the sole group advocating the passage of an equal rights amendment.[21] Indeed, as Alexander Keyssar notes, "The largest movement for voting rights in the nation's history did not spark the revolution that some had feared but instead coincided with the return to 'normalcy' in American politics."[22] The political and cultural climate of the 1920s was hostile to women's political campaigning, even though many were active in various organizations. Progressive women not only disagreed on policies, preventing a women's voting bloc from emerging, but were also attacked by conservative women's groups, such as the Daughters of the American Revolution and the Woman Patriot Corporation, organized in March 1922 after the National Association Opposed to Woman Suffrage disbanded, achieving influence in Washington. The latter group's newspaper *The Patriot* accused the NWP of being led by Communists.[23] In this climate, Alice Paul lamented in 1924, women were not recruited as candidates for Congress by the parties, and if they were, they were in "hopeless" districts.[24] For the rest of the decade, the NWP conducted research on the legal discrimination of women, tirelessly raised awareness about and lobbied for the passage of the ERA, and tried to convince other women to join their cause.[25] In this politically divisive period, commemorations served as an additional and essential strategy to build social cohesion and to assuage tensions within and outside the NWP. Representations of the past, the group believed, could be controlled, as opposed to politics in the present. Theirs was a reactive impulse as much as a nostalgic enterprise, illustrating how the past "is a crucial symbolic resource for groups in political contestation."[26]

(Re)building a Movement by Transmitting History

Within the NWP, commemorations took on a didactic function, conveying instruction, information, and entertainment. Indeed, knowledge of the past and its transmission were deemed central to women's political involvement. Tributes to suffrage history reactivated members' networks, nurtured old friendships, and aimed at educating younger generations by relaying ideas and tactics. Former suffragists persistently underlined that their sacrifices were disregarded and that the youth were ungrateful. This generational disconnect highlighted both perceived and imagined lack of transmission of suffragists' history as well as their awareness of the patriarchal gatekeeping of history making, including in the area of women's historical remembrance. While frustrated by a seeming lack of recognition, NWP members also saw commemorations as a means to recruit new and younger members. This politics of legacy encouraged an intergenerational exchange even as aging suffragists sought to control the dialogue. For example, in June 1923, the NWP purposely organized its Inez Milholland's Memorial Committee to galvanize new militants, especially within colleges and universities. NWP's publications portrayed Milholland, a suffrage martyr who died in 1916 at age thirty while on a Western speaking tour, as a modern New Woman—adventurous, athletic, and fearless, who "ha[d] a tremendous appeal for the young."[27] The committee organized a Memorial Masque, an allegorical entertainment involving music, dancing, singing, and acting on Milholland's birthday August 6, 1924, near Mount Inez, where she is buried, "to reach the student bodies and to interest them in the work of our Committee."[28]

Former suffragists actively created opportunities for cross-generational exchange facilitated through the sharing of mementos, giving younger women a perceptual and affective experience of the past grounded in material culture. New members of NWP could see an exhibition in Seneca Falls during the 1923 NWP convention of "relics of 1848." Activists formed reading circles, recommended books, and published bibliographies. During ceremonies, they told stories, read the letters of former leaders, and delivered eulogies and tributes, linking to the past through the power of verbal imagery and music. Speeches highlighted the exemplary lives of pioneers, such as Susan B. Anthony, whose life was described as "an epic poem, a tale of heroism, of faithfulness, of patience, and of great reward."[29] Hagiographical stories were repeated, circulated, and formed as a history was spun that focused on symbolic biographical moments. As monuments were scarce, history-minded former suffragists recognized the importance of the written word as a vehicle of commemoration.

The history of suffrage became a performance, a spectacle to be consumed. "In the beautiful Garden of the Gods, where great rocks rise like altars, the Woman's Party carried its banners, and thousands who witnessed their pageant shared in the desire and the demand of women to be free," the NWP recalled of one pageant performance held in Colorado.[30] Art made history more easily appropriated, and cognitive, didactic, and aesthetic functions were inextricably linked. Plays and pageants had been a key device used to bring attention to the suffrage cause, and were once again deployed to commemorate the movement. What once were political props and uniforms—costumes, banners, and other markers of suffrage identity used in suffrage demonstrations—were displayed again.[31]

The NWP headquarters itself in this moment was newly conceived as a "museum and laboratory of feminism," where preserving historical memory and forging a new political program were dual interests.[32] The NWP headquarters had been a succession of historic buildings, "venerable structures" selected because of their closeness to the White House and the halls of Congress.[33] Former suffragists were intentional in their consecration of a new geography of memory. Their strategic establishment of significant suffrage historic sites in proximity to political institutions in Washington, DC, sought to make a clear visual connection between women's struggle for the vote and representation in the federal government. However, the government's spatial interests did not always match suffragists commemorative needs. On May 21, 1922, the NWP dedicated their new headquarters in "Old Brick Capitol," a building donated by Alva Belmont that the organization described as a "shrine for women."[34] The building was constructed after the British torched the US Capitol in 1814 and was the site where Congress met from 1815 to 1819. Sold to the US government in March 1929, it was razed for the new Supreme Court Building. For a lot of NWP members, this trauma suggested possible erasure of the NWP from national memory. Regrouping that October, the NWP moved to a new building still at the doorstep of Congress at 144 B Street, NE (Constitution Avenue), renamed the Alva Belmont House, one of the oldest houses still standing on Capitol Hill.[35]

Former suffragists saw their work as a nationalizing project and sought to integrate women's suffrage into the narrative of nation building. Alice Paul believed that suffragist Lucretia Mott's birthday should become a national celebration, envisioning "to bring her before the country as a national character."[36] Monumentalizing suffrage history was especially a white women's project, reflecting their belief that the Nineteenth Amendment was a triumph. They promoted this message through a wide national awareness campaign forwarded in "schools, churches, fraternal societies, and other organizations."[37] NWP organizers lobbied and sent letters to state departments of education, to superintendent of schools, to professional organizations of teachers, to librarians, and to the National Education Association. Strategies to increase national visibility also included radio broadcasts, donations of busts, circulation of postcards, posters and photographs, and campaigns to name parks, playgrounds, lakes, and schools.[38] These campaigns sought to make women visible in history but also to refocus public attention on the NWP's current political goals and legitimize the group's power. Indeed, the NWP revised history to relocate the suffrage legacy in the center of their equal rights campaign.[39] This intention was underlined frequently in the NWP's newspaper *Equal Rights*. In one instance, it read:

> We turned to the past with a view to finding out for ourselves whether history showed any precedent for our odd vagaries, and whether we were really the first women in the world to agitate for Equal Rights as distinct from Equal Suffrage. Our researches showed that the movement for Equal Rights presents one continuous line of endeavor from the time of the first Equal Rights meeting in 1848 in Seneca Falls down to the recent Equal Rights Conference held by the Woman's Party at this same place on the seventy-fifth anniversary date of the first meeting.[40]

The past was a tool to empower women by educating them, giving them political momentum, and justifying their demands. Public representations of suffrage history were central to political work. The NWP always coupled commemorations with political meetings and invited political allies to its ceremonies. For example, it organized a meeting with President Coolidge on Susan B. Anthony's birthday in 1927. Commemorations were part of collective actions and forms of protests. They could be subversive, because they went beyond the act of remembering to comment on current politics or postulate the possibility of political change. As such, commemorations could be viewed as anamorphoses of political celebrations.[41]

The Exclusionary Memory Making of the NWP

Commemorations helped the NWP consolidate their collective identity and refresh their political momentum, while reproducing processes of exclusion. NWP official histories were carefully crafted to focus on white suffrage leaders and white women in general. Inez Irwin's *The Story of the National Woman's Party* and Doris Stevens's *Jailed for Freedom* paid tribute to the diversity of the NWP, which had welcomed unionists, immigrants, and working-class women, who are referred to in these historical accounts. Yet African American activists remained mostly invisible.[42] The only African American women who are explicitly mentioned in both accounts are the suffragists' prison inmates. Irwin and Stevens reprinted affidavits of white suffrage prisoners, and some complained about being forced to mingle with "diseased negro women" or to share the same bathrooms or dormitories.[43] The only photograph in *Jailed for Freedom* representing two African American women is one of two fellow prisoners.[44] Another revealing example of exclusionary memory making is the slide selection for NWP slideshow performances, which included portraits of icons, but also group pictures, parades, and delegations.[45] Slide lists indicated that pictures of socialist women, nurses, lawyers, college women, and labor organizers were shown. But the selection inconspicuously overlooked activists such as Mary Church Terrell, who had picketed the White House with the NWP. Much like the group's exclusionary programmatic decisions, their commemorative activities ignored the contributions of African American suffragists. However, African American women were invited to participate in the pilgrimage to the grave of Susan B. Anthony in Rochester on July 22, 1923. As the program indicates, they were at the back of the procession, including "groups that owe debt to Miss Anthony."[46]

The dynamics of racism, memory making, and political campaigns were on display in high relief at the 1924 NWP conference and its tribute to Inez Milholland. That June, the NWP had lobbied Republicans and Democrats to include an ERA plank on their platform, which failed. In August, the organization convened its annual gathering in Westport, New York, where participants discussed plans to elect more women to Congress and increase support for the ERA. Festivities that brought the convention to a close included a "Forward into Light" pageant, a memorial service, and a pilgrimage to Milholland's grave. During the ceremony at the grave, the revered suffragist's father accused NWP leaders of "drawing the color line" and "refusing to permit negro women who were his guests to pay tribute to his daughter."[47] The issue was widely reported in the papers and gave negative publicity to the NWP.[48] The National Association for the Advancement of Colored People sent a telegram to Alice Paul, chastising her for "capitulation to race prejudice . . . to the price of election of women to office."[49] The NWP tried to defend its position by revisiting its history and explaining that it did not discriminate against African American women. The debate resurfaced concerning the treatment of African American women in the March 3, 1913, parade, and Paul claimed that these women had not been barred from marching.[50] To respond to criticisms, the NWP reproduced an earlier interview with Mary Church Terrell, who stressed that the NWP was "one of the few organizations that ha[d] opened its membership to the colored people." But Terrell spoke out, highlighting her disappointment in hearing that NWP leaders believed the group was not "organized to take sides on the race question."[51] Moreover, NWP leaders "admitted they felt prominence given representatives of the negro race in any affair connected with the party campaign might work against chances of electing women nominated for Congress from the Southern States."[52] This episode shows that the NWP prioritized its legislative goals and chose to ignore the plight of African Americans as a strategy to rally white southern men and women to the cause of equal rights. Its commemorative activities were thus racialized to serve its political interests. And, in the end, the choice of Inez Milholland as the

NWP's ultimate icon suggests that the group believed only a young, white woman could serve as model for new generations of activists.

The NWP stands out as a significant vehicle of suffrage commemoration activity in the years after the ratification of the Nineteenth Amendment. The group had the skills and resources to create influential history-making vehicles capitalizing on a committed membership focused on preservation work alongside policy campaigns, political and media connections maintained after suffrage, a supple public preoccupied with memory politics, and the economic resources to forward monument-building thanks to effective fundraising.

Memory work was a way for NWP to give order to and brace the postsuffrage environment. But the creation of historical genealogy was also an expression of power in which certain figures were actively made visible and others invisible. Through protean commemorations, the NWP promoted a view of history that intertwined American exceptionalism and white supremacy. This whitewashed portrayal of suffrage memory has had long-lasting consequences, as shown by recent debates surrounding the establishment of a monument for women's rights in New York City's Central Park.[53] That is why there is a further need to deconstruct such representations and the dynamics of exclusionary memory making, which has erased minorities from images, narratives, and archives. These early suffrage commemoration activities must be understood as white women's active pursuit and not an accident of history.

Notes

1. Adelaide Johnson to Ida Husted Harper, October 17, 1920, Adelaide Johnson Papers, Manuscript Division, Library of Congress (hereafter "LOC"), Washington, DC. On the history of the *Portrait Monument*, see Sandra Weber, *The Woman Suffrage Statue: A History of Adelaide Johnson's Portrait Monument at the United States Capitol* (Jefferson, NC: McFarland, 2016). The author wishes to thank the French Association for American Studies and the Kluge Center at the Library of Congress for funding archival research that has been crucial for the completion of this piece.

2. As of February 1921, Alice Mary Robertson was the only woman in Congress. She was a Republican representative from Oklahoma hostile to woman suffrage.

3. Inez Irwin, *The Story of the Woman's Party* (New York: Harcourt, Brace, 1921).

4. Lisa Tetrault, *The Myth of Seneca Falls: Memory and the Women's Suffrage Movement, 1848–1898* (Chapel Hill: University of North Carolina Press, 2014), 1.

5. Tetrault, *The Myth of Seneca Falls*, 4.

6. Julie Des Jardins, *Women and the Historical Enterprise in America: Gender, Race, and the Politics of Memory, 1880–1945* (Chapel Hill: University of North Carolina Press, 2003), 177.

7. Christine Lunardini, *From Equal Suffrage to Equal Rights: Alice Paul and the National Woman's Party, 1910–1928* (1986; San Jose, CA: toExcel Press, 2000), 157.

8. Lunardini, *From Equal Suffrage*, 151.

9. Freda Kirchwey, "Alice Paul Pulls the Strings," *The Nation*, March 2, 1921, 332–333. The papers of the NWP show that many had written to the organization to alert it on the terrorizing of African Americans in the South and to request immediate action. See, for example, Anna A. Clemons to Emma Wold, October 24, 1920, National Woman's Party Papers, 1913–1974, Manuscript Division, LOC, microfilm (1979), reel 5; Mary White Ovington to Lucy Burns, December 17, 1920, National Woman's Party Papers, 1913–1974, Manuscript Division, LOC, microfilm (1979), reel 5; George B. Lockwood to Florence Boeckel, November 1, 1920, National Woman's Party Papers, 1913–1974, Manuscript Division, LOC, microfilm (1981), reel 83.

10. "Woman's Party Aids Porto Rican Women," *Equal Rights*, May 16, 1925; Allison L. Sneider, *Suffragists in an Imperial Age: U.S. Expansion and the Woman Question, 1870–1929* (New York: Oxford University Press, 2008), 131.

11. Lunardini, *From Equal Suffrage*, 160–162.

12. Lisa M. Budreau, *Bodies of War: World War I and the Politics of Commemoration in America, 1919–1933* (New York: New York University Press, 2010); Steven Trout, *On the Battlefield of Memory: The First World War and American Remembrance, 1919–1941* (Tuscaloosa: University of Alabama Press, 2010).

13. In 1922, the US Senate approved a proposal from the United Daughters of the Confederacy to create the Faithful Slave Mammies of the South memorial in Washington, DC, which infuriated African American communities. The UDC included suffragists.

14. Emily Westkaemper, *Selling Women's History: Packaging Feminism in Twentieth-Century American Popular Culture* (New Brunswick, NJ: Rutgers University Press, 2017), 1.

15. "114th Anniversary of the Birth of Elizabeth Cady Stanton, November 12, 1929," box 214, Anna Kelton Wiley Papers, Manuscript Division, LOC.

16. National Woman's Party Papers, 1913–1974, Manuscript Division, LOC, microfilm (1981), reel 83; "National Woman's Party Membership Report," September 1, 1923, to October 1, 1923, box 238, Anna Kelton Wiley Papers, Manuscript Division, LOC.

17. The press was already mentioning the Equal Rights Amendment in 1921, "Woman's Party All Ready for Equality Fight," *Baltimore Sun*, September 26, 1921. Amy E. Butler, *Two Paths to Equality: Alice Paul and Ethel M. Smith in the ERA Debate, 1921–1929* (Albany: State University of New York Press, 2002), 59.

18. "Opposes Equality Bill," *New York Times*, November 19, 1922. The National Consumers' League had announced it could not "cooperate with the NWP in the promotion of legislation to do away with discriminations against women." It added that the equality bill "would endanger even acts that already had been passed for the protection of working women and women in their homes."

19. The amendment read: "Men and women shall have equal rights throughout the United States and every place subject to its jurisdiction. Congress shall have power to enforce this article by appropriate legislation."

20. The ERA was reintroduced in every session of Congress for forty-nine consecutive years, although Alice Paul revised original 1923 wording in 1943.

21. US Congress, House of Representatives, Committee on the Judiciary, *Equal Rights Amendment to the Constitution: Hearing before Committee on the Judiciary House of Representatives*, Sixty Eighth Congress, 2nd Session (Washington, DC: Government Printing Office, 1925).

22. Alexander Keyssar, *The Right to Vote: The Contested History of Democracy in the United States* (New York: Basic Books, 2000), 218.

23. Dorothy Sue Cobble, Linda Gordon, and Astrid Henry, *Feminism Unfinished: A Short, Surprising History of American Women's Movements* (New York: Liveright, 2014), 12; "Are Not Reds, Woman's Party Leader Retorts," *Washington Post*, September 5, 1922. *The Woman Patriot* was described as "a national newspaper for home and national defense against woman suffrage, feminism and socialism" and was published from 1918 until 1932.

24. "Women Will Strive for a Congress Bloc," *New York Times*, August 17, 1924.

25. "Cite 50 Ways Laws Hold Women to Be Inferior," *New York Times*, March 2, 1924; "Finds Women Here Submerged by Law," *New York Times*, October 10, 1929.

26. Robert S. Jansen, "Resurrection and Appropriation: Reputational Trajectories, Memory Work, and the Political Use of Historical Figures," *American Journal of Sociology* 112, no. 4 (January 2007), 958.

27. "In Memory of Inez Milholland," November 1923, box 38, Anna Kelton Wiley Papers, Manuscript Division, LOC.

28. Lucy Branham to members of the Inez Milholland Memorial Fund Committee, January 5, 1924, box 38, Anna Kelton Wiley Papers, Manuscript Division, LOC. The year indicated on the document is 1923, but it is 1924.

29. 110th anniversary of the birth of Susan B. Anthony, February 16, 1930, box 214, Anna Kelton Wiley Papers, Manuscript Division, LOC.

30. Harvard University–Schlesinger Library on the History of Women in America/Alice Paul Papers Series II, Suffrage, Suffrage-related, post-1920: pamphlets, clippings, . . . , 1924–1976, MC 399, folder 279, Schlesinger Library, Radcliffe Institute, Harvard University, Cambridge, Massachusetts.

31. In a 1933 pageant dramatizing a national campaign for women's economic rights, militants carrying old banners previously used to picket the White House for suffrage were described as "memorializing women's rights pioneers." "Ask Roosevelt Aid for Women's Jobs," *New York Times*, July 9, 1933.

32. "National Woman's Party: Ava Belmont House," box 39, Anna Kelton Wiley Papers, Manuscript Division, LOC.

33. "Reception at Headquarters," January 29, 1930, box 214, Anna Kelton Wiley Papers, Manuscript Division, LOC.

34. "Make Old Capitol Shrine for Women," *Washington Post*, May 22, 1922.

35. Anna E. Hendley to Theodore W. Noyes, January 27, 1924, Susan B. Anthony Foundation, Washington, DC, records, correspondence, January–May 1924, box 3, Manuscript Division, LOC.

36. "Minutes of the Meeting of the National Council of the National Woman's Party," December 5, 1927, box 121, Anna Kelton Wiley Papers, Manuscript Division, LOC.

37. "Resolution passed by the All Americanism Conference held in Washington, DC, in May, 1924" Susan B. Anthony Foundation, Washington, DC, records, chronological file 1925–1926, box 1, Manuscript Division, LOC.

38. "From Susan B. Anthony Memorial Committee of the National Woman's Party," January 1, 1936, box 116, Anna Kelton Wiley Papers, Manuscript Division, LOC.

39. This was made obvious in a speech Belmont delivered on November 18, 1923, at a mass meeting held in the Crypt of the Capitol, which was the closing ceremony in its celebration of the seventy-fifth anniversary of the equal rights movement. "Equal Rights Meeting Held in Capitol Crypt," *New York Times*, November 19, 1923.

40. Carol Rehfisch, "Historical Background of the Equal Rights Campaign," *Equal Rights*, September 15, 1923, http://harvey.binghamton.edu/~hist266/era/historical.htm.

41. Louis Moreau de Bellaing, "Mémoire de la mémoire: la commémoration," *L'Homme et la société* 75–76 (1985): 238.

42. The only exception seems to be Nell Mercer, who is briefly mentioned in both Irwin's and Stevens's accounts.

43. Irwin, *The Story of the Woman's Party*, 264–269, 288.

44. Doris Stevens, *Jailed for Freedom* (New York: Boni & Liveright, 1920), 115.

45. Handbill, "The National Woman's Party presents Historic Lantern Slides," box 238, Anna Kelton Wiley Papers, Manuscript Division, LOC.

46. "National Woman's Party Celebration on July 20th and 21st at Seneca Falls, N.Y.," National Woman's Party Records, group IV, box 14, Manuscript Division, LOC.

47. "Women Pay Honor at Leader's Grave," *Evening Star*, August 18, 1924. Chronicling America: Historic American Newspapers, LOC, https://chronic lingamerica.loc.gov/lccn/sn83045462/1924-08-18/ed-1/seq-10/.

48. "Race Issue Hits Feminist Party," *New York World*, August 17–18, 1924, National Woman's Party Papers, 1913–1974, Manuscript Division, LOC, microfilm (1979), reel 28.

49. Telegram from Walter White to Alice Paul, August 18, 1924, National Woman's Party Papers, 1913–1974, Manuscript Division, LOC, microfilm (1979), reel 28.

50. Alice Paul to Miss L. J. C. Daniels, August 25, 1924, National Woman's Party Papers, 1913–1974, Manuscript Division, LOC, microfilm (1979), reel 28.

51. "Immediate Release," National Woman's Party to Walter White, September 2, 1924, Mary Church Terrell Papers, reel 13, Manuscript Division, LOC.

52. "Women Pay Honor at Leader's Grave."

53. Martha Jones, "How New York's New Monument Whitewashes the Women's Rights Movement," *Washington Post*, March 22, 2019.

Women's votes were not universally welcomed: "Beware, you are in danger it is a shame that a pretty and honorable girl had to get mixed up in politics—stay home Tuesday November 8th. A Friend." The recipient of this anonymous threat, dated 1932, reported it to federal authorities. US Department of Justice Central Files, Classified Subject Files, RG 60, Archives II, College Park, MD.

CHAPTER 3

After the "Century of Struggle"

The Nineteenth Amendment,
Southern African American Women, and the
Problem of Female Disenfranchisement after 1920

LIETTE GIDLOW

O N AN OCTOBER day in 1920, Susie W. Fountain fumed as she made her way home from the Elizabeth City County registrar's office in Phoebus, Virginia. Two months earlier, Tennessee had ratified the Nineteenth Amendment, making woman suffrage the law of the land and setting off celebrations from Boston to Los Angeles. Mrs. Fountain, fifty-one years old and college educated, was a pillar of the African American community there in her hometown. Her husband, John, was the only proprietor on their block on County Street in a neighborhood that was home to construction laborers, laundresses, and shipyard work-ers. The mother of four children, Mrs. Fountain presided over a "very pretty and comfortable home" that she and Mr. Fountain owned free and clear. They had paid taxes in the county for thirty-five years.[1]

Earlier that day, Mrs. Fountain had presented herself to the county registrar and taken the literacy test for prospective voters as required by Virginia law. The registrar looked over her answers, but then shook his head, saying she "did not pass altho she did very well." Registrars possessed the power to decide whether an applicant's answers were cor-rect, or correct enough, to pass, and anyone within earshot understood that the Commonwealth of Virginia was declaring that she was illiter-ate. The confetti from Nineteenth Amendment celebrations had barely settled, but Mrs. Fountain's trip home from the registrar's office was no ticker tape parade. As she told an NAACP investigator a few days later, she was "too humiliated and angry to try again."[2]

Mrs. Fountain was hardly alone in her effort to vote, and though she became discouraged, many other southern black women did not. The files of the US Department of Justice, the records of the NAACP, and African American newspapers are bursting with letters of complaint, investigative reports, and affidavits that demonstrate, contrary to prevailing understandings, that multitudes of southern black women made courageous efforts, individually and collectively, to cast ballots after the Nineteenth Amendment was ratified. Their efforts to vote were part of a surge to the polls in 1920 and beyond by southern African Americans, women and men, to claim or reclaim the voting rights that they, their fathers, or their grandfathers had lost. Sometimes their efforts succeeded. Often, however, they met with resistance, and, in some cases, outright violence. All the same, many in the community persisted. They banded together with family members and neighbors to approach election officials; they organized new groups and petitioned for redress; they sought allies among white women who had worked for suffrage; and they worked through political party organizations, especially the Republican Party, to cultivate their clout. These efforts frequently failed, but southern African Americans, once enfranchised by the Fifteenth and Nineteenth Amendments, never stopped trying to vote.[3]

Nor were southern black women the only women unable to freely vote after ratification. Women from other racial and ethnic minorities, women who lived in poll tax states, American women who married foreign nationals—these women and others also found that, despite the ratification of the Nineteenth Amendment, they still could not vote. These diverse women's stories of disenfranchisement after 1920 call into question the conclusion that the Nineteenth Amendment ended what historians once termed a "century of struggle."[4] For many women, it turns out, the struggle to vote lasted much more than a hundred years. Indeed, for some, it is not over yet.

. . .

The surge of southern black women to registration offices and polls in the fall of 1920 caught many contemporaries by surprise. Nationally, many white suffragists had worked hard to keep their black counterparts out of view during the ratification struggle, concerned that "the race question" might injure the cause and convinced that African Americans were unprepared to cast intelligent ballots. Inside the South, many whites had convinced themselves that African Americans had given up on dreams of "political equality." But show up these women did, by the thousands, in September and October to register and in November to vote in that presidential year. They celebrated their successes, often out of public view, and used their ballots to promote the community's interests. Frequently, however, they failed in their mission, blocked by obstructionist tactics, outright refusals, barely veiled threats, or threats made good.

African American women in fact succeeded in some locations in registering and voting. In Charles County, Maryland, some 247 African Americans added their names to the rolls during the September registration period, more than two-thirds of them women and every last one a Republican loyal to the party of Lincoln, the "Great Emancipator." In North Carolina, a total of about a thousand women succeeded in registering in Charlotte, Greensboro, Asheville, Salisbury, Southport, New Bern, and elsewhere. In Chatham County, Georgia, "an astonishingly large number of negro women—more than 1,000—" succeeded in getting themselves on the books, and in Atlanta, African American women "in every ward in the city" showed up to vote on election day. In Duval County, Florida, a remarkable number of African American women— some 6,400—put their names in the registration books. In Richmond, Virginia, an estimated 10 percent of voting-age black women succeeded in registering. Reports from Norfolk, Birmingham, Mobile, Shreveport, and Houston all testified to major collective mobilizations by African American women.[5]

Caught off guard, white registrars sometimes permitted the first few applicants to succeed; confronted with more, they developed tactics to obstruct them. An Alabama county registrar recounted this in an interview with political scientist Ralph Bunche as he traveled through the South while researching *The American Dilemma* with Gunnar Myrdal. "Way back in 1920," the Alabamian recalled, "we had a world of n* women coming in to register. There was a dozen of them, I reckon, come in one registration period. We registered a few of them and then we put them off . . . tell them they had to bring in white witnesses. . . . Tell them how much poll tax it was going to cost them." Permitting a few African Americans to register also allowed white supremacists to claim that they had not excluded on the basis of race at all, and that other applicants simply had failed to meet the standard of the "qualified voter." Such was the situation in Shreveport, Louisiana. Resident T. G. Garrett reported to the NAACP that "six hundred of our most learned race women of Caddo Parish" turned up to register; of these, only four succeeded—three on account of "thair propity" and one "under the edicational test."[6]

Pressure from black women compelled election officials to resort to other fraudulent tactics. When women in Americus, Georgia, approached the county office, the registrar "would hide the book or himself." Other women were given the runaround until the registration period ran out. In Hampton, Virginia, Mrs. Allen Washington complained that she and a friend had made repeated visits to the registrar's office, each time being told to return at a later date. On the last day of the registration period, they were simply refused, the clerk finally admitting to her as the clock ran out that "to tell you the truth[,] we are not going to be bothered with a lot of colored women." In Fulton County, Georgia, registrar Lucien Harris "suspended the registration of women" altogether, claiming that he needed to redeploy his staff to more pressing matters. In Muskogee, Oklahoma, when the registrar was approached by a group of African American women, he resigned.[7]

Perhaps part of the reason for the apparent panic was the fact that, when African American women turned up to register and vote, they often brought a group of people with them. Spouses and other family members, pastors, neighbors, coworkers, and friends often accompanied them when they approached election officials. The practice had long roots, for, as historian Elsa Barkley Brown found, African American male voters during and after Reconstruction had often brought their families and neighbors with them when they went to the polls. In both eras, the company was welcome because it offered a measure of safety and because the presence of "respectable" associates might reduce the odds that applicants would be treated with discourtesy. Moreover, the presence of a group enacted the idea, also with a long history in African American communities, that the ballot expressed the interest of the community and not just that of the individual who cast it. And the people who joined these women often intended to register and vote themselves.[8]

Even with assistance and support, however, women's efforts to register and vote often foundered. In Richmond, Virginia, registrars turned away women who brought "friends" with them "to help fill out forms." In Montgomery, Alabama, registrars turned away three pairs of husbands and wives: the Reverend P. W. Walls, the pastor of the A.M.E. Church, "and wife"; Professor Harry S. Murphy, a former secretary of the Montgomery NAACP, "and wife"; and Dr. A. W. West, "and wife." The wives were unnamed, but apparently the ratification of the Nineteenth Amendment drew not only them but also their husbands to the polls. These men were described as "prominent members of the race," a status their wives presumably shared. That status, however, did not shield them from discrimination at the registrar's office.[9]

White supremacists tried to block black voters from the polls, but their efforts at obstruction did not always work. When it failed, they sometimes turned to intimidation and violence, just as white supremacists had done to prevent black men from voting during and after Reconstruction. In November 1920, in the town of Ocoee, Florida, voting by a single black man triggered a pogrom that reduced a whole community to ashes. A few miles west of Orlando, Ocoee was home to about a thousand residents, a third of them African American. The Jacksonville *Times-Union* blamed election day violence there on "unregistered negroes [who] demanded ballots," including a man reported elsewhere to be Mr. July Perry, an orchard supervisor and a registered Republican. Perry was reported to have threatened to return to the polls after being denied registration, next time with his gun, but Alexander Akerman, a Republican campaign official from Florida who investigated the events afterward, came to a different conclusion. Akerman found instead that the situation in Ocoee had been brewing for some time. He wrote to a Republican US senator that "at Ocoee it was rumored for weeks in advance that not a single Negro would be permitted to vote." Akerman believed that Perry tried to vote but left quietly when he was turned down and that the violence started when "a number of armed men went to [Perry's] house [after the polls closed] without a warrant and without authority of law . . . to arrest him." When the white men approached Perry's property, apparently two of them were shot and injured, including Sam Saulsbury, Orlando's former police chief, who was shot in the arm.[10]

Newspapers from as far away as New York quickly reported the events that followed. White "reinforcements" began to arrive, men from nearby Crown Point and Winter Garden and "fifty carloads of men" from Orlando. Their purpose, in the words of a Jacksonville paper, was to "help preserve order." The New York *Dispatch* on November 2 described the scene as "a bloody battle." "The colored men engaged in the battle are barricaded in the house of July Perry," the paper said, and "their dead and wounded cannot be gotten to." The "white forces" are "said to be fighting at a great disadvantage to dislodge the colored forces"—a preposterous claim given that Perry and the men with him were surrounded and trapped. A November 3 update in the same paper reported that fighting was continuing and repeated that "the Negroes . . . are . . . heavily armed with every advantage in their favor." Once the violence subsided, the *Dispatch* reported that a total of six people had been killed, two African American and four white, but Akerman disagreed in a chilling report. "For two or three days the community ran riot. I do not believe it will ever be known how many Negroes were killed. Every Negro schoolhouse, church and lodge room in that vicinity was burned, in some instances with women and children occupying the house, and thus burned to death." Remaining members of the community fled and relocated to nearby towns including Orlando, Apopka, and Zellwood. The African American community in Ocoee was eradicated, and apparently the town remained all white for another forty years. Together, African American families and community members tried to vote; together, they also suffered violent retribution.[11]

. . .

Despite obstruction, threats, and violence, African American activists continued to struggle mightily throughout the 1920s to maintain the possibilities for black voting opened up by woman suffrage. They worked through women's clubs to collect poll taxes and register voters. They asked former suffragists to support their efforts. They flexed their electoral muscle where they could. They worked to rebuild ties to a tattered Republican Party in the South that had embraced "lily-whitism" and largely abandoned "Black and Tans." As they reached out, they continued to rely on family members, neighbors, and community organizations for protection and support.

Leading African American women insisted that the Nineteenth Amendment was not being enforced, and they raised the issue with their club networks and white allies. As early as 1921, National Association of Colored Women cofounder Mary Church Terrell pointed out that though not all African American women "live in those sections where their votes are counted," they must push forward by participating "in politics wherever, whenever, and however they can." That same year, Jennie B. Moton, Margaret Murray Washington, and other elite black clubwomen asked white allies in the Methodist Episcopal Church's Committee on Interracial Relations to step up. "We believe that the ballot is the safe-guard of the Nation, and that every qualified citizen in the Nation should have the right to use it. We believe that if there is ever to be any Justice before the law, the Negro must have the right to exercise the vote. We ask, therefore, that white women, for the protection of their homes as well as ours, sanction the ballot for all citizens."[12]

African American clubwomen also reached out to former suffragists for help. The League of Women Voters, as the successor organization to the National American Woman Suffrage Association, was deeply invested in showing that woman suffrage was a success and organized massive, nonpartisan voter turnout campaigns in the 1920s to try to prove it. League membership also included small numbers of African American women, most of whom participated in segregated chapters. Even so, the national organization did not encourage African American women to join, nor did it challenge the disenfranchisement of black women in the South. Evelyn Brooks Higginbotham concluded that "by the end of the decade the League of Women Voters had lost, largely by its own choice, the potential for being an important mobilizing force among Black women."[13]

Nor did the National Woman's Party (NWP) offer aid. Despite protests by some members, the NWP pointedly declined to take up "race questions," insisting that discrimination faced by African American women fell wholly outside their mission to eradicate inequalities of sex. Amid criticism of this narrow view of their mission, the treasurer of the NWP defended the decision to duck the problem in an open letter to *The Nation*. "The Woman's Party policy has always been to concentrate on its own issue and not take up other issues. The Woman's Party had nothing to do with the race issue and naturally never thought of taking it up in the South or anywhere else."[14]

Despite the lack of support from white former suffragists, African American women could claim some electoral success. Where it was possible to vote, they sometimes took credit for tipping the balance of power. This was the case in several states after the Dyer antilynching bill went down to defeat. The bill, which would have made lynching a federal crime and rendered perpetrators vulnerable to federal prosecution, passed the House but foundered in the Senate, filibustered to death by southern Democrats in 1922, 1923, and 1924. In part because of organizing work by Mary B. Talbert and the Anti-Lynching Crusaders, African American women voters claimed credit for defeating Dyer bill opponents in the border state of Delaware as well as Michigan and New Jersey. Alice Ruth Moore Dunbar-Nelson congratulated them in a 1927 article in *The Messenger*, the publication founded by labor activist A. Philip Randolph: "The women's votes unquestionably had the deciding influence in the three states mentioned, and the campaign as conducted by them was of a most commendable kind."[15]

Though occasionally African American women worked their will at the polls, neither major political party embraced the cause of voting rights—not even the Republican Party, which stood to benefit from their votes. African American women took up Republican Party work at the national level with Hallie Q. Brown, Nannie Burroughs, Mary Church Terrell, Jeannette Carter, and others assuming leadership roles in the party apparatus and at the local level outside the South through the efforts of women such as Lethia Fleming in Cleveland and Irene Goins in Chicago. In the South, however, the post-ratification push by African Americans to register and vote forced the Republican Party to make plain that it was "lily white" and did not want black votes. Certainly that is what African Americans in North Carolina discovered, as Republican office seekers appealed to new white women voters by assuring them that they "were not joining a 'Negro' party."[16]

Rejected by the very organizations that should have been most eager to help, still they pressed forward. African American women worked through civic clubs to prepare themselves for the responsibility of voting, demonstrate they were worthy of the privilege, and point out violations of the law. In Mississippi, for example, the state's Colored Women's Clubs in 1924 urged women to pay their poll taxes to bolster their argument that they should be permitted to register. Clubwomen in Birmingham—members of the Cosmos Club, Inter Se, the Joy Crafters, and Pierian Club—all took part in the county League of Women Voters' campaign to "get out the vote." In 1926, Terrell urged women of the National Association of Colored Women to inform themselves about candidates and pending legislation, write members of Congress to convey their opinions, and learn from people with more political experience. "No wom[e]n should work harder to have their ballots count for something worth while than colored women, because no group of women in the United States has more serious problems confronting them than they do."[17]

Black communities across the South continued to enlist family, neighbors, and friends to advance the cause of voting rights. Between 1925 and 1926, the "Ex-Soldiers Co-Operative Association" of Birmingham, Alabama, mobilized these ties to push for black access to the ballot box.

When the chairman of the Jefferson County Board of Registrars prevented registration, they called on the president and the attorney general to protect their right to vote. In her letter of protest to Washington officials, Executive Cabinet member Lula B. Murry divulged only a few details of an apparently unpleasant encounter. The registrar barred them from entering the office, requiring them to "make application on the outside doors" and then "turned down" the whole group. The rest of the ordeal she declined to recount. "If the whole detail upon the merits of this subject was explained[,] this sheet of paper could not hold the wordings." Surely they deserved better, for each letter writer in the association justified his or her claim to the ballot by recalling their own military service in the Great War, or as Murry's letter did, the service of a family member. "I am a sister of a deceased Ex-Soldier," Murry insisted. Other petitioners included Murry's brothers, Jim and Ozzie McNab; a husband and wife, Gus and Alice Stewart; and neighbors with addresses on the same Birmingham streets.[18]

As African American women pressed for voting rights into the 1920s, they risked violent reprisals, including sexual violence. This was the terrible experience of Indiana Little, a Birmingham schoolteacher who in January 1926 led "as many as one thousand Black women and a few men" in a registration march on the Jefferson County Board of Registrars. Though the march was widely reported in the black press, only two published historical accounts note the event, both in brief, and both indicate that Little was arrested for vagrancy. Justice Department records, however, tell a more detailed and tragic story: not only did the march fail to secure registration for a single black voter, but Little was sexually assaulted while in custody. Little swore in an affidavit that after her arrest, she was "carried by an officer that took her out of the Board of Registrars' office and locked her up," where she was "beat over the head unmercifully and . . . forced upon the officer's demand to yield to him in an unbecoming manner." A DOJ official dismissed the marchers' grievances as the complaints of "some troublesome colored folk," but a US senator intervened on Little's behalf and asked the attorney general to investigate. When the attorney general's office referred the case to a regional FBI officer in Alabama, the officer told his boss in Washington that he had no agent to whom he might assign the task. There the paper trail on this affair ends. Perhaps the investigation ended there as well, as law enforcement officials had long refused to prosecute sexual violence by white men against African American women. Soon Indiana Little herself largely disappeared from the historical record.[19]

* * *

African American women were not the only women denied the right to vote after the Nineteenth Amendment was enacted. For diverse women in substantial numbers, in particular women of color and poor women, the Anthony Amendment offered no guarantee that they would be able to cast ballots. The evidence of female disenfranchisement after 1920 is scattered but abundant.

Disenfranchisement of women among communities of color apparently was not unusual in the Southwest and West. Historian Cynthia Orozco concluded that "Mexico Texanas remained outside of electoral politics in the 1920s" and, in most of Texas, for the 1930s as well. Activist Ed Idar from Austin recalled the disfranchising effects of poll taxes on Mexican American women and men in the 1940s. "To the working people, the ones that had to pick cotton and all that, $1.75 was quite a bit of money. And for two people in a marriage, husband and wife, to come up with $3.50 or what have you, that was money, you know. It was a big hindrance, no question about it." Historian Thomas Guglielmo documented the exclusion in the 1940s of Mexican Americans from Texas's white primaries. In some states, exclusionary policies may have dated back to the territorial period. Arizona granted women suffrage when it became a state in 1912, but Mexican Americans there, including women, still were largely barred from voting. Idaho enfranchised women in 1896 but specifically excluded persons of Chinese descent. California did not formally enfranchise American-born persons of Chinese descent until 1926, Oregon until 1927. Voting rights for immigrants from Asia was a nonstarter. By 1926, every state required voters to be US citizens, and Chinese immigrants were barred from naturalizing until 1943 and Japanese until 1952. US-born women who married foreign nationals after 1907 lost their American citizenship, and even after passage of the Cable Act in 1922, these women had to naturalize to regain their US citizenship and access to the ballot.[20]

Class and marital status mattered too. In the fifteen states that in the 1920s required poll taxes or permitted municipalities to levy them—and in an era in which few women enjoyed financial autonomy—any woman who lacked an independent income might find herself disenfranchised. In households in which men controlled the family finances, women could not vote unless their husbands agreed to pay the tax. Field organizers from the League of Women Voters found in the 1920s that "throughout the South," white men blocked their wives from voting, one going so far as to burn his wife's poll tax receipt.[21]

For women for whom class, race, ethnicity, and citizenship status did not pose a barrier, partisan opponents sometimes blocked their access to the polls. Mrs. Mary Doran, a white woman and a Democrat from Johnstown, Pennsylvania, took such a complaint to the US Supreme Court in 1925, not by filing suit, but by writing directly to Justice Harlan Fiske Stone. Stone, a Republican appointee to the court, nonetheless dissented often from the court's conservative majority, quickly earning a reputation for nonpartisanship that President Roosevelt would capitalize on when he elevated Stone to chief justice in 1941. In Stone, Doran expected to find a sympathetic audience for her complaint that when she and like-minded women in Johnstown tried to mobilize voters for a Democratic candidate, Republican elections officials "left [us] off assessment lists." "As women we made a concerted effort in the 'Get Out the Vote Movement,'" Doran reported, but "we were blocked all along the way."[22]

The circumstances varied, but the outcome was the same: despite the "triumph" of the Nineteenth Amendment, many women, African American and otherwise, found that after 1920 they still could not vote. To understand their stories, we need to consider their experiences intersectionally, in the full, rich range of their complex identities and in the context of their families and communities. Their stories make it clear that, for many women, the "century of struggle" lasted much longer than a hundred years. Nor is that struggle confined to the past, as the racialized and partisan voter suppression campaigns in elections since the Supreme Court's 2013 *Shelby County v. Holder* decision make clear. Ratification ended the quest for voting rights for some, but for many others, it served as a new beginning, one more step in a long and ongoing struggle for a fully inclusive democracy.

Notes

The author thanks Lisa Materson, Tom Dublin, Ellen Hartigan O'Connor, Leah Zarnow, and Stacie Taranto for their careful readings and suggestions at various stages of this work, and Karen Barwick of the Greater Birmingham, Alabama League of Women Voters for research leads. Portions of this work appeared under the title "Resistance after Ratification: The Nineteenth Amendment, African American Women, and the Problem of Female Disfranchisement after 1920," in *Women and Social Movements in the United States, 1600–2000*, ed. Kathryn Kish Sklar and Thomas Dublin, 21 (March 2017).

1. US Bureau of the Census, *Sixteenth Census of the United States* (1940), *Twelfth Census of the U.S.* (1900), *Fourteenth Census of the U.S.* (1920), all available at Ancestry.com; typescript, [Addie W. Hunton], "Phoebus," [October 25, 1920], Records of the National Association for the Advancement of Colored People (hereafter "NAACP Records"), Manuscript Division, Library of Congress, Washington, DC.

2. [Hunton], "Phoebus," NAACP Records.

3. On the importance of pairing the Fifteenth and Nineteenth Amendments, see Liette Gidlow, "The Sequel: The Fifteenth Amendment, the Nineteenth Amendment, and Southern Black Women's Struggle to Vote, 1900s–1920s," *Journal of the Gilded Age and Progressive Era* 17 (July 2018): 433–449. On African American women's efforts to vote between the World Wars, see Ann D. Gordon and Bettye Collier-Thomas, eds., *African American Women and the Vote, 1837–1965* (Amherst: University of Massachusetts Press, 1997); Lisa G. Materson, *For the Freedom of Her Race: Black Women and Electoral Politics in Illinois, 1877–1932* (Chapel Hill: University of North Carolina Press, 2009); Glenda Elizabeth Gilmore, *Gender and Jim Crow: Women and the Politics of White Supremacy in North Carolina, 1896–1920* (Chapel Hill: University of North Carolina Press, 1996); Lorraine Gates Schuyler, *The Weight of Their Votes: Southern Women and Political Leverage in the 1920s* (Chapel Hill: University of North Carolina Press, 2006); Nikki Brown, *Private Politics and Public Voices: Black Women's Activism from World War I to the New Deal* (Bloomington: Indiana University Press, 2006).

4. Eleanor Flexner, *The Century of Struggle: The Woman's Rights Movement in the United States* (New York: Atheneum, 1974).

5. *Baltimore Morning Sun*, September 30, 1920, in Tuskegee News Clipping Files (hereafter "TNCF") (Sanford, NC: Microfilming Corp. of America, 1976); Gilmore, *Gender and Jim Crow*, 218–24; NAACP, "Disfranchisement of Colored Americans in the Presidential Election of 1920," [December 1920], NAACP Records; Jacksonville *Metropolis*, September 30, 1920, TNCF; Andrew Buni, *The Negro in Virginia Politics, 1902–1965* (Charlottesville: University Press of Virginia, 1967), 79; Schuyler, *The Weight of Their Votes*, 28–36; Brown, *Private Politics and Public Voices*, 147–148.

6. Ralph J. Bunche, "The Negro in the Political Life of the United States," *Journal of Negro Education* 10, no. 3 (1941): 571; T. G. Garrett to "The N.A.A.C.P.," October 30, 1920, NAACP Records.

7. S. S. Humbert to NAACP, November 9, 1920, NAACP Records; [Atlanta, GA] *Journal*, October 19, 1920, NAACP Records; [New York] *News*, February 27, 1919 [?], TNCF.

8. Elsa Barkley Brown, "To Catch the Vision of Freedom: Reconstructing Southern Black Women's Political History, 1865–1880," in Gordon and Collier-Thomas, *African American Women and the Vote*, 82–85.

9. NAACP, "Disfranchisement," NAACP Records; N. G. Langford to Hubert Seligman, November 8, 1920, NAACP Records.

10. Jacksonville, FL, *Times-Union*, November 3, 1920, NAACP Records; [Alexander Akerman] to Sen. Kenyon, November 6, 1920, NAACP Records.

11. [New York] *Dispatch*, November 6, 1920, NAACP Records (the *Dispatch* misreports the name of the town as "Ocoll"); Jacksonville, FL, *Times-Union*, November 3, 1920, NAACP Records; [Akerman] to Sen. Kenyon, November 6, 1920, NAACP Records.

12. Mary Church Terrell, "An Appeal to Colored Women to Vote and Do Their Duty in Politics," in Alison M. Parker, "What Was the Relationship between Mary Church Terrell's International Experience and Her Work against Racism in the United States?," *Women and Social Movements in the United States, 1600–2000* (hereafter "*WASM*"), ed. Kathryn Kish Sklar and Thomas Dublin, accessed through University of Michigan Libraries at http://www.lib.umich.edu/.

13. Liette Gidlow, *The Big Vote: Gender, Consumer Culture, and the Politics of Exclusion, 1890s–1920s* (Baltimore: Johns Hopkins University Press, 2004), 78–89; Evelyn Brooks Higginbotham, "Clubwomen and Electoral Politics in the 1920s," in Gordon and Collier-Thomas, *African American Women and the Vote*, 150.

14. Mrs. Lawrence Lewis to editor of *The Nation*, March 26, 1921, National Woman's Party Papers, 1913–1974, Library of Congress, microfilm (1979), in Kathryn Kish Sklar and Jill Dias, "How Did the National Woman's Party Address the Issue of the Enfranchisement of Black Women, 1919–1924?," *WASM*.

15. Alice Ruth Moore Dunbar-Nelson, "The Negro Woman and the Ballot," *The Messenger* 9 (April 1927): 111.

16. Glenda Elizabeth Gilmore, "False Friends and Avowed Enemies: Southern African Americans and Party Allegiances in the 1920s," in *Jumpin' Jim Crow: Southern Politics from Civil War to Civil Rights*, ed. Jane Daily, Glenda Elizabeth Gilmore, and Bryant Simon (Princeton, NJ: Princeton University Press, 2000), 222.

17. Mrs. Laurence C. Jones, "Outstanding Features of the Mississippi State Work," *National Notes*, July 1924, 14; Gidlow, *The Big Vote*, 60; Mary Church Terrell, "Department of Legislation," *National Notes*, November 1926, 4.

18. Petition, Executive Representatives of the Ex-Soldiers Co-operative Association to Hon. Calvin Coolidge, February 1, 1926, and Lula B. Murry to [US] Department of Justice, [ca. January 6, 1926], both in RG60, Department of Justice Central Files, Classified Subject Files, Archives II, College Park, MD (hereafter, "DOJ Files").

19. Joseph Matt Brittain, "Negro Suffrage and Politics in Alabama Since 1870" (PhD diss., Indiana University, 1958), 177; *Pittsburgh Courier*, January 30, 1926, 8; *Chicago Defender* (National Edition), January 30, 1926, 4; *Philadelphia Tribune*, February 6, 1926, sec. 2, 9; *Baltimore Sun,* January 19, 1926, 1; Charles M. Christian and Sari Bennett, *Black Saga: The African American Experience; A Chronology* (Boston: Houghton Mifflin, 1995), 339; Virginia Van Der Veer Hamilton, *Alabama: A History* (New York: W. W. Norton, 1984), 98; O. R. Luhring to Charles B. Kennamer, March 11, 1926; "SMP" to Luhring, ca. March 8, 1926; Sen. Lynn Frazier to John G. Sargent, February 23, 1926; Kennamer to "Attorney General," March 18, 1926, all in DOJ Files.

20. Cynthia Orozco, *No Mexicans, Women, or Dogs Allowed: The Rise of the Mexican American Civil Rights Movement* (Austin: University of Texas Press, 2009), 38; "'Our First Poll Tax Drive': The American G.I. Forum Fights Disenfranchisement of Mexican Americans in Texas," History Matters, http://historymatters.gmu.edu/d/6582/; Thomas Guglielmo, "Fighting for Caucasian Rights: Mexicans, Mexican Americans, and the Transnational Struggle for Civil Rights in World War II Texas," *Journal of American History* 92 (March 2006), 1221; Bertha Rembaugh, comp., *The Political Status of Women in the United States: A Digest of the Laws Concerning Women in the Various States and Territories* (New York: G. P. Putnam's Sons, 1911), 28–29; Alexander Keyssar, *The Right to Vote: The Contested History of Democracy in the United States* (New York: Basic Books, 2008), 229, 141; Candice Lewis Bredbenner, *A Nationality of Her Own: Women, Marriage, and the Law of Citizenship* (Berkeley: University of California Press, 1998).

21. Keyssar, *The Right to Vote,* 356–357. On the disparate, gendered consequences of the poll tax, see Sarah Wilkerson-Freeman, "The Second Battle for Woman Suffrage: Alabama White Women, the Poll Tax, and V. O. Key's Master Narrative of Southern Politics," *Journal of Southern History* 68 (2002): 333–374.

22. Mary H. Doran to Justice Harlan Fiske Stone, January 12, 1925, DOJ Files.

Representative Ruth Hanna McCormick, her fist clenched for emphasis, addresses a large audience on the campaign trail in Chicago in 1928. Chicago History Museum/Getty Images.

CHAPTER 4

"My Money's on the Mare"

Lessons from the 1930 US Senate Campaign of Ruth Hanna McCormick

JOHANNA NEUMAN

RUTH HANNA MCCORMICK was the darling of the Washington establishment, a figure of great political pedigree. Her father, Mark Hanna, had conceived the "front porch" campaign that in 1896 catapulted William McKinley to the White House—and crowned Hanna as "presidential kingmaker."[1] A wealthy businessman, Mark Hanna declined a position in McKinley's cabinet to become a politician in his own right, serving in the US Senate, and as chairman of the Republican National Committee, until his death in 1904. Seven months earlier, Ruth married Medill McCormick, whose grandfather owned the *Chicago Tribune*. Like Ruth's father, Medill would be drawn to the art and ordeal of politics.

Ruth McCormick was deeply involved in both men's political careers, absorbing partisan tactics from the front row. After high school, she worked as her father's secretary, learning parliamentary procedure from the Senate gallery as she took notes for him on floor debates; she also hosted his political breakfasts, must-attend events on every politico's calendar.[2] In 1913, she applied her considerable skills to advocating for woman suffrage in Illinois, an early success story in the state-by-state campaign that helped double the number of women who could vote in their states for president. When McCormick's husband first ran for the state House of Representatives in 1911, she became his top advisor. And when Medill volunteered to lead western efforts for Theodore Roosevelt's quixotic 1912 presidential bid, Ruth was co-manager in all but name. The former president appreciated Medill's reform instincts but valued Ruth's political judgment more. A guest at their wedding, Roosevelt said of the McCormick partnership, "My money's on the mare."[3]

. . .

Roosevelt's betting hand proved prescient. In 1928, three years after Medill's death, forty-eight-year-old Ruth Hanna McCormick won election as an at-large member of the House from Illinois. She defeated six candidates in the Republican primary, including the incumbent, by almost one hundred thousand votes. In November, she became the first woman in Illinois history to win election to Congress. *Time* magazine put her picture on its cover, the first female politician to gain this top billing since the magazine created the covers seven years earlier. Seeking to explain the anomaly of a woman succeeding in a man's world, the magazine noted in its caption, "She learned the law of the jungle."[4]

Ambitious, McCormick announced her candidacy for the Senate after one term in Congress and defeated incumbent Charles Deneen in the Republican primary by more than two hundred thousand votes. It was a bittersweet victory, as Deneen, twice governor of Illinois, had defeated her husband, Medill, in his Senate reelection bid in 1924, which may have led to his suicide.[5] Poised to become the first woman ever elected to the US Senate—Illinois had not sent a Democrat to the Senate in nearly twenty years—McCormick returned to Washington, triumphant. "Mrs. McCormick has demonstrated that political acumen is not reserved for the male sex," editorialized the *Washington Post*. "If she wins, it will be on her own merit. If she should lose, she would nevertheless be credited with the most remarkable campaign ever conducted by a woman."[6] One letter writer to the *Post* predicted that after her "inevitable" Senate victory, it would "not be surprising if, later on, she should enter the lists for the presidency of the United States, possibly in 1932."[7]

Yet, beneath these accolades was a rumble of gendered dissent. There was no more sacred site of male power than the US Senate, and many within its hushed walls were rattled at the very idea that a woman might sit among them. Hiram Johnson, vice presidential candidate on Roosevelt's 1912 Progressive Party ticket, called McCormick's primary victory "a punch in the eye," presaging the institution's "thorough breakdown and demoralization."[8] Still, lawmakers recognized political skill when they saw it, and when she entered the House chambers on her return to Washington in April, she received a standing ovation—the entire Republican side of the chamber rose, as did some Democrats. "For some minutes she was a center of an impromptu reception," reported one news agency.[9] No doubt many men shared Hiram Johnson's fear that a female senator would topple political institutions, but for those who saw McCormick's political acumen, she looked like a winner.

Instead, on Election Day in 1930, McCormick was crushed in a landslide, beaten by her Democratic opponent James Hamilton Lewis by nearly seven hundred fifty thousand votes. Many explanations have been offered by commentators of the day and historians ever since. Her attempt to straddle the middle on Prohibition, charges that she violated campaign laws by overspending in the primary, and the impact of a year-old Depression that was bankrupting Illinois farmers as well as disproportionately hurting African American wage earners—all took their toll on her candidacy. That fall, Democrats picked up fifty-four seats in the House and twelve in the Senate. By 1936, Democratic wins would realign the two major political parties and convince African American voters to leave the Republican Party of Abraham Lincoln, the Great Emancipator, for the Democratic Party of Franklin Delano Roosevelt, father of the New Deal.

If McCormick's defeat was a harbinger of the coming Democratic turn, her legacy was oddly nonpartisan. Like Hillary Rodham Clinton in 2016, Ruth Hanna McCormick in 1930 was a candidate of political celebrity, with deep history in the nation's politics and great credibility in its reform movements. She and Medill had lived at the University of Chicago Settlement House early in their marriage, under assumed names, to learn conditions for immigrant families. An activist for the pure foods movement, she purchased a large dairy farm in Byron, to teach good farming methods and provide healthy milk for the community. Eager to win on male terms, she rarely mentioned her status as the first viable female candidate for the Senate. After the Nineteenth Amendment was ratified, other suffragists lobbied for separate female slots within the

Republican Party hierarchy. She never did. The real power, to her, was not segregated in a parallel structure but earned in the main arena. "I am a suffragist," she said, "not a feminist."[10]

Of her two patrons in politics, her father, Mark Hanna, had advocated organization and endurance. "To succeed in politics you must have the hide of a rhinoceros," he said, "and a sense of the ridiculous."[11] After her husband's Senate loss in 1924, she decided Medill had faltered for lack of female voters. Adopting techniques Ruth had learned from her father, she spent four years organizing Republican women's clubs in 90 of Illinois's 102 counties, seeking to bolster the party, and her own electoral chances. But if her father had taught her discipline in the face of politics' cruelties, Teddy Roosevelt had modeled the bully pulpit. His cult of personality now became her lodestar.[12] Ruth Hanna McCormick's campaign slogan—"No Favors, and No Bunk"—was meant to advertise her character. It proved a miscalculation. In seeking to buck a national trend during a period of political turbulence, McCormick, already burdened by male chauvinism, could not rely on character alone. At a time of economic hardship, when many were without work or hope, voters did not want a political personality, man or woman. They wanted an agent of change. In the meantime, opponents were only too ready to remind voters that she was "a lady candidate," given to bursts of indecisiveness, hardly the jungle beast of reputation.

"Wonder Woman of the Country"

From the beginning, McCormick's general election opponent, Democrat James Hamilton Lewis, targeted her as a woman; he rarely used her name, instead referring to her as "the lady candidate." During the primary, the *New York Times* likewise described her candidacy in gender terms, routinely labeling her opponent as "Senator Deneen," while calling her not Congresswoman McCormick but "Mrs. McCormick."[13] As a columnist for the *Appleton (WI) Post-Crescent* explained, Lewis was appealing to "the latent prejudices of certain classes of voters against the woman in office."[14] He conflated the privilege of her class with the perceived weakness of her gender. "The great prize of a seat in the United States Senate is not a doll to be cast into the lap of an aspirant for fame as the wonder woman of the country," he said. Men might be "misled" or "beguiled" into voting for her, but women—presumably he meant those resentful of her public fame—would not reward "the aspirations of feminine vanity."[15]

A female candidate on the stump was still a novelty in 1930, and voters often traveled great distances "to listen or gawk at her." She told audiences, "I don't want anybody to vote for me because I'm a woman. But I don't want anybody to vote against me because I'm a woman." She tried to ignore the slurs, but occasionally she fought back. Once, during a speech at a college, a professor heckled her, and she deftly turned the moment to her advantage. "Wearing a tailored blouse with cuff links, she snapped the links and pretended to roll up her sleeves, saying as she did so, 'I was invited here; I believe these students want to hear me. Do you want to fight it out with me like a man?'" As one journalist reported, "A roar of appreciation went up from the students."[16]

Unlike other female candidates McCormick did not campaign under the banner of "municipal housekeeping," the idea that women, guardians of morality in the home, would have a similar impact on the public sphere. Though she ran against corruption, she did so as a good-government progressive, not as a female reformer intent on sweeping clean the political sphere. If some within the party sought to derail her candidacy on gender grounds, fearing "petticoat rule," and a female invasion of the all-male Senate, she would win on their terms, on political terms, not gender ones. As journalist Joseph Alsop said of her career, "It was uncommon then, as now, to meet a woman who talked politics, not morals."[17]

By the end of her Senate run, McCormick grew introspective about the role gender had played in the campaign, musing about the lessons she had absorbed while watching politics at her father's side. "When [William Jennings] Bryan was running for president in 1896, I stole away from my father's house and went down the street to the big tent into which he was piling them in," she recalled. Of Bryan's populist thunder, she observed, "They laughed with him and they cried with him, but they voted with McKinley." Ever since, she had favored a "crisp clear statement over flowery language." As one reporter noted, "She avoids fluttery draperies in her speech as carefully as she avoids [bling] in her dress."[18] If she thought refined speech or dress would ease the burden of gender, she underestimated the rampant sexism of male politicians. One confidante later told her of a conversation in which politicians in the state capitol in Springfield sat around speculating that, if McCormick were elected to the Senate, she would one day become governor. And that, wrote the informant, is what alarmed them. They "were just a little disturbed about the possibility of extending petticoat rule."[19]

The Patriarchy Targets Her Campaign Spending

Believing her husband had underspent in his failed campaign for the Senate, but eager to convey the impression of a clean candidate not beholden to special interests, Ruth Hanna McCormick largely self-funded her primary campaign. Looking back, it is clear that is precisely what riled Washington's establishment, the idea that a woman with wealth could upset the gendered power imbalance preferred. So its gatekeepers put up a new hurdle.

Shortly after her triumphant victory in the primary, Senator Gerald Nye of North Dakota, chairman of a Senate investigative committee, announced he was sending staffers to Illinois to look into complaints McCormick had overspent.[20] Cognizant of her husband's mistake of underestimating the need of money in politics, she spent her own funds. This action worried the guardians of the patriarchy in Washington—Republican as well as Democratic—concerned about the advantage women such as McCormick in their efforts to invade the bastions of male power. Nye had arrived in Washington, DC, in 1926 as a thirty-three-year-old freshman senator with a bowl haircut and an unsophisticated air, known as "the ten-cent senator" for the ten-cent donor fund set up by local farmers to finance his campaign.[21] With her wealth and pedigree, McCormick represented everything the populist Nye resented.

Nothing that happened in the campaign would undercut her candidacy more than his investigation, which robbed her of standing as a good-government reformer.

The rules on campaign spending were murky, and the US Senate's authority to investigate and disqualify successful candidates from being seated even more questionable. In 1913, the Seventeenth Amendment had been ratified, for the first time providing for direct election of US senators rather than their appointment by state legislatures. Ever since, the Senate had grown more zealous about guarding access to its club. When, in 1918, Republican Truman Handy Newberry, a former secretary of the navy, ran for the Senate in Michigan, he spent $100,000—about $1.6 million in current dollars.[22] His primary opponent was the wealthy automotive pioneer Henry Ford. At Ford's urging the Senate investigated, finding Newberry guilty of excessive spending. He appealed his conviction to the Supreme Court in 1921, and the court ruled in his favor, saying primary election spending was a matter for states to regulate. McCormick challenged Nye's inquiry, noting the court decision still stood.[23] Still, Nye persisted, looking into primary overspending in Illinois, Nebraska, and Pennsylvania.[24]

The hearings opened in July 1930 in a crowded courtroom at the Federal Building. Like Hillary Clinton facing the Benghazi investigation, McCormick testified alone, without pretense or counsel, for many hours. She told the committee she had spent $252,572 on the primary—about $3.7 million in today's dollars.[25] By contrast, Deneen had spent just under $25,000. Nye argued that "the vast sums expended" for her by Chicago's political machine should also count as her tally. She parried that she had no choice but to marshal powerful allies because Deneen, a sitting senator, could offer patronage—naming postmasters, census takers, and marshals.[26] To applause, she proclaimed, "You cannot buy an Illinois landslide."[27]

In September, after a summer of damning headlines, McCormick fought back. "Why have I been made the special target of the chairman of this committee . . . in the hope that one damaging fact against Ruth Hanna McCormick might be disclosed?" Charging that committee sleuths had tapped her phone wires, invaded her home, and ransacked her desk, she noted, "They have not been able to find one single thing against me."[28] She acknowledged she had hired detectives to spy on Nye, a sort of espionage tit-for-tat that prompted the *Milwaukee Journal* to decry these "Chicago methods"[29] and the *New York Times* to quip, "Were it not for an occasional dispatch" about a Lewis speech, "the impression would be that Mrs. McCormick is running against Senator Nye of North Dakota."[30]

McCormick had testified that she paid for her own campaign to avoid the taint of special interests. That, wrote a columnist for the United Press, was the real rub. "This bid certain members of the Committee pause. What be, if women were permitted to spend their money like that?" he asked. "There would be no political sanctuary for men if such carryings on were allowed."[31] As the Depression worsened, the optics of a wealthy woman spending money to buy a Senate seat bruised her image. McCormick sunk to his level by hiring spies to investigate him, which only underscored the expanse of her bank account. Her opponent Lewis wasted no time trying to take advantage of this dissonance, contrasting her wealth to the precarious economic situation of thousands in the manufacturing and farming sectors. "Cook County will cast a big vote against a woman whose inherited riches were wrung from the poor," he said.[32] The very basis of McCormick's campaign, that she was a person of character, was under attack. She was angry, and in defiance, she gave the impression of a woman with a sense of entitlement. The next storm would undercut her image as a woman of conviction.

Prohibition Pains: "An Ad Interim Dry"

In her victory speech after the Republican primary in April 1930, McCormick credited her win to her campaign against the Court of International Justice, convinced isolationism would carry the day in Illinois. "I am against this court because I think it is the inevitable vestibule leading us into the League of Nations," she had said.[33] After the election, the *New York Times*, found it "difficult to believe" McCormick had turned her opposition to the World Court "into a 200,000 majority."[34] By the general election, the drumbeat of World War I had long faded. What hurt her more was a decision by her party to test public opinion on Prohibition.

In June, the Republican Central Committee of Cook County put three initiatives on the November ballot to weaken Prohibition. The Eighteenth Amendment, passed in 1919, had, at first, reduced alcohol consumption—so dangerous to women and children abused by workingmen who drank their paychecks. But enforcement was near impossible. Organized crime figures—none more infamous than Chicago's still at-large Al Capone—took up bootlegging, and local saloons ran speakeasies where wealthy patrons who could afford the high cost of smuggled liquor defied the law. With Capone said to be bribing the mayor and the police, Prohibition seemed a flawed if noble experiment. It would be repealed nationally in 1933. McCormick, who had been in favor of Prohibition, in popular parlance a "dry," now faced political headwinds toward the "wets." She was in an untenable position. Either she changed her position, offending temperance advocates, or she clung to her principles, losing voters in Chicago's beer-and-wine-loving German, Irish, and Italian wards.

In a much-anticipated speech at the state Republican convention, McCormick announced her decision: she would abide by the will of the people, deferring to the decision by voters on whether to repeal the state's Prohibition laws. Editorial opinion was harsh. "Mrs. McCormick was a good Dry in the Spring when she was nominated for Senator," wrote the *New York Times*. "She is now an ad interim Dry, subject to the will of the people."[35] Even more damning was the reaction of German-language newspapers. Calling her a candidate "who tries to carry water on both shoulders in regard to one of the most important questions of today,"[36] the German language *Abendpost* said voters expect "the candidate to show his true colors."[37] In truth, this newspaper's editorial board would likely have been happy only if she had become a wet, but in protesting her attempt to straddle a middle ground, it charged her with abetting the large-scale corruption and mass civil disobedience touched off by Prohibition.

For McCormick, a stance against alcoholism was personal. Medill had been a depressive, one who turned to alcohol to cope with mood swings. The experience had made her a dry, though she thought the government should either "enforce the law or repeal it." Since Frances Willard had taken the reins of the Woman's Christian Temperance Union in 1879, Prohibition had been seen as the cause of female reformers. In kind, female candidates were more often called on to defend their prohibition position, and female temperance advocates were, in McCormick's view, "so much harder on another woman."[38] The liquor industry, the fiercest opponent of women's suffrage, had effectively changed the Prohibition narrative. Alcoholism was no longer the bogeyman. Female reformers were. Lewis criticized McCormick's turnaround, calling hers a "now you see it, now you don't policy."[39] Calling her indecisive was another coded sexist slight.[40]

Temperance advocates also pounced. The Anti-Saloon League encouraged McCormick's old nemesis Lottie Holman O'Neill to jump into the race as an independent. Elected in 1922 to the Illinois General Assembly, O'Neill had been the state's first female state representative. In January, she resigned as vice president of the Illinois Republican Women's Club, calling on the rank-and-file Republican women to align themselves against the "bossism of Mark Hanna's daughter." Denying any personal animus, O'Neill complained that McCormick had quashed her efforts to win a committee chairmanship, a charge both McCormick and House Speaker David Shanahan denied. Still, O'Neill suggested McCormick was in the race for power, not the people. "She balked me at every possible turn," O'Neill complained. "Her personal ambition for power brooks no interference."[41]

Republican leaders warned the Anti-Saloon League that its endorsement would only split the dry vote, in effect helping to elect Lewis, a wet. "While Mrs. McCormick may not measure up to the demand of the league in all respects, Mrs. O'Neill or no other candidate can hope to poll enough votes to defeat Mrs. McCormick," wrote D. W. Grandon, editor of the *Sterling (IL) Daily Gazette*.[42] His words proved prophetic. O'Neill won nearly 5 percent of the vote, not enough to flip the race but plenty to rob McCormick of some campaign excitement.

. . .

In a speech before the Illinois Republican Service Men's League, a veterans group, McCormick defended her decision, saying the Anti-Saloon League was ignoring "the orgy of crime and corruption which has been going on for the last few years."[43] Acknowledging she was a dry, she said she respected the right of four hundred thousand citizens to petition for a referendum on prohibition. In endorsing O'Neill, she said, the Anti-Saloon League was shutting its eyes to the problems of bootlegging. Crowds were not always receptive. At one stop, voters laughed out loud at her assertion that "the wet and dry question is not a political issue."[44] Speaking to a "noisy" gathering at Chicago's Apollo Theater, she was heckled for even mentioning the issue.[45] Unfriendly newspapers speared her for hypocrisy, with one noting sarcastically, "McCormick's Oratory Turns a Bit Moist."[46]

On the Wrong Side of the Great Depression

In the primary, McCormick had won easily, thanks to the support of Mayor "Big Bill" Thompson's political machine in Chicago and that of the governor downstate. She did best in northern Illinois while opponent Charles Deneen fared well in southern counties. Where both would falter, and where it would hurt McCormick in the general election, was the farm vote predominant in central Illinois.[47] McCormick owned a large dairy farm near Byron. "Farming means more than just some bitter times with account books," she said. "I think, at least I hope, I have learned all the ways there are to lose money on a farm. Now I want my community and farmers . . . to get as much good as possible out of my experience."[48] Yet, by 1930, low prices were sending many farmers into bankruptcy, and as economic news worsened, McCormick stood by President Herbert Hoover's promise that "prosperity" would soon return through his tariff policy.[49] This decision helped ensure that Mc-Cormick would not win a single county in the Corn Belt.[50]

McCormick's campaign received plenty of clues about the dire straits of Illinois voters. Campaign worker James Snyder sifted through piles of job requests, two hundred in one month. "I am gradually going mad," he noted, "This office has averaged 15–20 people a day in search of jobs or work, and an equal number of letters for help in the way of clothes. I have practically used all the old clothes and shoes on the Gold Coast during the last campaign."[51] These letters crackled with the sheer desperation of its authors. "I need work badly," Robert E. Holmes wrote to McCormick and several other officials, requesting, "There is a good position that I can fill with grace to the Governor, and the Republican Party owes it or something to me for my loyalty and delivering stability."[52] McCormick's campaign apparently responded, tasking him with tallying the votes in his own precinct. Snyder attempted to place him at Marshall Field's, at the Merchandise Mart, and at "various other places, among your friends and mine," but the task was overwhelming.[53]

No community was more harshly affected by the Depression than Chicago's African American population. Fueled by the Great Migration from the Deep South to jobs and educational opportunities in the North and Midwest, Chicago's black population had skyrocketed from 44,103 in 1910 to 233,803 in 1930. During primaries, black voters were especially influential, making up one-fifth of the Republican base.[54] Now, on the bottom rung of opportunity, they were victims in the last-hired, first-fired dicta of the business world. Women in Illinois had been voting locally since 1891, when the legislature enabled them to participate in school board elections. African American activists in Chicago's First and Fourth Wards canvassed for Lucy Flower, a white candidate running for the University of Illinois Trustees. Given her pledge to pursue scholarships for black students, they overlooked her elitism to make her the first woman elected to statewide office.[55]

During her term in Congress, McCormick had impressed black voters with her commitment to equal rights. While first campaigning for a seat in the House of Representatives, she had "raised her right hand and pledged . . . to fight for enforcement of the Fourteenth and Fifteenth Amendments," which had enfranchised black men after the Civil War.[56] Once in office, she helped quash a move by southern congressmen not to seat Oscar DePriest, the first black man elected to Congress from Illinois. She was one of the few Republicans in Congress who tried to enfranchise black Americans still denied the vote in the South.[57] But during her Senate bid, black supporters hesitated. In the fall of 1929, McCormick had named Washington, DC, leader Mary Church Terrell as her campaign's liaison to the black community, stoking resentment among local black activists who felt the plum job should have gone to one of them.[58] Terrell was no outsider to black causes—she had been active in the fight for black female educational and electoral rights. Still, Effie Humphrey Hale, organizer for the Colored Women's Republican Clubs, had expected the job, "due to my knowledge of work among the colored women of this state." Aggrieved, her organization wrote McCormick, "We resent the slight thus put upon the Negro women of Illinois whose vote she solicits, by the employment of an outsider to influence that vote."[59]

By October, McCormick acknowledged to friends the urgency of the economic collapse. Writing to Will Carson, editor and publisher of the *Greenville (IL) Advocate* and a longtime supporter, McCormick predicted, "I believe the campaign is going to swing our way, but I confess to you that it is 'sticky' at the present time. There is no enthusiasm because there are not enough jobs to go around, or enough cash in the banks to give people a sense of security." She shared Hoover's view that the stock market would recover without an infusion of government aid but was mindful that the voting public was not so sure. As she observed, "The unrest of the people and the strong combinations of factional feuds which are building their fences for two years now make an unusually difficult campaign for an off-year election."[60]

Sensing vulnerability, Lewis delivered a gender-inflected economic critique of McCormick at this opportune moment. "I cannot understand why the lady is content to remain silent on the present day crying necessities, silent on employment, or restoration of hope. I regret that her board of elocution and oratory that writes her daily manuscript for her, that board of straddling strategy, has abandoned these matters," he asserted.[61] By campaign's end, McCormick was on board with remedial measures that could lift farmers and the poor from poverty. She told one crowd, "The question is not whether everybody gets a bottle of beer but whether everybody gets a job." Calling Prohibition "a red herring across the trail," she charged Democrats with "calamity-shouting"[62] and argued that in hard times it was better to retain Republicans, since it was Democrats who had increased breadlines during the financial panic of 1893.[63]

Chicago Mayor "Big Bill" Thompson had backed her in the primary but switched to Lewis in the general. As Lewis observed, "He left the lady waiting at the altar." Now the mayor exploited her vulnerabilities among African Americans. Two Sundays before the election, Thompson posted police officers at black churches, distributing an anti-McCormick brochure. In campaign appearances at the Apollo Theater, and in Rockford, she seemed to delight in distancing herself from Thompson, whose support in the primaries was used against her in the Nye hearings. Now she cast him as incompetent, saying, "The mayor found no difficulty in mobilizing our police force to peddle Lewis handbills, but he and his entire force of policemen cannot find Al Capone." She pointed out that while Thompson was dry, Lewis was wet, and Thompson was a Republican, while Lewis a Democrat. McCormick also accused Thompson of corruption, suggesting, "Today Mr. Thompson is advertising that he has $100,000 in cash ready to give to ward leaders for the purpose of manning the polls on November 4. The larger wards will receive $5000."[64] She was flailing. As the *New York Times* sagely noted, "If this were a private quarrel, Mrs. McCormick might be congratulated on the enemy she has made. But if Big Bill's hold on the South Side is anything like what it used to be, his open defection may put the finishing touches to her ambition to be the first woman elected a United States Senator."[65]

Lessons from McCormick

Asked the day after the election to pinpoint the cause of her defeat, McCormick laughed and said, "What causes anybody's defeat but the fact that somebody else got more votes? Mr. Lewis got the votes. I still believe in majority rule, so there's no use whining, is there?"[66] Writing a friend a week later, she acknowledged a lingering bewilderment. "The tidal wave [that had] swept over the country" had engulfed her too, she wrote. "It undoubtedly means something more than most of us are able to analyze now."[67] Rewriting his sexist campaign attacks, James Hamilton Lewis, now Senator-elect, offered a veiled compliment, concluding, "Mrs. McCormick fought as valiant a fight as any man ever did."[68]

. . .

Lewis had a talent for stoking the gender fears that voters brought to the election. Yet, it was more than gender that impacted McCormick's doomed Senate bid. She was hurt by her own flawed reaction to internal party politics—first welcoming the endorsement of Thompson's Chicago City Machine, then distancing herself from him, and flailing on the issue of Prohibition. As Depression anxieties set in, she was smeared for overspending and misreading the warning signs of a deepening Depression. For African American women, the McCormick race tested the alliance with white activists to win suffrage. Her slighting of local black leaders, her tin ear to the searing cruelties of the Depression, especially for her black constituents, these issues of economics and race weighed down her candidacy. But it was the wave election that wrote her political obituary. Democrats had gained control of the House. Among the pick-ups were seven seats in the twenty-seven-member Illinois House delegation, all of them in favor of repealing Prohibition. As one headline writer put it, "Country Goes Democratic . . . Bad Times, Wet Issue Are Blamed."[69]

McCormick was charming, assertive, brilliant, and glamorous. Enemies within and outside her party targeted her because she was a woman who threatened their interests—not because she was weak but precisely because she was strong. A Republican Senate had sent Gerald Nye to spy on her, the drip, drip, drip of his accusations making her just another compromised politician. A Republican Party in Cook County had put Prohibition on the ballot, muddying her chances. Republican pols in Springfield and Washington, DC, disparaged her behind closed doors. Affiliated with the party of Teddy Roosevelt, which once stood for progressive reform, she clung to the party standard as Republicans became the party of heartless capitalism. She had run on character at a time when voters pined for real-life solutions. Her slogan—"No Favors, No Bunk"—was meant to tap into a nongendered claim of competency, but to those standing in line at soup kitchens, this anticorruption argument proved irrelevant.

Ten years later, after marrying Albert Gallatin Simms and moving to Albuquerque, New Mexico, McCormack became the first woman to manage a presidential candidacy, spearheading Thomas Dewey's 1940 campaign to win the Republican nomination. The thirty-seven-year-old Dewey lost that year to Wendell Willkie. He called on McCormick again when he ran for governor of New York and when he successfully won the GOP nomination for president in 1944. She passed away shortly after, a figure of note since forgotten. Four years after her death, Margaret Chase Smith ran for Senate from Maine. With an echo of McCormick's 1930 campaign, the wife of one of Smith's opponents asked, "Why [send] a woman to Washington when you can get a man?"[70] Overcoming this insistent sexism, Smith won, becoming the first woman to serve in both the House and the Senate, an honor that had earlier eluded Ruth Hanna McCormick, forever known as the first "lady candidate."

Notes

1. Quentin R. Skrabec Jr., *The Ohio Presidents: Eight Men and a Binding Political Philosophy in the White House, 1841–1923* (Jefferson, NC: McFarland, 2018), 88.

2. Kristie Miller, "Ruth Hanna McCormick and the Senatorial Election of 1930," *Illinois Historical Journal* 81 (August 1988): 192.

3. Hermann Hagedorn, *The Roosevelt Family of Sagamore Hill* (New York: Macmillan, 1954), 311, cited in Miller, "Ruth Hanna McCormick."

4. "In Illinois," *Time*, April 23, 1928.

5. Donald Tigley, *The Structuring of a State: The History of Illinois, 1899–1928* (Urbana: University of Illinois Press, 1980), 375–380, cited in Miller, "Ruth Hanna McCormick."

6. "Ruth McCormick," *Washington Post*, April 10, 1930, 6.

7. E. P. Evans, "Letters to the Editor," *Washington Post*, April 12, 1930, 6.

8. Kristie Miller, *Ruth Hanna McCormick: A Life in Politics, 1880–1944* (Albuquerque: University of New Mexico Press, 1992), 223.

9. "Great Ovation for Ruth McCormick in House Session Today," *New Castle (PA) News*, April 11, 1930, 27.

10. Miller, *Ruth Hanna McCormick,* 2.

11. Margaret Leech, *In the Days of McKinley* (Norwalk, CT: Easton Press, 1986), 76.

12. Miller, *Ruth Hanna McCormick*, 20, 52.

13. "Press Fight on Eve of Illinois Voting," *New York Times*, April 8, 1930, 3.

14. Owen L. Scott, "Two Ladies, One Gentleman after Seat in Senate," *Appleton (WI) Post-Crescent*, October 23, 1930, 18.

15. Arvarh E. Strickland, "'The Lady Candidate': Ruth Hanna McCormick and the Senatorial Election of 1930," *Illinois Historical Journal* 88, no. 3 (Autumn 1995): 197–199.

16. "Mrs. McCormick Fights for Toga as Man to Man: Wants No Preference Because of Sex," *Chicago Daily Tribune*, April 6, 1930, G1.

17. Miller, *Ruth Hanna McCormick,* 2.

18. Genevieve Forbes Herrick, "Mrs. M'Cormick as She Is Seen in Campaign," *Chicago Daily Tribune,* October 31, 1930, 1.

19. Miller, *Ruth Hanna McCormick,* 231–232.

20. Nye is best known for his mid-1930s investigation into the wartime profits of banking and munitions industries during World War I.

21. "The 'Ten Cent' Senator Sits in Judgement [*sic*] on Million Dollar Senators," Williams County (N.D.) Farmers Press, August 7, 1930, box 86, Clippings Scrapbook, Gerald Nye Papers, Herbert Hoover Presidential Library-Museum.

22. https://www.measuringworth.com/calculators/uscompare/relativevalue.php.

23. Letter to Editor from Ruth Hanna McCormick, *Peoria Star,* September 22, 1930, box 95, Hanna-McCormick Papers, Library of Congress.

24. "Sleuth for Nye Here on 2 Day Secret Mission," *Chicago Daily Tribune,* February 12, 1931.

25. This figure reflects estimates in 2018, https://www.measuringworth.com/calculators/uscompare/result.php?year_source=1930&amount=250,000&year_result=2018.

26. Miller, *Ruth Hanna McCormick,* 225–226.

27. "Mrs. M'Cormick and Nye Clash in Fund Inquiry," *Chicago Daily Tribune,* July 15, 1930, 1.

28. Arthur Evans, "Mrs. McCormick Defies Nye in Campaign Speeches Downstate," *Chicago Daily Tribune,* September 23, 1930, 4.

29. "Mrs. McCormick Snoops a Bit," *Milwaukee Journal,* September 4, 1930, box 86, Clippings Scrapbook, Gerald Nye Papers, Clippings Scrapbook, Herbert Hoover Presidential Library-Museum.

30. "Campaign of a Lady," *New York Times*, September 17, 1930, 22.

31. Miller, *Ruth Hanna McCormick,* 227.

32. Miller, *Ruth Hanna McCormick,* 227–233.

33. "Mrs. McCormick Fights for Toga as Man to Man: Wants No Preference Because of Sex," *Chicago Daily Tribune*, April 6, 1930, G1.

34. "Mrs. M'Cormick Is Winner over Deneen in Primary for Illinois Senatorship," *New York Times*, April 9, 1930, 1.

35. "Smart Work in Illinois," *New York Times,* August 25, 1930, 16.

36. Translation of editorial of *Abendpost* from September 12, 1930, box 96, Hanna-McCormick Papers, LOC.

37. Translation of editorial of *Abendpost* from September 10, 1930, LOC.

38. Miller, *Ruth Hanna McCormick,* 187.

39. S. J. Duncan-Clark, "Illinois G.O.P. Vote Faces Heavy Loss," *New York Times*, October 19, 1930, 55.

40. "Lewis Assails Prohibition in County Opener," *Chicago Daily Tribune*, September 15, 1930, 5.

41. "Mrs. M'Cormick Imputed a Czar by Mrs. O'Neill," *Chicago Daily Tribune*, January 31, 1929, 2.

42. Parke Brown, "Drys Indorse Candidacy of Lottie O'Neill," *Chicago Daily Tribune*, September 7, 1930, 1.

43. "Ruth McCormick Defends Stand on Prohibition," *Chicago Daily Tribune*, September 18, 1930, 9.

44. Strickland, "'The Lady Candidate,'" 195 (see n. 15).

45. "Big Bill's Tarquins," *New York Times*, October 25, 1930, 11.

46. Newspaper clippings, box 102, Hanna-McCormick Papers, LOC.

47. Strickland, "'The Lady Candidate,'" 190, 193.

48. Winifred Mallon, "Another Hanna Looks to the Senate," *New York Times*, June 9, 1929, 6.

49. Strickland, "'The Lady Candidate,'" 197.

50. https://uselectionatlas.org/RESULTS/.

51. Letter from Jim Snyder to Mabel Reinecke, May 21, 1930, box 88, Hanna-McCormick Papers, LOC.

52. "Dear Friend" letter from Robert E. Holmes, n.d., box 102, Hanna-McCormick Papers, LOC.

53. Letter from Jim Snyder to RHM, June 21, 1930, box 90, Hanna-McCormick Papers, LOC.

54. Lisa G. Materson, *For the Freedom of Her Race: Black Women and Electoral Politics in Illinois, 1877–1932* (Chapel Hill: University of North Carolina Press, 2009), 187–188.

55. Materson, *For the Freedom of Her Race*, 21–26.

56. "Ruth Hanna McCormick Opens Campaign Office," *Chicago Bee*, October 20, 1929.

57. Materson, *For the Freedom of Her Race*, 204.

58. "Leaders at Breakfast Conference," *Chicago Defender*, November 9, 1929.

59. Materson, *For the Freedom of Her Race*, 208.

60. Letter from Ruth Hanna McCormick to Will C. Carson, October 6, 1930, box 99, Hanna-McCormick Papers, LOC.

61. Philip Kinsley, "Back 'New Deal' for West, Lewis Urges Voters: Chides Rival on Issue of Unemployment," *Chicago Daily Tribune*, November 1, 1930, 2.

62. "Last-Minute Drives Made in Illinois," *New York Times*, November 4, 1930, 19.

63. Arthur Evans, "Jobs, Not Liquor, Called Issue by Mrs. McCormick," *Chicago Daily Tribune*, October 21, 1930, 9.

64. Arthur Evans, "Ruth McCormick Tears into Foes at Loop Rallies," *Chicago Daily Tribune*, October 28, 1930, 7.

65. "Big Bill's Tarquins," *New York Times*, October 25, 1930, 11.

66. Genevieve Forbes Herrick, "Mrs. McCormick Sees Defeat as Affair of Party," *Chicago Daily Tribune*, November 5, 1930, 7.

67. Ruth Hanna McCormick to Letitia Myles, November 12, 1930, box 102, Hanna-McCormick Papers, LOC.

68. "What They Said the Morning After," *Chicago Daily Tribune*, November 6, 1930, 3.

69. Arthur Sears Henning, "Country Goes Democratic," *Chicago Daily Tribune*, November 5, 1930, 1.

70. Tom Daschle and Charles Robbins, *The U.S. Senate: Fundamentals of American Government* (New York: Macmillan, 2013), 196.

Women Are City "Dads"
—They Run the Town

Women Who Will Govern Thayer, Kansas—Center, Mrs. A. H. Forest, mayor; Upper Left, Mrs. Daisy Savage; Lower Left, Mrs. Ina Craig; Right, Reading Down, Miss Alice Lambertson, Mrs. Eunice Rash, Mrs. Iva Cross.

Newspaper and magazine articles occasionally featured photographs and line drawings of female politicians. In this example, featuring several widowed women, they struggle to reconcile the women's identities as political leaders, acknowledging that "They Run the Town," but characterizing them as "City 'Dads.'" "Women Are City 'Dads'; They Run the Town," *Buffalo Times*, April 28, 1921.

CHAPTER 5

"A Dead Husband Is a Better Ticket to Congress Than a Log Cabin"

The Public Discourse of Widows in Office, 1920–1940

KATHERINE PARKIN

IN THE TWO decades after women secured the right to vote, a minuscule number of women found their way into political office. Heralded by history as pioneering politicians, a significant portion of the women in office at local, state, and national levels only found themselves elected or appointed to hold the seat of their dead husbands. Instead of reflecting real change, male political leaders used the widows of deceased politicians to hold on to the political machine's greatest asset: political power. Moreover, the women sought their positions not on the basis of being equal citizens; instead, they asserted a gendered identity as involuntarily dependent. Despite their transient status, widows who served in their husbands' stead were largely criticized in public discourse, dismissed as illegitimate politicians by virtue of their gender. Additionally, critics castigated the process that put widows into office as undemocratic and unfair.[1]

After the decades-long battle to win the vote, the League of Women Voters shifted their energies toward educating voters and compelling them to vote, in part because in 1920 voting declined among men, and "only about one-third of the eligible women voted." However, no national effort existed to encourage women to run for political office. In advance of securing national suffrage, small numbers of women pursued open seats, particularly in educationally focused, local positions. After national suffrage, some women found success in local and county races, but a considerable percentage of those elected to more prominent positions followed a deceased husband or father. More than half of the women who served in the US House of Representatives between 1920 and 1940, for example, did so only because of the death of their husbands. This false empowerment led to an exaggerated sense of women's achievement and disguised how little political voice and representation women had.[2]

Across party lines around the country, women's best bet to access a political seat was to be a widow. One 1925 newspaper columnist acknowledged as much, noting, "Just now a dead husband is a better ticket to Congress than a log cabin." Politically connected widows introduced a new way for male politicians to deliver seats to their party and to do so without disrupting people's narrow expectations of women in politics. Widows were assumed to be aligned to their husband's politics and considered easy pawns to be played by his political advisors and party leadership. The underlying supposition about widow politicians was that women did not want to be in politics, and their service would be short lived.[3]

Scholars have long understood widowhood to be one of the paths that enabled women to enter political office in the decades following suffrage. Less considered is how this practice was perceived at the time and its lasting social and political implications. This study explores how the American public reacted to this new crop of widow politicians, from local sheriffs to US senators. Women elected as widows, as daughters of deceased male politicians, and as stand-ins for their still-alive husbands all informed a public discourse about the limitations of women's political agency. Seen as a stand-in for men, widows in office were not recognized in their own right, their voices and positions muted, both literally and figuratively.[4] Looking at newspaper coverage, this chapter assesses the extent to which women were not seen as competitors but, rather, as placeholders in politics. As one reporter noted in a 1925 story, "Women who have ambitions to be elected to Congress should get married to men who will be elected and have the thoughtfulness to die in office." Indeed, in this period, most widowed women were relegated to a symbolic place in politics, denied an identity as politicians.[5]

Women were appointed to open US Senate positions, but these appointments were usually brief and held until a special election or the next election cycle. Often widows and bereaved daughters served in name only, as was the case with Rebecca Latimer Felton, the first woman to serve as a US senator. The antisuffrage governor of Georgia who appointed her to a vacant seat in 1922 hoped this stunt would allow him to feign his support for women voters. Felton's short-lived moment, farcically serving only twenty-four hours because a man had already been elected, was predicated on a woman's usefulness as a "sacrificial lamb" or a "bereaved benchwarmer." Likewise, from the time the widow Elizabeth Hawley Gasque took the oath of office in September 1938 to when she stepped down on January 3, 1939, Congress was never in session, and she never cast a vote. While the record books categorize her as a US congresswoman, the truth of many women's roles, such as Felton's and Gasque's, was that it was more shadow than substance. Widowed women appointed and elected to such effectively fictitious positions came to dominate the public's consciousness about women and politics between 1920 and 1940.[6]

Political widows helped Americans imagine a woman as politically capable but only by association with the assumed de facto competence of her deceased husband. After the ratification of the Nineteenth Amendment, the nation had not yet resolved whether women could engage in political leadership independently as equals. In fact, after being forced to allow women to vote, some "states initially tried to prevent women from running for public office." Oklahoma was the last state to finally amend its constitution in 1942. Voters held a largely skeptical and at times misogynistic view of female candidates. Therefore, the political machines that embraced widows as candidates or appointees generally did not base their decision on an expectation of a woman's competence. Instead, the selection of widows emerged out of a combined expectation that she would carry on her husband's legacy and hold the seat until a "real" candidate could be found. Thus, men in politics and an approving wider electorate remained reluctant to bestow on women the power of elected office, much as they had been reluctant to grant women the right to vote.[7]

Negative coverage of widows in politics spread fears of what would happen if these women stayed in office too long. In the 1920s and 1930s, newspapers and magazines across the country frequently ran stories that focused on "widow's succession." Columnists suggested that "passing along" the political seat from husband to wife smacked of a European monarchy. Instead of a duly elected, representative system of government, critics feared that men would pass along political seats in a dynasty, one that now included the potential for men to pass on political power to wives and daughters. Instead of seeing "widow's succession" as an unusual occurrence, concerns grew that the practice of appointing or electing widows would subvert democracy.[8]

Most critical editorials were penned by male leaders of political parties, but women also voiced opposition to women running for office. Fear of widows as politicians was compounded by the fear of women as incompetent and powerless representatives. As one *Ladies' Home Journal* article directed, "If you are a woman yourself you had better vote for a man who is afraid of your tongue than for another woman who has a tongue of her own," contending that women would be better off pressuring male politicians than supporting female politicians with limited power.[9]

Some widowed women withstood these critics and bucked expectations by sticking with politics, finding that their husband's death enabled them to actively engage in the political system for the first time. For some, it was only at their husband's death that they recognized their own political aptitude, concluded they were capable of the job, and gained the confidence to campaign and even seek reelection.[10] For example, Florence Khan, the wife of Congressman Julius Khan (California), had worked as his secretary until she stepped into his role when he became ill. Once a candidate herself, newspapers homed in on her identity as a woman and a widow and on her ability to represent the San Francisco area. Most stories did not center on her religious and ethnic identity, which was remarkable because she was Jewish and running in an era of intense anti-Semitism. Accordingly, despite the overwhelming trend in reporting to call candidacies like Kahn's a "distinctly unstatesmanlike precedent," she was elected in 1924 as the first Jewish US congresswoman. Soon thereafter, in 1928, the first African American woman to serve in a state legislature, Minnie Buckingham Harper, was elected to her deceased husband's West Virginia seat.[11] Thus, for some women, widowhood not only proved to be a way to overcome gender limitations but also let them break through nearly insurmountable racial and ethnic barriers.

To be reelected as a widow was truly exceptional. A few, such as US Representatives Kahn, Hattie Caraway (Arkansas), and Edith Nourse Rogers (Massachusetts), successfully made this leap. Political scientist Irwin N. Gertzog observed in his study of these cases that there were strong differences in nomination trends for second terms. Most notable, women outside of the South fared better in reelection campaigns because southern political patronage networks primarily used widows to bridge the gap to a male candidate.[12] And for those who did campaign, widows faced personal and political barriers. The energy, drive, and organization required to campaign was difficult for widows, often still mourning the loss of a partner, breadwinner, and experienced politician. A low-visibility strategy worked better for local and statewide races, whereas in campaigns for national office, women had to publicly prove themselves against strong male competitors. At times, widows' political acumen exceeded journalists' expectation, leading the candidates to receive favorable press. Reporters covering the congressional races of Edith Nourse Rogers and Florence Kahn, noted that, while sentimentality "prompted the candidacy," the women "surprised all by her grasp of national questions and the working of congress" and "rolled up votes on merit."[13]

Reporters grappled with how to cover these widow-to-office races. Columnist John Dickinson Sherman speculated that the dictionary would likely expand when more women achieved office and offered new terms—"Her Excellency, the Governess"—titles that negatively signaled antidemocratic royalty and cast women as maternal caregivers.[14] Other critics suggested that widowhood held inordinate cultural cachet. Sentimentality for a new widow was believed to be so powerful that there was no way to counter it in a political campaign; widowhood led people to vote irrationally. As one *El Paso Times* editorial condemning the practice contended in 1925, "What can the opposition do against a widow? To question her qualifications for office is to insult her sorrow. Even to inflict a debate of policies upon her fresh grief has the taint of bad taste."[15] A critic in the *Wilkes-Barre Times* denounced it as "an old-fashioned, not a 'modern' sentiment." In 1932, reflecting on the twelve years since suffrage, one critique in the *Times Leader*, published in Staunton, Virginia, lamented that the current crop of "five heirs to their husbands' seats" were doing irreparable harm to women's political progress. "Unless they show far more talent than any of them has done so far, are bound to injure the case for women in public office—bound, in the end, to keep intelligent women from seeking public office and to keep intelligent voters from supporting them," the story editorialized. Even in the late 1930s, a newspaper column on widow politicians disparaged "'lady'" sheriffs and discussed "women congressmen" as self-evident absurdities.[16]

Media coverage of widows in office did not generally cast them as successful independent actors and feminist pioneers. In 1936, the *Ladies' Home Journal* published a fictional account of a widowed "Stateswoman" that provided women readers with a cautionary tale. The male author made clear that the men who had stayed on from her husband's staff imagined that they were running her Senate office and even believed that they *were* the senator; one described his role as "the priest pulling the wires on the sacred image." This discourse, a mix of fact and fiction, allowed skeptics to publicly advance their hatred of widows in politics and denounce them as "mere figureheads."[17]

One tactic used in the press to limit women in politics was to spotlight widows who said no to politics. Newspaper columns showered attention on women who shunned or declined real or imagined offers to campaign for their deceased husbands' seats; these stories increased in frequency in the 1930s after appearing only occasionally in the 1920s. The leading message was, as one article opined, "sober-thinking people will think more rather than less of these bereft ones [who] would decline to try to capitalize their bereavement." Headlines such as, "Omaha Mayor's Widow Declines Succession," suggested a salve to soothe the fear that women would be passed the scepter of power, subverting the democratic process of elections. Other stories made examples of widows, like the extraordinarily wealthy Elizabeth Morrow (New Jersey), which maintained that a candidate "should be chosen solely for their own attainments and capabilities." Highlighting Morrow's case, skeptics bemoaned what a "pity" it was that others did not "emulate her wise example."[18]

A minor thread of public discourse around widows in office did comment optimistically about their prospects and at the very least suggested that "there is no real danger discernable in what has happened." Flatly rejecting the argument that women's status as widows duped the public, these writers sought to dispel the myth that widows were inept or out of their depth, had secured their offices in clear contests, and "served with distinction." One proponent went so far as to criticize those who called widows unfit for office: "Such an argument betrays a profound ignorance of politics and politicians." This editorial further noted, "When a woman can win an election because of her fitness and ability, she has as much right to it as any man." Occasionally, bold headlines— "On Their Merit, Not on Sentiment"—and published photographs featuring women in office heralded the accomplishments of widows in the face of critics.[19]

Sometimes articles were accompanied by illustrations portraying women in office speaking directly and assertively to men. The illustrations allowed Americans to imagine women standing and speaking to a group of men. "Will Women Upset Congress?" a 1933 *Charleston (WV) Daily Mail* article asked in its headline. The photographs accompanying the article highlighted congresswomen from across the country, heralded by veterans like Indiana's Virginia Jenckes or in formal poses behind their desks. However, the large line drawing of an anonymous woman in formal hat and a feminine, tailored suit and tie standing and speaking in a meeting with four seated men, reveals the power women asserted in engaging politics. Using fictionalized representations had the added advantage of expanding the discourse about who could represent Americans in the halls of power and stand up for their constituents. These unusual portrayals had the potential to broaden positive perceptions about female politicians.[20] This combination of support-ive language and visual substantiation was significant, for women in office had to reconcile that their new positions were within a social structure suited to male identity and male leadership. Coverage of women elected in Thayer, Kansas, in 1921—a widow became mayor and a police judge alongside five other women elected to city council—made clear how even in positive coverage gendered articulations of leadership remained. "Women Are City 'Dads'; They Run the Town," a headline proclaimed, accompanied by a collage of headshots suggesting that women were focused and in charge. Yet to capture the elected women's political acumen, the headline described them as men.[21]

Indeed, many articles showcased women in more domestic settings. In one story featuring a widow-turned-politician, she was photographed in her kitchen. The accompanying caption assured the reader that Mae E. Nolan "made an enviable record as a lawmaker, but she is much more interested in her home than in politics." While these domestic descrip-tions had the effect of softening women's political presence and assuring some that it was only temporary, they also had negative consequences. In softening women's political landing, homemaking references may ulti-mately have augmented the skeptical public's perception that widowed politicians had skewed priorities.[22] Thus, portrayals of women in office often affirmed proscribed gender roles, particularly with regard to public speaking, assertiveness, and political aptitude. Accordingly, the leading sentiment continued: "Most women are too ladylike for the job of president. Politics, patronage and other forms of economic chicanery are strictly masculine rackets." The gendered language of politics, and accom-panying public expectation, did not greatly evolve in this period even as more women exhibited their political ambition and agency.[23]

Widows played their part in limiting political speech. Some like Gov-ernor Nellie Tayloe Ross (Wyoming) used silence as a tactic, making "no speeches during the campaign" to replace her husband. Likewise, coverage of women noted how unusual it was for them to speak out. "She has never made a political speech in her life or taken much part in politics, except to assist at her husband's campaign headquarters," one article noted of Senator Hattie Caraway, "but if a neighbor is sick, she likes to go over with some hot biscuits and broth and help things along." This vignette had the effect of selling Caraway's pure femininity and womanhood, confirming that she preferred homemaking and was "not a politician."[24]

Still, surprisingly, in one area, widows had an advantage, skirting the usual trend in political coverage of women in politics that focused on their appearances. Descriptions of widow's physicality, including one's hairstyle, clothing, and accessories, did not generally pervade accounts until the late 1930s. The widows' adoption of the "somber garb of mourning" had the advantage of being sober and nondescript by design, leaving reporters with little to adorn their stories. It is possible that social mores around older women and widows also tempered reporters' physical descriptions.[25]

Epitomizing both the rationale for putting women in office and an idealized outcome, a 1933 newspaper account in the *Waterloo (IA) Courier* claimed that the "county recorders of Jackson county are elected as widows and marry as soon as their terms expire." In this unusual story, they reported that women entered into politics seemingly out of necessity, as widows, and retired from office having secured a husband.

The political endgame for widowed women was generally financial survival. The discourse between 1920 and 1940 revealed that many widows entered into political office as substitutes for their husbands. Sometimes, their standing as a "bereaved benchwarmer" was fleeting and drew the ire of critics who saw the practice as subverting democracy. However, there were also times when appointing and electing widows temporarily advanced their husband's legacy and his political party. Putting widows in office was thus touted as a way for voters and political leaders to honor deceased men and help secure the financial livelihood of their families. For this reason, some reports commented on not only the politician's widow but also his children. Such was the case with one story about "a young widow with a 9-month-old baby was elected sheriff of a Kentucky county to fill out her dead husband's term" or an ad that ran in the *El Paso Herald-Post* in 1938, encouraging voters to "Do the Job Right" and elect Mrs. W. D. Greet. The ad touted her husband's significant accomplishments as county clerk and reminded the community, "She needs this job. With a 14 year old daughter . . . she faces her responsibilities alone." Thus, it was women's widowhood and dependency that brought them into office.[26]

News coverage of widows in politics during the 1920s and the 1930s makes clear how difficult it was for the majority of Americans to imagine women as fully capable of political independence. Even so, women's presence in political coverage did help open the possibility for women to enter into politics. Indeed, widows themselves and constituents following them discovered that women could be astute, successful politicians. While not intended to extend power to women, widowhood helped introduce women to the political arena and awakened Americans to their political potential.[27]

Notes

The author thanks Chris DeRosa, Trish Maloney, Michael Phillips-Anderson, Melissa Ziobro, Stacie Taranto, and Leandra Zarnow for their helpful suggestions and feedback.

1. Nancy F. Cott, *The Grounding of Modern Feminism* (New Haven, CT: Yale University Press, 1987), 110–111. Cott compares minuscule numbers of women state legislators, 33 (1921) and 149 (1929) to almost 10,000 men in such offices.

2. Cott, *Grounding of Modern Feminism*; Barbara C. Burrell, *Women and Political Participation: A Reference Handbook* (Santa Barbara, CA: ABC-CLIO, 2004), 91, 130–132; Barbara Palmer and Dennis Simon, *Breaking the Political Glass Ceiling: Women and Congressional Elections* (New York: Routledge, 2006), 6–8; Liette Gidlow, "Delegitimizing Democracy: 'Civic Slackers,' the Cultural Turn, and the Possibilities of Politics," *Journal of American History* 89, no. 3 (December 2002): 922–957.

3. "New Vocation for Widows: Succeeding Their Late Husbands in Political Office Now the Vogue in American Political Life," *Abilene (TX) Morning Reporter*, March 8, 1925; "The Widow's Might," *Vernon (TX) Record*, August 21, 1925; Kathleen A. Dolan, *Voting for Women* (Boulder, CO: Westview Press, 2004), 37–38, 41; Suzanne O'Dea Schenken, *From Suffrage to the Senate: An Encyclopedia of American Women in Politics,* vol. 1 (Santa Barbara, CA: ABC-CLIO, 1999), 260–261; Kristi Anderson, *After Suffrage: Women in Partisan*

and Electoral Politics before the New Deal (Chicago: University of Chicago Press, 1996), 77–8, 111–114, 117; Cott, *Grounding of Modern Feminism*, 7.

4. Diane D. Kincaid, "Over His Dead Body: A Positive Perspective on Widows in the U.S. Congress," *Western Political Quarterly* 31, no. 1 (1978): 97; Farida Jalalzai and Chad Hankinson, "Political Womanhood in the United States: An Empirical Assessment of Underlying Assumptions of Representation," *Journal of Women, Politics & Policy* 29, no. 3 (2008): 395–426; "The North Dakota Vacancy," *Butte (MT) Miner*, August 19, 1925; "Widows in Public Service," *Indianapolis Star*, March 7, 1934; "A Baptism, a Tom Heflin and a New Woman Senator," *Life*, August 30, 1937; Palmer and Simon, *Breaking the Political Glass Ceiling*, 21.

5. Mark Sullivan, "LaFollette's Death Gives Borah Power," *Palladium-Item* (Richmond, IA), June 22, 1925, and "Woman Feature of Political Year," *Hartford Courant*, April 6, 1930; "The Widow's Might"; Charles S. Bullock III and Patricia Lee Findley Heys, "Recruitment of Women for Congress: A Research Note," *Western Political Quarterly* 25, no. 3 (September 1972): 418.

6. "Rebecca Latimer Felton" and "Elizabeth H. Gasque" in *Women in Congress, 1917–2006*, edited by US House of Representatives and Committee on House Administration (Washington, DC: Joint Committee on Printing, 2007), 53–55 and 171–175; Dolan, *Voting for Women*, 36; Schenken, *From Suffrage to the Senate*, 260–261; Anderson, *After Suffrage*, 114. Political scientist Diane Kincaid noted we must distinguish between appointments, which are temporary, and elections, which are contested. The US Constitution ensures that a special election is held to fill vacancies in the House of Representatives, while individual states govern the laws of appointment for Senate seats. In most instances, appointments sought to keep a seat in the same political party and not to circumvent duly-elected representatives. Moreover, most appointees at every level of office were men (Kincaid, "Over His Dead Body," 97–98).

7. Burrell, *Women and Political Participation*, 129–130; Kincaid, "Over His Dead Body," 97; Donlan, *Voting for Women*; "The North Dakota Vacancy"; "Widows in Public Service"; Irwin N. Gertzog, "The Matrimonial Connection: The Nomination of Congressmen's Widows for the House of Representatives," *Journal of Politics* 42, no. 3 (1980): 821–822, 830; Bullock and Heys, "Recruitment of Women," 417; Timothy Bledsoe and Mary Herring, "Victims of Circumstances: Women in Pursuit of Political Office," *American Political Science Review* 84, no. 1 (1990): 219; "Women Representatives and Senators by Congress, 1917–Present," United States House of Representatives, https://history.house.gov/Exhibitions-and-Publications/WIC/Historical-Data /Women-Representatives-and-Senators-by-Congress/; Anderson, *After Suffrage*, 122–125; Palmer and Simon, *Breaking the Political Glass Ceiling*, 52; Cott, *Grounding of Modern Feminism*, 107–108.

8. "Sun's Eclipse Delight of Pessimist," *Davenport (IA) Democrat and Leader*, January 25, 1925; "Debate Rights of Widows in Congress," *San Bernardino County (CA) Sun*, November 27, 1931; "Widows in Public Service"; "Mrs. Rainey to Be Different," *Daily Notes* (Canonsburg, PA), August 30, 1934; Eleanor Morton, "More Correspondents Believe Women Should Not Fill Public Offices without Training; Widow Succession Is Being Overdone," *Philadelphia Inquirer*, April 17, 1936; "On Her Own," *Baltimore Sun*, February 2, 1937; "Shuns 'Widow Succession,'" *Indianapolis Star*, September 22, 1940; Lisa Solowiej and Thomas L. Brunell, "The Entrance of Women to the U.S. Congress: The Widow Effect," *Political Research Quarterly* 56, no. 3 (September 2003): 286.

9. "Practical Politics for Gentlewomen," *Ladies' Home Journal (LHJ)*, September 1921, 16, 155; "A Sensible Precedent," *El Paso (TX) Times*, July 29, 1925; "Widows in Public"; Cott, *Grounding of Modern Feminism*, 266.

10. "Widow's Might"; "Sun's Eclipse."

11. "The Value of Family Prestige," *Montgomery (AL) Advertiser*, July 19, 1922; "Widow Will Run for Office Once Held by Husband," *Sheboygan (WI) Press Telegram*, December 22, 1924; "Widows in Office," *Asheville (NC) Citizen-Times*, January 16, 1925; Nellie Tayloe Ross, "The Governor Lady," *Good Housekeeping*, August 1927; Glenna Matthews, "There Is No Sex in Citizenship": The Career of Congresswoman Florence Prag Kahn," in *We Have Come to Stay: American Women and Political Parties, 1880–1960*, ed. Melanie Gustafson, Kristie Miller, and Elisabeth Perry (Albuquerque: University of New Mexico Press, 1999); Linda Van Ingren, *Gendered Politics: Campaign Strategies of California Women Candidates, 1912–1970* (Lanham, MD: Lexington Books, 2017), 45–48; Anderson, *After Suffrage*, 116.

12. Gertzog, "Matrimonial Connection," 823–828; "A Baptism"; Dolan, *Voting for Women*, 40; Palmer and Simon, *Breaking the Political Glass Ceiling*, 72–73.

13. "A Valuable Collection," *Des Moines (IA) Tribune*, July 7, 1925; Robert Fuller, "On Their Merit, Not on Sentiment," *Winona (MS) Times*, July 17, 1925.

14. "Another Woman for Governor," *Minneapolis Star*, October 15, 1924; Sherman, "Her Excellency"; "Families in Politics," *News Journal* (Wilmington, DE), April 16, 1925.

15. "A Sensible Precedent."

16. "A Sensible Precedent"; "Widows to Congress," *Wilkes-Barre (PA) Times Leader*, August 3, 1925; "Senatorial Widows," *Eugene (OR) Guard*, August 22, 1925; "Women, Brains and Politics," *Adams County Independent* (Littlestown, PA), February 11, 1926; "Another Congressional Widow," *News Leader* (Staunton, VA), August 9, 1932, 4; "Widows in Public"; "Arkansas Election," *Des Moines Tribune*, July 27, 1937; Cott, *Grounding of Modern Feminism*, 37.

17. Elmer Davis, "Stateswoman," *LHJ*, February 1936, 10–11, 50, 52–53, 55–56; "Widow's Might"; Morton, "More Correspondents."

18. "Omaha Mayor's Widow Declines Succession," *Detroit Free Press*, January 30, 1930; "Heirs Apparent," *Millville (NJ) Daily*, November 20, 1931; "Another Congressional Widow."

19. "Widows in Office"; "On Their Merit"; Rodney Dutcher, "Daily Washington Letter," *Evening Democrat* (Fort Madison, IA), July 1, 1929; "Women Members of Seventy-Third Congress," *Circleville (OH) Herald*, January 9, 1934; Drew Pearson and Robert Allen, "Ladies of the Congress," *Red Book*, March 1936, 12, 75–76; "Republicans Jubilant at Victories in Ohio," *Philadelphia Inquirer*, February 29, 1940; "Five Women Members of Congress Want to Return," *Corsicana (TX) Daily Sun*, March 19, 1940.

20. "New Vocation"; Corinne Reid Frazier, "Will Women Upset Congress?," *Charleston (WV) Daily Mail*, December 30, 1933, 25.

21. "Women Are City 'Dads'; They Run the Town," *Buffalo Times*, April 28, 1921; "Representative's Widow Elected," *Anaconda (MT) Standard*, March 3, 1925; "On Their Merit"; "Will Run for Office," *Muscatine Journal*, September 28, 1927.

22. "Capital Sidelights," *Hattiesburg (MS) American*, April 15, 1924; Ewing Johnson, "Meet Nation's Woman Senator!," *Burlington (NC) Daily Times-News*, November 25, 1931; "Will Women Upset Congress?"; "Women Members"; "No Woman Dictator," *The Courier* (Waterloo, IA), April 18, 1937; Cal Tinney, "Mrs. Norton Has Proudest Moment as Wage, Hour Measure OK'd by Senate," *Ogden-Standard Examiner* (UT), June 19, 1938; Teva J. Scheer, *Governor Lady: The Life and Times of Nellie Tayloe Ross* (Columbia: University of Missouri Press, 2005), 93; "Senator's Widow Expected to Fill Unexpired Term," *Corsicana (TX) Daily Sun*, January 13, 1932; Anderson, *After Suffrage*, 132–133.

23. "No Woman Dictator."

24. Johnson, "Meet Nation's Woman Senator!"; "No Woman Dictator"; "Mrs. Ross to Run Again," *Huntington (IN) Herald*, March 2, 1926, 8; Kirke Simpson, "Mrs. Hattie Caraway Faces New Experience for Women," *Bluefield (WV) Daily Telegram*, November 28, 1931; Kincaid, "Over His Dead Body," 101; Bledsoe and Herring, "Victims of Circumstances," 214, 217–218; Susan J. Carroll, *Women as Candidates in American Politics* (Bloomington: Indiana University Press, 1985), 137. See Karlyn Kohrs Campbell's *Man Cannot Speak for Her: A Critical Study of Early Feminist Rhetoric* (New York: Praeger, 1989) for analysis of the "feminine style" of political women (12–13).

25. "Mrs. Mae E. Nolan, Only Congresswoman, Lives Up to Her Brilliant Red Hair," *Cincinnati Enquirer*, December 27, 1923; "Mrs. Ross Accepts Election to Governorship as Tribute to Late Husband," *Casper (WY) Star-Tribune*, November 6, 1924; Harry B. Hunt, "Hunt's Daily Letter," *Edwardsville (IL) Intelligencer*, December 4, 1924; Pearson and Allen, "Ladies of the Congress," 13, 76; "Labor Concerns the Woman, Too," *Jefferson City (MO) Post-Tribune*,

June 23, 1937; Tinney, "Mrs. Norton"; Scheer, *Governor Lady*, 93; Anderson, *After Suffrage*, 126.

26. "Ex-Soldier Wins Office for His Colonel's Widow," *New York Tribune*, April 8, 1920; "Value of Family," July 19, 1922; "Slain Sheriff's Widow Elected," *Pittsburgh Daily Post*, June 25, 1927; "Widow Is Elected Wilson Sheriff to Succeed Husband," *The Tennessean* (Nashville, TN), April 3, 1928; "Mrs. Evans Elected to Vacant Position on Education Board," *Scranton (PA) Republican*, June 27, 1933; "Mrs. Ross to Run Again"; "Let's Do the Job Right!," *El Paso Herald-Post*, July 21, 1938; "Mayor's Widow Elected," *Clarion-Ledger* (Jackson, MS), October 27, 1938; "A Woman Supervisor," *Middletown (NY) Times Herald*, April 4, 1939; Anderson, *After Suffrage*, 118.

27. "Jackson Officers Elected as Widow, Retire to Marry," *The Courier* (Waterloo, IA), August 23, 1933.

Mary Elizabeth Switzer accepting congratulations from Paul V. McNutt in 1946, when she received the President's Certificate of Merit for civilian service during World War II. Courtesy Schlesinger Library, Radcliffe Institute, Harvard University.

CHAPTER 6

Beyond the New Deal Network

Mary Elizabeth Switzer at the
Federal Security Agency, 1939–1945

DEAN J. KOTLOWSKI

A DEPARTMENT OF Health and Human Services building in Washington, DC, presently and fittingly bears the name of Mary Elizabeth Switzer, a "frontline bureaucrat" and "resourceful administrator" during the middle decades of the twentieth century.[1] At a time when women only recently had won the right to vote and when elected office seemed, to many women, unthinkable, Switzer emerged as a dynamic presence at the Federal Security Agency (FSA) between 1939 and 1945. President Franklin D. Roosevelt formed the FSA in 1939 to oversee key New Deal programs, including Social Security, and to underscore the federal government's newfound commitment to promoting economic security for Americans. Switzer joined the agency at its inception as assistant to the administrator, the politically ambitious but managerially lax former governor of Indiana, Paul V. McNutt, who headed the FSA until 1945. Yet, for many, it was clear that Switzer was essential to the agency's operations. In 1949, Charles Phelps Taft, a son of a former US president and a onetime official at the FSA, contemplated replacing McNutt's photograph in his office with one of Switzer because, as he told her: "You really ran the show, anyhow."[2] Moving on from the FSA, Switzer directed the federal government's vocational rehabilitation program from 1950 until her retirement in 1970. Overseeing an office budget exceeding $8 billion, she was "the woman executive with the largest responsibility in the Government."[3]

Three aspects of Switzer's early career are critical to understanding her ascent in the federal bureaucracy. First, she benefited marginally from, and remained tangentially connected with, an orbit of reform-minded female officials active during FDR's first and second terms. Consisting of women approximately two decades older than Switzer, this New Deal network included officeholders who had attended women's colleges, fought for women's suffrage, and championed minimum-wage and maximum-hour laws to protect women workers. Led by Secretary of Labor (1933–1945) Frances Perkins and Mary Williams "Molly" Dewson, chair of the Women's Division of the Democratic National Committee (officially, 1933–1934, and informally until 1937), they drew inspiration from the activism of Eleanor Roosevelt, obtained ranking positions in the New Deal State, and helped implement such reforms as Social Security. Switzer received mentorship from one of the administration's most notable reformers: Assistant Secretary of the Treasury (1934–1937) Josephine Roche. Yet Switzer loved working in the civil service, where she served under both Republican and Democratic presidents beginning in 1922. "Switzer had been in Washington long before the 'New Deal' women arrived, and she stayed long after they left," her biographer, Martha Lentz Walker, observed. "Still, this network strengthened Mary Switzer's hand."[4] Personal relationships at times overlaid professional ones: while at Treasury, Switzer met her lifelong partner, Isabella Stevenson Diamond.

Second, Switzer's greatest professional breakthrough occurred when she went to work for McNutt at FSA. As historian Susan Ware noted, "Women generally do better in the formative periods of organizations when there typically is less prejudice against using female talent."[5] The newly formed FSA proved one such agency. With McNutt focused on a White House run in 1940 and then on chairing the War Manpower Commission (WMC) between 1942 and 1945 (in addition to heading the FSA), Switzer's responsibilities expanded, as she oversaw critical aspects of her boss's widening bureaucratic domain during wartime. Her diligence, know-how, and professionalism saved McNutt "from making embarrassing mistakes" and freed the Hoosier to concentrate on his national political ambitions, which went unfulfilled.[6] McNutt acknowledged his "overwhelming indebtedness" to Switzer.[7] She, in turn, earned his confidence as well as increasing authority at the FSA and the WMC. Drawing on her past experience at Treasury, burgeoning expertise in public health, and service to the World War II State, Switzer balanced liberal ideals, fiscal discipline, and managerial proficiency in ways that won the notice of coworkers and superiors. By 1950, she was the natural candidate to head the Office of Vocational Rehabilitation.

Finally, gender-specific limitations, and a promotional ceiling, accompanied Switzer's breakthroughs at the FSA. To be sure, the relationship between Switzer and McNutt underscores the inclusiveness, pragmatic administration, and day-to-day alliances that formed under New Deal liberalism—perhaps best exemplified by FDR's dealings with Perkins and Dewson, who were instruments of presidential will rather than Roosevelt confidants and increasingly sidelined as war approached.[8] Like Perkins and Dewson, Switzer made her mark in government by, as one observer explained, "being better than [her] male competitors." Yet, the "almost insuperable handicap," of functioning as a female public servant "in a male chauvinistic society," haunted Switzer no less than Perkins or Dewson.[9] Taft's remark, that Switzer essentially ran the FSA, suggested that she had not occupied a position commensurate with her lofty abilities.

Switzer benefited from the advent of the New Deal network and then accommodated, rather than contested, the gendered strictures of leadership prevalent in FDR's administration. Switzer's early contacts with radicalism, her humanitarian ideals, and her connections to women reformers eased her embrace of New Deal liberalism. More important to Switzer's success and advancement in the civil service, however, was her expanding interest in public health and ties to the medical profession, widening managerial authority, pragmatism in resolving problems, skill in implementing initiatives, and service to superiors, especially McNutt. As the FSA transitioned into the Department of Health, Education, and Welfare (HEW), Switzer's reputation endured. HEW Secretary (1970–1973) Elliot L. Richardson hailed her as a "great bureaucrat" for balancing "professional accountability and appropriate responsiveness to political leadership."[10] One thus senses a generational shift away from the New Deal network, whose members "identified themselves as social reformers rather than as feminists," toward a proud career bureaucrat who put into practice liberal-style reforms without self-consciously voicing a feminist perspective—before the emergence of second-wave feminism.[11]

Before, Within, and Beyond the New Deal Network (1900–1940)

Switzer's background differed somewhat from that of the women who composed the New Deal network—a group of twenty-eight female officeholders who supported one another's career aspirations and pushed social welfare policies and employment of women in FDR's first two administrations. With few exceptions, these women were born around 1880 into old-stock, white, Protestant, middle-class families. Seventy percent of them had attended college, and one-fourth of them matriculated at Seven Sisters institutions: Perkins at Mount Holyoke, Dewson at Wellesley, and Roche at Vassar. During the Progressive Era, they campaigned for women's suffrage, social justice, and legislation to protect female workers through such organizations as the National Consumers League (NCL) and Women's Trade Union League (WTUL). Yet they opposed the Equal Rights Amendment, deeming it a threat to protective legislation for women.[12]

The much younger Switzer, in contrast, hailed from modest circumstances and worked to obtain an education. Born in 1900 into a working-class family in the Irish American community of Upper Newton Falls, Massachusetts, Switzer attended a women's college—Radcliffe—via a scholarship and money she earned from wages. Her college years (1917–1921) spanned a time when momentum for Progressive reforms had slowed, when the women's suffrage amendment won ratification, and when the Great War and Bolshevik Revolution captured national attention. Her outlook was distinct from other women of the New Deal network as well. Switzer recalled holding radical beliefs in college, and she later expressed some sympathy for the Soviet Union, as did many idealistic Americans during the 1930s.[13] She joined Radcliffe's Liberal Club and remained close to her uncle, Irish-born Michael Jeremiah Moore, who championed socialism and Irish independence. Yet, pragmatic instincts balanced Switzer's leftist leanings. Scott Nearing, an economist and advisor to the Liberal Club, told her to "take only one step at a time" in pushing reform.[14] She later identified two motivations deriving from her youth. The first, reflective of her class origins, was "the desire for financial security" for herself. The second was an obligation "to make the world better."[15]

During the 1920s, Switzer blended devotion to liberal causes with pursuit of a career. After graduating from Radcliffe in 1921 with a degree in Government, History, and Economics, she relocated to Washington, where she worked for the District of Columbia's Minimum Wage Board, the Carnegie Endowment for International Peace, and the Women's International League for Peace and Freedom—all causes or organizations associated with female reformers.[16] Philosophical and financial considerations then led her to seek employment in government. "The futility of reformers and revolutionaries like her Uncle Mike led Mary to the decision to work for change from within the social structure," her biographer explained.[17] While many of the women who later entered the New Deal network continued to press for the rights of workers and women through the NCL and WTUL during the 1920s, Switzer in 1922 joined the Treasury Department as a junior economist. She subsequently held "numerous research and administrative positions" under Secretary of the Treasury Andrew Mellon, including handling press relations.[18] Working in the Republican administrations of the 1920s fostered a conservative streak in Switzer exemplified by her unease with centralized power and acceptance of the prevailing political order.[19] She came to regard the Treasury building as her "spiritual home" and later chose to remain in government rather than accept the presidency of the Connecticut College of Women.[20]

Ties to two female government employees, Tracy Copp and Isabella Stevenson Diamond, enabled Switzer to enjoy a rich personal life and brace the strains of work. A member of the Federal Board of Vocational

Rehabilitation, formed in 1917 to assist disabled service personnel, Copp introduced Switzer to the program that later became her own and to activists in the WTUL, some of whom, such as Rose Schneiderman, entered the New Deal network.[21] Both mentor and inspiration, Copp showed Switzer that it was possible to excel professionally and to enjoy life's finer points.[22] As with Copp, Switzer's interests "were many."[23] Her reading covered Shakespeare, Egyptology, archaeology, whodunits, novels, and histories. Switzer relished plays, films, football games, travel, cocktails, and gatherings with friends. Her correspondence conveyed good cheer at Christmastime, fond memories of her native New England, and delight in her house in Virginia, where she found happiness "growing things" with her partner, Isabella Diamond.[24] Switzer met Diamond at the Treasury Department, where she worked as a librarian. A graduate of Bryn Mawr who was nine years older than Switzer, Diamond brought Switzer into a circle of female civil servants known as the "Treasury bunch."[25] The two became housemates in 1928 and remained devoted to one another until Switzer's death in 1971. Diamond played a role in documenting Switzer's professional accomplishments. Stimulating exchanges with Diamond at home doubtless enabled Switzer to leave problems at the office.[26]

Same-sex relationships were not uncommon among women who obtained leading positions in FDR's administration, as Molly Dewson's lifelong romantic friendship with Polly Porter illustrated. In addition to providing emotional support, such associations, as Susan Ware has noted, "allowed women to pursue their professional callings free of the responsibilities of managing children and a large household."[27] They were known to, and accepted by, Americans as Boston marriages—a form of long-term companionship between unmarried women. Dewson and Switzer proved open about their relationships: Dewson called Porter her "partner," while Switzer referred to Diamond as "my companion."[28]

For Switzer, the New Deal brought a reform spirit, career advancement, and a new mentor: Progressive-Era activist Josephine Roche. In 1934, Secretary of the Treasury Henry Morgenthau Jr. appointed Roche to be assistant secretary in charge of the Public Health Service (PHS), a program administered by Treasury since the early years of the republic. Roche worked with Secretary of Labor Perkins to draft the Social Security Act of 1935, and she extended the orbit of female officeholders into the next generation by naming Switzer, fourteen years her junior, as her assistant.[29]

Roche empowered and inspired Switzer. The Social Security Act appropriated $10 million to improve public health services, and Roche determined which locales received funds. Switzer stepped in to provide guidance. When a report surfaced that officials in Westchester and Rockland Counties (New York) had claimed dollars from the Works Progress Administration to fight malaria, Switzer denied that these ventures were "Treasury or Public Health projects in any sense."[30] Switzer watched Roche use Social Security funds to expand the PHS's reach and prod federal agencies to improve hygiene in industry and public health.[31] Roche chaired an executive-branch panel that proposed a wide-ranging attack on health problems, and Switzer organized a follow-up conference to implement its recommendations.[32] Yet, Roche's committee did not recommend a nationwide system of government-run health insurance nor did Switzer favor "outright federal control of public health services."[33] "Traveling over the country as Roche's assistant," one historian observed, "she had become acquainted with the nature of localized delivery systems for public health."[34] Nevertheless, health care had caught Switzer's attention, and she regretted Roche's resignation as assistant secretary in 1937. "I can't believe the three grand years of work together by the Treasury columns are really over," Switzer wrote Roche. "The immeasurable opportunity of being touched by your mind—guided by your true and undeviating standards is to have an immortal influence that will never leave me."[35] Switzer reconciled herself to Roche's resignation. "My work is at the moment not quite as exciting as when Miss Roche was in the Treasury," she told a friend in 1939, "but it still has to do with the Public Health Service and I enjoy it thoroughly and feel very settled now in the civil service."[36]

Gender inequities within the Roosevelt administration partially forced Roche from Treasury and kept her from returning to the administration.

Roche had disliked Morgenthau's budget-balancing agenda and his "petulant condescension," and she no doubt resented having to pour tea for cabinet members at official functions, a task also performed by Perkins.[37] Switzer's awareness of these specific inequities is unknown. Nevertheless, she, like Roche, dealt with the "ferociously male" PHS and gender-inspired indignities, such as when doctors misremembered her name.[38] She responded by remaining at her post and, as an observer later reflected, by outperforming "her competitors, almost all of whom were male" as she rose through the civil service.[39] Yet Switzer never attained the highest position at a cabinet-level agency or department. Neither did Roche. When FDR established the FSA, the obvious candidate to head it was Roche, for she had overseen the PHS and had helped to set up the Social Security Board and National Youth Administration—all offices within the FSA. Although Roche remained Switzer's choice for the position, Roosevelt selected McNutt instead.[40] The president hoped McNutt would replicate the record he had compiled as governor of Indiana (1933–1937), combining support for Social Security and work relief with fiscal discipline—a priority for Roosevelt in his second term. And, if McNutt somehow faltered, he would be unable to contest FDR's re-nomination in 1940.[41] Gender politics thus influenced the FSA appointment, for "neither Roche nor any other woman could have challenged or fully aided FDR in the electoral ring."[42]

Switzer adapted to, then reaped benefits from, McNutt's appointment. McNutt designated Wayne Coy as assistant FSA administrator, someone who had run work relief in Indiana and had functioned as McNutt's de facto chief of staff when he was governor of Indiana and high commissioner to the Philippines (1937–1939). After being named assistant administrator, Coy—with McNutt's approval—recruited Switzer for a lesser, albeit similarly named, position: assistant to the administrator of the FSA.[43] Whether the job offer sought to assuage Roche and her allies or merely to tap Switzer's experience is unclear. Her appointment represented a departure from the all-male, heterosexual makeup of McNutt's circle. Even so, Switzer worked well with people of "differing philosophies, towards a practical goal" and was, like Mc-Nutt, a pragmatic liberal.[44]

Switzer gained influence at the FSA, between 1939 and 1940, for three reasons. First, McNutt proved a slack administrator. A counsel at the Social Security Board recalled: "You'd go in there and say, 'Governor, I think we should do . . . this and [for] that reason,' and he'd say, 'Fine, go right ahead.'" Such an exchange left one uncertain "whether he knew what you were talking about."[45] Second, an administrative vacuum opened at the FSA when a kidney ailment sidelined Coy between 1939 and 1940. Coy's absence, Switzer observed, enabled "individual staff members to get to know the Governor."[46] Third, McNutt's presidential bid allowed Switzer to demonstrate loyalty to her boss and to ease his burdens. She joined a McNutt-for-President Club and hoped that McNutt would receive "what he desires to have so strongly": the presidency. Yet she also conceded that McNutt's absenteeism caused "difficulties," as the FSA's staff "tried to pull together five [very] big agencies."[47]

Switzer moved forward to fill the void formed by McNutt's distractions and Coy's illness, recognizing that his absence "necessitated considerable readjustment in the kind of work" she did.[48] She coordinated among the FSA's subagencies and worked to thwart designs by the Social Security Board "to unify all welfare services."[49] Along with overseeing the PHS, Food and Drug Administration, and Office of Vocational Rehabilitation, she collaborated with Tracy Copp to "push along some things [Tracy and I] have been interested in," presumably in Copp's field of vocational rehabilitation. Switzer found working at the FSA "tremendously exciting" and "all absorbing," consuming "28 hours of every 24."[50] But she also complained of "running around in circles here at the new Agency."[51] Such grievances never reached McNutt, who Switzer found a "very interesting and satisfying person to work for." The taciturn McNutt responded favorably to Switzer's exuberance and loyalty, which he regarded as "a source of strength." Switzer remained grateful for the opportunities McNutt had given her.[52] "Those were exciting, busy years," Isabella Diamond emphasized, in a retrospective she wrote on Switzer's career. "Mary's responsibilities grew and grew and grew!"[53]

Not unlike FDR with Roche, McNutt expanded Switzer's responsibilities without promoting her to a position of higher rank. When Coy departed the FSA for the White House in 1941, McNutt named as assistant administrator Watson B. Miller, the national rehabilitation director of the American Legion, an overwhelmingly male organization that McNutt earlier had headed.[54] Switzer retained her secondary position as assistant to the administrator. The onset of World War II brought added titles and charges to McNutt along with further work and responsibilities—but no promotion—for Switzer.

Expanded Duties in Wartime (1940–1945)

Since health policy remained Switzer's "first love," it was not surprising that she became, by World War II's end, "the liaison with all groups working on medical problems in and out of government."[55] She did so, in part, in her expanded role as assistant to the coordinator of the Office of Defense Health and Welfare Services (ODHWS), also headed by McNutt and a companion office to the FSA. FDR in 1941 established the ODHWS to make Americans fit and ready for a possible war. Since McNutt remained chiefly interested in national politics, foreign and defense policy, and speechmaking, the daily doings of the FSA and the ODHWS fell to staff members. Charles Taft, assistant coordinator of the ODHWS, located sites for day care centers and pushed campaigns to improve nutrition and physical fitness. To fight venereal disease, the ODHWS worked with local and private authorities to close brothels, arrest women considered promiscuous, and promote wholesome recreation through the United Service Organizations.[56] Such enterprises drew upon the expertise and resources of the health-related subagencies of the FSA, where Switzer continued on as assistant to the administrator. The ODHWS swelled Switzer's workload, sending McNutt's office into what she characterized as "constant turmoil."[57]

Switzer became the point person on medical-related issues. Taft deferred to Switzer on ties to the medical profession because, as he put it, "she knows these people and has a good common sense."[58] After Switzer raised the problem of "medical care in industrial areas," Taft directed the PHS and the War Production Board "to discuss this question."[59] She organized a conference on the relationship between proper nutrition and national defense and dispensed federal grants to study military medicine and hygiene.[60] Switzer dove into policy questions such as nutrition, where she wrote a detailed memorandum on "dietary food regulations."[61] She even became involved in the fight against venereal disease by helping to set up quarantine camps.[62] Switzer's public profile grew almost simultaneously. Beginning in 1941, she accompanied Taft to engagements at which he spoke.[63] But because Switzer enjoyed travel, exuded warmth, and knew her field, she too—in 1941—spoke on defense-related priorities: "venereal disease control," "improvement of nutrition among the civilian population," and "promotion of physical fitness."[64] She extolled the value of good health, telling a Catholic audience: "the whole nation must be fit to see [this war] through."[65] Switzer's appeals at times proved gender specific. "National health during the war depends almost entirely on how we women meet our own problems," she declared. "We don't see a 'health problem' in terms of figures—we see a sick child." She celebrated the efforts of women in medicine: "Women are working in industrial hygiene, in cancer, and in the study of chemicals used for the treatment of disease."[66] Such rhetoric bolstered US government propaganda, which encouraged women to seek employment in defense-related industries.

By the early 1940s, the women associated with the New Deal had either departed government or lost influence, and Switzer thus adapted to an increasingly masculine federal arena. She did what she could for the women who remained, even rallying female officials behind an effort to help Mary Anderson, chief of the US Women's Bureau (1920–1944), earn an honorary degree from Smith College. The women still in government supported one another, and they later nominated Switzer as a delegate to a major health conference.[67] Yet Switzer's greater loyalty lay with the male and female medical professionals with whom she corresponded.[68] Within this narrowing environment, Switzer at times negotiated office power dynamics by adopting a gendered model of familial care toward her male coworkers.[69] (When Taft later lost a rosette from a medal he had received, he turned to Switzer, who helped locate a replacement.)[70] Switzer may have played a role analogous to that of a younger sister to Taft and McNutt—not unlike Perkins, who comported herself "in a way that reminded men of their mothers," and Dewson, who joshed that male colleagues looked upon her as an aunt.[71] Yet workplace inequities persisted. While Switzer made a point of signing her communiqués "Mary E. Switzer," male coworkers often wrote to "Miss Switzer."[72]

Switzer focused most intently on the recruitment of military doctors and nurses for McNutt's War Manpower Commission. Through its branch, the Procurement and Assignment Service (PAS), formed in 1941, she worked with leaders in the medical profession to bring these professionals into the armed forces without causing a shortfall of medical services at home.[73] In so doing, Switzer further cultivated her reputation as an insider expert on public health. Frank H. Lahey, chair of the PAS, appreciated Switzer's understanding of the medical profession and her "capacity to make friends in and out of official life in Washington and in and out of the Army."[74] The PAS succeeded so well that the Army, by October 1944, no longer required the enlistment of civilian physicians.[75]

Switzer's ties to the PHS led her, somewhat unexpectedly, to help develop America's biological warfare program. Beginning in 1942, a top-secret government enterprise, the War Research Service (WRS), studied how to defend against a biological attack and how to use such weaponry against the enemy. The WRS, led by the pharmaceutical mogul George W. Merck Jr., found a home alongside the PHS in the FSA. Fluency in health policy made Switzer an asset to Merck, and she became one of four people in McNutt's shop who knew of Merck's work. Switzer monitored the expenditure of government funds by scientists with

WRS contracts, smoothed relations between medical researchers and their home institutions, oversaw the transfer of most WRS projects to the War Department in 1944, and briefly served as acting director of the WRS.[76] She had "confidential dealings with our most prominent scientific people" and was the member of McNutt's staff at the FSA with "responsibility to act for the Administrator in this field."[77] Merck considered Switzer a "grand help." McNutt trusted her completely.[78]

The WRS diverted Switzer from the archetypally feminine fields of health and social welfare policy and toward the more masculine terrain of combat, which she came to lament. When the WRS ceased operations in 1947, Switzer's files housed two of the four copies of the agency's official history. Although neither FDR nor the military brass seriously considered unleashing a biological attack, the WRS examined ways to protect crops and livestock from pathogens, developed vaccines, urged plant quarantines at the US border, and pondered launching an assault on Japan's rice fields.[79] Switzer later regretted her participation in the biological warfare program. "I've often thought how terrible it was, that I did that, although I don't know. I don't see much difference between one weapon and another," she told an interviewer. "Anyway, we developed some good medical information valuable to researchers later on, so I suppose some good came out of it."[80] Switzer doubtless also saw the doings of the WRS as a necessary evil, essential to winning the war against global fascism.

Postwar Years (1945–1971) and Reflections

As World War II came to an end, Switzer foresaw the FSA becoming a cabinet-level department. In 1944, she asserted: "the Federal Security Agency is really the health, education, and welfare department of the Federal government."[81] Congress in 1953 elevated the FSA to a cabinet department—under the name Switzer suggested, transitioning into the Department of Health, Education, and Welfare. She maintained that during wartime the FSA had proven its importance by fighting venereal disease, expanding recreation, improving community facilities, and assigning doctors and nurses.[82] The agency's eventual transformation into HEW affirmed, as other FSA officials pointed out, "the national interest in health, education and security as components of the general welfare."[83] Switzer spent the last stretch of her career at HEW, after she became director of the Office of Vocational Rehabilitation in 1950.

Switzer's final act in government was that of a disability advocate, lecturing widely to challenge the stigma associated with disabled people.[84] She strove to ensure that disabled people received the opportunity to lead productive lives through physical rehabilitation and employment rather than subsistence as public charges. From 1950 to her retirement in 1970, the number of disabled people rehabilitated into jobs rose annually from fifty-six thousand to two hundred forty thousand.[85] She disbursed federal dollars to assist people, in line with her New Deal roots; did so prudently, as moderate Republicans liked; and insisted that "people shouldn't get something for nothing"—music to conservatives.[86] Republicans Richard M. Nixon, Elliot Richardson, and Nelson A. Rockefeller paid tribute to Switzer when she died in 1971. And Democrat Hubert H. Humphrey introduced legislation to rename the Railroad Retirement Board Building the "Mary Switzer Memorial Building," which the Department of Health and Human Services presently occupies.[87]

A glass ceiling remained in place throughout Switzer's public service. Following her appointment to head the Office of Vocational Rehabilitation, Charles Taft wrote: "Three cheers for you, except that you ought to be Assistant Administrator [of the FSA]."[88] He did not posit that she become the agency's administrator. Switzer never held that job or that of secretary of HEW. Indeed, as director (and later commissioner) of the vocational rehabilitation program, Switzer served under eight HEW secretaries, only one a woman: Oveta Culp Hobby, the former director of the Women's Army Corps who was appointed by President Dwight D. Eisenhower and was the sole female cabinet member between 1945 and 1975.

Switzer's career stands as an admixture of accommodation with a male-led government and female empowerment. On the surface, Switzer's service to male political leaders, her lack of interest in a political career for herself, and her expertise in health-related matters adds weight to Molly Dewson's dictum that "men focused on power and personalities, while women were more interested in social issues and programs."[89] In point of fact, however, power, personalities (female and male), social issues, and government programs all became important and useful to Switzer. She exemplifies how women carved out a space for themselves in government in the decades that followed the ratification of the Nineteenth Amendment. She endured gender-based inequities while building a bureaucratic domain—"Switzerland"—in the area of vocational rehabilitation, a field deemed acceptable for women and one introduced to Switzer by her mentor Tracy Copp.[90] Switzer did not regard the pursuit of professional success as a women's rights challenge but instead as a natural progression from obtaining the right to vote. The expanding calls for women's liberation at the close of her career felt like another world. As Isabella Diamond observed: "She would have said to the 'women's libbers,' if they had asked her advice, 'Beware of what you are giving up in order to become equal.'"[91] Switzer demonstrated that it was possible for a woman to gain authority, to implement policy, to achieve professional longevity, and to relish one's success in an environment that prioritized male leadership. "Mary Switzer," her biographer averred, "savored the power she wielded."[92]

Notes

1. Edward D. Berkowitz, "Rehabilitation: The Federal Government's Response to Disability, 1935–1954" (PhD diss., Northwestern University, 1976), 247 and 250.

2. Charles P. Taft to Mary Elizabeth Switzer, August 1, 1949, folder: "S" Miscellany 1949, box I:68, Charles P. Taft Papers, Library of Congress, Washington, DC (hereafter "TP").

3. "Mary Elizabeth Switzer Dies," *New York Times*, October 17, 1971, 77.

4. Martha Lentz Walker, *Beyond Bureaucracy: Mary Elizabeth Switzer and Rehabilitation* (Lanham, MD: University Press of America, 1985), xiv.

5. Susan Ware, *Beyond Suffrage: Women in the New Deal* (Cambridge, MA: Harvard University Press, 1981), 61.

6. Walker, *Beyond Bureaucracy,* 70.

7. Paul V. McNutt to Switzer, August 20, 1952, folder 515, box 53, Mary Elizabeth Switzer Papers, Arthur and Elizabeth Schlesinger Library, Cambridge, MA (hereafter "SP").

8. Ware, *Beyond Suffrage,* 58–59, 125.

9. "Tribute to Mary Elizabeth Switzer," ca. 1971, folder: "S" Miscellany 1968–71, box I:65, TP.

10. Elliot Richardson, foreword to *Beyond Bureaucracy,* by Martha Lentz Walker, ix.

11. Ware, *Beyond Suffrage,* 7.

12. Ware, *Beyond Suffrage,* 137–157, 16, 7.

13. Switzer to Maurice Neufeld, August 12, 1937, folder 525, and Switzer to Pat Powers, ca. 1937, folder 533, box 54, SP.

14. Walker, *Beyond Bureaucracy,* 23.

15. Walker, *Beyond Bureaucracy,* 11.

16. Walker, *Beyond Bureaucracy,* xii–xiii, 14–16.

17. Walker, *Beyond Bureaucracy,* xiii.

18. Undated biography of Switzer, folder 182, box 14, SP.

19. Jonathan Hughes, *The Vital Few: The Entrepreneur and American Economic Progress* (New York: Oxford University Press, 1986), 493.

20. Undated clipping, "Treasury Aide Loves Work," microfilm reel M-53 and Switzer to Elizabeth Brandeis Rauschenbush, August 11, 1943, folder 633, box 61, SP.

21. Hughes, *The Vital Few,* 466.

22. Walker, *Beyond Bureaucracy,* 26, 36.

23. Isabella Diamond to Taft, October 28, 1971, folder: "S" Miscellany 1968–71, box I:65, TP.

24. Switzer to "Joan and Milton," July 29, 1942, folder 463, box 49, SP; Dean J. Kotlowski, *Paul V. McNutt and the Age of FDR* (Bloomington: Indiana University Press, 2015), 317.

25. Walker, *Beyond Bureaucracy,* xiv.

26. Switzer to Richard King, September 25 and December 9, 1939, folder 491, box 51, SP.

27. Susan Ware, *Partner and I: Molly Dewson, Feminism, and New Deal Politics* (New Haven, CT: Yale University Press, 1987), 57.

28. Ware, *Partner and I,* 60; Switzer to "Joan and Milton," July 29, 1942, folder 463, box 49, SP.

29. Robyn Muncy, *Relentless Reformer: Josephine Roche and Progressivism in Twentieth-Century America* (Princeton, NJ: Princeton University Press, 2015), 160.

30. Switzer to Mrs. Klotz, November 18, 1935, folder 3, box 277, Henry Morgenthau, Jr. Papers, Franklin D. Roosevelt Library, Hyde Park, NY.

31. Muncy, *Relentless Reformer*, 181.

32. Undated biography of Switzer, folder 182, box 14, SP.

33. "The Need for a National Health Program: Report of the Technical Committee on Health Care," 1938, 34–36, box 277, folder 3, Morgenthau Papers; Berkowitz, "Rehabilitation," 240.

34. Hughes, *The Vital Few*, 474.

35. Muncy, *Relentless Reformer*, 185.

36. Switzer to Margaret Hunt, April 13, 1939, folder 477, box 50, SP.

37. Muncy, *Relentless Reformer*, 170.

38. Muncy, *Relentless Reformer*, 164 (quotation); Allan M. Butler to John P. Peters, May 23, 1941, folder 45, box I:2, John Punnett Peters Papers, Yale University Library, New Haven, CT.

39. Tribute to Switzer (1971), folder: "S" Miscellany 1968–71, box I:65, TP.

40. Walker, *Beyond Bureaucracy*, 69.

41. Kotlowski, *Paul V. McNutt*, 259–261.

42. Robyn Muncy, "Women, Gender, and Politics in the New Deal Government: Josephine Roche and the Federal Security Agency," *Journal of Women's History* 21 (Fall 2009): 73.

43. Walker, *Beyond Bureaucracy*, 69.

44. Berkowitz, "Rehabilitation," 241.

45. Jack B. Tate Oral History, June 3, 1965, 94, Oral History Research Office, Columbia University, New York.

46. Switzer to Estelle Warren, October 27, 1939, folder 578, box 57, SP.

47. Kotlowski, *Paul V. McNutt*, 318 (quotations); Walker, *Beyond Bureaucracy*, 70.

48. Switzer to Warren, October 27, 1939, folder 578, box 57, SP.

49. Hughes, *The Vital Few*, 476.

50. Switzer to Warren, October 27, 1939, folder 578, box 57, SP.

51. Switzer to Neufeld, September 12, 1939, folder 525, box 54, SP.

52. Kotlowski, *Paul V. McNutt*, 318.

53. Isabella Stevenson Diamond, *Mary Elizabeth Switzer: "The Dedicated Bureaucrat,"* 5, pamphlet, Duke University Libraries, Durham, NC.

54. Undated memorandum on Watson B. Miller, folder 39, box 4, SP.

55. Switzer to Erwin Schuller, July 7, 1944, folder 553, box 56, SP.

56. Kotlowski, *Paul V. McNutt*, 325–330.

57. Switzer to Dr. and Mrs. John Trask, August 30, 1941, folder 648, box 62, SP.

58. Taft diary, January 27, 1943, box I:2, TP.

59. Taft diary, July 13, 1942, box I:1, TP.

60. Kotlowski, *Paul V. McNutt*, 328.

61. Switzer to McNutt, August 6, 1941, folder 38, box 4, SP.

62. Taft diary, July 7, 1943 (p. 289), box I:2, TP.

63. Taft diary, April 8, 1941, and December 9, 1941, box I:1, TP.

64. Switzer address, March 10, 1941, folder 177, box 14, SP.

65. Switzer, "Health Facilities," October 21, 1941, folder 177, box 14, SP.

66. Switzer interview, January 31, 1943, folder 179, box 14, SP.

67. Walker, *Beyond Bureaucracy*, 76–78.

68. Muncy, "Women, Gender, and Politics," 75.

69. Walker, *Beyond Bureaucracy*, 99.

70. Taft to Switzer, June 26, 1947; Josephine Coe to Taft, July 3, 1947, folder: "S" Miscellany 1946–47, box I:68, TP.

71. Kirstin Downey, *The Woman behind the New Deal: The Life and Legacy of Frances Perkins* (New York: Anchor Books, 2009), 45; Ware, *Partner and I*, 167.

72. Switzer to Watson B. Miller, May 4, 1943, folder 126, box 10; Switzer to Schuller, July 7, 1944, folder 553, box 56; George P. Larrick to Switzer, May 14, 1942, folder 96, box 8; J. L. Kaukonen to Switzer, May 14, 1946, folder 100, box 8, SP.

73. Switzer to Frank Lahey, July 17, 1943, folder 97, box 8, SP.

74. Editorial, *Wisconsin Medical Journal*, October 1944, folder 181, box 14, SP.

75. War Manpower Commission press release, October 31, 1944, folder 93, box 7, SP.

76. Kotlowski, *Paul V. McNutt*, 335–336.

77. Undated biography of Switzer, folder 182, box 14, SP.

78. Kotlowski, *Paul V. McNutt*, 336.

79. Kotlowski, *Paul V. McNutt*, 336–338.

80. Walker, *Beyond Bureaucracy*, 97.

81. Switzer to Schuller, July 7, 1944, folder 553, box 56, SP.

82. Switzer to Leonard A'Hearn, June 12, 1946, folder 8, box 1, SP.

83. Kotlowski, *Paul V. McNutt*, 339.

84. Berkowitz, "Rehabilitation," 250; "Mary Switzer Named Lasker Award Winner," *Washington Post*, August 24, 1960, C1.

85. "Mary Switzer, HEW Official, Dies," *Washington Post*, October 17, 1971, B8.

86. "Welfare, Work and Wisdom," *Washington Post*, December 18, 1969, B2.

87. Tribute to Switzer (1971) and Irving M. Friedman to "Friend," October 29, 1971, folder: "S" Miscellany 1968–71, box I:65, TP; "Mary Elizabeth Switzer Dies," *New York Times*, October 17, 1971, 77; Switzer Memorial Building History, Department of Health and Human Services website, https://www.acf.hhs.gov/switzer-building, accessed January 28, 2019.

88. Taft to Switzer, November 17, 1950, folder: "S" Miscellany 1950, box
I:67, TP.

89. Ware, *Beyond Suffrage*, 14.

90. Walker, *Beyond Bureaucracy*, xii.

91. Diamond, *Mary Elizabeth Switzer*, 7.

92. Walker, *Beyond Bureaucracy*, xii.

Portrait of Elizabeth Peratrovich, ca. 1950. Courtesy
of Alaska State Library Portrait File Photographs,
ASL-P01-3294.

CHAPTER 7

Elizabeth Peratrovich, the Alaska Native Sisterhood, and Indigenous Women's Activism, 1943–1947

HOLLY MIOWAK GUISE

A S A THIRTY-THREE-YEAR-OLD MOTHER, Tlingit activist, and president of the Alaska Native Sisterhood (ANS), Elizabeth Wanamaker Peratrovich helped compel the Alaskan territorial senate to pass the 1945 Alaska Equal Rights Act to prohibit racial segregation. She dedicated her life to fighting for Indigenous rights for the Native community.[1] Her activism began when she enrolled her children in a segregated Alaskan territorial school in Juneau, and she subsequently convinced Native parents to join her school integration efforts. Bertrand Adams Sr., a writer known by his Tlingit name, Kadashan, explained that Elizabeth Peratrovich and her husband, Roy, had talked his parents into this school integration effort in 1944.[2] Uncovering the many facets of Elizabeth Peratrovich's community activism, and the alliances that Native women like her built, illuminates that Indigenous women uniquely positioned themselves as mothers to argue for racial equality, greater inclusion, and Indigenous land rights. The Alaska Equal Rights Act campaign exemplifies how Indigenous women navigated and manipulated US legislatures within a colonial system to advance Native rights.

Elizabeth Peratrovich epitomizes what sociologist Belinda Robnett has called women "bridge leaders" or "critical mobilizers of civil rights activities."[3] Elizabeth Peratrovich wrote to political leaders, worked with community members, traveled across Alaska to establish ANS and ANB (Alaska Native Brotherhood) chapters, and met with government officials to advocate for Native people. Alaska Governor Ernest Gruening believed that the Alaska Equal Rights Act would never have passed without Elizabeth Peratrovich's efforts.[4] Gruening recalled: "Had it not been for that beautiful Tlingit woman, Elizabeth Peratrovich, being on hand every day in the hallways, it would have never passed."[5] Roy Peratrovich (Tlingit) referred to his wife as a catalyst for his own activism. He once stated of Elizabeth, "She got me started and suggested we move to where we could be of more use [Juneau]. She was the manager. She saw the possibilities. She never once stepped out in front . . . [but] made it look as if I made my own way."[6]

Native mothers, Native women, and the members of the ANS played an integral role in asserting Indigenous Alaskan rights in the 1940s. Prior to the passage of the 1945 Alaska Equal Rights Act, Alaska Natives and other minorities were legally segregated in places of business and education.[7] Yet, during the war, when the United States militarized the Alaskan landscape, Native and white race relations reached a watershed. Native women were active and savvy participants in this fight. Alaskan activists pushed for Indigenous rights that prioritized an integrated education system in addition to land rights, civil rights, and human rights. The ANS and ANB were partner organizations that advanced Indigenous rights and improved educational opportunities, employment, social services, health services, and housing for Alaska Natives.[8] Oftentimes, the ANS has been characterized as tangential to the ANB fraternal organization. This marginalization undervalues the ways that the ANS brought positive changes for Native people. When Native women advocated for the well-being of their families, they augmented the political power held by the Native community and they changed the Alaskan social sphere.

Native women from across the Alaskan territory defined and challenged injustices, particularly within the domestic realm where the intimacies of colonial empire had emerged.[9] Indigenous domesticity was a central site for settler colonial efforts at Native assimilation and where Indigenous people resisted Western assimilation.[10] The domestic realm therefore served as a key site of power within Indigenous communities and adds importance to understanding the domestic projects advanced by Alaska Native women as part of a larger understanding of women's political movements.

The ANS's advocacy extended a long tradition of Indigenous demands for personal sovereignty alongside US voting and political rights. During the termination era of federal-Indian relations, in which the federal government attempted to eliminate tribal sovereignty, Alaska Natives asserted equal citizenship rights and maintained sovereignty to their land as well as economic self-determination.[11] This quest to preserve Indigenous resources aligned with citizenship rights.[12] Voting rights remained a contested issue, alongside the struggle for civil rights and Indigenous land rights.[13] Alaska Natives adopted and used the language of the US Constitution as a tool to demand equal rights. The Indigenous navigated Western bureaucracy and fought for voting rights and sovereignty into the twentieth century.

After the ratification of the Nineteenth Amendment in 1920, voting rights were not extended to American Indians until the passage of the 1924 Snyder Act.[14] Yet, certain states still excluded the American Indigenous from the right to vote.[15] In Alaska, for example, in accordance with the Alaska Voters' Literacy Act of 1925, the Alaska legislature required voters to speak and read the English language.[16] Such a law excluded many Alaska Natives from voting. The Alaska literacy law persisted until statehood and the adoption of the Alaska State Constitution in 1959.[17] In other regions, such as the American Southwest, New Mexico was the last state to enfranchise American Indians in 1962.[18] States strategized to diminish the Indian right to vote. Idaho, Maine, Mississippi, New Mexico, and Washington replicated US constitutional language and withheld the right to vote from "Indians not taxed."[19] Indigenous voting rights activism was, "much like the struggle for black voting rights in the South . . . long, arduous, and often bitter."[20] Likewise, Indigenous women's engagement in and around traditional political spaces should be seen as part of the long and wide struggle for women's suffrage.

Alaska Native activism escalated in the decades prior to the passage of the 1945 Alaska Equal Rights Act.[21] Established in 1912, the ANB and ANS lobbied for citizenship rights. From its inception, the ANB and ANS adopted US constitutional language for equality. For example, they deployed the familiar slogan "No taxation without representation."[22] With ANB and ANS chapters established across the Alaskan territory, Native people advocated for citizenship and voting rights. Outside these chapter organizations, Native leaders, such as the Tanana Chiefs of Interior Alaska, met with congressional representatives to advocate for Indigenous resources.[23] World War II offered an opportunity to draw greater attention to the US government's shortfall of commitment to Native equality. As the respective leaders of the ANS and ANB, Elizabeth Peratrovich and Roy Peratrovich invoked imagery of Indigenous American patriotism during the war. The pen proved mighty when the Peratrovichs wrote letters to territorial officials to call attention to racial injustice. In one such letter that they cowrote, dated December 1941, they called on Governor Gruening to address the exclusion at the Douglas Inn exemplified by the sign on the door that read: "No Natives Allowed."[24] Similar to the African American campaign for Double Victory, the letter identified discriminatory signs that excluded Native patrons, and it argued for racial equality during a war against fascism.[25] According to the Peratrovichs' arguments, Native people fought fascism abroad while they paradoxically confronted discrimination on the home front. This letter highlighted a settler colonial paradox that solicited the inclusion of minorities for military service while it excluded them from shared social spaces.

Alongside efforts at dismantling exclusion from businesses, as the leader of the ANS Elizabeth Peratrovich emerged as a key voice in the Alaskan desegregation movement challenging educational equalities. The 1905 Nelson Act bifurcated the Alaskan education system along a Native and white binary. As a result, the Bureau of Indian Affairs and the missionaries instructed Native students, and the Alaskan territorial schools instructed white students.[26] The Peratrovichs were among those who adopted the slogan "No taxation without representation," drawing on rhetoric from the American Revolution to highlight this central irony in US democracy. "Our Native people pay the school tax each year to educate the white children, yet they try to exclude our children from these schools," they argued. It took more than letter writing to move the Alaska legislature into action. Elizabeth Peratrovich served as a vocal leader when she spoke on behalf of Alaska Native people on the senate floor.

One of Elizabeth Peratrovich's most influential speeches contributed to the eventual adoption of the Alaska Equal Rights Act. Also known as the antidiscrimination act, the Alaska Equal Rights Act had failed to pass in 1943. The act provided equal accommodation in the Alaskan territory and enacted penalties for businesses that failed to comply.[27] Edward Anderson, the former mayor of Nome, introduced the act after mixed-race teenage activists Alberta Schenck (Iñupiaq) and Holger "Jorgy" Jorgensen (Iñupiaq) staged a sit-in at the Nome Dream Theater, refusing to move to the Native side of the theater from the white side.[28] When the Alaska Equal Rights Act came up for a vote in 1943, it passed the House with a vote of 19 to 5, but it encountered resistance from the Senate.[29] Disappointed, Roy Peratrovich blamed what he identified as "double cross politics" for the reason why the act failed to pass at that time. These double-cross politics stemmed from certain legislators who had promised to support the act and then changed their minds at the last moment.[30] Undeterred, Indigenous activists seized their next opportunity to put political pressure on politicians in order to achieve their desired result.

The annual ANB and ANS convention provided a platform to rally the Native community, and non-Native politicians began to recognize their influence. In 1943, at the convention in Hoonah, Governor Gruening delivered a guest speech that highlighted the fact that Alaska Natives comprised three-sevenths of the territory's population. Despite his opposition to Alaskan Indian reservations that would have protected Indigenous lands from settlers, Gruening spoke of equal treatment of the races, and he encouraged Alaska Natives to run for legislative positions.[31] In response to the failed antidiscrimination act, in 1944, at the annual convention in Kake, the organizations passed Resolution No. 2 titled: "DISCRIMINATION."[32] This resolution affirmed Native allegiance to terminate segregation in the Alaskan territory and laid the groundwork for a revote on the Alaska Equal Rights Act.

On February 5, 1945, when the Alaska Equal Rights Act came to a vote for the second time, Alaska Natives turned out in full force.[33] They were guided by the voice of one woman: Elizabeth Peratrovich. According to ANS member and personal friend Cecelia Kunz (Tlingit), ANS and ANB members and Juneau residents filled the meeting space of the Alaskan legislature and overflowed into the hallway as onlookers stood outside the open gallery doors.[34] During this time, some senators expressed racially motivated anxieties. For example, opponent to the act, Allen Shattuck, argued that "the races should be kept further apart. Who are these people, barely out of savagery, who want to associate with us whites with 5,000 years of recorded civilization behind us?"[35] Another challenger, Senator Frank Whaley, of Fairbanks, claimed that Eskimos smelled and that he did not want to sit next to them in a movie theater.[36] After these discriminatory remarks, Elizabeth Peratrovich took advantage of legislative custom in Alaska that allowed anyone, including women, to speak. She calmly responded, "I would not have expected, that I, who am barely out of savagery, would have to remind gentlemen with five thousand years of recorded civilization behind them of our Bill of Rights."[37] Elizabeth Peratrovich asked the senators why her family was compelled to live in the Juneau slums when a neighborhood denied them a home on the basis of their indigeneity.[38] As such, she invoked imagery of motherhood to provide adequate housing for her children. According to her son, Roy Peratrovich Jr., after her speech she held her daughter, Lori, highlighting her caregiving role.[39] Many identify Elizabeth Peratrovich's speech before the Alaska legislature as the primary reason why the Alaska Equal Rights Act of 1945 passed.[40]

The Daily Alaska Empire emphasized the importance of her performance: "Mrs. Roy Peratrovich, Grand President of the Alaska Native Sisterhood, the last speaker to testify, climaxed the hearing by wringing volleying applause from the galleries of the senate floor alike, with a biting condemnation of the 'superior race' attitude."[41] The arguments that Elizabeth Peratrovich presented on the legislative floor upheld ANS values that emphasized maternal care for family and the Alaska Native community. She used the United States' claims of cultural and political accomplishment, including foundational documents such as the Bill of Rights as a means to assert Indigenous rights. Her speech swayed the senate to pass the act 11 to 5.[42] Elizabeth Peratrovich's speech on the senate floor illustrates Native women's influential power. She had cleverly woven together language of maternal care with US constitutional language to persuade a settler colonial audience into legislative action.

Two days after the passage of the Alaska Equal Rights Act, Elizabeth Peratrovich declared, "For the first time in the history of our race under the democratic form of government we look toward a future filled with confidence and hope."[43] She saw this law as a major step for Native people to assert their rights within the democracy of a Western government. However, she was also somber in her assessment: "But let us not be jubilant that we shall forget that there is much work to be done, that we, as a Native race, must make a decided move to better the health and sanitary conditions of our homes and villages." She cautioned, "We must start now and put on the biggest drive we have ever sponsored."[44] Invoking maternalist imagery she intoned: "The future health and happiness of our children depends on our willingness to take the initiative in a problem that has long been neglected."[45]

The Alaska Equal Rights Act was one component of ANS's larger campaign to bring full equality to Native families. For instance, ANS members collaborated on a project to protect Native children from unfair media coverage. The ANS tried to stop the newspaper from publishing the names and ages of Indian children whenever Native youth encountered the police. Cecelia Kunz, who joined the ANS in 1925 and was close to Elizabeth Peratrovich, asserted that ANS members visit the *Daily Alaska Empire* and demand that Indian children be treated the same as white children.[46] Using their maternal role as protectors of Native children allowed ANS members to actively challenge segregationist practices.

Improving health care on the home front and abroad remained another important goal for Native women. In addition to upholding wellness programs for Native children, Elizabeth Peratrovich promoted the American Red Cross.[47] In March 1944, she wrote to all ANB and ANS camps and requested $2.50 from each member for the American Red

Cross War Fund.[48] She closed her letter by reminding activists that "you and I have done a lot of talking about the rights of each and every one of us. Let us show that we can adequately take care of such rights by first backing our Armed Forces through the American Red Cross." This sentiment aligned with actions by women across the country who contributed to the war efforts.[49] Native women leveraged their role as family caretakers into large-scale health care efforts.

As an organizer for the ANS Home Improvement Committee, Elizabeth Peratrovich linked higher education and the federal government to supply resources for Native women and their families. She advocated for support of domestic projects that would improve the Native community. In October 1944, Elizabeth Peratrovich wrote on behalf of the ANS Home Improvement Committee to invite Lydia Fohn-Hansen, the Home Demonstration Leader of the Department of Agriculture at the University of Alaska, to lecture at the annual ANB and ANS convention in Kake, Alaska.[50] Elizabeth Peratrovich outlined how Native women financially supported their families: "Native women do a great deal of sewing and canning in order to survive during the long winter months. I say, 'survive,' because there is practically no employment during the winter months." Her request highlighted that Native families depended on housewives. While the nature of this letter seemed to advocate for domestic spaces, it did so in the context of seeking resources for projects to improve the economic standard of Native households. Lydia Fohn-Hansen sent a colleague to the ANS convention, and she agreed to travel to Southeast Alaska to work with Native women on food issues.[51] She also committed to work with the Bureau of Indian Affairs to send an extension worker to Southeast Alaska.

During her tenure as ANS president in the early 1940s, Elizabeth Peratrovich empowered Native women within the domestic realm.[52] She worked within institutional structures of support to link Native women with resources in agricultural development that benefited the domestic sphere.[53] She advocated for Alaska Native women to use federal and territorial grants reserved for homemakers and children. For example, she believed that a 4-H Club could benefit boys and girls with sewing, gardening, health, childcare, livestock, and handicraft. She recognized that Alaska Native women could engage in Western organizations like the 4-H Club to seize more resources to assist Native families.

Childcare and home improvement projects emerged as repeated arenas where Native women could benefit in their domestic work. A letter from Boy Scouts of America revealed that the ANS Grand Council sought to adopt the Boy Scouts Program within the community.[54] Native homemakers could access newsletters and receive free bulletins on topics that ranged from nutrition and recipes to "repairing inner spring cushions" and "directions for knitting an Eskimo doll." Villages could benefit from hosting 4-H specialists on demonstrations like "jellies and jams from Native berries," "how to press a man's suit," and "how to clean and dress a turkey."[55] While these demonstrations appear more catered to Western tastes, such workshops clearly fused Indigenous values with Western US customs. In this regard, Elizabeth Peratrovich cleverly used colonial organizations to facilitate traditional Indigenous activities, including knitting Native dolls and making jams from Native berries.

Elizabeth Peratrovich integrated her role as a mother and a community organizer to propel Native activism forward. A skilled recruiter, she was instrumental in helping establish new chapters of the ANB and ANS across Alaska and partnering beyond the region with the American Indian activist organization known as the National Council of American Indians.[56] She went to great lengths to organize three new chapters of the ANB and ANS in the predominantly Iñupiat towns of Kotzebue, Selawik, and Deering in northern Alaska.[57] To accomplish this goal, she approached Alaskan pilot Shell Simmons, who gave her a spare seat on his plane to visit these distant towns. Bridging advocacy work and caregiving, she brought her young daughter along, who sat on her lap on these flights. This effort was supported by the community as well. When away on recruiting trips, she relied on friends like Minnie Field to watch her two older sons, who "seemed to understand their mother was doing something important."[58]

The ANS advanced their work beyond the domestic sphere by focusing on land rights. Working alongside Elizabeth Peratrovich, Amy

Hallingstad (Tlingit) helped integrate Alaska territorial schools and ad-vocated for increased Indigenous resources. Amy Hallingstad resented that her children had to attend a Native school in Petersburg when she paid taxes used for public schools. To combat this, Amy Hallingstad helped to close the Native school and to force integration of the Peters-burg territorial school in the early 1930s.[59] Her activism began at the Petersburg ANS Camp 16, and she later served as the grand president of the ANS from 1947 to 1949 and then again from 1953 to 1956.[60] In addition to her efforts to integrate Alaskan schools, Amy Hallingstad supported the Native land claims movement.

The ANS facilitated partnerships that allied Native organizations while it promoted the preservation of Indigenous livelihood that in-cluded control over Native land and subsistence activities. Prominent Indian law attorney Felix Cohen saved a letter from ANS president Amy Hallingstad. In this letter, Amy Hallingstad wrote to the National Con-gress of American Indians (NCAI), and she implored them to help pre-serve Indigenous Alaskan lands and resources. Established in 1944, the NCAI principally fought to protect Indigenous treaty and sovereign rights during the termination era and continued to promote a shared Indigenous identity in the post–World War II era.[61] In this letter to NCAI secretary Ruth Bronson (Cherokee) dated December 1947, Amy Halling-stad outlined the needs of Alaska Natives to protect their resources from colonialism. Thirty-five thousand Alaskan Indigenous, roughly half of Alaska's population, needed federal assistance to preserve Native lands. Amy Hallingstad noted as much saying, "Our homes and lands, our fish-eries and trees, our trap-lines and reindeer, everything we possess is being seized or threatened by unscrupulous white men, who tell us that what they are doing to us has been approved by Washington."[62] Here, Amy Hallingstad identified that bureaucrats in Washington either passed laws or ignored cases of stolen Indigenous resources. Fitting with maternalist arguments, such as those of former ANS president Elizabeth Peratrovich, Hallingstad referenced the roles of mothers to nurture their children. She noted that Secretary of the Interior Julius Albert Krug promised in June 1946 "that the boundaries of all our lands would be marked out clearly so that no trespasser would take the fish and game and furs that we need to keep our children warm and well fed throughout the long Alaskan winters." Amy Hallingstad referenced a larger network of not only Indigenous activism but also a collective Native female activism that permeated pan-Indigenous political organizations.[63]

Through their service to the ANS, Native women upheld Indigenous rights while they promoted racial equality in Alaska. This rendered activism for land sovereignty and racial equality as not mutually exclusive. The women in the ANS used their identities as Native mothers to advocate for resources for their families that benefited the entire Native community. When they used language that paralleled the eighteenth-century American Revolution against the British, Alaska Natives demanded equality while they resisted colonialism. Native women activists such as Elizabeth Peratrovich made powerful cases for Alaskan racial integration and the passage of the 1945 Alaska Equal Rights Act. This act brought change to Alaskan race relations, yet it did not terminate discrimination.[64] Much work remained to advance Native rights. Within organizational structures, Alaska Native women relentlessly advocated for Indigenous rights.

Revisiting the story of Kadashan's first day of integrating the Juneau school provides an important touchstone to understand the role of Native motherhood and Indigenous social activism. Kadashan recalled that his first day included a girl who called him an "Indian" and another girl who stood by him in defense. At home that evening, Kadashan turned to his mother for advice. He stated, "I went home after school and I asked my mom, I says, 'Mom, what's an Indian?'" Kadashan detailed. "She sat me down and explained to me what my heritage was and who I really was, and that sometimes during my lifetime I would have to deal with those issues. And she wanted us to—she talked to my brother as well—she wanted us to deal with those." Elizabeth Peratrovich reflected on her legacy when impacted by breast cancer, writing her college-aged son Roy Peratrovich Jr. a year before she passed away in 1957. "A few times some people tried to discriminate against us but that is almost impossible to do when the object of such action feels no inferiority," she wrote.[65] Whether advocating before the senate, working to gain resources and protect Native land, or advising her children, Elizabeth Peratrovich's actions show that Native motherhood played an integral role in the promotion of Indigenous rights and the advancement of Indigenous social activism.

Notes

1. Annie Boochever and Roy Peratrovich Jr., *Fighter in Velvet Gloves* (Fairbanks: University of Alaska Press, 2019).

2. Bertrand Adams's Indigenous name, "Kadashan," is also how he identifies as a writer. Bertrand "Bert" Adams Sr., oral history interview by Holly Guise, July 11, 2008, First Alaskans Institute, Anchorage. Excerpts from his oral history were previously published in Holly Miowak Guise, "Alaskan Segregation and the Paradox of Exclusion, Separation, and Integration," in *Transforming the University: Alaska Native Studies in the 21st Century*, ed. Beth Ginondidoy Leonard et al. (Minneapolis: Two Harbors Press, 2014), 274–304. Kadashan wrote about his story in Kadashan, "Thanks to an Old Friend from School," *Tundra Times*, January 18, 1995, http://ttip.tuzzy.org/collect/ttimes/index/assoc/HASH0181/c7861d5d.dir/doc11.pdf#xml=http://ttip.tuzzy.org:80/cgi-bin/ttimes.exe?a=pdfh&pdfxml=1&qbare=Kadashan&d=HASH0181c7861d5d738da76e308c.2.5.

3. Belinda Robnett, *How Long? How Long? African-American Women in the Struggle for Civil Rights* (New York: Oxford University Press, 1997), 20.

4. Ernest Gruening, *Many Battles: The Autobiography of Ernest Gruening* (New York: Liveright, 1973), 329–330.

5. Vern Metcalfe, "Roy Peratrovich Sets Columnist Straight," *Tundra Times*, September 14, 1987, Tuzzy Consortium Library Database.

6. Central Council of Tlingit and Haida Indian Tribes of Alaska, *A Recollection of Civil Rights Leader Elizabeth Peratrovich, 1911–1958* (Juneau, AK: Central Council, 1991) (hereafter *A Recollection*).

7. Terrence Cole, "Jim Crow in Alaska: The Passage of the Alaska Equal Rights Act of 1945," *Western Historical Quarterly* 23, no. 4 (1992): 429–449.

8. Boochever and Peratrovich, *Fighter in Velvet Gloves*, 10.

9. On colonial intimacies, see Margaret Jacobs, *White Mother to a Dark Race: Settler Colonialism, Maternalism, and the Removal of Indigenous Children in the American West and Australia, 1880–1940* (Lincoln: University of Nebraska Press, 2009); Anne McClintock, *Imperial Leather: Race, Gender, and Sexuality in the Colonial Contest* (New York: Routledge, 1995); Beth Piatote, *Domestic Subjects: Gender, Citizenship, and Law in Native American Literature* (New Haven, CT:

Yale University Press, 2013); Ann Laura Stoler, *Carnal Knowledge and Imperial Power: Race and the Intimate in Colonial Rule* (Berkeley: University of California Press, 2002); and Laura Wexler, *Tender Violence: Domestic Visions in an Age of U.S. Imperialism* (Chapel Hill: University of North Carolina Press, 2000).

10. Piatote, *Domestic Subjects*, 9.

11. Jessica Leslie Arnett, "Unsettled Rights in Territorial Alaska: Native Land, Sovereignty, and Citizenship from the Indian Reorganization Act to Termination," *Western Historical Quarterly* 48 (Autumn 2017): 233–254, 253. On asserting aboriginal claims and sovereignty through New Deal totem parks, see Emily L. Moore, *Proud Raven, Panting Wolf: Carving Alaska's New Deal Totem Parks* (Seattle: University of Washington Press, 2018).

12. Arnett, "Unsettled Rights in Territorial Alaska," 254; Thomas Michael Swensen, "The Relationship between Indigenous Rights, Citizenship, and Land in Territorial Alaska: How the Past Opened the Door to the Future," *Alaska Native Studies Journal* 2 (2015): 44–58.

13. A great source on litigation for Indigenous resources and sovereign rights, see Charles Wilkinson, *Blood Struggle: The Rise of Modern Indian Nations* (New York: W. W. Norton, 2005).

14. On the Snyder Act in Alaska, see David Case and David Voluck, *Alaska Natives and American Laws* (Fairbanks: University of Alaska Press, 2002), 46–48.

15. Daniel McCool, Susan M. Olson, and Jennifer L. Robinson, *Native Vote: American Indians, the Voting Rights Act, and the Right to Vote* (Cambridge: Cambridge University Press, 2007), x.

16. Stephen W. Haycox, "William Paul, Sr., and the Alaska Voters' Literacy Act of 1925," *Alaska History* 2, no. 1 (Winter 1986/87): 17–38.

17. Haycox, "William Paul, Sr."

18. Library of Congress, "Elections . . . the American Way: Voting Rights for Native Americans," https://www.loc.gov/teachers/classroommaterials/presentation sandactivities/presentations/elections/voting-rights-native-americans.html.

19. McCool et al., *Native Vote*, 10–12.

20. McCool et al., *Native Vote*, x.

21. Peter Metcalfe, *A Dangerous Idea: The Alaska Native Brotherhood and the Struggle for Indigenous Rights* (Fairbanks: University of Alaska Press, 2014).

22. *A Recollection.*

23. William Schneider, *The Tanana Chiefs: Native Rights and Western Laws* (Fairbanks: University of Alaska Press, 2018).

24. Elizabeth Peratrovich and Roy Peratrovich to Governor Ernest Gruening, December 30, 1941, Record Group 101, series 79–35, folder 461-6, box 461, Alaska State Archives, Juneau, Alaska. Document also published in Daniel M. Cobb, *Say We Are Nations: Documents of Politics and Protest in*

Indigenous America since 1887 (Chapel Hill: University of North Carolina Press, 2015), 78–79, Project MUSE.

25. Lawrence P. Scott and William M. Womack Sr., *Double V: The Civil Rights Struggle of the Tuskegee Airmen* (East Lansing: Michigan State University Press, 1992 and 1994); Ronald Takaki, *Double Victory: A Multicultural History of America in World War II* (Boston: Little, Brown, 2000).

26. On Bureau of Indian Affairs schooling, see Margaret Archuleta, Brenda J. Child, and K. Tsianina Lomawaima, eds., *Away from Home: American Indian Boarding School Experiences 1879–2000* (Phoenix, AZ: Heard Museum, 2000); Brenda Child, *Boarding School Seasons: American Indian Families 1900–1940* (Lincoln: University of Nebraska Press, 1998).

27. A Recollection.

28. Gruening, *Many Battles*, 329. On Alberta Schenck, see Muktuk Marston, *Men of the Tundra: Alaska Eskimos at War*, 2nd ed. (1969; New York: October House, 1972), 132–136; Jeffry Silverman, *For the Rights of All: Ending Jim Crow in Alaska* (Blueberry Productions, 2009), DVD; and Swensen, "The Relationship between Indigenous Rights." On Holger "Jorgy" Jorgensen, see Holly Guise, "From Haycock to Anchorage: Connecting the Wartime Landscape with Stories by Holger 'Jorgy' Jorgensen," in *Imagining Anchorage: The Making of America's Northernmost Metropolis*, ed. James K. Barnett and Ian C. Hartman (Fairbanks: University of Alaska Press, 2018), 340–355; and Holger "Jorgy" Jorgensen and Jean Lester, *Jorgy: The Life of Native Alaskan Bush Pilot and Airline Captain Holger "Jorgy" Jorgensen* (Ester, AK: Ester Republic Press, 2007), 72–77.

29. Gruening, *Many Battles*, 329.

30. A Recollection.

31. On Gruening who rejected aboriginal land rights yet upheld citizenship rights, see Peter Metcalfe, *A Dangerous Idea: The Alaska Native Brotherhood and the Struggle for Indigenous Rights* (Fairbanks: University of Alaska Press, 2014), 72; Gruening, *Many Battles*, 321. Andrew Hope (Tlingit) and Frank Peratrovich (Tlingit) answered the call and were elected as legislators in 1945. Gruening, *Many Battles*, 329.

32. A Recollection.

33. This date is according to "Superior Race Theory Hit in Hearing," *Daily Alaska Empire*, February 6, 1945, https://vilda.alaska.edu/digital/collection/cdmg21/id/2058/rec/1.

34. A Recollection.

35. A Recollection.

36. A Recollection.

37. A Recollection.

38. A Recollection.

39. Boochever and Peratrovich, *Fighter in Velvet Gloves*, 57.

40. Metcalfe, *A Dangerous Idea*, 58–59; Gruening, *Many Battles*, 329; Silverman, *For the Rights of All*.

41. "Superior Race Theory Hit in Hearing," *Daily Alaska Empire*, February 6, 1945, https://vilda.alaska.edu/digital/collection/cdmg21/id/2058/rec/1.

42. Gruening, *Many Battles*, 330.

43. Elizabeth Peratrovich to the Executive Committee, February 10, 1945, folder "ANS 1943–44," box 3, University of Washington Libraries Special Collections (hereafter UWLSC), William Lackey Paul Collection, Seattle.

44. Roy Peratrovich announcement, March 20, 1945, series 1, folder 10, box 1, Sealaska Heritage Institute (hereafter SHI), Walter Soboleff Collection.

45. This refers to documents on the US Indian Service Program Home Care of Tuberculosis in Alaska that linked tuberculosis to the Native community. Alaska State Archives, Record Group 101, series 79–35, folder 461-2, box 461, Juneau.

46. Boochever and Peratrovich, *Fighter in Velvet Gloves*, 53, 62.

47. Boochever and Peratrovich, *Fighter in Velvet Gloves*, 31.

48. Elizabeth Peratrovich to all ANB and ANS camps, March 1, 1944, folder "ANS 1943–44," box 3, UWLSC, William Lackey Paul Collection, Seattle.

49. On Native women's efforts on the home front, see Grace Mary Gouveia, "We Also Serve: American Indian Women's Role in World War II," *Michigan Historical Review* 20, no. 2 (Fall 1994): 153–182; Patty Loew, "Back of the Homefront: Oral Histories of Native American and African-American Wisconsin Women during World War Two," *Wisconsin Magazine of History* 82, no. 2 (Winter 1998–99).

50. Elizabeth Peratrovich to Miss Fohn-Hansen, October 5, 1944, series 1, folder 1, box 6, SHI, Walter Soboleff Collection.

51. Lydia Fohn-Hansen to Elizabeth Peratrovich, October 14, 1944, folder "ANS 1943–44," box 3, UWLSC, William Lackey Paul Collection, Seattle.

52. It has been difficult to pinpoint the exact years that Elizabeth Peratrovich served as ANS grand president. She was "elected grand president in the early 1940s." Boochever and Peratrovich, *Fighter in Velvet Gloves*, 20.

53. Elizabeth Peratrovich to ANS, Feb 6, 1945, series 1, folder 1, box 6, SHI, Walter Soboleff Collection.

54. Delbert R. Hanks to Elizabeth Peratrovich, December 21, 1945, series 1, folder 1, box 6, SHI, Walter Soboleff Collection.

55. Elizabeth Peratrovich to ANS, February 6, 1945, series 1, folder 1, box 6, SHI, Walter Soboleff Collection.

56. Elizabeth Peratrovich and Roy Peratrovich to the National Council of American Indians, October 20, 1945, series 1, folder 10, box 1, SHI, Walter Soboleff Collection.

57. Alfred Widmark announcement to ANB/ANS camps, June 11, 1946, series 1, folder 11, box 1, SHI, Walter Soboleff Collection.

58. Boochever and Peratrovich, *Fighter in Velvet Gloves*, 41, 38–45.

59. Zachary R. Jones, "Amy Hallingstad Documents Collection, 1973–1990: Sealaska Heritage Institute Archives," Sealaska Heritage Institute Archives, accessed April 2, 2019, http://shicollections.org/index.php?p=collections /findingaid&id=34&q=&rootcontentid=300.

60. Jones, "Amy Hallingstad Documents Collection."

61. Thomas W. Cowger, *The National Congress of American Indians: The Founding Years* (Lincoln: University of Nebraska Press, 1999), 3, 10.

62. Felix Cohen Collection, folder 400, box 24, Beinecke Rare Book and Manuscript Library, Yale University, New Haven, CT.

63. Cowger, *The National Congress of American Indians*, 5.

64. Discrimination, housing segregation, and job exclusion persisted after the 1945 Alaska Equal Rights Act. See, for example, Ian C. Hartman, "'A Bonanza for Blacks?' Limits and Opportunities for African Americans in Southcentral Alaska," in Barnett and Hartman, *Imagining Anchorage*, 356–373.

65. Boochever and Peratrovich, *Fighter in Velvet Gloves*, 65.

Three leaders of the Women's Committee for Educational Freedom attend the Texas State Democratic Executive Committee meeting on February 23, 1946, in Fort Worth, Texas. Minnie Fisher Cunningham (*center left*), Marion Storm (*center right*), and Lillian Collier (*far right*) are seated with a young, liberal Democrat, Jim Wright (*far left*), who went on to serve for thirty-four years in Congress, including briefly as Speaker of the House of Representatives. Courtesy *Fort Worth Star-Telegram* Collection, Special Collections, The University of Texas at Arlington Libraries, Arlington.

CHAPTER 8

"These Men Have Such Dominant Positions"

The Women's Committee for Educational Freedom and the Gendered Battle for Liberalism in the 1940s

NANCY BECK YOUNG

W AS IT SEX, Christian morality, or economic justice? Something in John Dos Passos's trilogy, *U.S.A.—The 42nd Parallel* (1930), *1919* (1932), and *The Big Money* (1936)—offended the sensibilities of Texas conservatives. The latter volume, these primarily male critics charged, was not the material for sophomore English classes at University of Texas at Austin (UT). It was, they argued, "indecent, vulgar and filthy," chalked with "obscene sex stories and blasphemous expressions" that could corrupt impressionable young minds.[1] When this controversy erupted in 1944, it dredged up a long-simmering battle that pitted Texas liberals and conservatives in a culture war. The one-party Democratic state was already enmeshed in conflict about New Deal Keynesian economics and the regulatory state. While liberal Democrats saw colleges and universities as a bulwark for social and economic liberalism, conservative Democrats attacked higher education for fostering radicalism.

Embroiled in this fight, politically active Texas women used defense of academic freedom at UT to forge a campaign for their own economic, social, and political equality. Feminists from the suffrage generation joined with younger liberals to rebut conservative men and seek academic freedom. Their feminism was as important as their liberalism. The women who led this challenge—including prominent suffragist Minnie Fisher Cunningham—employed this occasion to press for increasing the number of women working in state government. Cunningham and her fellow organizers embodied the expectation, energy, and skill of post-suffrage, premodern feminists. They recognized that World War II had created a vacuum of leadership, and tried to claim political power to advance a feminist, liberal agenda, making this an important chapter in a wider story of women in politics.

The problems began when UT's president, Homer Price Rainey, was fired on November 1, 1944, a penalty for permitting *The Big Money* to be assigned. Rainey was a liberal Democrat, a devout Christian, an ordained minister, and a University of Chicago trained PhD. In this controversy, the first and the last points governed his fate. Rainey argued that the "ruling political group" in Texas had tried to "subvert" the university for "their own purposes." He was right. The ultraconservative Texas Regulars—big oil and big business, small government, segregation, and strong moralism—attacked academic freedom. They saw it as culpable for the spreading of liberalism. Rainey had been clear in his opposing view: he believed that educated youth could lead the social regeneration of the nation and thus protect liberal democracy.[2]

Women's rights were a key point of tension in this battle over academic freedom, an element easily missed. Not coincidentally, many of the conservatives who challenged Rainey also opposed women's rights, and likewise, Rainey's leading defenders were liberal feminists. In response to Rainey's firing, these advocates formed the Women's Committee for Educational Freedom (WCEF). This particular social movement evolved gradually from connections among liberal and mostly rural, Texas women. The background of this group reminds that there has been a long-standing tradition in American politics of mixing Christianity with liberal reform, from antebellum antislavery and women's rights movements to the social gospel movement of the Progressive Era. Leaders of the Gleaners Sunday School Class at the First Baptist Church in Hearne, Texas, population 3,511, decided enough was enough. These religious reformers rejected the politics of socially and economically conservative segregationists who dominated the one-party Democratic South. They saw the Rainey matter for what it was—an assault on academic freedom and on liberalism. The church women countered: "[Rainey] seeks to promote . . . God-given and blood-defended principles of freedom. . . . On wings of believing prayer . . . we lift him up."[3]

Two interwoven convictions motivated liberal Texas women: without gender equality, political democracy was not possible, and without respect for Christian teachings, economic democracy was not possible. They did not explore the racial implications of the conservative attack on academic freedom, but that does not mean they practiced whitewashed feminism and liberalism. In other midcentury social movements, these same women pursued civil rights. In their cautious approach, the WCEF exposed the ease with which academic freedom had been attacked and thus the fragility of the liberal experiment in Texas.

The members of WCEF coupled this religiously grounded defense of liberalism with another transformative goal: achieving lasting guarantees of gender equality. Doing so, they believed, would fulfill many suffragists' long-term goal of increasing female political representation. In the 1940s, issue advocacy at the grassroots—and not party politics—was the better way to attract women to partisan concerns. At the same time, female activists found that advancing liberalism was a prerequisite for feminism. Bringing forward the lessons they learned during the suffrage movement, they avowed that a political solution could not be achieved without female leadership. Starting at the local county commissioner precinct, women were recruited with the ambition of training tomorrow's state leaders. This local story reveals how intergenerational exchange and mentorship were characteristics of women's political activism at midcentury. Indeed, the WCEF both kept alive the suffrage tradition and laid the roots for modern feminist politics in Texas in the 1960s and 1970s.

Defense of the state's flagship educational institution had long been important to progressive Democrats, who equated a good university education with the cause of social and economic liberalism. They had lived through demagogic attacks on higher education in the 1910s when then governor James E. Ferguson attempted to eliminate all funding for the University of Texas. This earlier fight coincided with the push for suffrage in Texas. In the 1910s, Cunningham had fought Ferguson, a mortal foe of woman suffrage and other Progressive Era reforms.[4]

Cunningham remained a potent force in liberal politics. She had helped found the National League of Women Voters in 1920 and the Women's National Democratic Club. By the time Cunningham came to UT President Homer Rainey's defense, she had an unsuccessful run for the US Senate in 1928 behind her, as well as work in New Deal agencies. In 1944, she helped form the liberal Texas Social and Legislative Conference to unite farmers, labor, and progressives.[5] This group was primed to support Rainey, as were others to which WCEF members belonged, such as the Texas Federation of Women's Clubs.

When appointed in 1939, Rainey, a native Texan, had a well-known history as a Christian liberal reformer in higher education. He advocated on behalf of American youth, who suffered because of the Great Depression. For Texas liberals, his selection signaled the university would play a role in reform politics. In an urbanizing state, they viewed UT and the equal educational opportunities that it provided to all-white Texans as a bulwark against conservative encroachment into state politics. For this reason, Cunningham assured Rainey she was "standing fully with [him] in [his] magnificent fight to give Texas that 'University of the first class.'" The public, she said, cared more about education than "private fortunes."[6]

Rainey faced pushback immediately from the Texas Regulars, who served the monied interests and had little sympathy for small farmers, independent business owners, workers, and poor people. Governor W. Lee "Pappy" O'Daniel, elected in 1938 and reelected in 1940, and his successor, Coke Stevenson, named a conservative majority to the regents. In a foreshadowing of postwar anticommunist tactics, O'Daniel plotted with the right-wing politicos about taking control of education throughout the state, including UT, which he believed the source of "radicalism."[7]

An incident in June 1942 was a prelude of more to come. D. F. Strickland, a conservative lobbyist and UT regent, asked Rainey to fire four full professors of economics, stating "we don't like what they are teaching." Their "sin" had been advocacy of the New Deal. The regents bowed to the tenure system and left the four men in place. Four of their untenured colleagues, known to argue that the government should protect the forty-hour workweek and labor union rights, were dismissed. Further academic freedom issues arose when the regents denied research grants to social sciences faculty for political reasons. Cunningham termed the regents' actions "intellectual terrorism."[8]

The controversy between Rainey and the regents simmered for three years, but on October 12, 1944, Rainey made the matter public. Earlier, Strickland and UT vice president Alton Burdine discussed giving Rainey an ultimatum. A frequent national orator, Rainey lambasted the chasm between America's claim to be a Christian nation and its failure to provide economic, social, and cultural justice for all, including people of color. Rainey was vice president of the Southern Regional Council, an interracial organization working to make "democracy a reality" in the South. The Texas Regulars reasoned from these facts that Rainey would push for integration at UT, but no such plan had been announced. After a two-day meeting of the regents, Rainey was fired in November. At this point, the WCEF sprang into action, for Rainey advocated social justice and equality and was worthy to defend. Marguerite Fairchild, a member of the board of regents who voted to sustain Rainey, received praise from women around Texas for her stand. Mrs. Albert T. Helbing declared, "We women have much at stake in this life. We bear children and train them for a happy life and must stand by and accept the rulings of a bigoted handful of men."[9]

The Rainey affair brought focus to Texas women's call for political recognition, a campaign already underway. Female political interest had intensified during World War II, and Texas women were no different from their sisters around the country. According to Cunningham, women desired "a greater share in shaping the policies of the Texas State government." Mothers, sisters, and wives used the military service–induced "disenfranchisement" of their sons, brothers, and husbands to assert their political influence. Cunningham quipped: "it even seemed as if some of the boys would rather have Mama safeguard their post-war future, than to have a well advertised nice Christmas box! So the Mamas came to Austin."[10]

More than two hundred women participated in a wartime rally at the state capitol on September 7, 1944. In addition to Cunningham, notables who attended this gathering included Jane Y. McCallum, the former secretary of state and former suffragist; Annie Webb Blanton, the former state superintendent of public instruction; Sarah T. Hughes, a Dallas County district judge; and Rae Files, a member of the state legislature. Speaking before this group, only a little over one month before his firing, Rainey told the audience that colleges and universities prepared women and men for a role in public affairs. Another speaker observed the power discrepancy facing Texas women: they counted as 60 percent of the voting population but wielded little political power. Few women served on the boards and commissions that decided state affairs.[11] Thus, it was not a stretch to connect defense of Rainey to being on the offense in promoting women's political rights.

After the September 7 meeting, Cunningham informed Texas women that, if they really wanted a political voice, they must be willing to "tackl[e] controversial public questions." She asserted that the most significant matter was the future of education. She pressed women to register their anger with the chair of the board of regents. She implored women to remind the governor of his responsibility to appoint good people as regents, and to offer Rainey their support. Write the *Houston Post*, she entreated, and complain about their pro-regents editorial policy.[12]

Democratic women's groups followed Cunningham's advice. In the first few months after Rainey's firing, female activists linked Rainey and academic freedom at UT with the Allied war cause. They asserted the regents aped the Axis Powers. McCallum shamed Texas political leaders for permitting "the gag rule" against Rainey who "dare to have 'great dreams' for the university." She avowed: "Hitler and Mussolini took over the great universities of Germany and Italy, established a gag rule and threw out all the professors who refused to approve their totalitarian doctrines."[13]

Lillian Collier and Margaret Reading, who together with Cunningham were termed the "three musketeers," recognized that a successful crusade for Rainey required rural backing; countryside voters still held the balance of power. Collier and Reading were members of a liberal organization that lobbied on behalf of farmers and, in this fight, attacked the regents for hindering academic freedom. Collier, Reading, and Cunningham sympathized with UT students, "many of them from poor families . . . making sacrifices to keep them in school."[14]

The WCEF also saw the UT academic freedom controversy as a national issue that linked the concerns of economic liberalism, academic freedom, and feminism. Margaret Carter, a Fort Worth Democratic Party strategist, stressed exactly that to Freda Kirchwey, the editor of the *Nation*. According to Carter, Rainey constructed his UT presidency as a response to Franklin D. Roosevelt's 1938 declaration of the South as being the "nation's No. 1 economic problem." Carter feared that Rainey was not the only target. She divulged to Kirchwey that the regents planned to dismiss more than three hundred persons from their academic posts. The anticommunist test was wide, with professors' subscriptions to the *Nation*, the *New Republic*, and *Common Sense* gaining their placement on a developing blacklist. Higher education had been a target of anticommunist investigation back to the Dies Committee in the late 1930s, but the WCEF's work complicates the idea that war-era liberals turned away from defense of progressive dissenters. Thus, the Texas Regulars' attack on academic freedom exemplified the burgeoning anticommunist, antiliberal movement that dominated postwar American politics.[15]

In early December 1944, McCallum and two other Austin women wrote a general letter circulated to legislators, Democratic county chairmen, and leading citizens condemning Rainey's firing. McCallum and her collaborators implored other women to follow their example, urging a broad operation of letter writing, holding meetings, passing resolutions, and talking to the press. They contended, "What you personally do in this crisis in its affairs may determine whether it is to continue to be the great institution . . . or whether . . . it is to degenerate into a tool of special, selfish interests." This encouragement incited controversy. One critic complained: "these liberals holler 'freedom of speech' but at the same time everyone who opposes them 'misrepresents facts', according to their idea, and 'tell untruths.'" Others celebrated the presence of businessmen in university affairs, noting their contributions during World War II. Another suggested, in addition to President Rainey, the entire UT English Department should be fired. These messages had two common threads: the belief "that the faculty of a University should [not] be allowed to control its destiny" and the commitment to an antiradicalism that led one writer to complain, "some influence at the University tended to inculcate in my children's minds some 'ism' that is wholly un-American."[16]

Facing these critics became a statewide calling for Texas liberals. In December 1944, a leading male liberal Democrat encouraged "the women of Texas" to "perfect an organization under the leadership of" Hughes, McCallum, and others "to help carry on this fight here at home for those great principles that our boys are fighting and dying for around the world." The women did exactly that. They organized. Cunningham urged women across the state to join the WCEF's "fighting" committee, kicked off at a meeting on January 18, 1945. To prep participants, Cunningham mailed a collection of newspaper clippings about the UT controversy, asking delegates to study "the whole background of the problem." For her, that included "the conspiracy to seize the Texas State Democratic Party machine," which Texas Regulars had unleashed in the summer of 1944. "We women of Texas have a solemn obligation to the sons and daughters of Texas to maintain and protect their educational opportunities," Cunningham asserted. "If we do not, those who live will accuse us, and justly, of having surrendered at home to the forces of tyranny and Fascism."[17]

Cunningham and her inner circle sought representation from each senatorial district to increase pressure on lawmakers. This goal mimicked a strategy Cunningham had used decades earlier in the suffrage fight. However, she realized that this campaign called for a more localized, county-level membership structure than the state senate district organization she had used for the suffrage fight. "If we average four persons to a county (and that should be easy building on the Senatorial

District set up that we now have) we can have a thousand members in the twinkling of an eye," she believed.[18]

The WCEF led a lobby numbering seventy-five "militant" women strong. Their campaign signaled, as local press characterized, the WCEF was in a "'do something' mood." They protested before the state senate and the governor, insisting that Rainey be reinstated. These male legislators did not want to contend with these determined women. Most legislators avoided comment. Some hid in phone booths rather than face the lobbyists' wrath. Others spent their interviews haranguing against Dos Passos's *U.S.A.* trilogy. WCEF lobbyists were ready for this. As Alice Taylor, active in WCEF and the Democratic Party, told legislators, Rainey was "a true Christian democrat who practices both phases of his belief." The WCEF demanded Governor Stevenson force the resignation of all regents in office when Rainey was dismissed.[19]

The WCEF lobbyists expected their pressure would lead to the regeneration of Texas politics as more liberal and feminist in orientation. "There is power enough in the women of Texas to do anything we desire to do," Cunningham insisted. Yet, this prediction was premature as Governor Stevenson evaded most of the WCEF's proposals. When the WCEF told the governor UT would be censured if Rainey were not reinstated, Stevenson replied, "It doesn't make any difference to us here in Texas what some people up North do." The American Association of University Professors blacklisted the university, where it remained until 1953. McCallum pushed for Rainey's reinstatement. Stevenson refused. The WCEF also implored a woman be named to replace exiting board member Marguerite Fairchild, who joined the WCEF. "Governor Coke," intoned Mrs. Walter Nixon, "we're looking to you to appoint not only women but also men of various political beliefs—that is, people other than Texas Regulars." Stevenson insisted that the new board waiting for senate confirmation was "fair" and "impartial." He ignored their pleas that he demand the resignation of anti-Rainey regents. Stevenson promised only to study the WCEF resolutions: "I don't know that I agree with all your objectives."[20]

At their January 18 meeting, the WCEF called for a new, nonpartisan system of appointing regents. They advocated granting appointment authority to the state supreme court and increasing the number of regents from nine to fifteen. They proposed the following requirements: one-third be women, one a businessman, one a laborer, one a miner or manufacturer, one a farmer, and one a scholar. The WCEF argued no regent should be eligible for reappointment. Finally, they insisted the term of service should be lengthened from six to fifteen years with one regent going off the board each year.[21] Such a system, Carter and her allies believed, would encourage political and economic democracy. The WCEF demands were also a direct attack on the Texas Regulars' dominance of the board of regents. However, other than attracting the media, the WCEF capitol visit failed to change the direction of public policy. The gendered balance of power still overwhelmingly favored elite conservative white men in Texas.

The WCEF's call for a reconfigured regents board was not realized; nor was Rainey reinstated as UT's president. After Governor Stevenson's 1944 reelection, he appointed six new members, all but one who were either Texas Regular Democrats or Republicans. The WCEF hoped to pressure the state senate into blocking their confirmation. McCallum and Cunningham avowed that the far-right appointees were unfair to the voters of Texas who in 1944 had polled eight hundred eleven thousand out of a million votes for the national Democratic Party, which was decidedly more liberal than the retrograde Texas Regulars. The women further noted that the state Democratic Party had included an academic freedom plank in its platform, which Stevenson and the state senate were obliged to obey. Taylor sent a circular letter urging "good Roosevelt supporters should be concerned about the domination of such state owned institutions as the University." She worried about the "standing of the University and the quality of its faculty. If he is not reinstated nearly all the really top-flight faculty and research men will begin to consider opportunities in other schools."[22]

By challenging Stevenson's appointment decisions and by campaigning for Rainey's reinstatement, the WCEF provided fodder for conservative newspapers throughout the state. The *Houston Post* lambasted the WCEF for "making a New Deal issue of the [Rainey] affair." That paper then chided the women for entering male spaces of politics: "Goodness gracious, don't tell us that the good women are dragging the university into politics!" Cunningham rebutted the *Post*'s snide treatment of women's activism: "'[I] regret [the] omission of [the] usual quote God Bless them unquote after quote good women unquote.'" Her friend and ally Margaret Reading complained to the *Post* about its lack of punctuation in one key phrase of the editorial. The paper derided the WCEF for suggesting that Rainey could get his job back with the assertion "however that could be done." Reading told the paper that it only needed to add a comma after the word "however."[23]

The *Post* intimated that the WCEF would have difficulty coming up with one thousand women willing to defend educational freedom, but Cunningham rebuffed their concerns. Indeed, Cunningham the organizer knew best; she and her colleagues had used their connections within women's voluntary culture to build a social movement for academic freedom that also—they hoped—would advance economic liberalism and gender equality, their ongoing concerns. She assured her readers in the *State Observer* that the four most important women's organizations in Texas—the Federation of Women's Clubs, the Business and Professional Women's Clubs, the Parent-Teacher Associations, and the American Association of University Women—were already supporting the WCEF as were the University Dames, a club for mothers of UT students, and religious groups throughout the state. Cunningham bragged of wide support for academic integrity among workers, farmers, and "feminine Texas-Exes eager to take a place in the ranks of the women's movement."[24]

Undeterred, McCallum and Cunningham urged WCEF organizers to "keep pounding away" at the senate and to help mobilize a "rapid expansion of the Committee membership." Membership numbers were such a priority that local and regional contacts were asked to "please send in your nominations as fast as possible." By 1946, the WCEF claimed approximately two thousand members. The point of this wide web was to make their lobbying pressure clear in each senate district. To this effect, they organized an Alert-Sub-Committee with a WCEF member assigned to each senator, who would "be sure there is always the 'personal touch'" in interactions. Still, members of the senate could not be persuaded. They held a secret session to approve Stevenson's appointees. Flummoxed but still driven, WCEF geared up for "a two year fight" leading to the 1946 elections. As McCallum told the press, "This is the real test—it will show that we are not just fighting when the going is good. Nobody expects the boys to turn back from the battlefield when the going gets tough—the fight to save the university is the same fight. But our battle cry instead of being 'On to Tokyo' is 'On to November, 1946.'"[25]

Until the Democratic primary of 1946, the WCEF talked less about academic freedom and spent more time electioneering. The WCEF touted Rainey as the ideal candidate for governor, but Texas voters disagreed, electing Beauford H. Jester instead. During their campaign, WCEF members forged a blatant attack on conservatives as the root of all evil in Texas. Yet, these conservatives, unfortunately for the WCEF, had the last word. As one critic retorted, "It would seem that the Cunningham-Collier female gang had selected small segments of the various Red groups in the state and succeeded in getting together a fairly representative cross section of the lunatic fringe of Texas." And yet, the women who led WCEF were far from the "lunatic fringe." Their efforts underscore the strong presence of women in Texas politics at this pivotal postwar moment where New Deal liberalism lost footing and women's representational concerns were voiced. This feminist activism nonetheless remained a hard sell statewide but one that scared conservatives. That same critic who renounced the WCEF as nothing more than a "lunatic fringe" admonished grassroots participation: "The old she red foxes of the outfit may have known what they were doing, but it is doubtful about the youngsters."[26]

. . .

The WCEF's long-term legacy was mixed. Between the 1960s and 1980s, UT entered a period of incongruence in which its faculty and student body exhibited tolerance of liberalism, while its administration remained associated with conservatives. Tensions on campus reached a fever pitch in the 1960s when students in the New Left rebelled against that same conservatism that had animated the WCEF to protest for a more just society in the 1940s.[27] Politically, the Democratic Party became more liberal and friendlier to women's issues, but the state as a whole followed the right wing out of the Democratic Party and into the resurgent Republican Party, an exodus in full effect by the 1980s. Thus, the WCEF's largest goal was unrealized, a permanent political and economic democracy that respected the rights of all Texans.

Some scholars might conclude gender-based politics failed, but this verdict avoids examination of why conservatives viewed these politics as a threat. The WCEF had used academic freedom as a vehicle to push a wider agenda, including feminism. Their organizing example highlights how highly engaged Texas liberal women were active in the political process and threatened the status quo. Indeed, the WCEF was one point on a continuum leading to Ann Richards, the second woman elected governor of Texas and the first without benefit of her husband's prior record as governor. Indeed, the grassroots lobbying organization helped create the space for more women in leadership in Texas politics. Careful probing of the WCEF reveals another layer to the complexities of twentieth-century southern politics, which, despite Democratic dominance, were not as simple as suggested by one-party rule. The lack of competition between the two parties, though, in addition to silencing African Americans, squelched women's attempts to foster either gender equality or the liberalism needed to support it.

The WCEF projected an alternate vision of what politics might look like in Texas, one that was briefly realized half a century later when Ann Richards was elected governor. Richards embodied the confluence of liberalism, economic equality, and feminism that had animated the WCEF. Her governorship reflected what partisan politics could look like when these forces were prioritized. She was unable, though, to institutionalize these accomplishments, showing just how prevalent and entrenched conservatism was in Texas, whether it was during the postwar years or at the end of the century. The story of the WCEF, then, is at its core an important window into Texas politics at a key crossroad of liberalism and conservatism, feminism and anticommunism. The liberal, feminist women of the WCEF projected strong voices in politics but voices that were muted by the emboldened far right.

Notes

1. Orville Bullington quoted in "An Educational Crisis . . . A Summary of Testimony before a Senate Committee Investigating the University of Texas Controversy," November 15–28, 1944, file 667, Homer P. Rainey Papers, Collection 32, Western History Manuscripts Collection, University of Missouri at Columbia (hereafter Rainey Papers).

2. Homer P. Rainey, *The Tower and the Dome: A Free University vs. Political Control* (Boulder, CO: Pruett Publishing, 1971), 1 (quotes); David L. Brown, "Homer Price Rainey and the Campaign of 1946" (senior honors thesis, University of Texas at Austin, 1989), 6; Judith N. McArthur and Harold L. Smith, *Minnie Fisher Cunningham: A Suffragist's Life in Politics* (New York: Oxford University Press, 2003), 177. For more details on the Rainey controversy, see Don E. Carleton, *A Breed So Rare: The Life of J.R. Parten, Liberal Texas Oil Man, 1896–1992* (Austin: Texas State Historical Association Press, 1998), 300–323; Alice Carol Cox, "The Rainey Affair: A History of the Academic Freedom Controversy at the University of Texas, 1938–1946" (PhD diss., University of Denver, 1970); George Norris Green, *The Establishment in Texas Politics: The Primitive Years, 1938–1957* (Norman: University of Oklahoma Press, 1984), 83–89.

3. Resolution signed by Mrs. E. R. Vaughan, president of the class, Lillian Collier, teacher of the class, and O. B. Barrow, pastor of the church, October 23, 1944, file 642, Rainey Papers.

4. Lewis L. Gould, *Progressives and Prohibitionists: Texas Democrats in the Wilson Era* (Austin: University of Texas Press, 1973), 185–221; Judith N. McArthur, *Creating the New Woman: The Rise of Southern Women's Progressive Culture in Texas, 1893–1918* (Urbana: University of Illinois Press, 1998), 97–142.

5. McArthur and Smith, *Minnie Fisher Cunningham*, 44–183.

6. Oral history interview with Margaret Carter, October 25, 1975, Interview A-0309-1, in Southern Oral History Program Collection, Southern Historical Collection, Wilson Library, University of North Carolina at Chapel Hill; Lillian Collier to Homer P. Rainey, February 28, 1939, and Mrs. Hilton R. Greet to Rainey, March 4, 1939, both file 814, and Cunningham to Rainey, October 13,

1944 (quotes), file 632, all in Rainey Papers. Integration began at UT after the Supreme Court decided *Sweatt v. Painter* (1950), and it did not include undergraduates until 1956.

7. Rainey, *Tower*, 7; Carleton, *A Breed So Rare*, 300–303; Brown, "Rainey," 9; Green, *The Establishment in Texas Politics*, 22–44.

8. Rainey, *The Tower and the Dome*, 1–14, 7 (first quote), 39–54; Rainey to Bullington, April 14, 1942, in "Orville Bullington, 1941–1944," box VF 23/B.a, President's Office Records, Dolph Briscoe Center for American History, University of Texas at Austin; Carleton, *A Breed So Rare*, 301; McArthur and Smith, *Minnie Fisher Cunningham*, 177 (last quote).

9. Rainey, *The Tower and the Dome*, 39, 109–123; Carleton, *A Breed So Rare*, 304–305; "New Council in South Aims to Promote Racial Harmony," *Christian Science Monitor*, May 2, 1944 (first quote); Mrs. Albert T. Helbing to Marguerite Fairchild, November 2, 1944, file 649, Rainey Papers (second quote).

10. Minnie Fisher Cunningham, "By Countryside and Town," *State Observer*, September 11, 1944, 3. For more on how World War II impelled women to undertake political activism, see Rebecca DeWolf, "The Equal Rights Amendment and the Rise of Emancipationism, 1932–1946," *Frontiers: A Journal of Women Studies* 38, no. 2 (2017): 47–80; John Thomas McGuire, "'Give Us Peace': Gladys Avery Tillett and the Search for Women's Political Activism in the United States, 1945–1950," *Women's History Review* 25 (December 2016): 887–902; Paige Meltzer, "'The Pulse and Conscience of America': The General Federation and Women's Citizenship, 1945–1960," *Frontiers: A Journal of Women Studies* 30, no. 3 (2009): 52–76.

11. "Texas Women Desire Wider Share in Government," *State Observer*, September 11, 1944, 1–2.

12. Cunningham to Dear Co-worker, October 18, 1944, box 44, part II, Jane Y. McCallum Papers, Austin History Center (quotes) (hereafter McCallum Papers); Fannie Coffey to Rainey, October 19, 1944, file 745, Rainey Papers.

13. Jane Y. McCallum, "Women and War: University Attack Challenges Dream of Texas Founders," *Austin American*, October 22, 1944.

14. "I Remember Margaret Reading," box 4J459, Lillian Collier Papers, Dolph Briscoe Center for American History, University of Texas at Austin (first quote); T.A.M.C. No. 16, October 23, 1944, box 44, part II, McCallum Papers (second quote).

15. Margaret Carter to Freda Kirchwey, November 1, 1944, file 723, Rainey Papers; William E. Leuchtenburg, *The White House Looks South: Franklin D. Roosevelt, Harry S. Truman, Lyndon B. Johnson* (Baton Rouge: Louisiana State University Press, 2005), 104 (quote).

16. McCallum, Mrs. Sam J. Smith, and Mrs. Will T. Decherd to Dear Citizen, December 9, 1944, box 44, part II, McCallum Papers (first quote);

Hervey M. Amsler to McCallum, December 15, 1944, file 674 (second quote), D. W. Thompson to McCallum, Smith, and Decherd, December 18, 1944, Paul D. Page to McCallum, Smith, and Decherd, December 18, 1944 (third quote), Russell Surles to McCallum, Smith, and Decherd, December 20, 1944 (last quote), all file 675, Rainey Papers.

17. Robert Lee Bobbitt to Sarah T. Hughes, December 13, 1944, file 673, Rainey Papers (first three quotes); Mrs. Alton Luckett to Cunningham, January 6, 1945, box 23, part II, McCallum Papers; Cunningham to Dear Committee Member, January 9, 1945, file 9, box 15, Collection 239, Margaret B. Carter Papers, Special Collections Division, University of Texas at Arlington Libraries (remaining quotes).

18. Cunningham to McCallum, January 11, 1945, box 23, part II, McCallum Papers; McArthur and Smith, *Minnie Fisher Cunningham,* 178.

19. "Texas Women to Plan Action on UT Dispute," *Austin American,* January 18, 1945 (first quote); "Militant Women Seek Rainey's Reinstatement," *San Antonio Light,* January 18, 1945 (second quote); "UT-Interested Women March on Capitol," *Austin American,* January 19, 1945 (last quote).

20. "UT-Interested Women March on Capitol," *Austin American,* January 19, 1945 (first quote); "Stevenson Pooh-Poohs Blacklisting as He's Closely Questioned by Women," *Austin American,* January 19, 1945 (remaining quotes); "Women Add Heat to University Row," *Dallas Morning News,* January 19, 1945; McArthur and Smith, *Minnie Fisher Cunningham,* 177.

21. Women's Committee on Educational Freedom, minutes of meeting held in Austin, January 18, 1945, file 7, box 2, part I, McCallum Papers.

22. Carleton, *A Breed So Rare,* 321–323; Green, *The Establishment in Texas Politics,* 88; McCallum and Cunningham to Dear Committee Member, January 20, 1945, file 7, box 2, part I, and Alice Taylor to Dear Friend, January 22, 1945, box 44, part II (quotes), both in McCallum Papers.

23. "University in Politics?," *Houston Post,* January 20, 1945 (first two quotes); Cunningham, "By Countryside and Town," *State Observer,* January 29, 1945, 3 (remaining quotes).

24. Cunningham, "By Countryside and Town," January 29, 1945, 3.

25. McCallum and Cunningham to Dear Member Committee for Educational Freedom, January 31, 1945, box 23, part II, McCallum Papers (first four quotes); McArthur and Smith, *Minnie Fisher Cunningham,* 179; "Demos Meet Monday on Rainey Case," *Dallas Morning News,* February 5, 1945; McCallum and Cunningham to Dear Member Committee for Educational Freedom, February 6, 1945, in "Women's Committee for Educational Freedom," box 2, Minnie Fisher Cunningham Papers, Special Collections and Archives, University of Houston, Main Campus (fifth quote); "Women Move into 2-Year Fight on UT Expected to End in November, 1946, Vote," n.p., February 7, 1945, box 23, part II, McCallum Papers (last quote).

26. "The Red's Attack the Educational Setup in Texas," statement by Lewis Valentine Ulrey, July 1, 1946, file 1346, Rainey Papers.

27. Sara M. Evans, *Personal Politics: The Roots of Women's Liberation in the Civil Rights Movement and the New Left* (New York: Vintage, 1980); Douglas C. Rossinow, *The Politics of Authenticity: Liberalism, Christianity, and the New Left in America* (New York: Columbia University Press, 1998).

During a 1952 campaign stop in Colorado, General Dwight D. Eisenhower talks with (*left to right*) Mary P. Lord, cochair of Citizens for Eisenhower; Bertha Adkins, Director of the Women's Division of the Republican National Committee; and Ivy Baker Priest, whom he would appoint as US treasurer in 1953. Photograph courtesy of AP.

CHAPTER 9

"I Have Talked to You Not as Women but as American Citizens"

The Gender Ideology of Presidential Campaigns, 1940–1956

MELISSA ESTES BLAIR

IN MARCH 1958, President Dwight D. Eisenhower spoke to a meeting of partisan women who worked within his administration as well as for Republicans in Congress and the Republican National Committee (RNC). To conclude his wide-ranging remarks, he noted, "I have talked to you not as women but as American citizens with a real responsibility in public affairs. You see, there is no 'women's angle' to the great issues of our day."[1] Political women, in other words, should rightfully be involved in everything.

In making this statement, Eisenhower operated from a belief held by presidential campaigns and administrations since at least the 1930s. Franklin D. Roosevelt's and Eisenhower's teams were leaders among them, seeking women's opinions on a variety of topics. They believed women's opinions were part of what FDR called the "collective wisdom of citizens," which informed government decisions not only on "women's issues" such as the Equal Rights Amendment or children's welfare but also on any policy area.[2] Their campaigns consulted women not because of their gender but often in spite of it. The generation of politically active women who came of age in the 1920s and 1930s, immediately after women gained the vote, cultivated an expanded vision of their role in politics. As they worked to earn women's votes, they tried to create spaces for themselves that were not restricted merely to "women's issues."

In the 1930s through the 1950s, a small group of women gained influence in diverse parts of the Roosevelt, Truman, and Eisenhower administrations, but outside this elite group of political insiders, women mattered in another, less explored way. All three midcentury presidents, Democrats and Republicans alike, believed that women formed an important bloc of swing voters, and their campaigns built robust mechanisms to reach these women. To secure women's votes, each campaign turned to the Women's Division of the Democratic National Committee (DNC) or the RNC. The work of Women's Divisions serves as an important window into how women voters were viewed by successful presidential campaigns. Their material, speaking largely to women's dominant role of the era as a housewife from 1944 onward, suggests their idealized constituent. The women behind Women's Division campaigns may not have had a particular "women's angle" on policy issues, but they and their bosses certainly believed the women whose votes they courted did. This chapter analyzes these outreach efforts, arguing that administrations and campaigns actively cultivated women voters, creating political media for women meant to speak to both "women's issues" as traditionally defined and broader political interests. This contradictory treatment—seeing women as housewives primarily, while at times acknowledging an interest in issues beyond the home and motherhood—defined campaigns for women's votes in the middle of the twentieth century.

Politically active women's lack of attention to (let alone success with) feminist issues in these decades has caused scholars to ignore the coinciding push by politicians to attract the support of women voters during this period. Historians have focused on the political work of women's civic organizations in the 1940s and 1950s rather than on voter behavior and recruitment efforts, while political scientists' studies end in the early 1930s due to gaps in available data.[3] Implicit, and occasionally explicit, throughout this literature is the assumption that national politicians ignored women voters as a distinct group from 1930 until the 1970s, since these were years when "women's issues" found little success.[4] However, when our focus shifts from policy success to campaign practices and beliefs and from statistical data to archival records, a rich story emerges that contradicts this position.

. . .

The Women's Division of the Democratic Party played a central part in FDR's victorious 1932, 1936, and 1940 campaigns, but very little of their work spoke only to women or used gendered language. The Women's Division developed a full-scale communication strategy that included speakers and radio broadcasts throughout the country, but their signature feature were nationally distributed Rainbow Fliers. These small posters addressed a wide range of issues; fliers from 1932 had titles like "The Forgotten Farmer" and "Why Wage Earners Want Roosevelt and Garner."[5] The format was enormously successful, making up 90 percent of the print media distributed during the 1936 campaign.[6] Seeking a repeat of that success, in May 1940, the division had planned one million each of eight fliers for that year's effort "so far."[7]

For the 1940 campaign, Women's Division director Dorothy McAllister and her staff returned to the Rainbow Flier format and once again did not restrict the fliers to women's issues. Indeed, these fliers were a central tool for outlining the president's position on all the major issues of that campaign. McAllister wrote eighteen fliers in all, with the help of media consultant Bess Furman, a former reporter who was a veteran of Eleanor Roosevelt's women-only press conferences.[8] Handwritten drafts of the fliers show McAllister and Furman trying out different ways to phrase information, and their text appears verbatim on the finished fliers. For instance, one flier, "That Third-Term Bugaboo," provided historical quotes and arguments on the subject of term limits.[9] This flier was essential as President Roosevelt ran for a third term in office, something no president had ever done before.[10] Other fliers created by McAllister had titles like "Social Gains Mean National Strength," "As Farmers Profit Cities also Prosper," and "The Truth about Taxes."[11] All of the fliers used gender-neutral language; there is no evidence that McAllister and her colleagues at the Women's Division imagined only women would read them. The Rainbow Fliers were distributed broadly to articulate the president's position on the major issues of the 1940 campaign to the entire nation, not just women. Approving of the division's work, FDR wrote to McAllister saying, "your program . . . is excellent. . . . I think your rainbow fliers are fine but I hope you will get out far more than one million of each in the long run."[12] As late as the final weeks of the campaign, flier production continued. On October 24, 1940, just ten days before the election, seven hundred fifty thousand copies of the flier "Roosevelt and Peace" were shipped nationwide.[13]

In 1944, FDR sought an unprecedented fourth term, and women voters played a substantially different role than they had during his earlier campaigns. During World War II, with millions of men deployed overseas, women made up a majority of the electorate for the first time. With women's votes more crucial to victory, media specifically targeting female voters appeared in large quantities for the first time since the late 1920s.[14] As one newspaper article acknowledged, "The consensus is that women will swing the pendulum in the 1944 elections."[15] The tone and content of media created by the Women's Division changed noticeably due to women voters' increasing influence. For the first time, Women's Division products spoke directly to women as women, emphasizing their roles as mothers and homemakers and outlining why and how those roles should shape their vote preference. In 1944, the division did not create Rainbow Fliers and therefore did not participate in the campaign's print media production. Instead, division leaders focused on radio programs designed for women that spoke to them in highly gendered language.[16] One script distributed to Democratic women nationwide instructed the female narrator to begin by stating, "We women always felt ourselves pretty important to our families. . . . We're USED to carrying the responsibilities of a home, and a family. We LIKE it. And, as a matter of fact, we DREAD the day when we have to give it up." The script then asserted that women understood that, due to the United States' role in World War II, they as American voters were responsible for "the health, the security, even the LIVES of millions of people all over the world."[17]

The focus on women voters meant that new Women's Division director Gladys Tillett had much greater public visibility than her predecessors. Tillett gave the opening night keynote address at the 1944 Democratic National Convention, the first Women's Division director to do so. In that spotlight, she struck a patriotic chord that drew on long-standing beliefs about women's support for peace, support grounded in women's position as mothers.[18] She argued that "American women" favored experienced leadership to conclude the war and create the terms of the peace and that "the women of America, in return for their suffering and sacrifice in this war, demand a future of opportunity and peace, and particularly better lives for the returning soldiers."[19]

During wartime, politicians increased their attention to women voters but narrowed their conception of those voters' interests. Women's Division media during World War II followed the dominant propaganda distributed by US government offices, which depicted women's work in defense industries and the military as critical but temporary. Ads, movie theater newsreels, and other sources all emphasized that the American woman's main identity was as a housewife, even during the emergency of the war. Nothing that women did during the war was supposed to diminish their femininity; women's domestic role "was supposed to govern all aspects of a woman's life" even while she worked for the war effort.[20] The shifting tone in Women's Division material was therefore in line with other government propaganda as it narrowed its vision of women voters' interests to focus on peace and stability—issues women were assumed to care about more deeply because they were mothers.

Was the increased attention to female voters a fluke in 1944? If the focus on women voters was driven exclusively by wartime demographics, then a return to the pre-1944 world and its lack of attention to women voters would be expected. Instead, the three presidential elections that coincided with the onset of the Cold War—in 1948, 1952, and 1956—maintained a focus on female voters. As domestic ideology became more pronounced, so did DNC and RNC attention to women as swing voters in close presidential elections. In these years, both Democrats and Republicans thought about women voters abstractly as a uniform identity group. They used "woman" and "housewife" as interchangeable terms in campaign materials that pursued women's votes.

This continuity with wartime ideas is unsurprising given the American housewife's centrality to Cold War ideology. One major demonstration of America's superiority to the Soviet Union, according to politicians and journalists, was the ability of American women to stay within the home, remaining feminine and disengaged from the "affairs of men."[21] Scholars have documented how ideas about "good" and "bad" mothers tracked onto policies regarding race and welfare throughout the postwar period, arguing that "gender conservatism" was at the center of American domestic politics as well as foreign policy.[22] A good mother who raised her children, participated in postwar consumerism, and provided a fulfilling sex life to her husband—this was the ideal and idealized American woman of the postwar period.[23] Yet, ironically, the politically active women who helped create this idealized woman voter archetype worked hard to forge an identity for themselves that went beyond the confines of housewife and mother. While using "woman" and "housewife" as synonyms when talking about women as a group, they worked on a wide range of issues in Washington and did so using gender-neutral language, as did other politically active women throughout the country and at every level of government.[24]

This consistency in messaging occurred despite a shake-up in leadership at the DNC Women's Division. In 1948, the role of women within the DNC and Harry Truman's reelection campaign was uncertain. Democratic losses in the 1946 congressional elections led to major upheavals, and the Women's Division was not spared from the turmoil. Chase Going Woodhouse, a Connecticut congresswoman who had just lost her reelection bid and had no prior experience working within the party mechanism, replaced Gladys Tillett as director. Woodhouse's ineffective leadership, and especially her December 1947 recommendation to dissolve the Women's Division, led to internal discussions about the best way to reach female voters. Eventually, the numbers won the debate. DNC executive secretary Gael Sullivan sent party chairman Howard McGrath a terse memo urging him to instruct state-level party officials to "give the strongest possible representation to women," noting that "the latest figures disclose a two million vote majority of women over men."[25]

In March 1948, McGrath appointed veteran party activist India Edwards as director of the Women's Division. As Women's Division director, Edwards was heavily involved in creating media—especially radio programs—targeting female voters. Most of this media focused on the 1948 campaign's top domestic issue: inflation. The Republican-controlled Congress ended wartime price controls in early 1947, and the cost of food, housing, and other necessities had risen rapidly.[26] Women's Division media zeroed in on this topic repeatedly, consistently drawing listeners' and readers' attention to the facts of rising prices and the Republicans' role in inflation. For example, a July 1948 radio broadcast featured Edwards "interviewing" Margery Clifford, wife of Clark Clifford, the White House counsel. She talked about how much the price of butter, shoes, and other necessities had increased. Edwards closed the broadcast by stating, "What can the American housewife do about high prices? The answer is to vote! And vote Democratic!"[27] In the last month of the campaign, the Women's Division wrote, recorded, and distributed nearly a dozen similar programs, all focused largely although not exclusively on the inflation issue.[28] They also sponsored "Housewives for Truman" trailers, traveling exhibits that toured rural areas demonstrating the differences between the price of goods in 1946 and 1948.[29]

During the 1948 election, inflation was a central domestic issue in the Truman campaign, discussed well beyond the confines of the Women's Division. Notes for a speech President Truman gave at a union hall in Flint, Michigan, largely to a male audience, listed "the price of meat" as the most important domestic issue for his audience.[30] In another speech just days before the election, Truman argued that the decision to eliminate price controls and the resulting inflation led to an increasing risk of communist influence in the United States, because this and other "Republican policies of the 80th Congress . . . threaten to put an end to American prosperity."[31] Therefore, what seemed on its face to be a women's issue—the price of food and other consumer goods—was a concern for everyone but discussed in gender-specific ways. When campaign media about inflation targeted women voters, the discussion was personal—Margery Clifford talking about three new pairs of shoes (one for each of her children) costing almost thirty dollars.[32] When the topic was broached to a gender-neutral or largely male audience, however, inflation was connected to global geopolitics, not to a housewife's shopping trip. Even when discussing the same issue, then, gendered appeals persisted.

The choices made by Eisenhower and his administration when Republicans regained the White House in 1952 demonstrate that both Republicans and Democrats believed in the importance of women as swing voters. Attention to female voters remained high, and women within the Republican Party steadily gained influence. Moreover, Eisenhower and the RNC were committed to consolidating the gains they made with female voters in 1952. They did so not only through highly gendered appeals but also by replicating the structures and methods that had worked so well for Democrats in the 1930s and 1940s.[33] Bertha Adkins, the incoming Women's Division director, prepared a detailed outline of her "Program for 1953." In it, she asked for a budget of $50,000 to create local "Schools of Politics," annual regional meetings, publications, and other events.[34] Max Rabb, the deputy to Eisenhower's chief of staff, endorsed Adkins' program: "Women in the 1952 election demonstrated their great interest and effectiveness in political activity. The Women's Division, Republican National Committee, would assume responsibility for maintaining this enthusiasm at the highest level possible. The 'Program for 1953,' outlined here, should accomplish this purpose and at the same time serve as a pilot plan of action for the years to come."[35] Clearly, aides throughout the Eisenhower administration believed in the importance of female voters to the continued success of the Republican Party after so many years out of the White House.

President Eisenhower himself was committed during his campaign to incorporating women into his administration and in the Republican Party. Vivian Kellems, host of a women's television program in Connecticut, wrote to Eisenhower during the campaign, stating that "millions of women" could have their votes swayed if he committed to employing women in government.[36] Eisenhower responded that "it would be impossible to carry out the responsibilities of the office without such help [from women]."[37] During a campaign event in Portland, Oregon, he also noted, "I want to speak for just a second about my honest belief, my deep conviction, that we should have more women in public life."[38] Throughout his time as president, Eisenhower repeated this sentiment frequently. Bertha Adkins attributed his policy of not putting "women to one side," his "awareness of the importance of women in the role of policy-maker as well as doer in government," to his time working with women in auxiliary military units during World War II.[39] Beyond this personal commitment, he also understood the partisan advantage he gained by making promises to increase women's government appointments. For this reason, Eisenhower's campaign orchestrated a photo op with the candidate and three leading women in his campaign, which ran in an August 1952 issue of the *Boston Herald* accompanying the headline "Ike Appoints Strategy Staff."[40] Letters sent with Eisenhower's signature to county-level party officials included a list of questions for canvassers to ask potential voters, including "will a temporary babysitter be needed on Election Day?"[41] Local party offices providing babysitters so that mothers of young children could vote was not new in 1952; the Truman administration had deployed half a million babysitters in one hundred thirty thousand precincts in 1948 to make it easier for women to get to the polls.[42] This program both recognized the realities of women's lives during the early baby boom and illustrated the centrality of housewives' votes to both parties' victory. Everyone in presidential politics understood housewives to be crucial swing voters.

The materials distributed by the Republican Women's Division run by Bertha Adkins from 1953 through the 1958 midterm election are strikingly similar to those used by the DNC throughout the 1930s. Women were sent a wide range of print material: newsletters which introduced them to campaign issues, fliers they could post in public places, and postcards titled "Let's Talk about It," which each featured brief talking points on topics such as "taxation," "agriculture," and "security."[43] Letters that accompanied the postcards instructed women to pass them out to neighbors and friends in order to generate conversation in support of Eisenhower's administration and its accomplishments. By creating cadres of women who were knowledgeable about a range of issues, Adkins and others at the Women's Division created a deep bench of women who could potentially be recruited to work professionally for the Republican Party. Both India Edwards and Adkins focused much of their time between elections on securing appointments for women within the government, and Adkins saw these Women's Division programs as a way to increase the number of Republican women who were qualified for professional government work.[44] Because government work required a different skill set than homemaking, Adkins and her colleagues saw their efforts to develop those skills in women throughout the country as critically important.[45]

Bertha Adkins and the Women's Division played a large role in the 1956 campaign as well. The division not only distributed more "Let's Talk about It" postcards, but also created material on how to do the work of campaigning. Pamphlets with titles such as "So You're Planning a Rally" and "How Women Win" were available through the division, enabling grassroots women to work more effectively to secure Eisenhower's reelection.[46] The division also inaugurated the Women's Finance Program, instructing grassroots women to do more fundraising than ever before.[47] Initiatives such as these were new in the 1950s and again indicate the ways in which the division under Adkins's leadership sought to build a professional cadre of grassroots Republican women. Adkins also assumed more responsibility in the 1956 campaign, becoming assistant chair of the RNC and the number two person running the entire reelection campaign for Eisenhower. In that role, she coordinated all the different divisions of the committee, not only the Women's Division but also the publicity and finance divisions, among others.[48] Because of Adkins's position, Women's Division activities were incorporated more closely into the overall operation of Eisenhower's reelection campaign than at any time since 1940.

While the Women's Division created expertise in topics like taxation and agriculture, however, they also supported efforts to appeal to women voters in gendered ways. In the months preceding the 1954 midterm elections, the RNC and the independent Citizens for Eisenhower committee wrote reports about women voters' continued importance to the Republican Party's success. Ellen Harris, the cochair of Citizens for Eisenhower, reported in April 1954 that women were a "major factor" in Eisenhower's 1952 victory. Harris showed that women were more than 50 percent of the voters in a majority of states. She informed party officials that women made up 52 percent of Eisenhower's 1952 vote but had only been 46 percent of Republican candidate Dewey's vote in 1948.[49] Their swing from the Democrats to the Republicans, in other words, was a central piece of the puzzle that allowed Eisenhower to become the first Republican president in two decades. Thus, Republican operatives throughout the administration and party structure recognized women as an important voting block that was key to their success.

Party officials also believed that women had particular interests as women. The cover sheet to the statistical report prepared by Harris asserted, "Women—as citizens, as homemakers, as mothers, and as wage earners—have a particular stake in continuing this administration."[50] The underlying assumption presented here was that women were most interested in social welfare and peace policies. Women's Division materials from the 1956 campaign also highlighted these themes. One pamphlet, for instance, comparing "the Democrat way" and "the Republican way" highlighted peace centrally. The "Republican way" section featured a drawing of a nuclear family in front of a two-story house and stated that Republicans "brought the family together again," a reference to Eisenhower's work in concluding the Korean War during his first term.[51] Campaign operatives also argued that radio remained the best way to reach women, rather than television, because "a housewife can listen to the radio while working, but TV requires a letdown in household chores."[52] Indeed, within Eisenhower campaign literature, "women" and "housewife" were frequently used as synonyms.

While Eisenhower's campaign literature promoted a domestic ideal, his staff worked alongside women who did not fit the housewife image and implicitly challenged that identity through their presence in national party offices and in the White House. However, those same women, who created much of the media that spoke to "women voters" as housewives, understood the cultural norms of the time in which they were living. Politically active women during World War II and the early Cold War often downplayed their gender in order to maintain a role in policy making. But as professional women, they saw themselves as exceptions to the rule and never challenged beliefs that most women were home-makers and viewed the world through that lens. Neither women in politics nor their male colleagues drew attention to the contradictions between these two positions that seem obvious to us today. Only by looking at the women behind the Roosevelt, Truman, and Eisenhower media outreach to women voters and the messages they created can we gain a complete picture of women's relationship to presidential politics in this era.

Notes

1. "Remarks of the President Delivered at Luncheon Meeting of the Sixth Annual Republican Women's National Conference," March 18, 1958, page 7, folder 2, box 596, White House Central Files Official File, Dwight D. Eisenhower Presidential Library, Abilene, KS.

2. FDR to Dorothy McAllister, Director of the Women's Division, April 4, 1938, Franklin D. Roosevelt Papers as President, President's Personal File, folder "DNC 1933–39," PPF 603 (Democratic National Committee), Franklin D. Roosevelt Presidential Library, Hyde Park, NY.

3. Historical works include Nancy F. Cott, *The Grounding of Modern Feminism* (New Haven, CT: Yale University Press, 1987); Cynthia Harrison, *On Account of Sex: The Politics of Women's Issues, 1945–1968* (Berkeley: University of California Press, 1988); and Robyn Muncy, *Creating a Female Dominion in American Reform, 1890–1935* (New York: Oxford University Press, 1991). Studies by political scientists include Kristi Anderson, *After Suffrage: Women in Partisan and Electoral Politics before the New Deal* (Chicago: University of Chicago Press, 1996); J. Kevin Corder and Christina Wolbrecht, *Counting Women's Ballots: Female Voters from Suffrage through the New Deal* (New

York: Cambridge University Press, 2016); and Anna L. Harvey, *Votes without Leverage: Women in American Electoral Politics, 1920–1970* (New York: Cambridge University Press, 1998).

4. Anderson, *After Suffrage,* 106–107, states this most directly.

5. 1932 Rainbow Fliers, folder 1, box 107, DNC Women's Division Papers, Franklin D. Roosevelt Presidential Library, Hyde Park, NY.

6. Susan Ware, *Partner and I: Molly Dewson, Feminism, and New Deal Politics* (New Haven, CT: Yale University Press, 1987), 220–221.

7. Jim Farley to FDR, May 2, 1940, Roosevelt Papers as President, folder "DNC 1940–44," PPF 603, FDR Library.

8. Ware, *Partner and I,* 198, for more on the press conferences.

9. "That Third-Term Bugaboo," folder 5, box 109, DNC Women's Division papers, FDR Library.

10. On the third-term issue, see John W. Jeffries, *A Third Term for FDR: The Election of 1940* (Lawrence: University of Kansas Press, 2017), chap. 3.

11. The entire set of 1940 Rainbow Fliers are in folder 4, box 108, DNC Women's Division papers, FDR Library.

12. FDR to Dorothy McAllister, August 15, 1940, folder "DNC 1940–44," PPF 603, FDR Library.

13. "Mailing of the Rainbow Flier Roosevelt and Peace," October 24, 1940, folder 4, box 108, DNC Women's Division papers, FDR Library.

14. Brian Balogh, "'Mirrors of Desire': Interest Groups, Elections, and the Targeted Style in Twentieth-Century American Politics," in *The Democratic Experiment: New Directions in American Political History,* ed. Meg Jacobs, William J. Novak, and Julian Zelizer (Princeton, NJ: Princeton University Press, 2003), 222–249, explores the 1928 appeals to women voters.

15. Clipping, Jane Eades, "Both Parties Woo Women as Decisive Election Factor," no paper, February 20, 1944, in scrapbook, box 138, DNC Women's Division Papers, FDR Library.

16. While the division had created radio programs in the past, they had not specifically targeted women.

17. Transcript of radio address, page 1, scrapbook, box 138, DNC Women's Division Papers, FDR Library. Capitalization in original.

18. Harriet Hyman Alonso, *Peace as a Women's Issue: A History of the U.S. Movement for World Peace and Women's Rights* (Syracuse, NY: Syracuse University Press, 1993) and Lelia J. Rupp, *Worlds of Women: The Making of an International Women's Movement* (Princeton, NJ: Princeton University Press, 1997).

19. Clipping, Emma Bulger, "Women's View Is Emphasized by Mrs. Tillett," *New York Herald Tribune,* n.d., scrapbook, box 138, DNC Women's Division Papers, FDR Library.

20. Melissa McEuen, *Making War, Making Women: Femininity and Duty on the American Home Front, 1941–1945* (Athens: University of Georgia Press, 2011), 4.

21. Elaine Tyler May, *Homeward Bound: American Families in the Cold War Era* (New York: Basic Books, 1988), 18–19.

22. Ruth Feldstein, *Motherhood in Black and White: Race and Sex in American Liberalism, 1930–1965* (Ithaca, NY: Cornell University Press, 2000), 3.

23. On consumerism, see Lizabeth Cohen, *A Consumer's Republic: The Politics of Mass Consumption in Cold War America* (New York: Vintage Books, 2003), chap. 3.

24. Kristin A. Goss, *The Paradox of Gender Equality: How American Women's Groups Gained and Lost Their Public Voice* (Ann Arbor: University of Michigan Press, 2013), 12; Sylvie Murray, *The Progressive Housewife: Community Activism in Suburban Queens, 1945–1965* (Philadelphia: University of Pennsylvania Press, 2003), chap. 6.

25. Gael Sullivan to Howard McGrath, February 3, 1948, folder 4, box 1, India Edwards Papers, Harry S. Truman Presidential Library, Independence, MO.

26. Several scholars have documented the woman-led consumer movement of the 1930s and 1940s on which these efforts built. See Annelise Orleck, "'We Are That Mythical Thing Called the Public': Militant Housewives during the Great Depression," *Feminist Studies* 19, no. 1 (Spring 1993): 147–172 and Emily E. LB. Twarog, *Politics of the Pantry: Housewives, Food, and Consumer Protest in Twentieth Century America* (New York: Oxford University Press, 2017), among others.

27. Transcript of radio broadcast featuring India Edwards and Mrs. Clark Clifford, July 27, 1948, folder 7, box 206, Records of the Democratic National Committee (DNC), Harry S. Truman Presidential Library, Independence, MO.

28. See, for example, transcript of "Democratic Record Show #6," October 22, 1948, folder 10, box 208, Records of the DNC, Truman Library.

29. "Housewives for Truman" report, November 1948, folder 4, box 3, India Edwards Papers, Truman Library. Also see India Edwards, *Pulling No Punches: Memoirs of a Woman in Politics* (New York: G. P. Putnam's Sons, 1977), 114.

30. "Vital Issues in Flint Michigan," accessed January 7, 2019, https://www.trumanlibrary.org/whistlestop/study_collections/1948campaign/large/docs/documents/index.php?documentdate=1948-09-06&documentid=10-3&page number=1.

31. Transcript of Boston campaign speech, October 27, 1948, folder 13, box 206, Records of the DNC, Truman Library.

32. Transcript of radio broadcast featuring India Edwards and Mrs. Clark Clifford, page 1, July 27, 1948, folder 7, box 206, Records of the DNC, Truman Library.

33. The 1930s DNC program is described in Ware, *Partner and I*, chap. 12. While the Republicans were copying 1930s Democratic structures, the Democratic Party was dismantling those same structures, dissolving the DNC Women's Division in 1953. Kimberly Brodkin, "'We Are Neither Male nor Female Democrats': Gender Difference and Women's Integration within the Democratic Party," *Journal of Women's History* 19, no. 2 (June 2007), 111–137.

34. "Program for 1953," January 3, 1953, page 1, folder 4, box 476, GF 139-A-1, White House Central Files General Files, Dwight D. Eisenhower Presidential Library, Abilene, KS.

35. "Program for 1953," page 20, folder 4, box 476, GF 139-A-1, White House Central Files General Files, Eisenhower Library.

36. Vivian Kellems to Gen. Eisenhower, August 9, 1952, folder 14, box 710, OF156-G, White House Central Files Official File, Eisenhower Library.

37. Eisenhower to Vivian Kellems, August 16, 1952, folder 14, box 710, OF156-G, White House Central Files Official File, Eisenhower Library.

38. "Excerpts from speeches by Gen. Eisenhower on the role of women in his campaign," page 2, folder 8, box 18, Katherine Howard Graham papers, Dwight D. Eisenhower Presidential Library, Abilene, KS.

39. Transcript, John T. Mason Jr. interview of Bertha Adkins, December 18, 1967, 48–49, Dwight D. Eisenhower Presidential Library, Abilene, KS.

40. Clipping, "Ike Appoints Strategy Staff," folder 1, box 19, Howard papers, Eisenhower Library.

41. Eisenhower to Mr. Gill, September 23, 1952, folder 2, box 872, PPF 49-B, White House Central File President's Personal Files, Dwight D. Eisenhower Presidential Library, Abilene, KS.

42. Clipping, "Mrs. Tillett Raps GOP Isolationists," *Philadelphia Daily News*, July 13, 1948, folder 14, box 3, India Edwards papers, Truman Library. While Tillett was no longer head of the Women's Division, she was still the vice-chair of the DNC.

43. "Let's Talk about It" postcards, folder 14, box 718, Republican National Committee papers, Dwight D. Eisenhower Presidential Library, Abilene, KS.

44. Harrison, *On Account of Sex*, chapter four, on appointments.

45. Adkins oral history, transcript pgs. 7, 23, Eisenhower Library.

46. "Literature of the Women's Division, RNC," n.d. (in folder labeled "Women's Division 1956"), folder 6, box 208, RNC Office of the Chairman papers, Dwight D. Eisenhower Presidential Library, Abilene, KS.

47. "Progress Report—Women's Finance Program," folder 19, box 104, RNC Office of the Chairman papers, Eisenhower Library.

48. Adkins oral history, transcript pages 55–56, Eisenhower Library.

49. Memorandum, Mrs. J. Ramsey Harris to the President, April 1, 1954, pgs. 1 & 3, folder 8, box 587 OF 138-A-2, White House Central Files Official Files, Eisenhower Library.

50. Memorandum, Mrs. J. Ramsey Harris to President, page 1.

51. "You Make the Choice" pamphlet, 1956, page 3, folder 14, box 718, RNC Research Division File Series, RNC Papers, Eisenhower Library.

52. "Campaign Clinic" report, April 1954, page 1, folder 7, box 587 OF 138-A-2, White House Central Files Official Files, Eisenhower Library.

PART TWO

Women's Political Leadership Takes Shape

Reform and Reaction, 1960s–1980s

Geraldine Ferraro and the "Political Time Bomb." Reprinted by permission of *Ms.* Magazine, © 1984.

CHAPTER 10

From Suffragist to Congresswoman

Celebrating Political Action, Women's History, and Feminist Intellectuals in Ms. *Magazine, 1972–1984*

ANA STEVENSON

Ms. MAGAZINE BECAME a cultural phenomenon and a voice of the women's movement during the 1970s. Its editorial team also, quite intentionally, ensured that it became a vibrant source of women's history. As editor Gloria Steinem wrote in its preview edition, inserted in *New York* magazine, "I have met brave women who are exploring the outer edge of possibility with no history to guide them, and a courage to make themselves vulnerable that I find moving beyond the words to express it."[1] Steinem, however, was well aware that some "brave women" were already contributing to political life. And, although her historical knowledge was still evolving, she recognized that the current upswing of women in politics built on the legacy of suffragist foremothers. For Steinem and the *Ms.* editorial team, women's political action and the recovery of women's history went together, offering a foundation for women's liberation.

As historian Amy Erdmann Farrell explains, *Ms.* embraced the genre and format of women's magazines to pursue its mission of popularizing feminism. But this goal was not without its challenges. The magazine's desire to emphasize a "sisterhood of all women" proved complex: it legitimated the women's movement while provoking questions about who represented the "norm" and how to approach difference.[2] When activists struggled to comprehend the problems of less privileged women, especially women of color, claims of "sisterhood" created tensions. However, the *Ms.* editorial team strove to appreciate the diversity of the women's movement and, sensing that something similar must have existed among earlier generations, to represent women's varied past—if at times falling short of this goal. Historical writing, they believed, would help foster dynamic feminist politics in the present, conveying an unbroken vision of women's political engagement with its roots in the nineteenth century.

This chapter situates *Ms.* Magazine as an important but overlooked political primer, born of the women's movement but very much engaged with political life. It makes the case that *Ms.* was a galvanizing vehicle that helped bridge the space between political knowledge and action. First, *Ms.* featured political narratives to demonstrate that women were already active in political life as congresswomen, senators, policy makers, and campaign volunteers. Second, its recovery of women's history cultivated a sense of belonging to and an understanding of prior political struggles, especially the woman suffrage movement, among readers. And third, *Ms.* traced the feminist intellectual path that was emerging alongside politics among a new generation of academics. Each initiative challenged the *Ms.* readership to think beyond the realm of the possible and to envision what women's large-scale political participation might achieve.

Women in Political Life

Just prior to *Ms.* Magazine's 1972 launch, journalist and cultural icon Gloria Steinem helped establish the National Women's Political Caucus alongside Congresswomen Bella Abzug and Shirley Chisholm and writer Betty Friedan. Its founders reflected the diverse currents and the fusion of grassroots and institutional politics emblematic of the women's movement, with Letty Cottin Pogrebin becoming a leading voice of Jewish feminism and Margaret Sloan active in the National Black Feminist Organization. Steinem, however, was the magazine's leading political voice and penned much of its political analysis across the next two decades. Fascinated by the meaning and implications of the Nineteenth Amendment, she actively sought to connect this history to the current feminist scene. Consequently, *Ms.* became a leading source for those interested in learning about women in political life.

Recognizing the timeliness of the magazine's debut in a presidential election year, its editors aimed to inspire more women to vote in 1972. Steinem sought to demystify pernicious myths about women's enfranchisement to encourage political action. Her feature article "Women Voters Can't Be Trusted" detailed the degree to which assumptions about women's voting patterns correlated with their internalized self-image "as non-political beings." Steinem drew upon the work of Eastern Michigan University political scientist Marjorie Lansing, translating her polls and findings for a lay audience. Steinem believed this growing body of academic research made it impossible to ignore that "women are voting." As she argued, "The myth that they are not should be finally shattered in '72." These statistics also suggested that women voted differently than men on a variety of topics, thus challenging the myth that "the 19th Amendment didn't amount to much, because women's vote is never going to make a fundamental difference anyway." Finally, Steinem highlighted an issue that remains controversial. Analyzing votes along racial lines, she observed that, contrary to the progressivism exhibited by black women and people of color, "white women's voting patterns are substantially different from their male counterparts, but often not different enough."[3] The relative conservatism of white women, she argued, needed to be addressed, not least because it could influence election outcomes. Steinem hoped to inspire women, as a heterogeneous class connected by gender, to vote in the interests of women and minorities.

Ms. offered readers rigorous political analysis across 1972.[4] However, the new magazine stopped short of outright endorsements, particularly when the candidacy of Democratic presidential candidate Shirley Chisholm became a source of friction within feminist circles. Although *Ms.* immediately fell short of unconditional support, "The Year of the Women Candidates" offered a guide to the platforms of prospective and incumbent women politicians, including Chisholm.[5] In 1968, she had become the first black woman elected to the US Congress, representing New York City's Twelfth Congressional District from 1969 until 1983. Chisholm supported black and women's liberation agendas, including the Black Panther Party, the "Free Angela Davis and All Political Prisoners" campaign, and the August 1970 Strike for Women's Equality, which commemorated the fiftieth anniversary of the Nineteenth Amendment.[6] Chisholm thus seemed like a natural choice to support, yet some feminists saw her candidacy as purely symbolic and instead elected to back Senator George McGovern, a progressive antiwar candidate who had greater momentum.

Steinem herself expressed divided loyalties, as she worked for Chisholm in the states where she ran and for McGovern elsewhere but ultimately became a Chisholm delegate. *Ms.*, however, only offered Chisholm tepid support, yet published an eleven-page diary entry detailing Steinem's personal experiences with McGovern since 1964. This included volunteering for his 1968 presidential campaign prior to her own "Feminist Realization." Acknowledging the "symbolic but important candidacy of Shirley Chisholm," Steinem described McGovern "as 'the best white male candidate.'"[7] This approach undermined coverage of Chisholm and was likely one of the reasons that undergirded later charges of racial bias against the magazine.

Only after the 1972 presidential election did *Ms.* publish a cover story—"The Ticket That Might Have Been"—about Chisholm and running mate Frances Tarlton "Sissy" Farenthold, a Texas state legislator also elected in 1968. Chisholm and Farenthold were the January 1973 "cover people"—the magazine's gender-neutral term for "cover girl." A close-up photograph featured the team cheek to cheek; a joyous Chisholm gazed directly at the camera while a more circumspect Farenthold looked away. Steinem presented a critical analysis of their campaign rather than an adulatory narrative of success, noting that "a familiar face, a familiar white and male face, [will be] in the White House for four more years." Had the rigors of 1972 been worthwhile, she asked? The media had "rarely analyzed" Chisholm's campaign, Steinem observed, either during or in its aftermath, but neither had her own magazine. This recap directed the most focus toward voters' impressions of a black woman becoming a presidential candidate and how her candidacy, while unsuccessful in establishing "a solid coalition . . . for social change," had inspired young people to participate in a political campaign.[8]

Steinem's close friend, New York Representative Bella Abzug, in Congress from 1971 to 1977, garnered more sustained political coverage. Abzug appeared as the February 1973 cover person. This was accompanied by a photographic series inside the fold that showcased her famous wide-brimmed hats, the colorful, stylized images recalling Andy Warhol's pop art. The feature article's prose, however, was somber. After Abzug's first congressional district had been rezoned, she faced a tough race against the terminally ill Representative William Fitts Ryan. Not without controversy, Abzug prevailed against his widow Priscilla Ryan. As former congressional staffer Judith Nies reflected in her *Ms.* profile, "It is in relatively liberal districts, and therefore perhaps against relatively liberal politicians, that women are most likely to run and win—since these constituencies have been more receptive to women politicians." But candidates like Abzug, she reasoned, should have no responsibility to bow to liberal men—or their widows. "Despite the media attention given to a Bella Abzug or a Shirley Chisholm," Nies reflected, "98 percent of the House is still male."[9]

Ms. staff used the magazine to raise awareness about important legislation, key among them the Equal Rights Amendment (ERA). Suffragist Alice Paul drafted this constitutional amendment, which the National Woman's Party debuted in 1923 at the seventy-fifth anniversary of the 1848 Seneca Falls women's rights convention; its purpose was to end sex discrimination by mandating gender-neutral law. After this law finally passed in Congress in 1972, *Ms.* staked a claim in the fight for its ratification. The magazine profiled still-living suffragists, including Paul, in July 1973 to help reinvigorate the campaign that quickly stalled after the majority of states ratified the ERA.[10] Other coverage included a report from the legislative vice president for the National Organization for Women, who predicted the ratification process would "not be as simple as the Nineteenth [Amendment], which gave women the vote 52 years ago" because Americans in 1920 believed that suffrage was more "tangible" than the ERA.[11] A seven-year deadline was introduced in 1971 as a necessary precursor to its passage, after which all previous state ratifications would be nullified. As this deadline approached with states still not acting, *Ms.* editor Mary Thom asked, "Should We Have Listened to Alice?"[12] Paul's original proposal had included no deadline, and she strongly disagreed with its later introduction, remembering the force of antisuffragists and fearing that anti-ERA proponents would derail the ratification campaign.[13] *Ms.* pursued new strategies to canvass support, especially after Paul's passing in July 1977.[14] Its editors prioritized "back to basics" factoids and garnered celebrity endorsements from Candice Bergen, Shirley MacLaine, Mary Tyler Moore, Robert Redford, Alan Alda, and Esther Rolle.[15]

Ms. continued to make connections between Paul's generation and that of its younger readers and staff in its coverage of the 1977 National Women's Conference. Held in Houston, Texas, in conjunction with the United Nations International Women's Year initiative, the conference was presaged by the "Relay for E.R.A."[16] The race kicked off on September 29 in Seneca Falls, New York, the site of a women's convention said to have initiated the suffrage struggle in 1848. More than two thousand runners carried the "Torch of Freedom" two thousand six hundred miles to Houston across fourteen states over fifteen days. *Ms.* described this as an event during which "thousands of cross-country relay runners carr[ied] . . . the flame kindled by our suffragist foremothers."[17] When it entered the city, the "relay slowed to a march" to evoke the suffrage marches of the 1910s.[18] Bella Abzug, Betty Friedan, and tennis legend Billie Jean King—featured as *Ms.*'s July 1973 cover person—walked alongside young students serving as final torchbearers. The torch was ultimately passed to Elizabeth Cady Stanton's great-niece Susan B. Anthony, the namesake of her friend and coadjutor.[19] Its arrival marked the beginning of the National Women's Conference, attended by key feminists and political figures such as Abzug and Friedan. *Ms.* published a guide to this conference, at which Steinem was a national commissioner and its staff held a strong presence, to frame women as bastions of political engagement—past, present, and future.[20]

The failure to ratify the ERA by two-thirds of state legislatures by the 1982 deadline led *Ms.* into a period of self-reflection. In conjunction with the election of President Ronald Reagan, the magazine's earlier political analysis of anti-ERA activist Phyllis Schlafly expanded into further examination of the rise of the New Right. As the 1984 presidential election approached, Steinem continued to advocate for women's political engagement.[21] But *Ms.* also began to reassess women's political behavior in terms of the "gender gap," that is, the gender-based difference in the percentage of votes for any given candidate.[22] Revisiting the Nineteenth Amendment stimulated this political analysis. Steinem recalled her "disappointment and surprise" when she discovered that "only a third of all eligible women actually voted in 1920: the first year that women, after more than a century of struggle and hunger strikes and marches by sisters and foremothers, were allowed to vote." Her conclusions were informed by a sweeping, if not particularly thorough, sense of women's history. Recent voting patterns, Steinem reflected, testified to "what women had been saying ever since Abigail Adams warned against excluding females from the U.S. Constitution, or since the suffragists of the 1800s talked about women's potential civilizing influence on political life: females as a group have measurably different opinions on many major issues from males as a group."[23] This slightly hackneyed *long durée* analysis—few women, if any, had been publicly advocating enfranchisement prior to 1848—emphasized women's capacity to facilitate change in 1984. To test these theories, *Ms.* again turned to political research, commissioning an Exclusive Louis Harris Survey and sharing its results in the July 1984 edition.[24] The magazine's cover boldly proclaimed: "Women in 1984: Political Time Bomb."

One of the contributors to this so-called time bomb was Democratic presidential nominee and Walter Mondale's vice presidential choice, Geraldine Ferraro.[25] Representing New York's Ninth District in Queens, Ferraro served in Congress between 1979 and 1985. Her selection was seen as groundbreaking and received wide coverage in *Ms.* However, mixed reviews about Ferraro's potential as a historic first reflected feminists' unsure footing in the political arena. "What Difference Can One Woman

Make?" Steinem asked, weighing for readers the possibilities. Despite her fervent support for Ferraro, Steinem expressed outright doubt about her power and capacity as vice president, echoing reservations she had about Chisholm eleven years earlier. Ferraro did offer "a sense of linkage that few women have ever felt to the White House," but, Steinem concluded, "win or lose, the Ferraro Factor is only one small step."[26]

Across the 1980s, the women's movement embraced a vision of a global sisterhood. This was, in part, a response to the frustration that followed the Mondale-Ferraro loss and the prospect of four more years of Reagan. Perhaps, *Ms.* considered, feminism could be invigorated by the dynamism of women's political engagement beyond the United States. *Ms.* profiled Israeli Prime Minister Golda Meir; Australia's Elizabeth Reid, the world's first political advisor on women's affairs, and Senator Susan Ryan; Argentinian first lady and cultural icon Eva Perón; New Zealand Member of Parliament Marilyn Waring; President Corazon Aquino of the Philippines; South African antiapartheid activist and political prisoner Winnie Madikizela-Mandela; Queen Noor of Jordan; and Myanmar political prisoner and politician Aung San Suu Kyi. Becoming a pulse point for the movement's shift from local to global politics and issue-centered organizing, *Ms.* illustrated that women were engaged in everything from electoral politics to social revolution all around the world.

Covering the History of Women's Political Struggle

In the early 1970s, the study of women's history was only just emerging as a nascent field. As historian Judith M. Bennett observes, "one of the battlefronts of feminism was women's history, where feminists— both in the academy and outside it—were reclaiming a lost past in their research, empowering students in their teaching, and using historical insight to inform feminist strategy."[27] Important connections existed between popular writing and revisionist academic history. Women's liberation groups published anthologies and journals that featured women's history alongside women's political manifestos. A 1970 edition of *Women: A Journal of Liberation*, for example, featured "Women in History: A Recreation of Our Past": academic historian Ellen Carol DuBois discussed antebellum abolitionists Sarah and Angelina Grimké alongside excerpts of Elizabeth Cady Stanton and Susan B. Anthony's writings.[28] However, neither women's liberation print culture nor academic scholarship could reach the same readership as a professionally printed magazine with a growing national and international circulation. *Ms.* played a pivotal role in challenging the assumption that women had "no history," contributing to this broader project by cultivating a historical awareness that linked contemporary congresswomen to their predecessors in the women's movement a century earlier.

Ms. envisaged historical recovery as central to women's liberation. Although Farrell suggests that history held "little place in a monthly magazine" for fear of becoming too "'repetitive,'" the *Ms.* editorial team never considered women's history to be a superficial or passing interest.[29] Alongside the emerging feminist historians who were beginning to write women into the historical record, *Ms.* projected the simple yet radical assertion that women's history mattered.[30] Approximating *Women* and the "Archives" section of *Signs: Journal of Women in Culture and Society*, *Ms.* published historical literature and archival sources.[31] For example, the magazine ran an excerpt from the 1973 edition of Harriet Jacobs's harrowing slave narrative, *Incidents in the Life of a Slave Girl* (1861), reprinted when rediscovered.[32] Visual as much as textual, *Ms.* included rich historical imagery—photographs, sketches, and other memorabilia. To celebrate the 1976 bicentenary, for example, the magazine published the famous 1776 correspondence between Abigail Adams and President John Adams and a photographic review of revolutionary women. Yet, like its women's magazine competitors, *Ms.* made many of their features entertaining. One "Ms. Quiz" highlighted history centrally: of its thirty questions about women of European, African, Native American, and Jewish ancestry, across fields such as literature, sports, suffrage, politics, and aviation, seventeen addressed US women's history. "Who was the outspoken suffragist who did not change her name when she married Henry Blackwell?" it asked.[33]

Central to this feminist project was "Lost Women," a regular feature series that showcased biographies of "historically significant women," often within the magazine's first few pages.[34] Most subjects—millworker Harriet Robinson, transcendentalist Margaret Fuller, novelist and theorist Charlotte Perkins Gilman, abolitionists Harriet Tubman and Frances Wright, westerners Nellie Cashman and Annie Oakley, anarchist Emma Goldman, businesswoman Madam C. J. Walker, suffragist Adella Hunt Logan—were little known at the time. Indeed, the "Lost Women" series did important recovery work; it "exposed . . . the outrageous omissions of history as it was then taught in schools and universities."[35] Fittingly, *Ms.* recruited pioneer women's historian Gerda Lerner to create a "Lost Women" quiz for the magazine in September 1972.[36] History, specifically women's history, therefore became pedagogical—a consciousness-raising tool that offered a blueprint for political action.

Ms. made direct connections between these historical women and ongoing legislative campaigns, from sex discrimination to abortion rights. For example, a September 1972 feature article about Victoria Woodhull's 1872 presidential campaign chronicled the flamboyant trailblazing of the "most notorious woman in the country." Miriam Schneir evoked parallels between 1960s counterculture and the women's movement a century earlier by describing Woodhull as "a lifestyle revolutionary in the cause of female liberation." This article detailed Woodhull's pioneering analyses of sexuality, abortion, and labor, as well as her understanding that the vote was a necessary but partial provision toward political influence.[37] While this article made only the briefest mention of Chisholm, another feature article about Susan B. Anthony overlooked her 1872 presidential campaign completely. Describing Anthony's arrest and trial for illegally voting in Rochester, New York, during the 1872 presidential election, the implicit historical lesson was that women should cherish their right to vote.[38] A December 1972 photo-essay, "So You Think We've Got Troubles . . . ," answered this presentist question with the pointed yet playful publication of misogynistic historical ephemera: antisuffrage cartoons, postcards, and newspaper clippings.[39] Archival material such as this poignantly illustrated what *Ms.* perceived as the bend toward justice of women's history.

Ms. featured the nineteenth-century woman suffrage movement most prominently in its historical writing, creating "rhetorical ties" between suffrage-era feminism and the present to "reclaim feminist history and provide greater grounding for feminist ideas and beliefs."[40] This fascination coalesced around the lives and achievements of Elizabeth Cady Stanton and Susan B. Anthony, contributing to what historian Lisa Tetrault describes as the mythological status of Seneca Falls in US women's history. Stanton and Anthony established this metanarrative in the *History of Woman Suffrage*, co-edited with Matilda Joslyn Gage and Ida Husted Harper. Published between 1881 and 1922, the *History* strategically situated the 1848 Seneca Falls convention as the beginning of the women's rights movement and concentrated its six volumes around the efforts of its editors and their compatriots—at the expense of many other suffragists.[41] *Ms.* retold what had become a conventional narrative in "125 Years Later . . . What Do You Know about Seneca Falls?": Stanton and abolitionist Lucretia Mott, having met in London at the 1840 World's Anti-Slavery Convention, sat together in Upstate New York eight years later to discuss their grievances as women.[42] *Ms.* profiled Stanton and Anthony in "A Feminist Friendship," helping to secure this political and emotional partnership as sacrosanct.[43]

Ms. also skirted the space between historical nostalgia and the commercialization of the past. Its classifieds featured products, such as reproductions of the 1948 Seneca Falls centennial commemorative stamp; reprints of Stanton's *The Woman's Bible* (1899); artist SuZanne BentOn's necklace busts of Anthony; the "Susan B. Anthony Pendant Watch" from the Pilgrim Watch Co.; and the Susan B. Anthony Dollar Coin, minted between 1979 and 1981.[44] But the *Ms.* editorial team also began to shift its focus from editorializing to fundraising. The magazine asked readers to make "An Investment in History . . ." by donating an Anthony Dollar to the Women's Hall of Fame to upgrade historical displays and develop "a research library for and about women in Seneca

Falls—where the women's Declaration of Sentiments was signed in 1848."[45] This endeavor highlighted how staff began to extend their mission from reporting to historical preservation, an initiative spurred on by encounters at Seneca Falls. It was a shock to find Stanton's former home "neglected" and dress reformer Amelia Bloomer's home for sale.[46]

Women's history is far from neutral interpretive ground. This became especially clear when the *Ms.* editorial team encouraged readers to consider how suffrage history might inspire new insights and political approaches. However, these feature articles did not always examine the important lessons to be found in the campaign's failures as much as its final success, often neglecting to examine the tensions present among nineteenth-century reformers. Celebrating the Nineteenth Amendment without much of a sense of its checkered legacy allowed *Ms.* to position the predominantly white, middle-class, and elite suffragists' achievements as the central guide for women's political action. As a result, this historical analysis often glossed over women's differences and assumed a universalist perspective.[47] While *Ms.* did not wholly overlook women of color, it remained largely uncritical of the suffrage movement's leadership or the racism of luminaries such as Stanton and Anthony. For *Ms.* to uncritically embrace the commemoration—and gradually the commercialization—of a specific historical narrative was to offer its readership a greater focus on white American women, an omission that reflected its own elision of Shirley Chisholm.

Feminist Intellectuals as Political Experts

Going beyond recovery work, *Ms.* began to report on the development of feminist scholarship during the 1980s, seeing what Gerda Lerner described as scholars' challenge of the "androcentric assumptions" of traditional historical inquiry as important.[48] Much of this content appeared in the *Ms. Gazette,* "a 'tear-out' section printed on newsprint."[49] Its December 1979 report, "Women's History—the Uses of Our Pasts," recounted the ideas presented at the Summer Institute on Women's History at Sarah Lawrence College, New York. Although unusual for a popular magazine to consider such an academic event newsworthy, *Ms.* provided its readers with a sense of what it was like to be at this historic meeting of women's minds. Lerner herself, whose book *The Majority Finds Its Past: Placing Women in History* appeared that year, highlighted the histories of nineteenth-century women reformers: physician Elizabeth Blackwell, educators Mary Lyon and Catharine Beecher, social worker Jane Addams, suffragist Alice Paul, and antilynching campaigner Ida B. Wells-Barnett.[50] In the coming years, *Ms.* reported about Women's History Week, an initiative championed by the Summer Institute, as well as black history and black women's history. The *Ms. Gazette* also offered recommendations for how to assemble "A Do-It-Yourself Women's Studies Course."[51]

The *Ms.* editorial team regularly invited feminist historians as guest authors to share their insights, archival discoveries, and personal reflections, suggesting an ongoing affinity between the magazine and its academic counterparts. As a result, *Ms.* published cutting-edge theoretical and conceptual work while also discussing novelist Barbara Chase-Riboud's revelatory historical novel *Sally Hemings* (1979), which explored the enslaved woman's relationship with Thomas Jefferson.[52] The magazine also sought to demystify women working in the ivory tower by promoting books about historical method and publishing interviews with historians such as Lerner; Barbara Haber, who was curator of the Arthur and Elizabeth Schlesinger Library on the History of Women in America; and Bettye Collier-Thomas, director of the Bethune Museum and Archives, which housed the National Archives for Black Women's History.

By promoting new academic monographs through its book reviews, *Ms.* offered its readership not only an introduction to emerging scholarship but also a sense of the exhilaration that could be gleaned from new historical findings. Describing Lerner's *The Female Experience: An American Documentary* (1977) as "History You Can't Put Down," *Ms.* assured its readership that the book offered "exciting proof that women's history remains still a secret treasure trove."[53] Many of the academic monographs *Ms.* reviewed would emerge as influential in women's history and women's studies: Ann Douglass's *The Feminization of American Culture* (1977); Ellen Carol DuBois's *Feminism and Suffrage: The Emergence of an Independent Women's Movement in America, 1848–1869* (1978); Cherríe Moraga and Gloria Anzaldúa's *This Bridge Called My Back* (1981); Angela Davis's *Women, Race & Class* (1981); and Paula Giddings's *When and Where I Enter: The Impact of Black Women on Race and Sex in America* (1984).

In its second decade, *Ms.* played an important role in helping raise awareness about women's intellectual expertise. In September 1980, *Ms.* appointed a board of feminist scholars—a quarter of whom were historians—as advisors to the magazine. Its "12 Wise Women" were Catharine R. Stimpson, Mary Brown Parlee, Kathryn Kish Sklar, Janet Boles, Marysa Navarro, Dorothy Smith, Danielle Bazin, Patricia Albjerg Graham, Gaye Tuchman, Constance Carroll, Rayna Rapp, and Florence Howe.[54] *Ms.* also created its own forums on current affairs, actively seeking to spark political dialogues in a period where women remained peripheral to most Americans' conception of the public intellectual. Accordingly, the influence it sought in both the political and the intellectual arenas spoke to a broader feminist mission of effecting change across society.

One key initiative was a roundtable held in June 1981 to address the leading questions of the day: the New Right, feminist backlash, reproductive rights, women's labor, and the potential for cross-racial and cross-class political alliances. At the table, prominent feminist historians and women's studies professors Linda Gordon, Kathryn Kish Sklar, Mary Lyndon Shanley, and Elizabeth Higginbotham were joined by New York State legislator Karen Burstein. "Historically," Sklar maintained, "we see that feminist movements have a much better chance of gaining momentum in periods of radicalism, when women can find issues to use to form coalitions."[55] This kind of historical assessment was essential to discussions about how to regenerate feminist energy during the 1980s, a point not lost on the *Ms.* editorial team.

Realizations about how much feminist historians had achieved in recent years impelled *Ms.* to gradually move away from its project of historical recovery. Perhaps, as Steinem indicated in 1972, the consolidation of the women's movement did indeed come with a greater sense of women's past. To effect political change, *Ms.* envisaged feminist historians as public intellectuals and political experts whose knowledge was pertinent in reconstructing women's past, understanding women's present, and determining women's future.

Conclusion

No longer a for-profit magazine, *Ms.* continues to be published and to offer political commentary. "Women Who Know Their Place (in the House)," the winter 2019 edition proclaimed as it showcased the ninety-one women in Congress, making light of gains made during the 2018 midterms. This followed the magazine's long tradition of celebrating the achievements of women engaged in political action and electoral politics. After Congresswomen Shirley Chisholm and Sissy Farenthold graced its cover in 1973, the next two decades featured Congresswomen Bella Abzug, Helen Gahagan Douglas, Geraldine Ferraro, and Pat Schroeder. More recent cover people include Secretary Hillary Rodham Clinton, Green Party vice presidential candidate Winona LaDuke, President Barack Obama, Senator Wendy Davis, and Speaker Nancy Pelosi.

Ms. has offered its readership an unbroken vision of women's political engagement since its inception in 1972. It has openly supported women politicians and feminist legislation, commemorated suffragist foremothers, and advanced feminist historians as political experts. Although it muted the racial divisions of the nineteenth-century women's movement, it also regarded the Nineteenth Amendment as a milestone for all American women. In framing women's history as primarily a political story, *Ms.* Magazine boldly chose to treat its readers as political consumers. This coverage played a crucial role in shifting women's self-perception as possible political actors. Not only presenting women as having the potential to be political, the magazine showed, by recounting a collective history, that they already are.

Notes

1. Gloria Steinem, "Sisterhood," *Ms.* Preview Edition, Spring 1972 (Hillman Library, University of Pittsburgh).

2. Amy Erdman Farrell, *Yours in Sisterhood*: Ms. *Magazine and the Promise of Popular Feminism* (Chapel Hill: University of North Carolina Press, 1998), 60, 20–21.

3. Gloria Steinem, "Women Voters Can't Be Trusted," *Ms.*, July 1972.

4. "The Bulletin Board: Memo for Election Day," *Ms.*, November 1972; Virginia Kerr and Elen Sudow, "A Legislative Agenda for the 93rd Congress," *Ms.*, January 1973.

5. "Barbara Marcus, "The Year of the Women Candidates," *Ms.*, September 1972.

6. Barbara Winslow, *Shirley Chisholm: Catalyst for Change* (Boulder, CO: Westview Press, 2014), 90–93.

7. Gloria Steinem, "Coming of Age with McGovern: Notes from A Political Diary," *Ms.*, October 1972.

8. Gloria Steinem, "The Ticket That Might Have Been . . . President Chisholm," *Ms.*, January 1973.

9. Judith Nies, "The Abzug Campaign: A Lesson in Politics," *Ms.*, February 1973.

10. Judy Gurovitz, "Suffragists Still Going Strong," *Ms.*, July 1973.

11. Ann Scott, "The Equal Rights Amendment: What's in It for You?," *Ms.*, July 1972.

12. Mary Thom, "A New Lease on Life for the ERA? The Case for Extension," *Ms.*, May 1978.

13. Susan Ware, "The Book I Couldn't Write: Alice Paul and the Challenge of Feminist Biography," *Journal of Women's History* 24, no. 2 (2012): 14–15.

14. Robin Morgan, "Alice Paul: Mother of the ERA," *Ms.*, October 1977.

15. Kathleen Willert Peratis and Susan Deller Ross, "A Primer on the ERA: Back to Basics for This Year's Fight," *Ms.*, January 1977; Letty Cottin Pogrebin, "Hollywood Mobilises for the ERA," *Ms.*, June 1978.

16. "Relay for E.R.A.," 1977, National Archives, Records of the US House of Representatives.

17. "A Participant's Guide to Houston," *Ms.*, November 1977.

18. Alyssa A. Samek, "Mobility, Citizenship, and 'American Women on the Move' in the 1977 International Women's Year Torch Relay," *Quarterly Journal of Speech* 103, no. 3 (2017): 221.

19. Sharon Crozier-De Rosa and Vera Mackie, *Remembering Women's Activism* (Abingdon, Oxon, UK: Routledge, 2019), 52.

20. Lindsy Van Gelder, "Countdown to Houston: Memo for the First National Women's Convention," *Ms.*, November 1977; Farrell, *Yours in Sisterhood*, 50–53.

21. Gloria Steinem, "Five Reasons to Vote, Any One of Which Should Be Enough," *Ms.*, November 1982.

22. Mary Thom, "The All-Time Definitive Map of the Gender Gap," *Ms.*, July 1984.

23. Gloria Steinem, "How Women Live, Vote, Think . . . ," *Ms.*, July 1984.

24. Gloria Steinem, "Exclusive Louis Harris National Survey: How Women Live, Vote and Think," *Ms.*, July 1984.

25. Sheila Caudle, "Geraldine Ferraro: A Woman for This Political Season?," *Ms.*, July 1984.

26. Gloria Steinem, "The Ferraro Factor: What Difference Can One Woman Make?," *Ms.*, October 1984.

27. Judith M. Bennett, *History Matters: Patriarchy and the Challenge of Feminism* (Philadelphia: University of Pennsylvania Press, 2006), 1, 6–7.

28. Ellen Carol DuBois, "Struggling into Existence: The Feminism of Sarah and Angelina Grimké," *Women: A Journal of Liberation* 1, no. 2 (1970): 4–11; "Message to Future Generations from Elizabeth Cady Stanton and Susan B. Anthony (1881)," *Women: A Journal of Liberation* 1, no. 2 (1970): 16.

29. Farrell, *Yours in Sisterhood*, 123.

30. Sheila Tobias, "Finding Women's History," *Ms.*, November 1972.

31. *Ms.* published *Signs* advertisements after its 1975 launch; see *Ms.*, May 1975, 106.

32. Linda Brent, "Incidents in the Life of a Slave Girl," *Ms.*, August 1974.

33. "Everything You Always Wanted to Know about 'Herstory'—but Never Learned in School," *Ms.*, October 1976. Answer: Lucy Stone.

34. Farrell, *Yours in Sisterhood*, 60. For the longer tradition of women's history and female biography, see: Mary Spongberg, *Writing Women's History since the Renaissance* (Basingstoke, UK: Palgrave Macmillan, 2002), chap. 5.

35. Bennett, *History Matters*, 65, 7.

36. Gerda Lerner, "So You Think You Know Women's History," *Ms.*, September 1972.

37. Miriam Schneir, "The Woman Who Ran for President in 1872," *Ms.*, September 1972.

38. Sophy Burnham and Janet Knight, "The United States of America vs. Susan B. Anthony," *Ms.*, November 1972.

39. "So You Think We've Got Troubles . . . ," *Ms.*, December 1972.

40. Sarah T. Partlow-Lefevre, "Bridging the First and Second Waves: Rhetorical Constructions of First Wave Feminism in *Ms.* Magazine, 1972–1980," *Relevant Rhetoric* 3 (2012): 2.

41. Lisa Tetrault, *The Myth of Seneca Falls: Memory and the Women's Suffrage Movement, 1848–1898* (Chapel Hill: University of North Carolina Press, 2014).

42. Anne Grant, "125 Years Later . . . What Do You Know about Seneca Falls?" *Ms.*, July 1973.

43. Alice S. Rossi, "A Feminist Friendship," *Ms.*, January 1974.

44. "1948 Stamp Reproduction: Stanton, Catt, Mott," *Ms.*, November 1975; "The Woman's Bible," *Ms.*, January 1976; SuZanne BentOn, "Susan B. Anthony," *Ms.*, September 1975; "The Golden 'Susan' Limited Edition," *Ms.*, October 1979; "Susan B. Anthony Pendant Watch," *Ms.*, July 1980.

45. Jane Bosveld, "An Investment in History . . ." *Ms. Gazette*, September 1979.

46. Barbara Moynehan, "Seneca Falls Rises: From Laundromat to Women's Rights National Park," *Ms. Gazette*, January 1980.

47. Bennett, *History Matters*, 65.

48. Gerda Lerner, *The Majority Finds Its Past: Placing Women in History* (New York: Oxford University Press, 1979), xiv.

49. Farrell, *Yours in Sisterhood*, 60.

50. Gerda Lerner, "Women's History—the Uses of Our Pasts: Lost from the 'Official' Record," *Ms. Gazette*, December 1979.

51. Ellen Sweet, "A Do-It-Yourself Women's Studies Course," *Ms. Gazette*, September 1980.

52. Susan McHenry, "Reading: 'Sally Hemings': A Key to Our National Identity," *Ms.*, October 1980.

53. Eve Merriam, "History You Can't Put Down," *Ms.*, May 1977.

54. Martha Nelson, "12 Wise Women: The Scholars Who Will Be Advising the New *Ms.*," Campus Special, *Ms.*, September 1980.

55. Lisa Cronin Wohl, "A *Ms.* Roundtable: Holding Our Own against a Conservative Tide," *Ms.*, June 1981.

Congresswoman Louise Day Hicks, ca. 1969. Photograph courtesy Library of Congress.

CHAPTER 11

"You Know Where I Stand"

Louise Day Hicks, and the Politics of Race, Class, and Gender, 1963–1975

KATHLEEN BANKS NUTTER

"Y OU KNOW WHERE I Stand" was the campaign slogan Louise Day Hicks used in her unsuccessful 1967 attempt to become the first female mayor of Boston. Beginning in the mid-1960s, for more than a decade, Hicks was the national "face of anti-busing" for her strident opposition to the desegregation of the Boston school system. Hicks was the chair of the Boston School Committee in the mid-1960s, as well as a member of the Boston City Council, of which she would be the first woman elected president in 1976, and even served one term in Congress (1971–1973). She left a complicated legacy of public service during one of the city's most tumultuous times. Her political career—its successes and eventual collapse by the end of the 1970s—became inextricably intertwined with the ultimately unsuccessful efforts to desegregate the Boston city schools. The public response to her death in 2003 only highlighted what Hicks achieved in life: the ability to project a political stance that made her the darling of some and an object of derision to others.

Recent scholarship on the rise of modern American conservatism has increasingly acknowledged the important role women have played in this movement, especially in terms of race. According to Elizabeth Gillespie McRae, "White women were the mass in massive resistance [to racial equality]."[1] While McRae's focus is on the American South through an examination of the activism of four women opposed to racial integration, her overarching arguments also apply to the North and certainly to Louise Day Hicks. McRae argues that "suffrage moved white women undeniably into electoral politics where they could use 'the weight of their votes' to shape the worlds in which they lived. . . . Some even ran for office."[2] And indeed Hicks did run, several times, not always successfully. As Matthew F. Delmot notes in *Why Busing Failed*, "Louise Day Hicks made opposition to 'busing' a center piece of her campaigns," rendering her "as a national icon of white resistance to civil rights."[3] In the 1970s, neoconservatives, especially women acting within their maternalistic duties, would rally around issues introduced by modern feminists, such as the Equal Rights Amendment and abortion rights, denouncing them as threats to the nuclear family. But, twenty years earlier, with the *Brown* decision in 1954 making segregated schools unconstitutional, what initially drew white conservative women into the movement was their maternal duty to protect their children against what they saw as the dangers of school integration through busing, in the North as well as in the South.[4]

For more than a decade, Hicks successfully used maternalist language to argue against school desegregation and was adept at pulling many other "concerned mothers" and their male companions into this racially charged debate. Even before the turn to so-called family values in the 1970s, especially in light of the growing abortion rights movement, and along with the impact of that decade's economic decline, many white working-class northerners would move away from the Democratic Party, which would pave the way for Republican Ronald Reagan's election as president in 1980. Hicks's political career was part of that trajectory.

Through a close examination of Hicks's campaigns, particularly her 1967 mayoral campaign, and the varied reactions to them, the nascent strands of a growing neoconservative movement in America are thus evident. Many white working-class Bostonians saw the efforts to desegregate the Boston schools as yet another example of liberal white middle-class politicians responding to the special interests of a few. But in doing so, they racialized their growing discontent and their increasing disconnect from government. Focusing on Hicks's political career in the city known as "The Cradle of Liberty" highlights not only the impact of white racism on this budding conservative movement but also the centrality of women's highly racialized white maternalism within that movement.

Anna Louise Day was born on October 16, 1916, in the South Boston manse that she would die in eighty-seven years later.[5] Her mother, Anna McCarron, who had been a fashion model, died when Louise was a teenager. She became even closer to her father, William J. Day, a wealthy and respected attorney, banker, and judge as well as a leading political force in this Irish American enclave. After graduating from Wheelock College and teaching first grade for a couple of years, the young woman known by her middle name of Louise worked in her father's law office until 1942 when she married John E. Hicks, a former ice skating champion who would later work as an engineer. They would have two sons, John Jr., who would disappear under "mysterious circumstances" likely related to mob violence in 1978, and William D. Hicks, now in his seventies, who manages the real estate holdings amassed by the family over the years.[6]

In 1950, Louise Day Hicks's father died with his only daughter, who felt she had now lost her "first and only hero," at his side. Hicks then decided, as she would later claim, to honor his memory by going to law school herself, though she had actually started at Boston College Law School a year or so before his death, attending sporadically until just after her father died. But then, after earning an additional education degree from Boston University, she finally entered BU's law school in the fall of 1952 as a full-time student—a bold move for a married thirty-six-year-old woman with children in the 1950s.

One of only nine women in the class of 1955, Hicks would have certainly been seen as an oddity by most of the other 211 male members of her law school cohort. Nor had she necessarily been groomed for this seemingly unconventional path. As one old friend would later say, "Louise loved being Judge Day's daughter. Growing up in South Boston, she'd been a princess." But when her oldest brother died in his late twenties and neither of her two surviving brothers showed much interest or ambition, Hicks, according to her friend, "decided the torch had been passed to her."[7] In his journalistic, and still highly regarded, account of the efforts to desegregate the Boston school system, J. Anthony Lukas says that Hicks's entry into Boston University Law School's class of 1955 was "extraordinary," especially "for a South Boston woman, steeped in the Irish mystique of home and family."[8] Hicks, the pious Catholic, Irish American "princess" and daughter of a judge, later emphasized that she spent most of her time in law school in the company of two other "female outcasts," one Jewish, the other African American.

Upon her graduation in 1955, Hicks opened a law firm with her brother, specializing in real estate transactions. She entered politics in 1961, running for the Boston School Committee as "the only mother on the ballot," though at the time her two teenaged sons attended parochial, not public, school and she herself was not a "stay-at-home mom" but a practicing attorney. She nonetheless established herself as the caring matriarch of Boston's public school children from the beginning of her political career. Hicks officially entered the Boston political scene at a somewhat tumultuous time. After a decade of urban renewal as part of the effort to create a "New Boston," white working-class neighborhoods such as the West End, the South End, and Charlestown felt under attack. Simultaneously, the burgeoning modern civil rights movement was moving North and the growing African American community, clustered primarily in Boston's Roxbury section and parts of Dorchester, was finding its voice. The Boston National Association for the Advancement of Colored People (NAACP) and the local chapter of the Congress of Racial Equality (CORE) teamed up with a growing number of local African American activists to address very real concerns regarding inadequate housing, employment discrimination, and the increasingly poor conditions African American public school students faced in Boston.[9]

Elected "Madam Chairman" in January 1963, Hicks led the fight against the efforts of local black community activists who began pushing the all-white Boston School Committee to address the de facto segregation within the city's schools.[10] While an estimated three hundred African Americans protested outside of City Hall, several members of the Boston NAACP, including the formidable Ruth Batson, met inside with the Boston School Committee on June 11, 1963. The initial exchange, as reported in the official minutes, was relatively polite. After Batson presented the NAACP's concerns regarding what they saw as the harmful effects of de facto segregation owing to residential racial patterns in Boston, Hicks tried to wrap up this segment of the committee's meeting by assuring Batson and her fellow NAACP members, "I feel that the Committee will meet with the leaders of your group and with the [school] administration to see if we can't straighten out those problems immediately." Batson replied, "I do want to thank you for your very cordial attention this evening, and I would like to ask you if you would do more than just say that we will meet. I would like to say that we will meet." Tersely, Hicks ended the discussion, repeating, "We will meet."[11]

Four days later, they did meet again. While the School Committee did vote to organize a "bi-racial Community Committee," half of whom were local NAACP members, the majority of Boston's African Americans still felt that not enough was being done to seriously address their demands. Black community activists and their white allies called for a one day "Stay Out for Freedom" action for June 16, 1963.[12] Almost eight thousand African American junior and senior high school students went instead to the multiple Freedom Schools organized for the day in the predominately black neighborhoods of Roxbury and Dorchester. While NAACP activist Ruth Batson deemed "Stay Out for Freedom Day" to be a success, the Boston School Committee, led by Hicks, felt otherwise.[13] The committee refused to admit that the Boston school system was either segregated or inferior, citing instead what they saw as voluntary residential patterns that shaped the racial composition of the city's schools rather than the long-established practice of redlining, buoyed by persistent racism.[14]

During the 1960s and into the 1970s, Hicks's electoral victories increased as she maintained her stand. Despite the hope of Boston's African American community of a different outcome, in 1963 Louise Day Hicks was reelected to the School Committee with a whopping 74 percent of the votes cast. She was again the top vote getter in her

1965 reelection to the committee. In the wake of what the *New York Times* referred to as "her smashing reelection as chairman of the Boston School Committee," Hicks was immediately seen "as a leading Boston mayoral candidate in 1967."[15]

Given the almost complete lack of personal papers currently available, the biographer of Louise Day Hicks must rely on the public record, which given the national attention even the possibility of her mayoral campaign generated, is ample if often hyperbolic. The title of a profile by Ira Mothner in *Look* in early 1966 set the tone: "Boston's Louise Day Hicks: Storm Center of the Busing Battle."[16] According to Mothner, Hicks, while "a big woman, her voice is small, almost piping, and it starts to break when she talks about 'civil rights leaders using our children, using our schools.'" Mothner quotes her as saying, "'If mothers didn't have me. . . .' she says, shaking her head slowly and the unspoken alternatives are clear." Mothner concludes: "Fear is her vehicle, but she didn't create it. It is a mindless panic, freshly felt in the North, and not only in Boston."[17] Her maternalistic duty was clear: maintain de facto segregation in the Boston public schools regardless of what the press might say about her or her supporters.

A few months later, author Peggy Lamson profiled Hicks in the *Atlantic Monthly*. Lamson asked "this shrewd, tough-minded, stubborn, and often likable woman" if she would be running as mayor of Boston in 1967. "When asked to comment on this possibility, Mrs. Hicks smiled and said, 'Well, if that Mrs. Gandhi can be prime minister, I don't see why a woman can't be mayor.'" Lamson went on to pose the question, "What about the men? Would they vote for her?" Hicks replied, "with a laugh, 'I'm very big with the longshoremen.'"[18] This exchange once again demonstrates Hicks's contradictory relationship with the evolving notions of women as public figures in the 1960s. Could a woman get involved in politics for reasons other than her maternalistic duties? For Hicks, it was both yes and no, but more often than not, she continued to rely on her identity as a mother to advance her political ambitions.

By early 1967, the question of whether Hicks would indeed run for mayor was getting even more press. The *Boston Herald* was relatively neutral in its reporting of a small fire that broke out at Hicks's South Boston home after a St. Patrick's Day parade party. Under the headline "A Blaze of Glory for Mrs. Hicks," the *Herald* noted that "the most notable thing Mrs. Hicks did during the evening was not to announce for Mayor." Speculation had been that Hicks would use the occasion of her party following the annual South Boston parade, in which she rode at the head, to announce her candidacy. But, according to the *Herald*, "she made it a non-occasion by stating that she would make an announcement May 1."[19]

On the appointed day, Hicks was quoted in the far less supportive *Boston Globe* as saying, "My chapeau . . . is in the ring."[20] The *Globe* would grow increasingly critical of Hicks as the campaign continued, particularly after the September primary. It was a crowded field throughout, with ten candidates, including two Republicans, on the open primary ballot. When Hicks came out on top with just over 28 percent of the total votes cast, even the *Globe* had to concede she "ran a commanding first."[21] A runoff was set for November 7, pitting Hicks against Kevin White, the secretary of the commonwealth, who came in a relatively distant second (Hicks: 43,719; White: 30,497). White, son and son-in-law of prominent Boston Democrats, was a rising politician in his own right, having first won election in 1960, when he was only thirty-one years old, as secretary of the commonwealth.[22] After Hicks's stunning win in the mayoral primary that September, the *Globe*'s coverage of her grew more and more harsh, as did the national coverage.

Time's piece entitled "Southies' Comfort," published a few days after the primary, began with: "Louise Day Hicks is a bulky grandmother who would not stand out in a supermarket crowd. Yet she stood out so far from nine male candidates in Boston's nonpartisan primary last week that she may well become the city's next mayor." The article went on to note that Hicks's rise to fame is both about class and race. "Mrs. Hicks collected 28.1% of last week's vote (compared to White's 19.8%), principally from the large blue-collar and lower-middle-class groups who feel bypassed by federal and city welfare programs and who support her unsuccessful attempts to block measures promoting public-school integration."[23] Any discussion of Hicks in the press was in very gendered terms—as it is unlikely that any of the male candidates would have been described as stout grandfathers.

Hicks embraced her maternalistic image as a justification for opposing desegregation. Writing in the *Reporter*, Martin Nolan likened Hicks to the well-known vitriolic supporter of racial segregation, Alabama governor George Wallace. Nolan pointed out that "like George Wallace of Alabama, she relies on an easily decipherable code. 'You know where I stand,' she tells crowds and they all cheer."[24] According to the *New York Times*, in a lengthy piece on Hicks in its *Sunday Magazine*, all this press "focused on her campaign because of one issue—her unyielding opposition to the desegregation of Boston's schools."[25] For Hicks, it was her duty as a mother and grandmother that justified that opposition, not just for her children but as she often said for "all the boys and girls in Boston."

Perhaps the most scathing coverage she received was the 1967 cover story in *Newsweek*, entitled "Backlash in Boston," that appeared on the eve of the Boston mayoral election. *Newsweek* described Hicks at a South Boston campaign rally by noting: "Her formidable 5 feet 10 inches and 175-odd pounds encased in a shimmering kelly-green suit, she planted herself stoutly before the microphone and spoke up in an unexpectedly small voice." *Newsweek* quoted her as saying, "'I seek this office to bring about change. . . . The greatest issue of all is that we feel alienated. No one in City Hall listens to us.'" According to *Newsweek*, "with those high-pitched words, the backlash had come of age." The article went on to describe her supporters as "a comic-strip gallery of tipplers and brawlers and their tinseled, overdressed dolls" who obviously adored *their* Louise. This fact puzzled many, including *Newsweek*, which could only credit such adoration to the parochial and racist nature of the audience.[26] Several pages later, after discussing her personal background, her political rise based on her stance against integration, and the ongoing and egregious de facto segregation of Boston's schools, *Newsweek* returned to critiquing Hicks's physical presence and appeal: "As a vigorous campaigner for high office, Louise has had no apparent difficulty overcoming the visible deficiencies of her appearance. She is nobody's Shirley Temple Black. The powdered, puffy face squared off by a beauty-parlor coif seems to sag from the eyes down, giving her a kind of St. Bernard's mournfulness. But to her more zealous supporters, her face shines with the beauty of truth and courage."[27]

Kevin White, her opponent and the eventual victor, who would serve as mayor of Boston for the next fifteen years, was described much more succinctly, and flatteringly, as an "amiable, craggily handsome Irishman of 38."[28] While being a concerned mother was socially acceptable, being female and opposed to desegregation were not qualities generally associated with the mainstream liberal, but still male-dominated, politics of the 1960s.

On November 6, the day before the mayoral election, the *Globe* broke its seventy-one year tradition of not endorsing candidates by backing Kevin White for mayor. For the *Globe*, the choice was quite stark. "Above all, Mr. White has a responsible and responsive position on civil rights. Mrs. Hicks, in our opinion, does not."[29] The next day, White would beat Hicks by more than twelve thousand votes out of the just over one hundred ninety thousand cast. Two weeks later, after noting the small margin of victory in the Boston mayoral race, the *Nation* editorialized: "The crowning irony of this election is that the bigoted Mrs. Hicks may have been defeated only by the measure of another form of bigotry: that which any woman must overcome when competing against a man for high office. Given Boston's particular ethnic character, the woman's-place-is-in-the-home vote is a considerable factor."[30] For her part, Louise Day Hicks did not see her gender as the reason for her narrow defeat in the mayor's race. The *Boston Globe* reported her saying, "Malicious rumors that my election would bring violence in the neighborhood . . . were circulated through Roxbury Negro districts, . . . turning those areas almost unanimously against [me]."[31] Indeed, voters in Boston, regardless of their race, class, or gender, knew where Louise Day Hicks stood regarding the desegregation of the Boston public school system. She lost not because she was a woman but because Boston's African American voters, along with more liberal white Bostonians, rallied against her. Nonetheless, her stance against integration would remain the driving force of her political career.

In 1968, there were briefly heard rumors that Hicks was being considered as George Wallace's running mate in his third party bid for that year's presidential campaign. Both Hicks and Wallace denied any such consideration, but it says much about the public perception of Hicks as a strident segregationist.[32] Nonetheless, her political success still was most easily achieved on the local level where she continued to be a top vote getter in her elections to the Boston City Council in 1969, 1973, and 1975; in 1976, Hicks would be elected by her fellow members as president of the City Council, the first woman to hold the office. In a crowded field of twelve, she won the 1970 Democratic primary race for the Ninth Congressional District and, as the Democratic candidate, easily went on to win in the general election. Serving only one term in Congress, Hicks supported the Equal Rights Amendment while proposing, unsuccessfully, an antibusing amendment at the same time.[33] While it may be difficult for us in hindsight to understand how one could support the Equal Rights Amendment and all it implied while at the same time opposing the integration of the nation's public schools, in Hicks's mind supporting equality for women in 1970 was about equal pay and did not necessarily lead to believing in full equality for all in terms of both gender and race.[34]

While serving her district in Congress, Hicks made a second run for mayor of Boston in 1971. This time the incumbent, Kevin White, easily beat his still controversial opponent. As historian Mark Robert Schneider deduced, "The fact that a congresswoman was running for mayor suggested that Hicks was not happy in Washington."[35] Hicks's home was in South Boston, and her identity as a person and a politician was inextricably bound to the neighborhood. A year later, she lost her reelection to Congress and was able to return home to much more familiar turf. In 1973, she was enthusiastically reelected to the Boston City Council, just in time for the final showdown in the effort to desegregate the Boston public schools.

In 1965, after a white Unitarian minister from Boston, James Reeb, was beaten to death by white southern segregationists during the historic

March to Selma, a stunned Massachusetts state legislature passed the Racial Imbalance Act, which sought to impose sanctions, including the loss of state funding, on any city in which there were individual schools with a student body more than 50 percent nonwhite.[36] That fall, Louise Day Hicks was resoundingly reelected to the Boston School Committee, which aggressively refused to enforce this new law, despite the loss of millions of dollars in much-needed state aid for education, until the city was ordered to do so by a federal district court judge in June 1974.

In his June 1974 decision, Judge W. Arthur Garrity not only ordered that the schools be desegregated by busing students, primarily between the all-black neighborhood of Roxbury and white South Boston, but that the process begin with the next school year, scheduled to commence in less than three months. As school and city officials scrambled to, literally, set the wheels in motion, and the black community organized to facilitate the transition, many in Boston's white community, especially the economically depressed neighborhood of South Boston, organized in opposition. Seeing this as a liberal, middle-class attack on the sanctity of their turf and their rights as parents, many working-class white Bostonians saw themselves as victims and their children as pawns. In this spirit, ROAR (Restore Our Alienated Rights) had been formed a few months before Garrity's June 1974 order.

Initially led by Hicks, who by this time was a Boston City Councilor, ROAR would at first be a rather loose, semisecret organization of both men and women opposed to "forced" busing.[37] They were inspired in part by the actions of those who brought revolutionary politics to the streets of colonial Boston in the 1770s and now, two centuries later, were willing to take to the streets to make their grievances heard. Over the next two years, ROAR would establish a more formal organizational structure and even attempt to build a national movement. But by 1976, it was divided by factional in-fighting.[38] Through it all, women—deploying maternalist ideology—played an active role as the majority of rank-and-file members of ROAR.[39]

When busing began in September 1974, two years of racial violence followed, tearing the city of Boston apart. Louise Day Hicks emerged, in the words of historian Ronald Formisano, as the "Mother Superior" of antibusing politics in Boston.[40] In reality, before the end of 1974, Hicks seemed to be losing control of the movement she had helped create. New, more virulently racist voices were drowning out her pleas for nonviolence. While Hicks won reelection to the city council in 1975, and was elected by her fellow councilors as the first female president of that body, she lost her seat in 1977 and never won another election. This once top vote getter seemed to have lost her base as Bostonians soured on the increasing violence and political strife paralyzing the city.

Hicks would always be remembered as the face of busing opposition in Boston. But who was she? A tall woman known for her flowery hats and her soft voice in which she often expressed concern for all "the boys and girls" in Boston's school system, Hicks had as School Committee chair steadfastly refused to implement the Racial Imbalance Act throughout the 1960s. Then, as a city council member in 1974, the fifty-eight-year-old grandmother maintained her polite but determined stance against desegregation and was a cofounder of ROAR, the leading antibusing organization in Boston. Dismissed by many, then and since, as a political opportunist who was merely pandering to the white racism of her South Boston constituency, Hicks and her stance were more complicated than that. Her political rise and eventual fall were very much a part of an increasingly pervasive trend toward white racist neoconservative politics, often shrouded in maternalistic terms that has ebbed and flowed in America over the last few decades. Despite a recent two-term president who was the first African American elected to the White House, race continues to be a divisive factor in the United States. A better understanding of historical racism, along with the complicated intertwining of class and gender, can only help eradicate it in the future.

Notes

1. Elizabeth Gillespie McRae, *Mothers of Massive Resistance: White Women and the Politics of White Supremacy* (New York: Oxford University Press, 2018), 3.
2. McRae, *Mothers of Massive Resistance*, 7.

3. Matthew F. Delmont, *Why Busing Failed: Race, Media, and the National Resistance to School Desegregation* (Oakland: University of California Press, 2016), 3, 16.

4. In addition to Delmont, for yet another most useful account of civil rights activism, including efforts to desegregate public schools in the North in the post–World War II era, see Thomas J. Sugrue, *Sweet Land of Liberty: The Forgotten Struggle for Civil Rights in the North* (New York: Random House, 2008).

5. Mark Feeney, "Louise Day Hicks, icon of tumult, dies," *Boston Globe*, Octobert 22, 2003, ProQuest Historical Newspapers.

6. Commonwealth of Massachusetts, the Trial Court, Probate and Family Court Department, Suffolk, ss, docket no. 01-P-0567, bk: 36679, pg. 107, retrieved March 5, 2008, http://www.masslandrecords.com/malr/controller?commandflag=searchByNameID&optflag=ImageSearchCommand&county=ma025&userid=null&userCategory=7&filename=&server=&namespace=&filePath=&instrumentnumber=35767&docId=5056811&ptrno=5056811&officeid=70&zoomprop=100&year=2005&convtype=2&volume=36679&volpage=107.

7. As quoted in J. Anthony Lukas, *Common Ground: A Turbulent Decade in the Lives of Three American Families* (New York: Vintage Books, 1986), 118.

8. Lukas, *Common Ground*, 119.

9. Jim Vrabel, *A People's History of the New Boston* (Amherst: University of Massachusetts Press, 2014), 41–43; see also Thomas H. O'Connor, *The Boston Irish: A Political History* (Boston: Back Bay Books, 1995), 241–242.

10. The classic scholarly examination of the Boston "busing crisis" remains Ronald P. Formisano, *Boston against Busing: Race, Class, and Ethnicity in the 1960s and 1970s* (Chapel Hill: University of North Carolina, 1991); see also Thomas M. Begley, "The Organization of Anti-busing Protest in Boston, 1973–1976" (PhD diss., Cornell University, 1981), and Jack Tager, *Boston Riots: Three Centuries of Social Violence* (Boston: Northeastern University Press, 2001), chaps. 9 and 10. Journalistic accounts abound as well; here, the standard-bearer is Lukas, *Common Ground*; see also Jon Hillson, *The Battle of Boston: Busing and the Struggle for School Desegregation* (New York: Pathfinder Press, 1977); Alan Lupo, *Liberty's Chosen Home: The Politics of Violence in Boston* (Boston: Beacon Press, 1988, first published 1977). Two memoirs have also enriched my understanding of this time and place: Michael Patrick MacDonald's haunting account of growing up in South Boston, *All Souls: A Family Story from Southie* (Boston: Beacon Press, 1999) and Ione Malloy, *Southie Won't Go: A Teacher's Diary of the Desegregation of South Boston High School* (Urbana: University of Illinois Press, 1986).

11. School Committee Secretary Desegregation Files, page 122, folder 1, box 1, City of Boston Archives and Records Center, West Roxbury, MA.

12. Vrabel, *A People's History*, 53.

13. Delmont, *Why Busing Failed*, 80.

14. See, for example, Richard Rothstein, *The Color of Law: A Forgotten History of How Our Government Segregated America* (New York: Liveright, 2018).

15. "Mrs. Hicks in Spotlight," *New York Times*, November 4, 1965, 55, ProQuest Historical Newspapers.

16. Ira Mothner, "Boston's Louise Day Hicks: Storm Center of the Busing Battle," *Look*, June 22, 1966, 72.

17. Mothner, "Boston's Louise Day Hicks," 72.

18. Peggy Lamson, "The White Northerner's Choice," *Atlantic Monthly* 217, no. 6 (June 1966), 62.

19. "A Blaze of Glory for Mrs. Hicks," *Boston Herald*, March 18, 1967, 1, 5.

20. "Louise Hicks in Mayor Race," *Boston Globe*, May 2, 1967, 1, ProQuest Historical Newspapers.

21. "Sears Beats Logue . . . ," *Boston Globe*, September 27, 1967, 1, ProQuest Historical Newspapers.

22. For an interesting discussion of White's sixteen years (1968–1984) as mayor of Boston, see George V. Higgins, *Style versus Substance: Boston, Kevin White and the Politics of Illusion* (New York: Macmillan, 1983).

23. "Southies' Comfort," *Time*, October 6, 1967.

24. Martin Nolan, "Louise Day Hicks Gets Out the Vote," *The Reporter*, October 19, 1967, 22.

25. Berkeley Rice, "BOSTON: 'I am a symbol of resistance'—Hicks," *New York Times Sunday Magazine*, November 5, 1967, 16, ProQuest Historical Newspapers.

26. "Backlash in Boston—and across the U.S.," *Newsweek*, 70, November 6, 1967, 29.

27. "Backlash in Boston," 33.

28. "Backlash in Boston," 34.

29. *Boston Globe*, November 6, 1967, 16, ProQuest Historical Newspapers.

30. "Editorials—Tuesday's News," *The Nation*, November 20, 1967, 515.

31. "Mrs. Hicks Analyzes Her Defeat," *Boston Globe*, November 14, 1967, 2, ProQuest Historical Newspapers.

32. "Mrs. Hicks Denies Report," *New York Times*, September 8, 1968, 41, ProQuest Historical Newspapers.

33. Joan Kuriansky, *Louise Day Hicks, Democratic Representative from Massachusetts* (Ralph Nadar Congress Project, 1972), 18.

34. For a nuanced discussion of the evolution of conservative women's political thought as increasingly shaped by "family values," see Stacie Taranto, *Kitchen Table Politics: Conservative Women and Family Values in New York* (Philadelphia: University of Pennsylvania Press, 2017).

35. Mark Robert Schneider, *Joe Moakley's Journey from South Boston to El Salvador* (Boston: Northeastern University Press, 2013), 69.

36. Formisano, *Boston against Busing*, 35–36.

37. Hillson, *The Battle of Boston*, 29.

38. Tager, *Boston Riots*, 219. ROAR would hold its first "national" convention—in Boston, of course—in May of 1975. See convention pamphlet, Fran Johnnene Papers, City of Boston Archives and Records Management, West Roxbury, MA.

39. Kathleen Banks Nutter, "'Militant Mothers': Boston, Busing, and the Bicentennial of 1976," *Historical Journal of Massachusetts* 38, no. 2 (Fall 2010): 52–75.

40. Formisano, *Boston Against Busing*, 2.

After her historic win in 1968 as the first African American woman elected to Congress, Shirley Chisholm greets constituents in her Bedford-Stuyvesant, Brooklyn, neighborhood. John Duricka/AP Photo.

CHAPTER 12

On the Shirley Chisholm Trail

The Legacy of Suffrage and Citizenship Engagement

BARBARA WINSLOW

WHILE CAMPAIGNING FOR the Democratic Party nomination for the US presidency in 1972, Shirley Chisholm's stump speech demonstrated her awareness of her place in history: that African American women had always been central in the struggle for equality. Chisholm always pointed out that "it took a little black woman, Harriet Tubman, to lead three hundred of her women out of slavery. . . . It may take another little black woman to bring us together in these troubled times of war and worry."[1]

Chisholm, daughter of working-class Caribbean immigrants, was born in 1924, in Brooklyn, New York. In 1968, she was the first African American woman elected to Congress. Four years later she ran for the Democratic Party nomination for the US presidency. Her audacious campaign came at a time when American women were not on equal grounds with men, and most African American women were domestic workers, nurses, or teachers. Her youthful experiences in Barbados, and her life in Brooklyn, shaped her racial, gender, and political consciousness. Her courageous run for the presidency opened the country's eyes to the possibility that women or people of color could be political leaders—even president of the United States. Chisholm's activism was part of the long arc of African American women such as Sojourner Truth, Harriet Tubman, Mary Church Terrell, Ida B. Wells-Barnett, and Nannie Helen Burroughs who fought for women's suffrage before and after the Nineteenth Amendment was ratified.

Women's campaign for suffrage was part of centuries of struggle for full citizenship rights regardless of class, race, gender, religion, ethnicity, employment, address, age, or citizenship status. Recent historians have challenged the long-standing narrative that argued that the struggle for women's suffrage began with the Seneca Falls Convention of 1848 and ended with the passage of the Nineteenth Amendment to the Constitution.[2] The Fourteenth (1868) and Fifteenth (1870) Amendments to the US Constitution defined citizenship as male, giving African American men the right to vote. After 1880, the Jim Crow laws in the South disenfranchised the overwhelming majority of black men. The Nineteenth Amendment constitutionally enfranchised women, but the existing Jim Crow legislation in the South disenfranchised African American women and men. The 1965 Voting Rights Act all but wiped out southern voter suppression. Further amendments extended the franchise.

The Great Migration that relocated more than six million African Americans from the rural South and the Caribbean to the cities of the North, Midwest, and West from about 1916 to 1970 transformed suffrage struggles. African American population growth, political upheaval, and institution building marked this period. The Urban League, the Association for the Protection of Colored Women, and the National Association for the Advancement of Colored People (1909) were formed. Along with a revitalized Brooklyn Negro YMCA and YWCA, these organizations were the backbone of black institutional life in Brooklyn, enabling the black population to participate in a wide range of social, cultural, political, and religious activities. These organizations and institutions served the black community until the 1960s when they were replaced by new government antipoverty agencies as well as the more radical Black Power organizations. Black women were the backbone of all these organizations.

Barbados and Brooklyn

Although Chisholm was born in Brooklyn in 1924, her early years were formed by her experience growing up in Barbados in the care of her grandmother and aunt. Her seven years in Barbados shaped her political, racial, and gender consciousness. Barbados, with a majority black population, was dominated by white British rule. But in Barbados, Shirley had daily role models—the black teachers, police officers, tradespeople, ministers, newspaper editors, even politicians who looked like her and her family. Her stay in Barbados coincided with the beginning of anticolonial, socialist, feminist, and trade union struggles. Living through these early years of the struggle for modern Barbadian independence, no doubt, gave her an understanding of the need to stand up and fight for one's principles, one's self-respect, as well as independence from oppressive gendered and racially unjust relationships—whether personal or imbedded in economic or social relationships.

Chisholm returned to Brooklyn in 1933 with little memory of her birthplace or urban politics dominated by hierarchies of class, ethnicity, gender, and race. Family influences and the larger Brooklyn community shaped Chisholm's politics. African American women in the North did not face the same hurdles as their sisters in the Jim Crow South, but the persistence of gendered racism in all ways of life made it difficult for women to find meaningful employment, decent housing, fresh food, police and firefighting protection and to participate fully in city and state politics. As a young girl in Brooklyn, Chisholm experienced racial slurs for the first time. New York City schools were as segregated as any in the South. Chisholm never had an African American teacher, or saw an African American police officer, bus driver, newspaper reporter, veterinarian, as she had in Barbados. While African American women, her grandmother and aunt in Barbados, her stern but loving mother in Brooklyn, were strong role models, she idolized her father, Charles St. Hill. A race conscious New Deal Democrat, he taught Chisholm about unionism, Marcus Garvey, anti-imperialism, and the importance of political engagement. He took Chisholm to black nationalist rallies. In addition, he was adamant that Chisholm read, study, and do well in school. After 1920, seventy-five thousand African American women were enfranchised in New York City alone. Chisholm, like the hundreds of thousands of other black women, engaged in a wide range of political activities, including registering people to vote; joining political, religious, immigrant, community, and school clubs and associations;

supporting candidates for political office; and lobbying municipal, state, and federal officials. Eventually, she became a candidate for the state legislature, US Congress, and even the presidency in 1972.[3]

Chisholm soon immersed herself in the struggle for greater black representation in New York City that began in earnest in the mid-1950s. For all its liberal veneer, New York was not at all progressive regarding race. In fact, New York City was as racially segregated as Birmingham, Alabama, not legally but structurally. The city's major institutions, schools, and police, fire, transit, and sanitation workforces were administered by white people and employed very few people of color. Racist practices such as redlining and restrictive covenants in the housing industry prevented African Americans from moving into white neighborhoods. African Americans in New York City suffered all the injustices of racism—de facto segregation, inadequate housing, and lack of police protection, social services, access to jobs, and decent food. But unlike their southern brethren, black Brooklynites could technically patronize all public spaces and did not face lynch mobs and other forms of day-to-day violence.

African Americans had supported the Republican Party because of the Civil War and emancipation, but beginning in the twentieth century, northern urban blacks shifted political loyalties to the Democratic Party. Adam Clayton Powell Jr. was the first and only African American congressman from Manhattan, where by 1950, he was one of only six black men in the House of Representatives. Powell was elected in 1945 and served until 1971. The New York State legislature was equally unrepresentative of New York's population with only eleven state representatives and two senators. Bessie Buchanan of Manhattan was the first African American woman elected to Albany, serving from 1955 to 1962.[4]

Shirley Chisholm's political journey began when she entered Brooklyn College in 1942. She immediately involved herself in a wide range of radical, socialist, and progressive political clubs. Along with almost every other African American student, Chisholm was active in the Harriet Tubman Society. The club took on the pressing issues of integrating the armed forces, creating black studies courses, and bringing black faculty to Brooklyn College. She loved being in the Debating Society, and she later credited that experience with preparing her to be a powerful public speaker.[5]

Since sororities refused to admit African American women, she organized a women's club called In Pursuit of the Highest in All. In 1943, she worked on the campaign of Georgia Pearl Graham, a Tubman Society member who unsuccessfully ran as an independent candidate for student government. Aware of the discrimination women faced at the college, for example, rarely elected to student offices (save as secretaries of student government or clubs), she supported almost all campaigns for women candidates, black or white, painting posters, organizing rallies, even speaking on a few occasions. In *Unbought and Unbossed*, Chisholm mainly wrote about racism at her college. She was highly critical of the Political Science Society when their speakers "gave us liberal sentiments as, 'We've got to help the Negro because the Negro is limited.'" Her experiences at Brooklyn College led her to believe that the country was racist all the way through, and concluded that "if I ever had a chance, somehow I would tell the world how things were as I saw them."[6] Her other extracurricular activities included membership in the Brooklyn chapter of the NAACP, the Brooklyn Urban League, and the Brooklyn League of Women Voters. A racially conscious New Deal Democrat, she joined her neighborhood Seventeenth Assembly Democratic Club in Bedford-Stuyvesant, Brooklyn.

After her graduation in 1946, she struggled to find employment. Realizing there were few opportunities for African American women, save teaching and nursing, she enrolled at Columbia Teachers College where she earned a master of arts in childhood education in 1951. While at school and working part time, she met and married Conrad Chisholm, a Jamaican immigrant, who was a private investigator. After being denied teaching jobs because of her race and age, she finally found full-time work as the director of the Friend in Need Nursery in Brooklyn and then the directorship of the Madison Child Care Center in Manhattan.

Chisholm continued her activities in Democratic Party politics. In New York City, all political activity worked through the political clubhouses, whose primary function was to support the party's candidate at election time. Nearly every Brooklyn neighborhood had a club, usually headed by a white and male district leader who selected nominees for public office. Having experienced race and gender discrimination while politically active at Brooklyn College, Chisholm was angered at the race and gender politics of the 17AD club. "Isn't that just like those corrupt politicians," Chisholm complained to her husband. "Bedford Stuyvesant is now an almost all-black neighborhood, and those politicians won't let a black man get a job."[7] Worse, there was an unwritten rule that blacks sat on one side of the meeting room, whites on the other, and women's involvement was primarily supportive, preparing food for the meetings and organizing socials and fundraisers.

Undaunted, Chisholm challenged the white male leaders of the club, demanding to know why trash was not picked up in black neighborhoods, why the Bedford-Stuyvesant neighborhoods did not have adequate police protection, or why housing codes in black neighborhoods were not enforced.[8] Their refusal to act propelled Chisholm's further involvement. She became such a persistent irritant that the AD district leader thought by putting Chisholm in charge of the women's activities, she would be placated. Instead, she organized other women to speak up at meetings, demanding recognition and respect. This collective clout was enough to secure Chisholm's election to the club's board of directors—no small accomplishment for a twenty-four-year-old black woman.

In 1953, a political vacancy opened up on the Bedford-Stuyvesant Second Municipal Court. Not surprisingly, the Democratic Party leadership passed over every qualified black jurist. They further enraged black Democrats when they nominated a white man who did not even live in the neighborhood. Immediately, Chisholm and other black activists organized a primary challenge against the white candidate. Drawing upon the African American experience, they ran an aggressive, confident campaign: "End Boss-ruled Plantation Politics," read one leaflet.

Chisholm threw herself into this primary campaign, ringing doorbells, stuffing envelopes, going to community, church, school, union, and political meetings. She talked to ordinary Brooklynites convincing them that they could challenge the all-white machine. The community's efforts paid off. Lewis Flagg Jr. was elected the first African American jurist in Brooklyn. In 1960, Chisholm joined the Unity Democratic Club (UDC), whose goal was to overthrow the white and male Democratic machine. The UDC was a somewhat remarkable political club in that it was racially integrated and hard-working, dedicated, politically connected and competent women, such as Shirley Chisholm, Ruth Goring, and Jocelyn Cooper, held leadership positions. Chisholm became a prominent political activist, leading delegations to City Hall, writing speeches, speaking at rallies, phone banking, and fundraising.

In 1964, forty-year-old Chisholm notified the Unity Democrats that she wanted the club's nomination for state representative. As a member and president of Brooklyn's Key Women of America, a civic organization committed to the protection of children, family services, and community needs, she called on them to "elect me to dramatize the problems of black women." She believed that after twenty years of Democratic Party activism, doing every conceivable job in Brooklyn party politics except run for elective office, she was the most qualified person to run. Challenging the entrenched male leadership, she vowed, "I was not going to be denied because of my sex." She won the election handily. The Key Women celebrated Chisholm's victory, "We salute a lady of color. . . . This is a year for dreams to come true. Dr. Martin Luther King receives the Nobel Peace prize and Shirley becomes our representative in Albany, New York."[9]

Unbought and Unbossed

Chisholm's first campaign planted the seeds of her later feminism. While not yet using the rhetoric of the women's movement, she campaigned as a voice for underrepresented women in Brooklyn. Second, she became more conscious of systematic as well as personal sexism. Once Chisholm made the decision to run for political office, she faced opposition from men, white and black alike. Men actively opposed her ambitions within the Democratic Party, her campaigns for state representative, congressional representative, and her nomination for the US presidency. Throughout her political career she would always have to face men who tried to infantilize, patronize, or demonize her. She constantly spoke and wrote that the greatest hurdle she would face for the rest of her political life was hostility because of her sex.

She was an effective legislator while in Albany. She worked most closely with Percy Sutton, a prominent African American civil rights activist, attorney, businessperson, and Manhattan borough president. Chisholm introduced bills calling for unemployment insurance for domestic workers, seniority protection for pregnant teachers who took maternity leave, extended unemployment insurance, and social security protections for agricultural workers. This legislation not only championed but connected the needs of the working class, women, and people of color, presaging the contemporary understanding of the importance of intersectionality in challenging inequality. She was most proud of the legislation that created the Search for Education, Elevation and Knowledge (SEEK) Program that sought out African American and Latinx high school students to give them state scholarships so that they could attend either the City University of New York (CUNY) or the State University of New York (SUNY) systems. SEEK provided students with financial assistance, tutoring, and counseling. Within two years CUNY's enrollment jumped from one hundred thousand to two hundred fifty thousand and reflected the enormous diversity of the New York metropolitan area.

She also became involved in the emerging women's movement. In 1967, she was the vice president of the New York City chapter of the National Organization for Women (NOW), although not an active day-to-day member. She pushed for a New York State equal rights amendment. She used her position as a state legislator to advocate legislation that considered "the right to terminate a pregnancy shall be deemed a civil right."[10] After four years in the state assembly, she was the top vote getter, winning two more primary and general elections handily. In her years in Albany, she built a power base in Brooklyn, with women as her staunchest supporters. Her politics were always deeply rooted in class, gender, and racial equality. The lessons she learned in Albany prepared her for her next challenge: Washington.

Electoral politics came front and center when redistricting changes, which had begun in 1964, resulted in the creation of a new congressional district in central Brooklyn. Wanting her place in history as the first African American woman in Congress, ambitious, and confident in her ability to be an effective national legislator, she announced her candidacy. Almost immediately, she faced opposition. Chisholm was one of two women running, and this gender imbalance worked to her advantage. Women in the New York State Democratic Party were pushing for more women in Congress. Bernice Brown, of the New York State Women's Democratic caucus, wanted to make sure "that we got some females in there because everything was male. Shirley Chisholm was the best we had."[11] Not surprisingly the Democratic Party county leadership, which was overwhelmingly white and male, fielded a white and male candidate, William C. Thompson, a former state senator.

Drawing on her well-crafted political persona as a renegade, she "wrote a slogan that said it all: 'Fighting Shirley Chisholm: Unbought and Unbossed.'"[12] She put the slogan on shopping bags, bumper stickers, and fliers that were distributed everywhere. Unbought meant more than her vote was not for sale; it referred to liberation from slavery and colonialism. Unbossed signified that she was not going to be dominated by any political faction, and that she was her own person, not beholden to obey orders at work, or within political organizations or at home.[13] Her political consciousness had been formed first in Barbados and then in Brooklyn, an anticolonial majority-black political setting. As a candidate, she continuously faced discrimination as a woman. Instead of being a liability, Chisholm used gender, ethnicity, class, and race as a political asset in these political campaigns.

The primary fight was grueling. Chisholm's district was 80 percent African American and Puerto Rican. She knew that the African American vote would be somewhat divided and that the vote would be close, so in order to win, she had to win over white voters. She campaigned seventeen hours a day, walking the streets of Bedford-Stuyvesant, Williamsburg, Crown Heights, and Bushwick. She went into every supermarket and housing project, in the parks and in all the women's, community, immigrant, social, and political clubs. She campaigned from a sound truck holding a bullhorn, exclaiming, "This is fighting Shirley Chisholm coming through." Not yet using the feminist language of the post–World War II women's movement, Chisholm was very explicit about focusing on the women's vote. Women held raffles, teas, bake sales, and barbecues. Chisholm knew she was transforming the meaning of women's work. Women were no longer working for "the man," or men. This time women were doing the same work but for a woman.

William Thompson, Chisholm's primary opponent, was so confident of his victory that he went on vacation in the middle of the campaign. Not for the first or last time, Chisholm astounded the pundits and won handily.[14] Chisholm carried all four majority white sections in the district. She had no time to savor her victory. Usually in Brooklyn, a Democratic stronghold, a Democratic primary win meant an easy electoral victory in the fall. But 1968 was no usual year. The New York State Republican Party drafted James Farmer, the former head of the civil rights organization, the Congress of Racial Equality (CORE), to run in Brooklyn's Twelfth District. The Republicans were confident Farmer could win because of his reputation as a courageous civil rights leader. Farmer agreed to run with the caveat that he would not have to campaign or endorse Richard Nixon, the presidential standard-bearer.[15]

Chisholm was furious that Farmer would be her opponent, exclaiming, "He doesn't even live in Brooklyn! . . . Why doesn't he run for something in Harlem?" At first glance, Farmer had all the advantages. He was male, a nationally known civil rights leader with impressive oratorical skills, and ran an in-your-face masculinist campaign, emphasizing gender differences. His literature proclaimed that the Twelfth District needed "a man's voice in Washington."[16] Chisholm was offended by his tactics: "He toured the district with sound trucks manned by young dudes with afros, beating tom-toms: the big black male image." She walked into one campaign meeting only to be heckled "here comes the Black matriarch."[17] Farmer was further aided by television and print media. One NBC weekend special reported only on Farmer, without mentioning Chisholm altogether. The *Village Voice* ignored her campaign, while a *New York Times* article about the Twelfth District race did not mention her name, referring to her only as "a woman."

Not yet using the language of post–World War II feminism, Chisholm ran an unabashed pro-woman campaign. She challenged the white and male political machine as well as the masculinist male chauvinist ideology of parts of the black freedom struggle. Her electoral triumph pushed Chisholm into the national and even international spotlight. Equally important, her election pushed issues she championed: racial and gender equality and justice, expansion of medical care, access to public education, an end to the war in Vietnam, and de-escalation of US militarism to the forefront of US politics.

During the campaign, Chisholm remained cautiously confident. She drew upon the strength and activism of Brooklyn's women. She knew the women of Bedford-Stuyvesant were already capable leaders, always organizing something—parent-teacher association, a civic club, a church social club. "Men always underestimate women . . . they underestimated me, and they underestimate women like me," she wrote. She used her gender as a campaign weapon. "I am a woman and you are a woman and let's show Farmer that woman power can beat him." Chisholm constantly stressed the importance of electing the first black woman to Congress. Finally, she used humor and a bit of braggadocio to shore up her persona, "They call me Fighting Shirley Chisholm. My mother tells me I was born fighting. I was kicking so hard in the womb she knew I was aching to get out and fight."[18] Her strategy of focusing on the women of central Brooklyn paid off. She won the election 21½ to 2.[19]

Chisholm's election and arrival in Washington created a huge sensation. She hired an all-woman staff, something that had never been done before. Not only did she arrive late to her congressional swearing in, referencing the struggle for women's suffrage, she wore all white and a hat. Up until then, congressional protocol barred representatives from wearing hats and coats on the house floor. After being sworn in, she broke another unwritten rule that junior legislators not speak to senior House members. She asked the Speaker of the House, John McCormack, to reenact her swearing in at a nearby hotel so that everyone who had come from Brooklyn could witness the ceremony. Most unheard of, she dared protest her first committee assignment.

In 1969, committee chairs were all-powerful, their positions were based on seniority; committee chairs were all older, white men, most of whom were southern. Hoping to be on the Education and Labor Committee, she wanted to be placed on the subcommittee considering food stamps, surplus food, and migrant workers. Instead, the committee chair assigned her to Rural Development and Forestry. Speaker McCormack urged her to be a "good soldier," suggesting perhaps after a few years she might get more relevant committee assignments. "All my forty-three years, I have been a good soldier . . . and I can't be a good soldier anymore. . . . If you do not assist me, I will have to do my own thing."[20] McCormack, nervous about what Chisholm's "thing" might be, tried to broker a compromise. Tired of waiting to be recognized on the floor of Congress, she walked down into the "well" (the open area near the House Speaker dais) and explained why she rejected her initial committee assignment. She argued that since there were so few African Americans in Congress, they should be put on committees where they could best represent her constituents. She won her battle and was reassigned to the Veterans Affairs Committee where, as she put it, "there are more veterans in my district than there are trees."[21]

She did not stop with this victory. Delivering her first congressional speech, she vowed to vote against every bill that provided money for the Department of Defense. This was both a stand against the war in Vietnam as well as a protest of the war's devastating impact on her constituents. Funding for the war cut back on funding for needed social programs; young black and brown men were disproportionally drafted, wounded, and killed in Vietnam; they came home unable to find work. Her work was not all confrontational. She was a founding member of the Congressional Black Caucus (CBC), which worked to push for legislation that would further civil rights for people of color. The opposition Chisholm faced as a local Brooklyn political activist was nothing compared to the outright racist and gendered hostility from men in Congress. One southern Democrat, in front of other congressional representatives, would ostentatiously wipe off the chair Chisholm sat on during committee meetings. Others sneered and hissed at her in public places.[22] Gendered and outright racist acts against her were commonplace. She also had a difficult time with her male CBC colleagues. She was the only woman in the original CBC, and just as she wouldn't take guff from white men, she took the same attitude with her African American male colleagues.

By 1972, Chisholm had gone from an unknown local Brooklyn Democratic Party activist to one of the most important, admired, and influential women in the United States. She had become a leading spokesperson on the issues of women's rights and along with Patsy Mink, representative from Hawai'i, and Bella Abzug from New York, were the only congressional representatives who connected class, ethnicity, and race in framing policies that had an impact on women's lives. She also began using the language of the 1960s and 1970s feminist movement. In a chapter, "Women and Their Revolution," in *Unbought and Unbossed*, she argued that "women must become revolutionaries," citing her approval of women's liberation activist Robin Morgan's call for women to rise up.[23] Gloria Steinem, a leading feminist activist, became an ally. When Chisholm ran for the Democratic Party nomination for the US presidency in 1972, Steinem wrote Chisholm's only televised speech.[24] On August 10, 1970, Chisholm reintroduced into the House of Representative the Equal Rights Amendment (ERA), which had first been brought to Congress by former suffragist and National Woman's Party president Alice Paul. She constantly tried to build coalitions between mainstream and radical feminists and women of color. A longtime member of the National Council of Negro Women, she joined the 100 Black Women and the National Black Feminist Organization. Along with Bella Abzug, Betty Friedan, and Gloria Steinem, she founded the National Women's Political Caucus. Since 1969, she was also the honorary president of the National Association for the Repeal of Abortion

Laws. She took the NARAL presidency to advocate for *all* women, poor, working class, and women of color. Knowing she was challenging the dominant black nationalist sentiment at the time, wrote articles and gave speeches challenging those African Americans who argued birth control and abortion was a form of genocide against blacks. "To label family planning and legal abortion 'genocide' is male rhetoric for male ears," asserting that "I do not know any black or Puerto Rican women who feels that way."[25]

On the Chisholm Trail

Chisholm is perhaps best known for being the first woman and the first African American to make a serious run for the Democratic Party nomination for the US presidency. College students gave her that idea first. "It began as far back as 1969. . . . Before the end of my second term in the House, I had spoken to well over one hundred campuses in forty-two states, and on most of them, someone had asked me, 'Why don't *you* run for president in 1972.'"[26] Chisholm also explained, "I ran because someone had to do it first."[27] Her intention was to shake up the political system, hoping to engage people of color, young people, the poor, the elderly, and women—the very people US society had marginalized in the struggle for a more just society. She was under no illusion that she could win either the nomination or the presidency; she ran because she believed that none of the all-white and male candidates could speak to those disaffected constituencies. Her campaign was nonstop, energetic, impassioned, unprofessionally but ardently staffed, underfunded, and very disorganized. People who worked on her campaign compared the enthusiasm to that of the 2008 Barack Obama presidential campaign. She ran in nine primaries and campaigned in over thirty states.

But most important, her campaign demonstrated her fierce courage. Just seven years after the passage of the Voting Rights Act, Chisholm campaigned in Marianna, Florida, at the site of a well-publicized 1934 lynching and race riot. She spoke on the steps of the county courthouse.

"Nearby, as everywhere, there was a statue of a Confederate soldier. . . . The rifle, the statue was holding seemed almost to be pointing at me." She remembered that an elderly black man approached her saying, "I never thought I'd live to see a black person speaking from the court house steps." Two hours later, George Wallace, the racist anti–civil rights candidate spoke at the same spot. [28]

She did not win endorsements from any major political figures. Bella Abzug, a radical and feminist representative from Manhattan who was Chisholm's close ally in Congress, opposed her candidacy. As organizations, NOW and the NWPC could not endorse any candidate, but individuals could. Their primary concern was electability—that is, who was the best candidate to defeat Richard Nixon in 1972. Chisholm had to fight for any news coverage, and when she got it, she was described in hostile, diminutive, and chauvinist terms—"prim," "pepper pot," "feisty."[29] No one from the CBC supported her, and worse, other civil rights figures openly attacked her. William Clay from Missouri called her crazy; Alcee Hastings from Florida claimed she was a disgrace to black people. Jessie Jackson refused to let her speak at the Operation PUSH office in Chicago; Julian Bond, the civil rights icon, explaining his dislike for Chisholm in a comment laced with sexism, didn't think her "gender had as much to do with it as her style."[30]

She did win support from a wide range of community and grassroots activists, such as the Black Panther Party, Gloria Steinem, Rosa Parks, the California chapter of the National Organization for Women, the Reverend Al Sharpton (her youth organizer), civil rights activist Fannie Lou Hamer of Mississippi, and prominent entertainers Ossie Davis and Harry Belafonte. She went to the 1972 Miami Convention with 151 delegates and a promise from congressional representative Ron Dellums to place her name in nomination. At the very last moment, under intense pressure from then San Francisco mayor Willie Brown, Dellums backed out. Even though she was heartbroken by this betrayal, civil rights activists Percy Sutton of New York and Charles Evers of Mississippi, both Democrats involved in local politics, placed her name in nomination. It is unsurprising given these circumstances that Chisholm constantly stated that she "met much more discrimination in terms of being a woman than being black, in the field of politics." She never regretted her presidential run. "I ran because somebody had to do it first. I ran *because* most people think the country is not ready for a black candidate, not ready for a woman candidate. Someday."[31]

Legacy

After 1972, Chisholm became a more conventional, less confrontational politician. She divorced, remarried, and gave up her seat in Congress in 1982. After her husband's death, she taught at Mt. Holyoke, gave lectures, and finally retired, moving to Florida and retreating from public life. At the time of her death in 2005, public awareness of her career as a champion of her Bedford-Stuyvesant community and civil rights fighter had faded. During the 2008 Democratic Party primary, very few pundits referred to the Chisholm campaign in 1972 as opening the door for Hillary Clinton or the historic election of President Barack Obama.

At a time when opportunities for all women, but especially for working-class women of color were severely limited, Chisholm broke a number of barriers and rules. Starting as a rank-and-file Democratic Party activist, she learned that willpower, hard work, coalition building, grassroots activism, and courage could bring about progressive social change. Unlike most black women in the civil rights struggle, she did not defer to the established black male leadership—mainly to her detriment at the time. She was a skilled legislator in Albany, but not as effective in Washington. This was in part due to her celebrity status, plus opposition by Republicans and Dixiecrats in Congress, many in her own party. With Bella Abzug, she crafted the most far-reaching day care legislation in 1971. Despite organizing a bipartisan congressional coalition that passed the bill in both the House and the Senate, President Nixon vetoed the childcare bill that ultimately emerged, arguing it would "Sovietize" America's children if federal funding were used to provide for their care outside the home while their mothers worked. As politics lurched rightward, Chisholm found that her effectiveness in Congress waned.

After her death in 2005, a new generation of social justice advocates rediscovered Chisholm. Shola Lynch's award-winning documentary *Chisholm 72: Unbought and Unbossed* brought Chisholm back to a national audience. The Shirley Chisholm Project of Brooklyn Women's Political Activism was launched in 2005; in that year, the New York State legislature proclaimed November 30, Shirley Chisholm Day. After years of invisibility, Chisholm's name now appears on New York State buildings, post offices, and day care centers throughout Brooklyn. In 2005, Brooklyn Borough President Marty Markowitz put a portrait of Shirley Chisholm up in Brooklyn Borough Hall. Four years later, Speaker Nancy Pelosi arranged for a portrait of Chisholm to hang in the Capitol. Hillary Clinton referenced Chisholm on a number of occasions during her 2016 presidential run. New York State governor Andrew Cuomo has named a state park in Brooklyn for her, and New York City mayor Bill De Blasio has commissioned a statue of her to grace the entrance to Prospect Park in Brooklyn. The Academy Award–winning actress Viola Davis has announced that she will produce and star in a feature film about Chisholm.[32]

The results of the 2018 congressional election, one in which 107 women were elected, many of whom were women of color, brought Chisholm's legacy front and center. Newly elected Democratic congresswomen made a point to pose under Chisholm's portrait. Referencing Chisholm as well as earlier suffragists, congresswomen of both parties wore white to the 2019 State of the Union speech. Thirty-eight-year-old Tamaya Dennard, a first-time candidate who won a seat on the Cincinnati City Council last fall, used another of Chisholm's famous quotes during her campaign: "If they don't give you a seat at the table, bring a folding chair," and when she showed up for her first council meeting, she brought a red folding chair.[33]

Chisholm's legacy will no doubt continue to be a "catalyst for change" as more women enter politics. But it will not be easy. The global climate crisis, growing inequality between rich and poor, the rise of extreme right-wing nationalism, racism, xenophobia, and attacks on women's rights present tremendous challenges. Chisholm fought for a more democratic and inclusive America all her adult life. "We can become a dynamic equilibrium, a harmony of different elements, in which the whole will be greater than all its parts and greater than any society the world has seen before."[34]

Notes

This chapter is dedicated to Rosalyn Terborg-Penn, who pioneered our understanding of African American women and women's suffrage. Special thanks to Brooklyn College as well as Irva Adams and Ivy Barrett Fox Bryan from the Brooklyn College Women's and Gender Studies program for their invaluable help.

1. Shirley Chisholm, *The Good Fight* (New York: Harper and Row, 1973), 80.

2. Lisa Tetrault, *The Myth of Seneca Falls: Memory and the Women's Suffrage Movement, 1848–1898* (Chapel Hill: University of North Carolina Press, 2014).

3. Barbara Winslow, *Shirley Chisholm: Catalyst for Change* (New York: Westview Press, 2013), 30.

4. Julie Gallagher, *Black Women and Politics in New York City* (Urbana: University of Illinois Press, 2012), 171.

5. There is no way to determine either the numbers or percentages of African American students or faculty at Brooklyn College in the 1940s. The college only recorded gender of students. Looking at Brooklyn College yearbooks, 1944–48, can only give an impression. Shirley Chisholm's sister Muriel said that she thought there were fewer than ten African American students when she attended in the late 1940s, but she could not be sure.

6. Shirley Chisholm, *Unbought and Unbossed*, ed. Scott Simpson, Expanded Fortieth Anniversary Edition (Washington, DC: Take Root Media, 2011), 42, 43.

7. Susan Brownmiller, *Shirley Chisholm: A Biography* (New York: Doubleday, 1970), 63.

8. Gallagher, *Black Women and Politics*, 178.

9. Winslow, *Shirley Chisholm*, 53.

10. Susan Brownmiller, "This Is Fighting Shirley Chisholm," *New York Times Magazine*, April 13, 1970, 83.

11. Gallagher, *Black Women and Politics*, 178.

12. Chisholm, *Unbought and Unbossed*, 86.

13. Josh Guild, "To Make That Someday Come: Shirley Chisholm's Radical Politics of Possibility," in *Want to Start a Revolution: Radical Women in the Black Freedom Struggle*, ed. Dayo F. Gore, Jeanne Theoharis, and Komozi Woodard (New York: New York University Press, 2009), 254.

14. *New York Times,* July 19, 1968, 31.

15. Brownmiller, *Shirley Chisholm,* 32.

16. Brownmiller, *Shirley Chisholm,* 107.

17. Chisholm, *Unbought and Unbossed,* 86.

18. James Haskins, *Fighting Shirley Chisholm* (New York: Dial Press, 1974), 86.

19. Chisholm, *Unbought and Unbossed,* 94.

20. Chisholm, *Unbought and Unbossed,* 99.

21. Chisholm, *Unbought and Unbossed,* 103.

22. *Chisholm 72: Unbought and Unbossed,* directed by Shola Lynch, documentary, January 18, 2004.

23. Chisholm, "Women and Their Liberation," in *Unbought and Unbossed,* 175–181.

24. Gloria Steinem, letter to the editor, *New York Times*, July 8, 2019, https://www.nytimes.com/2019/07/08/opinion/letters/gloria-steinem-shirley-chisolm.html.

25. Chisholm, "Facing the Abortion Question," in *Unbought and Unbossed,* 129–137.

26. Chisholm, *The Good Fight,* 13.

27. Chisholm, *The Good Fight,* 3.

28. Chisholm, *The Good Fight,* 69.

29. Winslow, *Shirley Chisholm,* 116.

30. Winslow, *Shirley Chisholm,* 99.

31. Chisholm, *The Good Fight,* 3.

32. Aris Folley, "Viola Davis to Play Shirley Chisholm, First Black Woman Elected to Congress," The Hill, December 1, 2018, https://thehill.com/blogs/in-the-know/in-the-know/419305-viola-davis-to-play-shirley-chisholm-first-black-woman-elected.

33. Vanessa Williams, "'Unbought and Unbossed': Shirley Chisholm's Feminist Mantra Is Still Relevant 50 Years Later," *Washington Post*, January 26, 2018, https://www.washingtonpost.com/news/post-nation/wp/2018/01/26/unbought-and-unbossed-shirley-chisholms-feminist-mantra-is-as-relevant-today-as-it-was-50-years-ago/?utm_term=.07f9807af8f7.

34. Chisholm, *The Good Fight,* 163.

Patsy Mink and Bella Abzug, ca. 1970s. Inscription: "Wendy dear—You've got the greatest mom—and you're pretty terrific, too. In sisterhood and love, Bella." With Permission from Gwendolyn Mink.

CHAPTER 13

Envisioning the National Women's Conference

Patsy Takemoto Mink and Pacific Feminism

JUDY TZU-CHUN WU

IN NOVEMBER 1977, approximately twenty thousand people arrived in Houston, Texas, for a federally funded conference to craft a national women's agenda. Inspired by the United Nations declaration of International Women's Year (IWY) in 1975 and the World Conference on Women held in Mexico City that summer, the 1977 IWY National Women's Conference (NWC) brought two thousand official delegates from the fifty states and six territories to discuss, debate, and vote on a platform of women's issues to be presented to the US president and Congress.[1] The four-day event also attracted an additional eighteen thousand observers from across the nation and representatives from fifty-six countries in Asia, Africa, the Caribbean, Eastern and Western Europe, Latin America, and the Middle East. This chapter offers a new interpretation of the political origins of the 1977 NWC in Houston by focusing on the leadership of Patsy Takemoto Mink, a third-generation Japanese American from Hawai'i and the first woman of color in the US House of Representatives. Bringing attention to Mink's efforts to envision and create a federal mandate for this historic gathering, an event described as the pinnacle of second-wave feminism, offers new insights regarding the significance of Pacific feminism for reimagining the US nation and the politics of representation.

The advocates of the NWC envisioned the event as a grassroots effort. The National Commission on the Observance of International Women's Year (National Commission), created by executive order under President Gerald Ford, a Republican, in 1975 and reauthorized in 1977 under President Jimmy Carter, a Democrat, oversaw the organizing of

both the national conference as well as the state and territorial preconferences. At these local meetings, an estimated one hundred fifty thousand individuals debated issues and elected delegates.[2] The participants
at the local and national levels included antifeminist men and women
who mobilized to assert their political priorities at gatherings that their
tax dollars helped to fund. They attended both the NWC at Houston's
Albert Thomas Convention Center and the counterprotest, which attracted an estimated fifteen thousand to twenty thousand people, at the
nearby Astrodome. Nevertheless, the NWC organizers emphasized the
importance of involving women of diverse backgrounds, both due to
their feminist commitment to inclusion and owing to the political mandate from receiving federal funds. Conference commissioners and staff
allocated money and made concerted attempts to include women with
low incomes, homemakers, rural women, lesbians, people of different
religious faiths and ages, and women of color. As a result, "over a third
of delegates (35.5%) were racial or ethnic minorities."[3] African Americans constituted the largest group (17.4%), followed by Latinas (8.3%),
Native Americans (3.4%), Asian Americans (2.7%), Alaskan (0.5%),
and Hawaiian (0.4%) natives.[4] At the conference, these women cau-
cused among those of similar backgrounds as well as collectively with
one another to craft a substitute plank on "minority women." Historian Marjorie Spruill argues that the phrase "women of color" was
coined at the NWC in Houston.[5]

This chapter explores the significance of the NWC for the development of Asian American and Pacific Islander (AAPI) feminisms.[6] The
NWC's fortieth anniversary in November 2017 prompted increasing
scholarly interest in the NWC as a moment that mobilized women's activism in diverse ways. Spruill's 2017 book, *Divided We Stand*, the first
monograph about the conference, emphasizes how the NWC ignited
both feminist and antifeminist organizing, thereby realigning political
parties along gendered lines and defining modern US politics as we know
it. Other scholars foreground the importance of the conference for African American and indigenous women as well as Latinas.[7] Little attention, however, is given to the eighty-three-plus Asian American and

Pacific Islander women who participated as delegates or commissioners. Nor is Patsy Takemoto Mink, who spearheaded and envisioned the scope of the conference, given due credit for her contributions.

Focusing on Mink and the legislative debates to sponsor the NWC makes two important contributions to the scholarship on the conference and 1970s feminisms more broadly. First, Mink's political leadership and vision challenge the common assumption of "liberal" and "second-wave feminism" as predominantly white, middle-class, and East Coast phenomena. Scholars of US feminism have critiqued simplistic understandings of the categorization and chronology of women's activism. Female activists during the 1960s and 1970s came from diverse backgrounds and drew political inspiration from various movements. Recognizing this challenges a sequential understanding of second-wave feminism as a white, middle-class women's movement giving rise to a third world, or women of color movement.[8] Women's activists held diverse and evolving perspectives that spilled beyond categories such as liberal, radical, socialist, lesbian, and third world.[9] As Chela Sandoval argues, women of color feminist methodology operates through a "differential consciousness" that refuses any singular approach to resisting multiple intersecting oppressions.[10]

Second, a focus on Mink's political vision reveals the influence of a Pacific World understanding of feminism. Mink's status as a racialized woman from Hawai'i fundamentally shaped her ideas for NWC as a bridging of the "top down" and the "bottom up." The federally funded conference served as a platform to channel activist energies and visions from across fifty states and six territories in order to develop a policy mandate for the president and Congress. Mink's positionality foregrounds how a Pacific World view fundamentally shaped both her feminist politics and the politics of representation at the NWC.

"Capitol Hill Feminism"[11]

As the first woman of color elected to the US House of Representatives, Mink broke gender and racial political barriers. She served for twenty-four years, first from 1965 to 1977 and again from 1990 to 2002, when she passed away at the age of seventy-four. In between these terms, Mink acted as President Carter's assistant secretary of state for Oceans and International Environmental and Scientific Affairs, as the national chair of Americans for Democratic Action (a progressive organization cofounded by Eleanor Roosevelt), and on the Honolulu City Council. Throughout her political career, Mink advocated for civil rights, the antiwar movement, environmental protection, and feminist policies. In fact, Mink ran for the US presidency as a peace candidate in 1972. A "bridge" feminist, Mink collaborated with activists to advocate for legislation, like Title IX (renamed after Patsy Mink), WEEA (the Women's Educational Equity Act), and federally funded childcare.[12] She also played a key and under-recognized role to envision and obtain fiscal allocations to support the NWC.

The idea of the NWC stemmed from the political merger of two bills, one offered by Representative Bella Abzug (D-NY) and the other sponsored by Mink. On March 6, 1975, Abzug argued before the House of Representatives that the United States should convene an American women's conference before the end of 1976 to assess "the progress ... made in the United States toward achieving the three goals of International Women's Year—equality between men and women, integration of women in total development effort, and recognition of women's contribution to world peace." Abzug argued that the US conference also could develop "specific recommendations for the elimination of all barriers to full and equal participation of women in all aspects of national life" and create a schedule to implement these changes. She noted that other nations, such as Canada and Australia, each appropriated $2 million for IWY-related programs, and that the United States could surely "afford to assign this important year an equally high priority."[13]

Abzug's leadership, more than Mink's, is remembered in connection with the NWC. In *Divided We Stand*, Marjorie Spruill largely credits Abzug for envisioning and implementing the idea of the conference. Abzug's critics also focused their blame on her, describing the conference as "Bella's Boondoggle" and the legislation to fund the event as "Bella's bill." Abzug, a lawyer and activist, emerged from the antinuclear, pro-peace maternalist organization Women Strike for Peace to serve in the House of Representatives from 1970 to 1976. She certainly played a central role in the NWC. Along with Margaret Heckler (R-MA), Abzug served as an official US delegate to the 1975 UN Conference in Mexico City. She also chaired the subcommittee that held hearings on legislation to authorize the NWC and shepherd the bill to passage and funding authorization. After Abzug lost a senatorial campaign in 1976, President Carter appointed her as chair of the national commission to organize the NWC. This focus on Abzug, however, obscures how Patsy Mink developed and advocated for the idea of a grassroots national women's conference.

Six days after Abzug, Mink introduced a joint House and Senate resolution calling for a White House Conference on Women. The proposals by Mink and Abzug shared some commonalities, which is why the two legislators, who also happened to be best friends in the House of Representatives, eventually collaborated on creating a cosponsored piece of legislation. Like Abzug, Mink argued that the United States has "unfinished business before us." She specifically cited the 1969 President's Task Force on Women's Rights and Responsibilities, convened by Nixon. Mink decried that "in the face of nearly universally stated support for equality of women that there are the inequalities in the laws which we still find today." The conference she envisioned would foster discussion "of these remaining inequalities and their early resolution."[14]

Similar to Abzug, Mink also highlighted the bicentennial of the United States' founding as a propitious moment to evaluate the history and progress of women in US society. She and other advocates of the conference pointed out that the planned national celebrations tended to overlook women's historic contributions. Instead, Mink called for an accurate accounting of history and argued that 1976 represented a "unique opportunity for self-examination . . . to reorient our priorities where necessary."[15] In other words, Mink argued that the NWC, originally planned for the two hundredth birthday of the nation's founding, represented an opportunity to retell the history of the United States and chart the future of the country by focusing on women's experiences. Her call for a bottom-up approach to historical commemoration paralleled grass-roots and activist critiques of the bicentennial celebration and their rejection of a nationally imposed common narrative of the country.[16]

Mink's plan primarily differed from Abzug's in the scale of the proposed conference and the amount of federal funding. Mink, too, referenced the IWY but more as a negative example of inadequate US investment. The United Nations announced plans for IWY in 1972, but the US federal government provided limited resources to foster attention to the proposed world conference in 1975. Although the United States sent an official delegation to Mexico City, and Congress passed legislation acknowledging and endorsing the goals of IWY, only $350,000 was authorized to foster attention on the conference and the global exchange of ideas related to women's issues. An IWY-US center opened in Washington, DC, in the fall of 1973, which served as a coordination and information network, but the staff largely depended on volunteer labor and even sold jewelry featuring the UN Conference logo of a white dove to raise funds.[17]

To bring more widespread attention to women's issues, Mink called for a White House Conference on the Status of Women. Such a conference brought national attention; previous White House conferences also provided the model of state and territorial preconferences. In other words, Mink envisioned the conferences as generating political discussions at the highest level and at the grassroots. To carry out this plan, Mink proposed an authorization of $10 million. Her emphasis on local and regional participation—particularly the use of government funds to facilitate the involvement of women of diverse class backgrounds, geographical locations, ages, races, ethnicities, and religions—is what distinguished the NWC as a historic event. It would be the first federally funded conference devoted to defining a national platform of women's issues through a process of widespread deliberation throughout the fifty-six states and territories that constituted the United States.

Mink's contributions to envisioning the NWC have received little historical attention, in part due to her approach to political advocacy.

Abzug, Mink, and their staff members, who were predominantly women, consulted with leading women's organizations and worked with one another to blend the two visions and bills. Despite the congresswomen's friendship and political synergy on feminist and antiwar politics, differences and conflicts also existed. Mink's key aide, a Japanese American woman from Hawai'i named Susan Kakesako, provided regular summaries of phone calls that Mink's office received. On April 8, 1975, Kakesako explained that Carol Burris, president and cofounder of the Women's Lobby, called to report Abzug's take on the two bills. The memo reflected the use of pidgin creole among Mink's staff: "Bella huffy about your bill. She no like WH Conf becuz doesn't want to give Ford an inch in election yr."[18] In addition to not wanting to share political credit with the Republican president running for reelection, Abzug also believed that her less expensive bill would receive faster approval from the Committee on Government Affairs. She served on the committee and had confidence that the chair would support the bill. Mink responded by pointing out the difference in their political visions: "Tell Carol not to worry about Bella. Bella has to decide for herself whether she wants or does not want a nationally prestigious conference with the name of the White House connected with it. . . . If all she can get is 1 million dollars, can't be White House type conf so might as well settle for just her small one-shot deal. My bill requires 10 million dlrs, no less no way you can have WH type conf for less money."[19]

Despite these pointed critiques, Mink also maintained that Abzug should take the lead and receive recognition for her work. Mink pointed out that Abzug, as "chair" of the subcommittee on Government Information and Individual Rights that would hold hearings on the bill, needed to decide for herself which version of the bill should proceed. In another exchange of memos, Mink encouraged Kakesako to informally contact women's organizations about upcoming hearings related to the bill but to do so by calling and not in writing. Kakesako recorded the instructions as: "No want Bella think I am trying to preempt her."[20] Mink's decision to pursue behind the scenes negotiation rather than upstage Abzug reflected their mutual friendship as well as Mink's recognition of Abzug's political status as the head of a significant committee that could approve the conference. Mink wanted to pass a bill substantive enough to support her vision of the NWC, not take public credit from her colleague and friend.

Eventually, fifteen out of the nineteen female legislators in the House of Representatives cosponsored the merged bill for a National Women's Conference (H.R. 8903).[21] Abzug and Mink, both Democrats, worked across party lines to include two prominent and moderate Republican representatives, Margaret Heckler of Massachusetts and Millicent Fenwick of New Jersey. Female congressional leaders tended to be Democrats, but the Republican National Committee adopted a women's rights plank at its 1972 convention. The RNC support for women's rights, however, would increasingly be attacked by "family values" and antifeminist conservatives within the party. By 1975, four more women of color, all African Americans, joined Mink in the House of Representatives.[22] The supporters of the bill consciously restricted their cosponsors to women only, although the revised bill (H.R. 9924), after hearings and amendments in committee, included male legislators who requested to serve as cosponsors. The bill distanced the conference slightly from President Ford by dropping the title of a White House conference, which also protected him from the conservative right in his own party in an election year. Instead, a national commission, appointed by the president, was authorized as the organizing body. Very importantly, the legislation retained the vision of grassroots involvement, which justified the $10 million request. To align with the IWY and the UN pronouncement of a Decade of Women, the bill also proposed a second conference to be held in 1985 to assess the progress of women's rights.

Critics of the NWC bill questioned the necessity of sponsoring local, regional, and national conferences devoted to women's issues. Empowered by antifeminist lobbying led by Phyllis Schlafly and her Eagle Forum organization, as well as other groups, conservative legislators lambasted the fiscal request, charging that the conference served special interests and provided a platform to politically mobilize against unwanted policies like the Equal Rights Amendment and abortion rights.

They argued that the expenditure of federal funds constituted a waste of taxpayer dollars, especially given the recessionary state of the economy in the mid-1970s and the suspicion that conference attendees were likely to spend their time sipping cocktails. Critics even charged sponsors of the bill with dishonesty for misrepresenting support from the Republican National Committee. Some Republicans did support the NWC and advocated for attention to issues related to women's rights. In response, the critics of the conference sought to delegitimize women's rights as a topic worthy of federal attention and funding and to redefine the agenda of the Republican Party as antithetical to feminism.

Senator Edward Brooke of Massachusetts, a moderate Republican and the first African American popularly elected to the Senate, offered one of the most poignant arguments for the conference. He highlighted the increasing gender gap in pay with "women earn[ing] 56 cents for every dollar men earn on the average," which represents "a decline from 64 cents in 1967."[23] Brooke further pointed out the educational disparity in pay, given that "a man with an eighth-grade education earns as much as a woman with a bachelor's degree." In addition, Brooke noted how race and gender compound their impact with "94 percent of the jobs paying $15,000 and over are held by white men." Brooke emphasized that these disparities increased during the period after Congress passed antidiscrimination laws—namely, the banning of sex discrimination in employment practices under Title VII of the 1964 Civil Rights Law. As Brooke noted, eliminating discrimination through legislative mandate did not necessarily result in deterring discrimination in practice. This distinction between de jure versus de facto inequality characterized both gender and race relations in the United States.

Female legislators in the House also rose to the challenge of demanding a National Women's Conference. Shirley Chisholm, the first African American female legislator in the House of Representatives, responded to the characterization of women's issues as a "special interest." She remarked during the deliberations that, "I really do sincerely hope that the gentlemen will, for once in their lives, as this country approaches its 200th anniversary, realize that 51 percent or 52 percent of the population is a very important segment of the population."[24] She also directly questioned the patriarchal fear and anxiety surrounding women convening a national meeting. Chisholm pointed out that the inadequacies of male legislative bodies necessitated a space for women of diverse backgrounds and interests to come together to deliberate policy recommendations. In 1975, women constituted 4 percent of the House of Representatives and 0 percent of the Senate. Chisholm underscored that she welcomed women of different backgrounds with various views to participate in the proposed women's conference. Again, this call for diversity both reflected her investment in including traditionally marginalized voices as well as a political strategy to receive federal authorization.

Through this collective support, which crossed party lines, the Senate finally approved funding to support the NWC by one vote. Rather than the requested $10 million, conference organizers received $5 million, a compromise offered by Mink. The cost of the conference, devoted to discussion of 52 percent of the population, represented an expenditure of approximately four cents for each of the 115 million women in the United States. Several congressional feminist leaders who had made the conference a reality faced hostile opposition that exposed the tenuousness of their so-called establishment status. In fact, both Abzug and Mink, who served multiple terms in the House of Representatives, ran and lost senatorial campaigns in 1976. President Carter appointed both to positions of leadership in his administration, but their electoral losses occurred during the bicentennial year in which they sought to celebrate women's achievements and assess how to continue women's progress toward greater equality.

A Pacific Vision of Feminism

The lack of recognition given to Mink for advocating for the NWC also erases how her worldview as a woman of color from Hawai'i profoundly shaped her vision and arguments for a grassroots NWC. Mink came from islands in the Pacific and that geographical locale framed how she understood various political issues, ranging from Cold War militarism, race relations, environmentalism, and women's politics. She inserted her perspectives into the national political debate, insisting that Americans reimagine their country to include those from the peripheries. Erasing Mink from the historical memory of the NWC also erases the contributions of Asian American and Pacific Islander feminisms to 1970s political culture. Mink's Pacific World view influenced the 1977 NWC in three main ways.

First, Mink emphasized the importance of involving women of diverse backgrounds and from places considered "small" and marginal to the national polity. She argued that states and territories with "small" populations nevertheless needed at least a minimum of ten delegates to the NWC.[25] Even in more sparsely populated areas, Mink recognized from her own experience, a diversity of views, races, ethnicities, classes, ages, and religions existed. While states with larger populations would receive more delegate slots, Mink nevertheless argued that states with smaller populations should have the right to have a diverse range of people and perspectives represented nationally.

This Pacific imaginary was a hallmark of Mink's political worldview, leading her to argue for the importance of territorial representation at the national gathering. Born in the territory of Hawai'i in 1927 and growing up in a starkly stratified plantation society, Mink recognized the unequal political power of people and lands who are part of but not full members of the United States. Japanese immigrants, for example, were designated "aliens ineligible for citizenship," and only became eligible for naturalization in 1952, when Japan became a Cold War ally of the United States. During World War II, Japanese immigrants and their US-born children in Hawai'i faced heightened racial hostility, suspected of collaborating with Japan to attack Pearl Harbor. Mink's father, in fact, was taken away. Wendy Mink, Patsy's daughter, recalled, "I know that that night spent with my grandfather away from home . . . made an enormous impression on my mother. . . . [She was] just sort of afraid that he wouldn't come back in the morning."[26] Although Japanese in Hawai'i were not incarcerated en masse, like those on the West Coast of the United States, they, like other residents of the island, lived through the war under martial law. The experiences and awareness of racialized and political exclusion led Mink to advocate for those on the margins of the US polity throughout her political career—whether advocating for the end of nuclear testing in Pacific Island territories or for better territorial participation (including for Washington, DC) at the NWC.

Third, Mink's argument for an accurate accounting of women's contributions to US history focused on exposing a gendered history of imperialism and colonization. When she testified at the hearings for the NWC legislation, Mink elaborated on an underrecognized historical figure, Queen Lili'uokalani. Mink pointed out that "American businessmen and religious leaders," forcibly deposed Lili'uokalani, the last monarch of the Kingdom of Hawai'i, and imprisoned her when she refused to give up her throne.[27] Mink underscored the need for similar historical recovery of women's contributions across the United States."[28] Mink's decision to focus on Queen Lili'uokalani is remarkable in many ways. No doubt, Mink may have used Lili'uokalani as a way to appeal to the constituency in Hawai'i. In doing so, however, Mink also foregrounded a history of gendered and racialized US colonialism. The forced incorporation of Hawai'i as a US territory resulted from the illegal displacement of a female political leader by *haole*, or white male businessmen, Christian missionaries, and military leaders. Mink's argument that similar stories could be found in each state could be read as a "flattening" of this history of violence and resistance into a multicultural or "cultural pluralist" history of women's achievements. Natasha Zaretsky pointed out how certain narratives were mobilized by organizers of the US bicentennial to defuse criticism of the US nation. They adopted "cultural pluralism" to enable divergent communities to recognize themselves in the commemorations. In addition, various "folk" festivals, including the Smithsonian's 1976 Festival of American Folklife, foregrounded Native American pageantry and appropriated the concept of the "tribe" to both acknowledge indigenous peoples and communicate the message that all Americans could belong to a collective community.[29] Mink's message, however, did not smooth over but instead illuminated a broader pattern of racialized, patriarchal settler colonialism that pervaded each part of the lands recognized as the United States. She did not overlook or gloss over this history but instead tried to use her status as an elected official to recognize the harms of the US nation and consider various forms of legislation to repair the past.

Conclusion

Mink's intervention in the 1977 NWC reimagines the US political project to include the small, the territorial, the Pacific, and the indigenous. Her relationship to the Pacific and the indigenous is not necessarily an easy subject position. Native Hawaiian sovereignty activist and scholar Haunani-Kay Trask has charged Asian Americans in Hawai'i as settlers.[30] Although discriminated against in the plantation economy and the political state, Asian Americans nevertheless gained economic and political power over time that contributed to the dispossession of Native Hawaiians. In fact, by advocating for statehood and the liberal project of national incorporation, Mink could be perceived by Native Hawaiians and other Pacific Islanders as furthering a colonial project of dispossession.

Mink's attention to those on the margins of the US empire reflects her status as an outsider as well as insider to the US nation. As a congressional representative from the newest state, located off the map of the continental United States, and one of the few women and people of color in national office, Mink believed in the promise and project of the US liberal state. She advocated for political forums, like the NWC, to include those traditionally left out of the US polity. She had faith that democratic dialogue could help the country live up to its ideals of equality and liberty. At the same time, Mink recognized the structural forms of violence and dispossession that the United States enacted, within and across national borders, in the name of democracy and equality. She believed in her role of exposing these inequalities and atrocities, of speaking truth to power, so that all who desired to do so could receive full recognition as political subjects and legitimate beneficiaries of state protection.

Mink was one of many who advocated support for and eventually participated in the NWC in Houston. Nevertheless, her leadership role in defining the vision for the conference and creating the federal mandate for a national assessment of women's issues needs to be more fully recognized. Doing so sheds light on the significant role of an Asian American woman in a whitewashed history of feminism and the importance of the Pacific World to foreground histories of exclusion, settler colonialism, and militarism in the US polity. Erasing this history also diminishes the meaning of the NWC. We must recognize how women of diverse backgrounds understood their relationship to the US nation in order to assess how they envisioned new political possibilities for themselves and their collective society.

Notes

1. The "territories" represented at the conference were American Samoa, the District of Columbia, Guam, Puerto Rico, Virgin Islands, and the Trust Territories. *American Women on the Move: National Women's Conference,* November 18–21, 1977, Houston, Texas Conference Program.

2. Shelah Gilbert Leader and Patricia Rusch Hyatt, *American Women on the Move: The Inside Story of the National Women's Conference, 1977* (Lanham, MD: Lexington Books, 2016).

3. Doreen J. Mattingly and Jessica L. Nare, "'A Rainbow of Women': Diversity and Unity at the 1977 U.S. International Women's Year Conference," *Journal of Women's History* 26, no. 2 (2014): 88.

4. Doreen J. Mattingly, *A Feminist in the White House: Midge Costanza, the Carter Years, and America's Culture Wars* (New York: Oxford University Press, 2016), 145.

5. Marjorie J. Spruill, *Divided We Stand: The Battle over Women's Rights and Family Values that Polarized American Politics* (New York: Bloomsbury, 2017), 7.

6. Some noteworthy anthologies on Asian American and Pacific Islander feminisms include Asian Women United of California, *Making Waves: An Anthology of Writings by and about Asian American Women* (Boston: Beacon Press, 1989); Leslie Bow, *Asian American Feminisms,* vol. 1–4 (London:

Routledge Press, 2013); Shirley Hune and Gail M. Nomura, *Asian/Pacific Islander American Women: A Historical Anthology* (New York: New York University Press, 2003); Lynn Fujiwara and Shireen Roshanravan, *Asian American Feminisms and Women of Color Politics* (Seattle: University of Washington Press, 2018); Sonia Shah, *Dragon Ladies: Asian American Feminists Breathe Fire* (Boston: South End Press, 1999); Mitsuye Yamada, Merle Woo, and Nellie Wong, *Three Asian American Writers Speak Out on Feminism* (Seattle: Red Letter Press Books, 2003). Please also see Shirley Hune and Gail Nomura, eds., *Our Voices, Our Lives: New Dimensions of Asian American and Pacific Islander Women's History* (New York: New York University Press, forthcoming); and Judy Tzu-Chun Wu, "Defining Asian American Feminisms: Intersectional Theorizations of Transnationalism," *Konan Research Institute Monograph* 30 (February 2018): 5–19.

7. Sherna Berger Gluck in collaboration with Maylei Blackwell, Sharon Cotrell, and Karen S. Harper, "Whose Feminism, Whose History? Reflections in Excavating the History of (the) U.S. Women's Movement(s)," in *Community Activism and Feminist Politics: Organizing across Race, Class, and Gender*, ed. Nancy Naples (New York: Routledge, 1998), 31–56; Mattingly and Nare, "'A Rainbow of Women.'"

8. Becky Thompson, "Multiracial Feminism: Recasting the Chronology of Second Wave Feminism," *Feminist Studies* 28, no. 2 (Summer 2002): 336–360.

9. Stephanie Gilmore and Sara Evans, *Feminist Coalitions: Historical Perspectives on Second-Wave Feminism in the United States* (Urbana: University of Illinois Press, 2008).

10. Chela Sandoval, "U.S. Third World Feminism: The Theory and Method of Oppositional Consciousness in the Postmodern World," *Genders*, no. 10 (Spring 1991): 1–24.

11. Rachel Pierce coined the phrase, "Capitol Hill feminism," to capture how "women on the Hill adopted and adapted the rhetoric, ideological precepts, and policy goals of the women's movement." Pierce, "Capitol Feminism: Work, Politics, and Gender in Congress, 1960–1980" (PhD diss., University of Virginia, 2014), 4.

12. Anastasia Curwood uses the term "bridge feminism" to describe how Shirley Chisholm (D-NY), the first African American woman to serve in the House of Representatives helped to bridge the African American civil rights movement and the women's movement as well as the grassroots and the legislative arena. Anastasia Curwood, "Black Feminism on Capitol Hill: Shirley Chisholm and Movement Politics, 1968–1984," *Meridians* 13, no. 1 (2015): 204–232.

13. Hon. Bella S. Abzug, "International Women's Year," *Congressional Record*, March 6, 1975, E946, folder 6, box 562, Patsy T. Mink Papers, Library of Congress, Washington, DC (hereafter "Mink Papers").

14. Patsy T. Mink, "Remarks in the U.S. House of Representatives Concerning a White House Conference on Women in 1976," March 10, 1975, p. 1, Mink Papers.

15. Mink, "Remarks in the U.S. House of Representatives."

16. M. J. Rymsza-Pawlowska, *History Comes Alive: Public History and Popular Culture in the 1970s* (Chapel Hill: University of North Carolina Press, 2017), and Natasha Zaretsky, *No Direction Home: The American Family and the Fear of National Decline, 1968–1980* (Chapel Hill: University of North Carolina Press, 2007).

17. "For US-IWY Activities," *Women's International Network News* 1:1 (January 1975), p. 9, folder 3, box 895, Mink Papers.

18. Susan Kakesako, "Note to Patsy T. Mink," April 8, 1975, folder 13, box 562, Mink Papers.

19. Patsy T. Mink, "Message to Susan Kakesako," most likely typed and recorded by Kakesako, April 8–9, 1975, folder 13, box 562, Mink Papers.

20. Mink, "Message to Susan Kakesako," April 8, 1975, Mink Papers.

21. The cosponsors included Bella Abzug (D-NY), Lindy Boggs (D-LA), Yvonne Burke (D-CA), Shirley Chisholm (D-NY), Cardiss Collins (D-IL), Millicent Fenwick (R-NJ), Margaret Heckler (R-MA), Elizabeth Holtzman (D-NY), Barbara Jordan (D-TX), Martha Keys (D-KS), Helen Meyner (D-NJ), Patsy Mink (D-HI), Shirley Pettis (R-CA), Patricia Schroeder (D-CO), Gladys Spellman (D-MD).

22. Chisholm, elected in 1968, was the first African American female representative in Congress. Collins was the first African American woman from the Midwest, Jordan from the South, and Burke from the West. All were elected in 1972. Burke, who became the first African American woman head of the Congressional Black Caucus, also became the first woman to give birth while in Congress and the first to use parental leave.

23. Edward Brooke, "National Women's Conference," *Congressional Record—Senate*, May 11, 1976, S6922, folder 11, box 562, Mink Papers. The remaining quotes in this paragraph all come from this speech.

24. Shirley Chisholm, "Providing for a National Women's Conference," *Congressional Record—House*, December 10, 1975, H12201–2, folder 7, box 562, Mink Papers.

25. Sparky Matsunaga, who served in the House of Representatives with Mink and who ran against her for the senatorial campaign in 1976, asked to be the person to insert this amendment into the legislation. However, Mink's office noted that Matsunaga initially only wanted to argue for a minimum of two, not ten, delegates. See "Amendment to H.R. 9924: Offered by Mr. Matsunaga," and "H.R. 9924: Amendment offered by Mrs. Mink," folder 10, box 562, Mink Papers.

26. Gwendolyn Mink, interviewed by Kimberlee Bassford, timecoded transcript, April 26, 2007, Washington, DC, take 592, p. 1.

27. Patsy T. Mink, "Statement to the Subcommittee on Government Information and Individual Rights of the House Committee on Government Operations on H.R. 8903, National Women's Conference," September 30, 1975, folder 6, box 562, Mink Papers.

28. Mink, "Statement to the Subcommittee on Government Information and Individual Rights," Mink Papers.

29. Zaretsky, *No Direction Home.*

30. Haunani-Kay Trask, *From a Native Daughter: Colonialism and Sovereignty in Hawaii* (Honolulu: University of Hawaii Press, 1999). Jodi Byrd distinguishes between those who landed in what became the United States as racialized subjects as "arrivants" rather than settlers. However, Dean Saranillio reminds us that being an "arrivant" does not absolve one of the responsibilities of challenging the settler state. Jodi A. Byrd, *The Transit of Empire: Indigenous Critiques of Colonialism* (Minneapolis: University of Minnesota Press, 2011); Dean Itsuji Saranillio, *Unsustainable Empire: Alternative Histories of Hawai'i Statehood* (Durham, NC: Duke University Press, 2018).

Rep. Pat Schroeder, accompanied by her husband, Jim, acknowledges her win over opponent Naomi Bradford for a fifth term in Congress, November 4, 1980. Photography by Duane Howell; courtesy of the *Denver Post*.

CHAPTER 14

Married Congresswomen and the New Breed of Political Husbands in 1970s Political Culture

SARAH B. ROWLEY

O N MARCH 20, 1971, the Inner Circle Press Club held its annual dinner. According to tradition, members of the press staged skits lampooning New York politicians. Like other events for the political and media elite, this was a sex-segregated affair, with men seated around tables on the main floor and women (many of whom were their wives) observing from the balcony above. In 1971, however, Bella Abzug, the fiery and famous first-term member of Congress from Manhattan, helped desegregate the event by sitting at the table of a lawyer friend on the main floor.[1] As one of only ten women serving in the House, Abzug was accustomed to operating in all—or predominately—male spaces, and she was not in the habit of being intimidated by dint of outsider status.

One skit in the show featured a male reporter dressed in drag, complete with extra padding and a floppy hat to mimic Abzug's signature accoutrement. He sang a song mocking Abzug's weight, fashion, and feminism. Following the song ("We'll burn a bra and girdle/But dammit there's one hurdle/When we take them off/We all look like hell"), a man dressed in a white frilly apron joined the skit as "Mrs." Martin Abzug. Already perturbed, it was this final jab at her husband of twenty-seven years that the congresswoman found the most offensive.[2] The frilly apron was intended to belittle and subordinate Martin by associating him with the feminine role of housewife. The inverse implication was that Bella was masculinized by virtue of her public role. That the satirist fashioned his costume to depict her body as fat, grotesque, and ugly—which is to say, outside the bounds of ideal feminine beauty standards—highlighted the gender disorder that the jokesters identified in the Abzugs' relationship. The lampoon followed a long tradition of American antifeminist humor predicated on a strict binary construction of gender roles and the assumption that a woman in (especially public) power necessarily emasculated her husband. But while it lacked originality, the skit struck a nerve.

Throughout the long 1970s, politics was understood by most to be a masculine realm, though one into which women were making important incursions. Serious scholars argued that women were underrepresented due to lack of will or perhaps even biological incompatibility. Given the rarity of elected women, the political scientist Jeane J. Kirkpatrick asked in the first major academic study of women in politics (1974) whether such a creature as "political woman" even existed. Congresswomen held few positions of power, in no small part due to the seniority system, which rewarded members of Congress who were first elected at a younger age, a time when most women were rearing children.[3]

By the early 1970s, women were running for office earlier than their predecessors. Several new candidates and eventual officeholders were married. Many were feminists. Observers noticed a "new breed of woman on the Hill" after Yvonne Burke (D-CA), Barbara Jordan (D-TX), Elizabeth Holtzman (D-NY), Patricia (Pat) Schroeder (D-CO), and Marjorie Holt (R-MD)—all lawyers running on independent professional reputations and younger than the average female lawmaker—were elected in 1972.[4] As mothers of young children, Burke and Schroeder particularly symbolized the new presence in Congress. When Schroeder first won election to represent Colorado's First Congressional District, her son, Scott, was six years old and her daughter, Jamie, was two. Burke gave birth to her daughter, Autumn, in 1974, making her the first woman to have a child while serving in Congress. They joined feminist colleagues already in the House, such as Patsy Mink (D-HI), Abzug (D-NY), Martha Griffiths (D-MI), and Margaret Heckler (R-MA).

Feminist congresswomen pushed for women's rights legislation on issues such as equal pay, reproductive freedom, homemakers' rights, education nondiscrimination, and federally funded childcare. This new women's political movement coincided with and helped shape reforms both within Congress and the parties that aimed to democratize decision making and weaken the hold of powerful conservative blocs.[5] The McGovern-Fraser Commission reforms that mandated proportional representation of women, young people, and racial minorities in the presidential selection process of the Democratic Party opened the door for women's increased visibility in national politics, and the National Women's Political Caucus (formed in 1971) further pressured both parties for equal representation.[6] Often full inclusion was not forthcoming. When Griffiths bypassed the labor-centered political machine in Detroit, and Schroeder won her first primary in Denver without even the support of organized Democratic women, they proved the potential that women candidates might harness to appeal directly to voters and challenge male-dominated power networks. However, it was not just partisans of the liberal and reformist "new politics" that rose in prominence. Across the political spectrum, women confronted established male power and drove both symbolic and policy change.[7] By the early 1980s, a *New York Times* article argued that "the promise of this 'second generation' and its potential for changing the image of women in politics [were] already being realized in all levels of government."[8]

By rejecting auxiliary status and claiming a right to run for office rather than just volunteer for male candidates, women politicians upset long-assumed gender roles. The outburst of public discussion over the existence, role, and psychological health of congresswomen's spouses over the long 1970s illustrates one aspect of the political culture that shaped women's experiences and opportunities during an era of significant changes in gender roles. Discussion of political spouses included reactionary antifeminist expressions such as the one mocking "Mrs." Martin Abzug, but the phenomenon also captivated people of many political and cultural persuasions, including feminist reporters. Studying the sustained cultural fascination with political husbands can therefore expand our understanding of the women's political movement. The political husband was "a rarity no longer," but he highlighted changing gender norms and resultant anxieties and transformations surrounding the roles of wives and husbands, both on and off Capitol Hill.[9]

Political husbands not only symbolized inverted power dynamics within specific marriages in Washington; they also represented a broad shift toward two-career families, working mothers, and the myriad manifestations of increased independence and challenges to traditional heterosexual marriage.[10] The changes were both symbolic and practical. In a series of challenges to state marriage laws, the Supreme Court institutionalized feminist critiques by reconceptualizing gendered rights and obligations of citizenship. By adopting what Alison Lefkovitz has termed a liberal feminist "expansionist" definition of equality, the court made spousal support benefits available regardless of gender and thereby "fundamentally altered" both marriage law and women's rights more broadly.[11] In this context, political watchers interpreted congresswomen's personal lives through explicitly political lenses. In both the realms of marriage and electoral politics, gendered contestations over paid-versus-unremunerated labor, domination and subordination, access to institutional resources, and the breadwinner model of masculinity upended traditional assumptions about men's and women's roles. In the figures of women politicians and their husbands, these realms intersected. They served as screens onto which to project larger cultural anxieties about gender, power, the home, and the state.

Because of structural inequalities, which led to fewer opportunities for women of color, the majority of women elected to Congress were white, as were their husbands. The hegemonic masculine role of the husband as sole breadwinner was also historically racialized as a white ideal. Thus, much of the public focus on congresswomen and their husbands occurred within the frame of a crisis of white masculinity. Women-of-color representatives such as Burke and Chisholm had additional concerns with which to contend, as they fought a particularly racialized set of gender assumptions. Even those figures who recognized the opportunity to shape public discourse, such as the Abzugs and the

Schroeders, were limited in their attempts to model a new, more egalitarian marital relationship. In rejecting the old trope of the feminist's husband as emasculated and domesticated, many congresswomen and their husbands ended up affirming hegemonic notions of manhood even when trying to reframe the traditional husband role.

Interesting Arrangements

Throughout the 1970s, major newspapers and style magazines alike published profiles of the handful of new high-profile transplants to the capital, while long-standing gender-specific social customs in Washington adjusted fitfully to the gender-neutral concept of the "political spouse." The most obvious model for the proper role of a congressional husband was that of the political wife, a figure that had long occupied an important symbolic and practical role in a politician's public career.

Washington Post journalist Myra MacPherson interviewed dozens of politicians, their spouses, and staffers for a 1975 book that cracked the traditional façade of the "happy political couple." Women whom she interviewed across Washington painted a vivid picture of high expectations for the political wife: she was expected to be polite and agreeable, self-sacrificing and acquiescent to political staff, available for campaign and ceremonial events, in accordance with her husband's views on the issues, ever-forgiving of frequent absences and other hardships or indignities, and happily willing to shoulder the majority of the domestic responsibilities. Above all else, she was seen as subordinate. And yet, MacPherson reported, "team player" wives who proclaimed happiness in their helpmate role often felt more ambivalent than they let on in public. Cathy Gilligan, whose father was a former governor of Ohio, explained why she stayed away from politics in her own adult life: "The woman's official role is as the man's wife. *Period.*" Joan Mondale, whose husband was a Minnesota senator at the time, told MacPherson that "women are absolutely trapped."[12]

While many women followed the preordained role, by the mid-1970s, others challenged the traditional model of the political wife. Some women insisted on Betty Ford–inspired candor and discussed difficulties, some obtained long-deferred and now-easier divorces, and an increasing few bucked the norm and maintained professional careers.

Meanwhile, while more married women, and especially feminists, were elected, there was no single, clearly defined mold for the husbands of officeholders. Even their physical presence in the capital was not taken for granted. In a culture that assumed both that a husband retained the right to determine where his family resided and that he would be the primary if not sole financial provider for the household, a married woman's election to the Congress posed a conundrum. "As far as I'm concerned, a woman's home is with her husband," one Kansas voter, speaking about a congresswoman married to someone from another state, told a *Wall Street Journal* reporter in 1976.[13]

Lee Novick, chair of the Connecticut Women's Political Caucus, highlighted how these questions came up for women candidates. She told the *Christian Science Monitor* that, "when a man runs, the public assumes he can neglect his family—drag them around or not with him. When a woman runs, they ask who is going to cook the meals, who will take care of the children. The question is, 'Can the family absorb the experience?'"[14] Running for Congress in 1980, Connie Morella "had to face the family issue squarely" and worried that voters would resent that her nine children "didn't have a momma," a double standard she did not think male candidates faced.[15] Virginia Shapard's plan to keep her children in their Georgia schools and visit them on weekends led her opponent in the 1978 Democratic congressional primary to emphasize that he would bring his children with him to Washington.[16] What these accounts make clear is that seeing married women campaign triggered fraught conversations over long-assumed gender roles.

Writing about her first campaign for the New York state assembly in 1964, Shirley Chisholm described an older man who scornfully accosted her, asking: "Young woman, what are you doing out here in this cold? Did you get your husband's breakfast this morning? Did you straighten up your house? What are you doing running for office? That is something for men."[17] Pat Schroeder likewise recalled regularly facing the "household question" during her first congressional election. After the same person asked about her husband and two young children at multiple events, Schroeder suspected that her opponent's campaign had planted this audience member in order to keep the issue front and center.[18]

The comments and questions did not stop after the campaign ended. When she got to Congress in 1969, several of Chisholm's new colleagues asked, "What does your husband think about all this?" Ostensibly joking, Chisholm interpreted their questions as not-so-subtle ways to convey to her that a woman's place was in the home and not in the legislature.[19] Schroeder likewise continued to hear incredulous comments and questions about her dual roles. In an oft-repeated tale, she is said to have wittily responded to an astonished older Democratic congressman, "I have a uterus and a brain, and I use both."[20] Whether apocryphal or not, the viral staying power of the defiant quip indicates that the need to dispel a restrictive definition of femininity's proper sphere resonated widely.

Unlike political wives, relatively few congressional husbands relocated to Washington. Martin Abzug remained in New York, where he was a stockbroker, and he saw his wife only on weekends. Helen S. Meyner's husband, Robert (a former governor), likewise stayed in New Jersey, and Martha Griffith's husband stayed in their native Michigan along with his law practice. Also unable to relocate his business, John Heckler stayed in Boston when Margaret brought their children to Washington after she was elected for her first of eight terms in 1966. Neither Duncan nor Marjorie Holt moved to Washington since she could commute from their Maryland home. William (Bill) Burke kept up his business in Los Angeles when Yvonne moved to Washington, and they traveled across the country every week with their young daughter to keep separation to a minimum. The norm was that congressmen's wives would defer to their spouses' careers while political husbands were provided more leeway to continue on as they had before. Marion Javits, wife of US senator Jacob Javits of New York, who refused to move to the capital and insisted on a separate daily life, was a heterodox anomaly in a political culture in which the all-American happy family served as key to a male politician's image.[21]

No political husband in this era garnered as much press attention as James (Jim) Schroeder, one of the few to move to Washington. A perennial press favorite, Schroeder left his position as a partner in a Denver law firm to follow his wife to Washington when she was elected to the first of her twelve terms in 1972. With two young children, Schroeder not only gave up his local practice, he made a point to prioritize flexibility in a new job so that he could spend more time with his family. With their often-photographed kids, dual Harvard Law School degrees, easy public demeanor, and mutual support, Pat and Jim represented a new model. They were willing to open their private lives to public comment, and they embodied the youthful energy and reformist zeal of the era's "new politics."[22] They self-consciously pioneered a two-career household based on gender equality and a modern approach to domestic life.

Focusing on Schroeder's sacrifice of his lucrative and prestigious Denver practice served to highlight both his departure from the norm and his devotion to offering a new marital model. While one career had to take precedence at a time, Jim explained, it did not necessarily have to be the husband's. Later, looking back on their political years, he further explored his philosophy: "It is inevitable—and I think necessary—that the wife will assume greater responsibility and require more time and effort with the children and on the home front than the husband. . . . The ladies can't and should not have to do it all. But they will do more."[23] In their memoirs, both Schroeders later joked about Pat's lack of cooking skills and affectionately recalled the state of semi-disorganization that characterized their parenting and housekeeping habits.[24] Even this paragon of an enlightened husband, who supported his wife's career and advocated for marriage as an equal partnership, still harbored conservative assumptions regarding gender-segregated labor among husbands and wives. Though intending to advocate egalitarian marriage and women's social equality, both Schroeders played on the assumption that the domestic realm was primarily the wife's responsibility. Tales of Pat Schroeder's kitchen woes were funny because they gently lampooned the idea that women should be mavens of the kitchen—and yet the joke served to reify the very same assumption it claimed to disprove.

When, every couple of years, a journalist wrote a profile of the "new political animal" that was the political husband, Jim Schroeder was inevitably included. During this transitional phase, reporters treated political husbands as a curiosity, who, in their oddity, might be ushering in a new norm or might remain abnormal. Typical to Schroeder's personality, he approached questions about his marriage with jocular humor, as if to imply that all the fuss was unnecessary. He joked in 1973 that he was "now in the role of wife."[25] He was more reflective about his "conflicting feelings" in another interview: "I was cast in the traditional role of the wife.... That was a source of disappointment. On the other hand, I couldn't help but feel that it would be a wonderful experience coming to Washington. That gave me an opportunity to start something new at a stage in life when a lot of people would like to try something but can't."[26] Here Schroeder reframed his experience not as one of dislocation or subordination but as opportunity, thereby shoring up his manly independence. For her part, Rep. Schroeder praised her husband for his support, but—typical of her humorous, informal style—was never overly precious about it. "He has no ego hangups, doesn't resent the attention paid to me," she told a reporter in 1974.[27]

Pat Schroeder was not alone: elected women and the sympathetic journalists that covered them were quick to praise husbands in public for supporting wives' political careers. Shirley Chisholm lauded her husband, Conrad, as unusually supportive in her 1970 memoir, which she dedicated to him "for his deep understanding."[28] Similarly, Bella Abzug proudly noted that "it takes a special kind of man to be able to cope with this kind of thing. A lot of men feel threatened by me, but that's obviously only because, unlike a man like Martin, they have feelings of insecurity."[29] The New York representative was infamous for her activism and iconoclasm, but she was not just referring to men who could not handle her unique brand of left-liberal feminism. Her comments reflected a larger cultural assumption that a woman's public success would potentially harm the men in her life. Both of the Abzugs agreed that balancing the domestic role and a political career took some negotiating. In 1971, Martin admitted that "all this"—presumably, her legal career, activism, and political ambitions—"inconveniences married life, but we've managed to make adjustments."[30]

Bill Burke was also often extolled for his flexibility in accommodating Yvonne Burke's career. A 1974 *Essence* writer described the Burkes' "interesting arrangement" whereby the couple split their time between the East and West Coasts. Yvonne praised her husband in the cover story, saying she felt "lucky" because "there are few men who would understand."[31] In a profile in *People* magazine the same year, Bill centered his own professional identity and assured readers that he was not overshadowed by his accomplished wife: "'We do the things Yvonne needs for her career,' Bill says, adding that he never feels like 'Mr. Yvonne Brathwaite Burke.' 'When she's meeting with my business associates and their wives, there's not that much feeling that she's even a congresswoman. We have a super marriage.' Burke does still maintain one chauvinist prerogative, regardless of other priorities of state: 'I insist that we have to be in Los Angeles for the 10 Rams' home games. The rest of the year I'm completely flexible.'"[32]

Here Bill Burke, as framed by the writer, blended a serious response about balancing two independent careers with a joke. Though the use of "chauvinist" was sarcastic, Bill's invocation of football fandom humorously reasserted his final marital authority using a common trope of hegemonic masculinity. Given the prevailing norm that men determined a family's place of residence, this joke was loaded with meaning. For all the effort that both Burkes put into presenting a public face of modern, two-career marriage, an edge remained in Bill's comments. He further reasserted his individual identity and masculine prerogative by pointing out that despite her higher public profile, in his business contexts, her status mattered little.

Like Bill Burke and Jim Schroeder, Gene Hawkins, married to Florida's Senator Paula Hawkins (a rare married female senator, who was elected in 1980), also deflected attention from his unusual status by using humor. Describing his assigned seat at Ronald Reagan's inauguration (next to other congressional spouses), Hawkins commented winkingly that "I was surrounded by wives, but it wasn't too bad. I had Elizabeth Taylor on my left and Nancy Thurmond on my right."[33] His quote comprised the final words of a report on political husbands in Washington, which imbued his comment with a certain poignancy—or, perhaps, irony. Taylor, a famous movie star, and Thurmond, a former beauty queen decades younger than her senator husband, were famous for their beauty. Rhetorically, his mobilization of the women's sex appeal reasserted his own masculinity, which might have been otherwise threatened by being grouped together with wives (subordinates). He laughed off the notion that he would socialize with traditional Senate wives and instead suggested that one benefit of his new position was access to attractive women. Of course, Hawkins was joking, but the particular humor that he and other political husbands used reified existing gendered expectations about heterosexual power relations.

Someone like Anthony Morella was seen as a "very supportive husband" to his candidate wife because "he [didn't] mind cooking meals, escorting her to political functions or being known, occasionally, as 'Mr. Connie Morella'"—all things, ostensibly, foreign to most husbands but common expectations for most wives.[34] The positive attention paid to these men illustrates that the notion of a husband rearranging his life around his wife's career was alien to 1970s American middle-class norms. Yet the long-term restructuring of the capitalist economy, in which the family wage–based model of the male breadwinner was cracking under the pressure of rampant inflation in the 1970s, meant that working wives were increasingly common. By 1976, even a majority of married women with school-age children participated in the paid labor force, a statistic that fueled growing, multidimensional anxieties about the current and future state of the family.[35] Viewed in this context, it is not surprising that women politicians attracted popular attention as potential harbingers of a new two-career family model among the professional class. One way to read the praise by sympathetic reporters and feminist congresswomen themselves is as a way to ease this transition. Theirs was an expansionist vision, a liberal attempt to gain equal access to the levers of government and to professional autonomy within existing familial, political, and economic norms, rather than a radical quest to overturn their underlying logic. Consequently, even when self-defined feminist lawmakers highlighted their unusually supportive marriages as egalitarian examples, the public discourse around these congressional husbands reinforced the idea that women should defer to men. Martin Abzug, Jim Schroeder, Conrad Chisholm, and Bill Burke proved the norm by being the exceptions.

Defending the Male Ego

In 1973, the *Chicago Tribune*'s Washington correspondent Louise Hutchinson marveled that Bill Burke's ego appeared "marvelously in tact," despite the fact that he commuted across the country every week to accommodate his wife's job.[36] This observation was repeated in a myriad of discussions about the new women in politics. In her 1974 study, Jeane Kirkpatrick found that "wives are expected to shield their spouse's egos especially from possible damage due to the wife's prominence," a finding reinforced by the larger political and popular culture.[37] Pat Schroeder, for example, remembered of her early years in politics, "The part I worried about the most was, what have I done to *him*?"[38] This presented a potential block to women's—especially younger women's—entrance into politics. How could women elected to Congress, the *New York Times*'s Barbara Gamarekian asked in 1975, "juggle the problems of geographical distances, housekeepers, children, schools, dirty laundry, and husbands with egos and careers of their own?"[39] These questions betrayed deeply held assumptions about male dominance and an uncritical acceptance of the gendered psychoanalytical framework of the ego. They suggested that a woman's public success and authority inherently threatened her husband's very sense of selfhood.

Dispelling the common stereotype of political husbands as "weak and demeaned," Myra MacPherson highlighted an alternative model: "Instead of being weak or subservient, the mates of female politicians seemed, although often unspectacular in personality, secure in their manhood, far more so than some of the power-obsessed, up-front male colleagues of their wives."[40] What might have seemed a threat was reframed as character advantage *for men*. In seeking to allay anxieties, sympathetic writers and political women emphasized political husbands' self-confidence. Bolstering the male ego was one way to assimilate the prevailing definition of middle-class masculinity (dominant, professional, breadwinning, independent) into the shifting structural realities of economic and social life.

The pattern was often repeated. Abzug wrote that many people wondered "what kind of man" her husband must be. Martin was "very mature and very stable," she insisted, and they were happy together.[41] Both Abzugs sought to dispel doubts by pointing to the hypocrisy of many of those people doing the questioning. They both publicly told the story of a client who called to invite Martin to dinner and felt free to judge his domestic arrangement: "What kind of life is that you lead? That's no kind of life, alone. Couples should be together," to which Martin replied by indignantly slamming down the phone. The punch line? "The guy is divorced."[42] In this example, Martin was the one adhering to traditional masculine standards of virtue and devotion to family.

At its core, the ego question centered on whether men could retain independent identities separate from their wives' prominent careers—a specifically masculine prerogative. In an interview with the *Chicago Tribune*'s female Washington correspondent, Bill Burke joked about threatening to knock down anyone who called him "Mr. Yvonne Burke."[43] To be called by the title of "Mr." in front of one's wife's name was represented as the ultimate insult. In the case of the Inner Circle Press Club's satire of Martin Abzug, putting a "Mrs." in front of his name inverted gender roles within his marriage, suggesting that he was emasculated by his wife. Dispensing with the man's first name altogether, as in the construction "Mr. Yvonne Burke" carried the insult further, to completely subsume the identity of the husband into that of the congresswoman wife.

Of course, the conventional naming practice within American marriages had long committed the same erasure but with the roles of men and women reversed. This was a fact not often acknowledged in mainstream political discourse. Husbands seemed particularly challenged: "a political husband needs an extra dose of masculinity and compassion to take in his stride the strains political life puts on his marriage," the political scientist and reporter married duo of Susan Tolchin and Martin Tolchin wrote in 1973.[44] Barbara Gamarekian observed in the *New York Times* that political husbands faced the same problems as wives, with added burdens. "Beyond the obvious disruptions of moving a household, finding new schools for the children and confronting career changes," she wrote, "there is the subtle and sensitive problem of suddenly taking second place behind a woman who has instant name recognition and upon whom attention is lavished. It helps to have a strong ego."[45] Gamarekian's comment betrayed a striking unwillingness to reckon with the gendered differences between men's and women's experiences as spouses. The public officials/wives' names, which were recognized, for example, *were their husband's names*. Bella Abzug, Shirley Chisholm, Pat Schroeder, Yvonne Burke, Paula Hawkins, Marjorie Holt: all of these figures took their husbands' last names when they married, whereas the reverse was not true. In Burke's case, the process played out in public, as she transitioned from being Yvonne Brathwaite (having taken her first husband's name) when she served in the California state legislature, to Yvonne Brathwaite Burke as she ran for Congress and was elected in 1972, to finally, simply, Yvonne Burke. No one expected women to have identities separate from their husbands.

A 1978 *Ebony* article by Bill Berry profiled five "strong black men who support and encourage famous wives" and laid out the ego issue: that "this role reversal where the woman is the star and the man plays a supporting role, could be an intimidating situation." He continued that "some men would feel hen-pecked" or would "resent" their wives' public attention while being relegated to the status of relative unknown. But, Berry assured readers, the five men profiled—four of them political husbands, including Bill Burke—were "secure in themselves and in their careers." The unusual public success of the wives was even *made possible* by their husbands, who "very often have provided the inspiration, encouragement and support vital to the success of the women in their lives." This construction served not only to reassert the "secure" selfhood of the men but also to recenter them in the narrative of their wives' public lives. Furthermore, Berry reminded readers that "long before" the many professional achievements and public recognition of someone like Secretary of Housing and Urban Development Patricia Roberts Harris, she was "Mrs. William Beasley Harris." In the way the article was constructed, then, the primary identification of this extraordinarily accomplished woman was as a wife, which reveals both resistance to the shifting gender roles and the resilience of traditional standards of masculinity.[46]

Fusing independent manhood with women's achievements was particularly important for the audience reading about Burke, Harris, and the other husbands in *Ebony*, because gendered racist stereotypes of the black matriarch, popularized in 1960s–1970s political and sociological discourse, shaped the public reception of black women politicians.[47] Moreover, racial discrimination prevented many black men from realizing the masculine breadwinning ideal. Shirley Chisholm felt it necessary to defend Conrad's strength of self against allegations that, in her words, "my husband would have to be a weak man who enjoys having me dominate him." To the contrary, she declared, "I don't think Conrad has ever had a moment of insecurity or jealousy. . . . Conrad is a strong, self-sufficient personality, and I do not dominate him." For Burke and Chisholm, this question of whether they "dominated" their husbands was inflected by both the deep-seated stereotype of the domineering black woman and the newer perception that women's liberation was a "white issue."[48] The only other black women in Congress throughout the 1970s were unmarried: Barbara Jordan, who was single, and Cardiss Collins, who took over her late husband's seat. As wives and congresswomen (and, in Burke's case, as a new mother), Chisholm and Burke regularly fielded questions about the relationship of race and gender or the relevance of feminism to black women. Many of these queries implicitly or explicitly referenced the idea that white supremacy worked to emasculate black men and that it would be a denial of race pride for women to upstage men.

Chisholm's defense of her husband was based on the familiar concerns about selfhood, identity, marriage, and gender roles. Even in her response to potential detractors, she betrayed a shared underlying assumption: men's "security" depended on primacy within the marital relationship. Chisholm insisted that she enjoyed public attention, while her husband was content to remain unknown to the general public: "Conrad is able to let me have the limelight without a thought," she wrote. To "let" is to give permission; it is to hold the power. In this construction, she did not so much reframe marriage as an equal partnership as insist that her unusual role could be integrated into the traditional concept of marriage. Conrad was framed as a benevolent man who was secure enough to withstand the challenge to his primacy that Shirley's career posed, whereas "a weak man's feelings of insecurity would long since have wrecked a marriage like ours."[49]

Interestingly, though ego was normally a concern for men, at least one male politician accused Chisholm of "ego tripping" by running for president during her second term in the House.[50] In running for president, Chisholm was undertaking a quintessentially masculine activity, which may have influenced this man's interpretation that it was merely an exercise in "ego tripping." Clearly, the ego "hang-up," to use the lingo of the era, reflected a deep concern about how changing gender roles might collectively destabilize people's (particularly men's) sense of self based on social belonging and professional success. The ego, in other words, was inextricably connected to the relationship between men and women, both in personal terms but also in their social roles. In subverting the traditional gender expectations, politician-wives had, in turn, according to the underlying logic of this discourse, upended their husband's place not only in the home but in the world.

Discussions happening within the political realm tapped into larger cultural conversations about heterosexual power relations. Press outlets across the spectrum reported regularly on the increasingly common phenomenon of middle- and upper-class working wives and mothers. Reporters investigated how "the ego problem" applied not just to the spouses of politicians but also to doctors and other women in male-dominated fields.[51] Even positive profiles of professional women repeated deeply held cultural norms about husbands' approval of their wives' careers and praised men willing to "help" with domestic duties.[52]

Conclusion

In the early 1970s, married women elected to Congress drew attention because they challenged bifurcated gender roles. The explicit feminism of married congresswomen such as Schroeder, Abzug, Chisholm, Griffiths, and Burke meant a potential reorientation of roles and policy priorities that would resonate deeper than the level of symbolic representation. As we begin to incorporate these pioneering women into the political history of the era, we must keep a critical view on how they navigated the complex ways that gender operated within the political culture, including through the framing of their own relationships. At the heart of the public discourse about their husbands was a skepticism toward the legitimacy of women's public service and positions of power. Whether overtly sexist, skeptical, curious, or even supportive, the attention paid to congresswomen's family and work balance and to their husbands made abundantly clear that their presence in Congress was unusual at best, and unnatural at worst. All political husbands, like political wives, were judged by how well they adhered to traditional gender roles. Even those feminist congresswomen who expanded the roles for women in public often seemed locked within ways of conceptualizing and communicating the marital relationship that reinforced the norm of women's subordination. When men such as Jim Schroeder ostensibly deviated from the traditional husband role, they still ended up affirming gendered perceptions of femininity/masculinity and domestic divisions of labor as normative. In particular, in acknowledging common misperceptions and bucking the norms, they named them and gave them power. Supporters of the new women's presence validated the idea that the discursive landscape for married women in politics and their husbands should feature such fraught gendered terrain as the ego. This was the bitter irony of the iterative power of gendered political discourse: even those actors hoping to shape a new model for women in public life faced the deep intractability of hegemonic gender norms.

Notes

1. "Roast Politico Served Up by Reporters," *New York Times,* March 21, 1971, 30; Bella Abzug, *Bella! Ms. Abzug Goes to Washington* (New York: Saturday Review Press, 1972), 71.

2. Abzug, *Bella!,* 72.

3. Irwin N. Gertzog, *Congressional Women: Their Recruitment, Treatment, and Behavior* (New York: Praeger, 1984), 6, 34–47; Jeane J. Kirkpatrick, *Political Woman* (New York: Basic Books, 1974).

4. Louise Hutchinson, "There's a New Breed of Woman on the Hill!," *Chicago Tribune,* December 7, 1972, B1; Mim Kelber, "How Women Are Changing Our Political Landscape," *Redbook,* November 1979, 82.

5. Julian Zelizer, *On Capitol Hill: The Struggle to Reform Congress and Its Consequences, 1948–2000* (Cambridge, UK: Cambridge University Press, 2004), 108–205; Bruce Miroff, *The Liberals' Moment: The McGovern Insurgency and the Identity Crisis of the Democratic Party* (Lawrence: University Press of Kansas, 2009), 11–24.

6. Jo Freeman, *The Politics of Women's Liberation* (New York: Longman, 1975), 159–162; Susan Tolchin and Martin Tolchin, *Clout: Womanpower and Politics* (New York: Coward, McCann, & Geoghegan, 1973), 31–59; Sara Evans, *Tidal Wave: How Women Changed America at Century's End* (New York: Free Press, 2003), 61–97.

7. Tolchin and Tolchin, *Clout,* 192, 197–198; Marjorie J. Spruill, *Divided We Stand: The Battle over Women's Rights and Family Values That Polarized American Politics* (New York: Bloomsbury, 2017); Catherine E. Rymph, *Republican Women: Feminism and Conservatism from Suffrage through the Rise of the New Right* (Chapel Hill: University of North Carolina Press, 2006), 188–238.

8. Anita Shreve and John Clemans, "The New Wave of Women Politicians," *New York Times,* October 19, 1980.

9. Barbara Gamarekian, "The Political Husband Is a Rarity No Longer," *New York Times,* November 16, 1981, A20.

10. Stephanie Coontz, *Marriage, a History: How Love Conquered Marriage* (New York: Penguin, 2005), 252–262; Nancy Cott, *Public Vows: A History of Marriage and the Nation* (Cambridge, MA: Harvard University Press, 2000), 200–215.

11. Alison Lefkovitz, *Strange Bedfellows: Marriage in the Age of Women's Liberation* (Philadelphia: University of Pennsylvania Press, 2018), 10.

12. Myra MacPherson, *The Power Lovers: An Intimate Look at Politics and Marriage* (New York: G. P. Putnam's Sons, 1975), 18, 87–104, 139, 59.

13. June Kronholz, "For Congresswoman, Issue in Kansas Race Is a 'Messy Divorce,'" *Wall Street Journal*, October 7, 1976, 17.

14. Jo Ann Levine, "Women Plot Campaign Course," *Christian Science Monitor*, August 2, 1974, 10.

15. Shreve and Clemans, "New Wave of Women Politicians."

16. Dennis Farney, "Uphill Race," *Wall Street Journal*, October 11, 1978, 41.

17. Shirley Chisholm, *Unbought and Unbossed* (New York: Avon Books, 1970), 65.

18. Tolchin and Tolchin, *Clout*, 88; Fred Brown, "McKevitt Unseated by Pat Schroeder," *Denver Post,* [November 1972], clipping, box 74, Pat Schroeder Papers, University of Colorado Libraries, Special Collections and Archives, Boulder.

19. Chisholm, *Unbought and Unbossed*, 93.

20. Tolchin and Tolchin, *Clout*, 87.

21. Barbara Gamarekian, "A Congresswoman's Life: Juggling Home and Politics Isn't Easy," *New York Times*, May 26, 1975; Dorothy Marks, "Men Pull Up Stakes to Join Their Wives: New Breed of Congressional Husband," *Baltimore Sun*, January 12, 1973, B4; Tolchin and Tolchin, *Clout*, 99; MacPherson, *Power Lovers*, 35–45.

22. Ilene Barth, "Our Five New Congresswomen," *Boston Globe*, February 25, 1973, C8.

23. James Schroeder, *Confessions of a Political Spouse* (Golden, CO: Fulcrum, 2009), 44, 45.

24. Pat Schroeder, *24 Years of House Work . . . and the Place Is Still a Mess* (Kansas City: Andrews McMeel, 1998), 131.

25. Jennings Parrott, "Colorado Lawmaker Makes Bustling Debut," *Los Angeles Times,* January 12, 1973, A2.

26. Louise Hutchinson, "Jim Goes to Washington, but His Wife's the Politician," *Chicago Tribune*, March 15, 1973, B1.

27. Karen Peterson, "Roles Reverse When Wives Take Up Politics," *Chicago Tribune*, September 19, 1974, B3.

28. Chisholm, *Unbought and Unbossed*, vii.

29. Abzug, *Bella!*, 34.

30. Abzug, *Bella!*, 34.

31. Betty Wisham, "Yvonne Brathwaite Burke: Day by Day," *Essence*, November 1974, 88.

32. "Rep. Brathwaite: She Married a Constituent," *People*, April 15, 1974, clipping, folder 6, box 396, Yvonne Burke Papers, University of Southern California Libraries, Special Collections, Los Angeles.

33. Gamarekian, "Political Husband," A20.

34. Shreve and Clemans, "New Wave of Women Politicians."

35. Natasha Zaretsky, *No Direction Home: The American Family and the Fear of National Decline* (Chapel Hill: University of North Carolina Press, 2007), 11.

36. Louise Hutchinson, "Bill Burke: Connubial Commuter," *Chicago Tribune*, March 31, 1973.

37. Kirkpatrick, *Political Woman*, 227.

38. Betty Cuniberti, "Lives of Congressional Spouses," *Los Angeles Times*, August 21, 1983, G13.

39. Gamarekian, "A Congresswoman's Life."

40. MacPherson, *Power Lovers*, 321, 327.

41. Abzug, *Bella!*, 75.

42. Abzug, *Bella!*, 33. Martin Abzug later repeated this anecdote to MacPherson. MacPherson, *Power Lovers*, 329.

43. Hutchinson, "Bill Burke."

44. Tolchin and Tolchin, *Clout*, 98.

45. Gamarekian, "Political Husband."

46. Bill Berry, "Husbands of Well Known Women: Behind Every Successful Woman There Is . . . ," *Ebony*, April 1978, 154, 155.

47. Anastasia Curwood, "Black Feminism on Capitol Hill: Shirley Chisholm and Movement Politics, 1968–1984," *Meridians* 13, no. 1 (2015), 204–232.

48. Hutchinson, "Bill Burke."

49. Chisholm, *Unbought and Unbossed*, 58.

50. Norman C. Miller, "Mrs. Chisholm Insists on Running, to Dismay of Many Politicians," *Wall Street Journal*, February 14, 1972, 1.

51. Lydia Chavez, "Doctors' Husbands Adjust to Roles," *New York Times*, August 26, 1979; Bernard Carragher, "Women Managed by Their Men," *Cosmopolitan*, November 1977, 248.

52. Mary Augusta Rodgers, "A Supportive Family Helps a Wife Who Wants to Work," *Woman's Day*, September 20, 1977, 102–104, 106–108.

President Ronald Reagan and his cabinet, February 1981. White House photo; courtesy Reagan Library, official government record.

CHAPTER 15

Madame Ambassador

Jeane J. Kirkpatrick and Global Diplomacy

BIANCA ROWLETT

D ESPITE THE PASSAGE of the Nineteenth Amendment, women
faced restrictions and limitations in the realm of politics, especially
the masculine-dominated world of global diplomacy. Until Ronald Reagan's appointment of Dr. Jeane J. Kirkpatrick as permanent ambassador to the United Nations in 1981, women were not widely known for
planning, creating, or implementing important foreign policy directives.
Kirkpatrick, a political science professor at Georgetown University, was
the first American woman appointed to the position of permanent ambassador to the UN, as well as the first female to serve on the National
Security Council (NSC) and the National Security Planning Group
(NSPG). This essay will emphasize the accomplishments of America's
first female diplomatic power broker by analyzing her contributions to
both foreign and domestic politics.

Kirkpatrick is best known for her "Kirkpatrick Doctrine," an argument for making distinctions between right-wing authoritarian and left-
wing totalitarian political systems that served as the intellectual rationale behind many of Reagan's foreign policies, including those associated
with the Reagan Doctrine and Central America. As UN ambassador,
Kirkpatrick was responsible for articulating, defending, and recruiting
support for American foreign policy goals and actions. Moreover, her
contributions to American domestic politics should not be marginalized.
She was actively engaged in both Democratic and Republican Party politics and a leader of the burgeoning neoconservative movement of the
1970s. Indeed, Kirkpatrick's political migration from the Democratic
to Republican Party was emblematic of the defection of many liberals

during that time. Though rejected by modern feminists due to her affiliation with Republican politics and her opposition to the methods, ideology, and policies promoted by feminist organizations, Kirkpatrick saw herself as a feminist who supported gender equality, specifically, the advancement of women in American politics, diplomacy, and society. Her influence and leadership helped break through gender barriers that previously prevented women from attaining the highest of diplomatic positions, thus paving the way for female secretaries of state from both parties, including Madeleine Albright, Condoleezza Rice, and Hillary Clinton.

Politics and Diplomacy

As a political scientist, Kirkpatrick took politics and political action seriously. Her own interest in politics began in her youth. Kirkpatrick was born in Duncan, Oklahoma, to yellow dog Democrats whose allegiance to the party was cemented during the Great Depression. As white middle-class Americans, they benefited from New Deal policies and viewed rural electrification, Social Security, and support for labor via unions and public works projects as "godsends" and President Roosevelt as a "savior."[1] Kirkpatrick thus became a dedicated member of the Democratic Party, casting her first vote in a presidential election for Harry S. Truman, her favorite president.[2] She became a regular attendee and active participant at the Democratic National Conventions (DNC) throughout the 1960s and 1970s. Kirkpatrick wrote articles and speeches and analyzed polling data for Democratic Senator Hubert Humphrey in 1960, 1964, 1968, and 1972. In 1976, she supported Henry "Scoop" Jackson as the Democratic presidential nominee, traveling with the senator across the country as a political advisor and polling analyst.

In the mid-1970s, Kirkpatrick broke with the Democrats and became an active leader in the neoconservative movement. The neoconservatives were appalled by the politics of the New Left, a revolutionary movement led by the nation's youth that embraced a myriad of causes, including civil rights and greater societal liberation for minorities, women, and those not identified as heteronormative. They rejected Cold War interventionism, in particular, the Vietnam War. New Left protests at the 1968 DNC caused the party to institute internal reforms via the McGovern-Frasier Commission allowing for greater participation from minority groups who had been underrepresented in the past. This influx of new members shifted the party left of center, culminating in the 1972 presidential nomination of the antiwar, left-leaning candidate George McGovern, a move that upset traditional party members like Kirkpatrick. Though neoconservatives expressed support for civil rights and gender equality, they broke with the party on policies supporting racial and gender quotas, affirmative action, and school busing. In the realm of global politics, neoconservatives were militant anticommunists whose worldview had been fashioned by the fight against totalitarianism and the threat of global communism. Accordingly, they rejected détente and isolationist policies and defended anticommunist interventionism.

In 1976, Kirkpatrick became a founding member and leader of the Committee on the Present Danger (CPD), a neoconservative foreign affairs lobbying group that argued the primary threat to the United States and the world was the Soviet drive for global domination and the unparalleled military buildup orchestrated by Moscow in the 1970s thanks to détente.[3] The group wrote pamphlets, articles, offered seminars and workshops, lobbied Congress, and gave interviews on radio and television in order to spread their message. Kirkpatrick's work at the CPD enhanced her reputation in academic and political circles, resulting in an invitation to join the American Enterprise Institute (AEI), a prominent conservative think tank. While at the AEI, she attended conferences on Latin American politics; met the future president of El Salvador, José Napoléon Duarte; and published an influential article, which brought her into Republican Party politics.[4]

In November 1979, Kirkpatrick published a scathing critique of President Jimmy Carter's foreign policies in a *Commentary* magazine article entitled "Dictatorships and Double Standards."[5] Kirkpatrick disagreed with the Carter administration's handling of Cold War affairs, in particular, the impact of his human rights' policies on revolutions in Iran, Nicaragua, and El Salvador. In her assessment of his diplomatic failures, Kirkpatrick outlined distinctions between nondemocratic governments and their relation to American foreign policy. These distinctions and their corresponding policy recommendations became known as the Kirkpatrick Doctrine.

Kirkpatrick claimed that the United States had lost two longtime allies in 1979, Iran and Nicaragua. She charged Carter with actively collaborating in the replacement of moderate autocrats, friendly to US interests, with less friendly totalitarian regimes.[6] She pointed out several similarities that existed between Iran and Nicaragua. Both were autocracies led by men who tolerated limited opposition and faced violent revolutions that threatened their power and the overall political stability of their countries. Carter had withdrawn military and economic aid to both nations due to charges of human rights abuses; however, Kirkpatrick claimed that Carter had taken such abuses out of context. She argued that violence wrought by revolutionaries had forced the leaders of Iran and Nicaragua to invoke martial law and arrest, imprison, exile, and occasionally torture their opponents.[7] She compared the course of events in these nations with those that had unfolded in China, Cuba, and Vietnam, arguing that in each case, the American effort to impose liberalization and democratization on governments confronted with violent internal opposition not only failed but also brought to power new regimes where ordinary people enjoyed fewer freedoms and less security.

According to Kirkpatrick, Carter unwittingly assisted in bringing to power such regimes due to several misconceptions. First, the administration had ignored or underestimated the Marxist presence among revolutionary insurgents, causing it to believe that a democratic alternative existed within the opposition. Second, Carter assumed that it was impossible to maintain the status quo in both nations. Third, Washington operated under the misguided belief that any change in the two nations was preferable to the current regimes.[8] Kirkpatrick chastised Carter for ignoring the lesson of Vietnam, which had presumably demonstrated the dangers of being the world's midwife to democracy, especially when that birth was set to occur amid insurgency.[9] She argued that it was impossible to democratize governments anytime, anywhere, and under any circumstances. Kirkpatrick insisted that democratic institutions were difficult to establish and preserve under any circumstances and that a functioning democracy was dependent on complex social, cultural, and economic conditions largely absent in Nicaragua and Iran. She noted that it took decades, if not centuries, for functioning democracies to develop.[10] Kirkpatrick then described the difficulties that ensued when rapid political change occurred within autocratic systems, stating the longer a dictator has held power, the more dependent on him a nation's fundamental institutions become. Thus, the overthrow of a dictator could lead to the collapse of government and society as a whole, a point that Carter did not appear to appreciate.[11]

Finally, Kirkpatrick condemned the administration for failing to understand the differences between traditional and left-wing revolutionary (totalitarian) autocracies. According to her, traditional autocracies were less repressive, more susceptible to liberalization, and more compatible with American interests than totalitarianism. Though she acknowledged that both were capable of producing "truly bestial" leaders who terrorized their own citizens, Kirkpatrick argued that there were systemic differences between the two.[12] In general, traditional autocrats *tolerated* social inequities, poverty, and brutality, whereas revolutionary autocracies *created* them. Traditional autocrats left in place existing allocations of wealth, power, status, and other resources, but they allowed for the worship of traditional gods and the observation of traditional taboos. They did not disturb the habitual rhythms of work and leisure, places of residence, or patterns of family and personal relations. Such societies, Kirkpatrick asserted, did not create refugees.[13] Conversely, totalitarian regimes created millions of refugees because they controlled and changed all aspects of society, culture, and politics in an effort to create ideological utopias.[14] Because of the incredibly repressive nature of such regimes, Kirkpatrick claimed that totalitarian governments could not transform into liberal, democratic states. Unlike totalitarian systems, traditional autocracies permitted limited contestation and participation. Thus, Kirkpatrick argued, given time, favorable economic, social, and political circumstances, talented leaders, and a strong indigenous demand for representative government, autocracies could develop into democracies.[15] She believed it was possible for American policies to encourage the process of liberalization in autocratic systems if proposed reforms were aimed at gradual change, not perfect democracy overnight, and were not attempted when the incumbent government was fighting for its life against insurgents.[16]

Since its articulation, the Kirkpatrick Doctrine has become the subject of much scrutiny and debate by academics and diplomatic analysts. Historian J. David Hoeveler described it as the "most influential contribution to foreign policy discussion in the conservative literature in two decades."[17] Her analysis, he argued, provided authoritarian states with a safety valve of tradition, history, and continuity by which one could measure them against the rending of social fabric caused by leftist revolutions and the total control over all aspects of life in communist states. Mark Gerson noted that Kirkpatrick's doctrine served as a reminder that there were degrees of evil in the world, and authoritarian regimes were the lesser of two evils when compared to governments of the totalitarian variety.[18] Others argued that her doctrine provided a rationale for ignoring bad behavior from right-wing dictators around the world as long as they were anticommunist.[19] Historian Walter LaFeber contended that, instead of liberalizing and democratizing, authoritarian regimes sometimes became more repressive. He argued that many authoritarian dictators were not as benign as Kirkpatrick portrayed them: they brought revolution upon themselves through their actions of repression, brutality, and exploitation.[20] Each of these analyses has value and deserves consideration, and the accuracy of the doctrine's tenets remain highly debatable. However, these assessments ignore the nuances of her argument in favor of an overly simplistic interpretation that reflexively accepts authoritarianism while rejecting totalitarianism. They disregard her acknowledgment that not all authoritarians are the same, her discussion of the prerequisites of democracy and the time it takes to develop, and her appraisal of the chaos that ensues once a dictator is overthrown.

"Dictatorships and Double Standards" was widely read, which advanced Kirkpatrick's growing reputation as a public intellectual. One reader, Republican presidential hopeful Ronald Reagan, was so impressed by her analysis that he recruited her to serve as a diplomatic advisor for his 1980 campaign. Once victorious, he appointed her permanent ambassador to the UN, a position he raised to cabinet-level rank, and assigned her to be part of his national security team. Like Kirkpatrick, Reagan was an ardent anticommunist, determined to prevent the spread of totalitarianism around the world. However, by the time he came to office, presidents could no longer rely on Congress and the American public to support Cold War policies such as backing authoritarian dictators based solely on their anticommunist stance. Unlike his Cold War presidential predecessors, Reagan was forced to provide moral justification for the support of authoritarian dictators that was not based solely on strict anticommunism or naked economic interests. Kirkpatrick provided this with her distinctions between authoritarian and totalitarian regimes. By investing authoritarians with political legitimacy and presenting them as transformative systems, the ambassador moved away from the previously accepted notion that the United States could only be safe if surrounded by like-minded political systems, effectively legitimizing a third option between democracy and totalitarianism.[21]

The Kirkpatrick Doctrine provided the intellectual rationale for support of authoritarian regimes and anticommunist insurgencies that became part of the Reagan Doctrine.[22] The doctrine was born out of the 1985 State of the Union address in which Reagan claimed that the United States could not break faith with freedom fighters who were risking their lives to resist communism.[23] Reagan promised to nourish and defend democracy by promoting trade, providing economic development to poor nations, standing by America's allies, and keeping faith with anticommunist revolutionaries.[24] His determination to support American allies, including those that were not democratic like the Philippines, South Africa, and El Salvador, was legitimized by Kirkpatrick's arguments regarding the transformative nature of authoritarian systems. His decision to support freedom fighters in Afghanistan, Nicaragua, Angola, and Cambodia was buttressed by her analysis of Carter's diplomatic failures. Moreover, historian Sean Wilentz argues that Reagan's Central American policies, the containment of communism by supporting authoritarian regimes and providing assistance to military insurgencies in pro-Soviet states, were part of a larger policy shift that led to the adoption of the Reagan Doctrine.[25] As a "key player" in many of the administration's policies toward Central America, Kirkpatrick again emerged as an influential figure in American diplomacy.[26]

In January 1981, Kirkpatrick's critique of US policies toward Central America was published in *Commentary* magazine. The article, "U.S. Security in Latin America," sounded the alarm over the spread of communism in the region. Kirkpatrick claimed that Marxist groups had come to power in Nicaragua and Grenada, were attempting to take power in El Salvador, as similar threats mounted in Guyana, Martinique, and Guadeloupe.[27] Kirkpatrick bemoaned the loss of the special relationship between the United States and Latin America, which she blamed on the "Vietnam Syndrome," beliefs that intervention in the affairs of other nations was immoral and that the United States should not support autocrats faced with revolutionary movements.[28] Kirkpatrick then described the unique characteristics shared by Latin American governments, offered a brief political history of both El Salvador and Nicaragua that highlighted Carter's mistakes, and concluded by offering suggestions for future policies in the region. Kirkpatrick argued that American national security interests should be prioritized and that policy makers must consider the history, economy, and culture of Latin American states, along with the unique characteristics of their political systems. This would enable the United States to determine the appropriate amount and types of aid to offer governments in Latin America, while also being more realistic about the time required for liberalization to occur.[29]

On assuming office, Reagan made Central America a top priority, which pleased Kirkpatrick. "In foreign affairs, geography is destiny," she declared.[30] Situated at the southernmost tip of North America, she designated Central America as the "fourth border" of the United States, making expansion of communism in the region a threat to American national security.[31] She argued that the Nicaraguan Sandinistas, aided by the Soviets and the Cubans, were exporting communist revolution to insurgents in neighboring El Salvador and that America must act to prevent another domino from falling.[32] Kirkpatrick recommended increasing military and economic aid to El Salvador in order to stabilize the nation. Once this was accomplished, the United States could increase its efforts at rolling back communism in Nicaragua. Meanwhile, covert action and proxy forces would "do the work for us" in fighting the Sandinistas.[33] Overall, many Reagan policies, including increased military and economic aid for the authoritarian Salvadoran government, opposition to a negotiated settlement in the Salvadoran Civil War, military and covert aid for the Contras in Nicaragua, and hostility toward the Sandinistas and the Cubans, were based on Kirkpatrick's assessment of Carter's mistakes in "Dictatorships and Double Standards" along with her recommendations for reconstructing regional security and stability in "U.S. Security and Latin America."

Outside of her influence on diplomatic strategies, Kirkpatrick was responsible for articulating and advocating for the administration's foreign policies to the United Nations. Historian Rhodri Jeffreys-Jones noted that typically "the U.N. Ambassador merely explains policy, as distinct from making it" and described the U.N. ambassadorship as having become disempowered and a "feminized space."[34] Yet, this was not the case with Kirkpatrick. Her inclusion within the NSC and NSPG gave her opportunities to influence and shape policy. Reagan admired Kirkpatrick and the two became close, allowing her to bypass normal diplomatic channels between the UN and the State Department in favor of direct access to the president. This did little to endear her to other members of Reagan's national security team and to the First Lady, causing them to block her promotion to national security advisor on two occasions.[35]

Overall assessments of Kirkpatrick's tenure as UN ambassador vary. She was commended for standing up for American interests, defending Israel, and challenging the actions of the Soviets and their allies but was criticized for her inexperience, confrontational style, and insistence on appointing team members from outside the established diplomatic bureaucracy. She was an outsider to the diplomatic community who was chastised for her inaccessibility. Critics deemed her willingness to bypass normal diplomatic channels and speak directly to the president as "unprofessional."[36] In response, Kirkpatrick acknowledged that she did hire outsiders to work for her, largely because she was an outsider and wanted to work with people whom she trusted. The ambassador conceded that she was sometimes unavailable, but she blamed this on her frequent travel between New York and Washington, arguing that her participation in the NSC and NSPG was essential for the US mission to function effectively.[37]

Kirkpatrick frequently criticized the UN, which she considered a "seriously bloated, overblown, international bureaucracy" that was ineffective in terms of its primary missions of conflict resolution, peacekeeping, and peacemaking.[38] She maintained that the United States had become relatively impotent there since the 1960s and blamed American ineffectiveness in part on the General Assembly's "one-nation, one-vote" structure that created a disjunction between power and responsibility. Kirkpatrick, along with other fiscal conservatives within the administration, were angered by the fact that the United States was responsible for paying a quarter of the UN budget while lacking commensurate voting clout.[39] Moreover, Kirkpatrick claimed that Americans had not practiced good politics at the UN. Following a decade of détente, the United States had isolated itself from international political blocs in an attempt to remain neutral. As a result, the United States had influence only when the blocs failed to act cohesively, which was rare. Kirkpatrick felt that this political isolation made the American ambassador's job difficult, requiring time and effort spent with each political bloc in an effort to influence their vote. When that failed, as it often did, the ambassador had to resort to casting a veto in the Security Council.[40]

Frustrated by this situation, Kirkpatrick was determined to increase American influence. When she was unable to gather enough support to block a resolution, she employed the veto, casting a total of nineteen in the Security Council, ten of which involved Israel and the Middle East. She made it clear to member nations that the United States took actions in the UN seriously, and votes against American interests would be taken into account in assessments of bilateral relations. Accordingly, during her tenure, voting records at the UN were placed under congressional oversight.[41] She maintained that the United States should use its control over the institution's budget in order to increase its influence. Kirkpatrick pointed out that several member nations refused to pay their fair share of dues and were not penalized; therefore, the United States could do the same. Kirkpatrick also argued that the United States could withdraw its voluntary contributions to the UN's specialized agencies.[42] Despite her many critiques of the UN, Kirkpatrick repeatedly praised its work with refugees, children, and efforts to address global health issues, and she recognized its importance as a global forum for small nations. Furthermore, she commended it for focusing world attention on important issues. For these reasons, she believed that the United States should remain active inside the international body.[43]

After four years, Kirkpatrick resigned as UN ambassador in April 1985, making her the longest serving UN ambassador since Adlai Stevenson in the early 1960s. Following her tenure as ambassador, she continued to be politically active. Kirkpatrick attended the 1984 Republican National Convention (RNC) where she gave a fiery speech in support of Reagan's reelection. She subsequently worked with Reagan throughout the campaign, prepping him for presidential debates.[44] In 1985, Kirkpatrick finally switched her political allegiance and became a registered member of the Republican Party. In 1988, she attended the RNC and gave a speech in support of George H. W. Bush. She worked for several advocacy groups, served on various government commissions under both Reagan and Bush, wrote a syndicated weekly column on foreign affairs for the *Los Angeles Times* (1985–1998), and lectured and wrote about government and policy from her position as a senior fellow at the AEI. Her last act of government service occurred in 2003 when she served as chair of the US Delegation to the UN Human Rights Commission where she worked to defeat a resolution that condemned American military action against Iraq.[45]

A Trailblazing Woman in Politics

Throughout her life, Kirkpatrick was an intelligent, determined individual who resisted familial and societal pressures to conform to stereotypical gender roles. As a young woman, she insisted on going to college after graduating high school and fought to attend graduate school. After she completed a master's degree in political science, her parents cut her off financially, claiming that she had received more than enough education for a woman and was in danger of becoming a spinster. Undeterred, Kirkpatrick took a job at the State Department in order to fund her own education.[46] There she met her future husband, the political scientist Evron Kirkpatrick. In subsequent years, she married, gave birth to three sons, finished her PhD in political science, published articles and books, remained active in domestic politics, and became a professor at Georgetown University. Kirkpatrick appeared to have it all: she was a wife and a working mother with a successful career.

Kirkpatrick's personal philosophy regarding women, family, and career was "refuse to choose," a seemingly feminist motto most readily embraced by more affluent women—a philosophy that might better be described as a racialized form of rugged female individualism.[47] Because of her race and affluence, Kirkpatrick was able to take advantage of educational and career opportunities normally reserved for white men and unavailable to working-class women and women of color. The dominant liberal feminist political goals were to give women more choices in their personal or professional lives, such as the right to choose to be a homemaker, to work outside the home in any occupation, to equal pay, and to equal access to education, jobs, and promotion. In that sense,

Kirkpatrick's career looked like the fulfillment of liberal choice feminism. Her privilege in early life enabled her to receive her education, yet her career was forged alongside the growth of modern feminism, which continuously opened up more opportunities for women. Thus, Kirkpatrick often found herself in the role of trailblazer in whatever path she chose.

Kirkpatrick hoped that, over time, other women would follow her lead to create a more equal America—an understanding that aligned far better with the individual-minded ethos of conservative Republicans than the increasingly feminist-backed Democratic Party. The modern feminist embrace of choice was a collective vision based on swift structural change; they aimed to eradicate systemic forms of societal inequality by using the levers of an expanded federal government to create opportunities and protections for all women. But as Kirkpatrick saw it, by the 1970s, Democrats and feminists were demanding instantaneous equality for racial minorities and women in all areas of American life. She claimed to favor equality of the sexes and races but only supported limited governmental action that would prevent discrimination. She believed that once political and social equality were protected, hard work, ambition, and ability would determine the success of an individual.[48] Furthermore, she spent years studying totalitarian political systems, in which attempts by revolutionaries to radically alter culture and society resulted in state terror and a loss of individual freedom. Kirkpatrick maintained that attitudes and beliefs could not be changed overnight by legislation and attempts to do so could result in a backlash that might undermine current advances toward equality. Consequently, Kirkpatrick supported the gradual change that would occur once more women and minorities took advantage of available opportunities to advance themselves individually in society.[49]

As America's first female UN ambassador, Kirkpatrick felt a tremendous amount of responsibility and pressure to excel at her job and not make political waves. Accordingly, she focused her attention on diplomacy and did not use her public platform to advance feminist goals. Neither did she discuss domestic political issues involving racial equality, unions and workers' rights, education, and Social Security, a difficult task for the former Democrat who remained loyal to the tenets of Truman's postwar liberalism. Critics, feminists in particular, perceived her silence on these issues as acquiescence and support for her party's conservative, antifeminist "family values" agenda and vilified her for it. As someone who saw herself as a feminist, breaking down barriers for women, and as the author of one of the first major works on American women in politics, Kirkpatrick was offended by their rejection. "Gloria Steinem called me a female impersonator. Can you believe that?" she said, "Naomi Wolf said I was 'a woman without a uterus.'"[50] Even a leading female academic dismissed her as "not someone I want to represent feminine accomplishment."[51]

In addition to facing criticism from feminist activists, Kirkpatrick had to overcome the gender bias and discrimination inherent within the male-dominated political system and media. Her alleged "lack of femininity" was criticized as she was forced into a makeover that included highlighting and styling her hair, makeup, and more fashionable clothing and jewelry. Kirkpatrick's academic background was mostly ignored, and her research on women went almost wholly unnoticed. Unlike males with advanced degrees in government, Kirkpatrick was almost always referred to as "Mrs. Kirkpatrick" rather than as "Doctor" or "Professor Kirkpatrick." She was called schoolmarmish or a teacher, never a professor or a scholar. In addition, she was frequently described as confrontational, tough, hawkish, temperamental, and Reagan's Iron Woman, all terms she claimed were rooted in sexism.[52] Historian Rhodri Jeffreys-Jones examined the development of the "Iron Lady," a common reference to female political leaders in the late twentieth century, and found that the "concept of an iron lady defined as a bloodthirsty self-made woman is a myth based on fiction."[53] He acknowledged that Kirkpatrick was not nearly as hawkish as she was portrayed, a point that the ambassador was forced to make several times in her own defense.[54]

Perhaps the most compelling evidence of gender discrimination toward Kirkpatrick is her absence or marginalization in diplomatic historiography. Insider accounts of Reagan diplomacy, like those by secretaries of state Al Haig and George Shultz, portray Kirkpatrick as being ideological, confrontational, and not a good team player. Other works reference her doctrine but claim her duties at the UN made her a part-time participant at national security meetings in Washington.[55] In a recent study of female diplomatic leaders, political scientist Sylvia Bashevkin argues that Kirkpatrick's relative absence in the historical literature is consistent with the findings of feminist diplomatic historiography.[56] She concludes that Kirkpatrick was a highly influential member of Reagan's national security team who held influence over the president but was not promoted to national security advisor because men in the administration envied her access to the president and resented the fact that she spoke her mind and refused to compromise her ideals.[57]

. . .

Overall, Kirkpatrick's contributions to foreign affairs and domestic politics make her an iconic figure in American history. Her assessments of Carter's foreign policy failures as outlined in her essay, "Dictatorships and Double Standards," provided the intellectual rationale behind Reagan Doctrine policies that included aid to anticommunist resistance groups around the world in Afghanistan, Nicaragua, Mozambique, and Cambodia. In addition, Kirkpatrick was a major player in the development of the administration's Central American policies. Her criticisms of Carter's policies there, along with her recommendations for restructuring American strategies in the region, became official administration policy. Furthermore, as UN ambassador, Kirkpatrick was responsible for articulating and defending the administration's policies to the global community. Thanks to her inclusion within the NSC and the NSPG, along with her personal access to Reagan, Kirkpatrick was privy to the development of policies as they evolved within the State and Defense Departments. Such direct access to the machinations of diplomacy was unique compared to previous UN ambassadors. This, along with Reagan's decision to raise the rank of the permanent ambassador to the United Nations to a cabinet-level position, further demonstrates her importance and influence within the administration. Moreover, Reagan endorsed Kirkpatrick's promotion to national security advisor on two occasions. In both instances, his male secretaries of state, Al Haig and George Shultz, threatened to quit if Kirkpatrick were promoted. Outside the realm of global diplomacy, Kirkpatrick's engagement with domestic politics was lifelong. She was active in both Democratic and Republican Party politics at the national level and was an important leader in the neoconservative movement. Indeed, her career and personal political transformation can be read as a history of one of the most significant shifts in American domestic and foreign politics in the late twentieth century.

Notes

1. Jeane Kirkpatrick, "An American Girlhood," *Weekly Standard*, February 5, 2007, 4.

2. Peter Collier, *Political Woman: The Big Little Life of Jeane Kirkpatrick* (New York: Encounter Books, 2012), 22. All biographical information was taken from Collier, *Political Woman*, and the following: Pat Harrison, *Jeane Kirkpatrick* (New York: Chelsea House, 1991); Kirkpatrick, "An American Girlhood."

3. Justin Vaïsse, *Neoconservatism: The Biography of a Movement* (Cambridge, MA: Harvard University Press), 2010, 163.

4. Collier, *Political Woman*, 94–95.

5. Collier, *Political Woman*, 100.

6. Jeane Kirkpatrick, *Dictatorships and Double Standards* (New York: AEI Press, 1982), 23.

7. Kirkpatrick, *Dictatorships*, 24.

8. Kirkpatrick, *Dictatorships*, 29–30.

9. Kirkpatrick, *Dictatorships*, 30, 34.

10. Kirkpatrick, *Dictatorships*, 30–31.

11. Kirkpatrick, *Dictatorships*, 32–33.

12. Kirkpatrick, *Dictatorships*, 49.

13. Kirkpatrick, *Dictatorships*.

14. Kirkpatrick, *Dictatorships*.

15. Kirkpatrick, *Dictatorships*, 32.

16. Kirkpatrick, *Dictatorships*, 51.

17. J. David Hoeveler, *Watch on the Right* (Madison: University of Wisconsin Press, 1991), 159.

18. Mark Gerson, *The Neoconservative Vision* (New York: Madison Books, 1996), 176.

19. See Sean Wilentz, *The Age of Reagan: A History, 1974–2008* (New York: HarperCollins, 2008), 153; Murray Friedman, *The Neoconservative Revolution: Jewish Intellectuals and the Shaping of Public Policy* (New York: Cambridge University Press, 2005), 145.

20. Walter LaFeber, "The Reagan Administration and Revolutions in Central America," *Political Science Quarterly* 99, no. 1 (1984): 6.

21. Bianca Joy Rowlett, "Jeane Kirkpatrick and Neoconservatism: The Intellectual Evolution of a Liberal" (PhD diss., University of Arkansas, 2014), *Theses and Dissertations*, no. 2114, 254, https://scholarworks.uark.edu/etd/2114.

22. Rowlett, "Jeane Kirkpatrick," 254. See also Sylvia Bashevkin, *Women as Foreign Policy Leaders: National Security and Gender Politics in Superpower America* (New York: Oxford University Press, 2018), 61–62.

23. Chester Pach, "The Reagan Doctrine: Principle, Pragmatism, and Policy," *Presidential Studies Quarterly* 36, no. 1 (2006): 76.

24. Pach, "Reagan Doctrine," 77.

25. Wilentz, *Age of Reagan*, 157.

26. Lou Cannon, *President Reagan: The Role of a Lifetime* (New York: Public Affairs, 2000), 304.

27. Kirkpatrick, *Dictatorships*, 54.

28. Kirkpatrick, *Dictatorships*, 55–56.

29. Kirkpatrick, *Dictatorships*, 89–90.

30. "Foreign Policy Issues," *Worldnet*, no. 225, July 23, 1986, National Archives and Records Administration, College Park, MD, 306-WNET-241.

31. "The Caribbean Basin," National Security Council meeting, February 10, 1982, http://www.thereaganfiles.com/19820210-nsc-40-on-cbi.pdf.

32. See Bianca Joy Rowlett, "Jeane Kirkpatrick, the Reagan Administration, and Neoconservative Policy in El Salvador" (master's thesis, University of Arkansas, 2007).

33. "Strategy toward Cuba and Central America," National Security Council meeting, November 10, 1981, http://www.thereaganfiles.com/19811110-nsc-42.pdf.

34. Rhodri Jeffreys-Jones, *Changing Differences: Women and the Shaping of American Foreign Policy, 1917–1994* (New Brunswick, NJ: Rutgers University Press, 1995), 175.

35. Bashevkin, *Women as Foreign Policy Leaders*, 61, 215. See also Cannon, *President Reagan*, 158–159, 327, 380.

36. See Cathal J. Nolan, ed., *Notable U.S. Ambassadors since 1775: A Biographical Dictionary* (Westport, CT: Greenwood Press, 1997); Seymour Maxwell Finger, *American Ambassadors at the United Nations: People, Politics, and Bureaucracy in Making Foreign Policy* (New York: UNITAR, 1992); Gary Ostrower, *The United Nations and the United States* (New York: Twayne,

1998); Linda Fasulo, *Representing America: Experiences of U.S. Diplomats at the UN* (New York: Praeger, 1984); Keith Hindell, "Madame Ambassador," *Passport* 39, no. 3, January 2009; Allan Gerson, *The Kirkpatrick Mission: Diplomacy without Apology; America at the United Nations, 1981–1985* (New York: Free Press, 1991); Ann Miller Morin, *Her Excellency: An Oral History of American Women Ambassadors* (New York: Twayne, 1995).

37. Morin, *Her Excellency*, 251.

38. Morin, *Her Excellency*, 260.

39. Jeane J. Kirkpatrick, *Legitimacy and Force: State Papers and Current Perspectives*, vol. 1, *Political and Moral Dimensions* (New Brunswick, NJ: Transaction Books, 1988), 217.

40. Kirkpatrick, *Legitimacy and Force*, 1:225–227.

41. Kirkpatrick, *Legitimacy and Force*, 1:276–277.

42. Kirkpatrick, *Legitimacy and Force*, 1:261, 1:268–270.

43. Kirkpatrick, *Legitimacy and Force*, 1:278–279.

44. Kirkpatrick, *Legitimacy and Force*, 1:165–166.

45. Collier, *Political Woman*, 201.

46. Collier, *Political Woman*, 25.

47. Harrison, *Jeane Kirkpatrick*, 58.

48. Jeane Kirkpatrick, *The New Presidential Elite: Men and Women in National Politics* (New York: Russell Sage Foundation, 1976), 83.

49. Kirkpatrick, *New Presidential Elite*, 83–85.

50. Collier, *Political Woman*, xiv.

51. "At Lunch with Jeane Kirkpatrick," *New York Times*, August 17, 1994.

52. Kirkpatrick, *Legitimacy and Force*, 1:456–458.

53. Jeffreys-Jones, *Changing Differences*, 158.

54. Jeffrey-Jones, *Changing Differences*, 190–191. See also Jeane Kirkpatrick, "Pardon Me, but Am I That 'Hard-Liner' the Anonymous Sources Are Talking About?," *Washington Post*, June 20, 1983.

55. Rowlett, "Jeane Kirkpatrick and Neoconservatism," 3; Bashevkin, *Women as Foreign Policy Leaders*, 59.

56. Bashevkin, *Women as Foreign Policy Leaders*, 59.

57. Bashevkin, *Women as Foreign Policy Leaders*, 59, 61, 210.

PART THREE

Looking Toward a New Century

Women in Politics, 1990s–2010s

CHAPTER 16

Palin versus Clinton

Feminism, Womanhood, and the 2008 Presidential Election

EMILY SUZANNE JOHNSON

WITH THE PASSAGE of the Nineteenth Amendment in August 1920, many observers predicted the emergence of a unified women's voting bloc, for better or worse. But contemporary ideas about the "woman vote" varied widely. Taken together, they actually highlighted the political diversity among women and undermined the idea of women's unified political interests. Journalist Emma Bugbee came closest to the truth when she observed on election day in 1920, "There are about twenty-six million women voters, but no woman voter. Much less is there a woman vote."[1]

A hundred years later, simplistic ideas about women's political interests continue to haunt our national discourse and pose serious problems for campaigners, candidates, and analysts alike. In 2008, these assumptions became unusually explicit in the rhetoric surrounding Hillary Clinton's bid for the Democratic presidential nomination and Sarah Palin's vice presidential candidacy on the Republican ticket. Across the political spectrum, observers revealed their expectations of female political solidarity even as they also demonstrated fundamentally different ideas about how women should think, feel, and vote. Many Clinton supporters scoffed at the notion that women would vote for Palin simply based on gender. At the same time, they lambasted women in their own party who failed to support Clinton, the only female candidate in the Democratic primary. Women who backed Barack Obama and those who supported the Republican Party found themselves in a position of defending not only their political choices but also themselves *as women* in light of those choices.

The cultural conversations that surrounded the candidacies of Clinton and Palin in 2008 offer an opportunity to unpack the often unspoken assumptions that inform our public and scholarly conversations about women's political engagement.[2] Groups across the political spectrum have persistently tried to reduce women's political interests to unified platforms that suit their own agendas. These arguments have appeal because they resonate with cultural understandings of fundamental gender differences and with the ideal of feminist solidarity. Women's political allegiances and interests, however, have always been complex, and attempts to reduce women to a single political constituency will always fail to adequately capture their political interests and contributions.

McCain's Folly: The Interchangeable Woman

When Republican presidential candidate John McCain announced his choice of running mate on August 29, 2008, most Americans were caught by surprise. At the time, Sarah Palin was a little-known politician from Alaska, serving her second year as the state's governor. In the rampant media speculation over vice presidential nominations, Palin's name had almost never come up. Yet there were good reasons for McCain to choose Palin. Both styled themselves as "mavericks" who relied on a tell-it-like-it-is charisma to connect with voters. Republicans had held the White House since 2001; in 2008, President George W. Bush was struggling against historically low approval ratings.[3] To distance himself from Bush, McCain leaned heavily on his reputation as an iconoclast and hoped that Palin would help bolster that image. Yet McCain's heterodoxy had often estranged him from religious conservatives in the Republican Party. The senator opposed a federal amendment banning same-sex marriage and had once referred to Christian Right luminaries Jerry Falwell and Pat Robertson as "agents of intolerance" whose tactics "shame our faith, our party, and our country."[4] Palin's evangelical background and record of social and fiscal conservatism helped assuage voters in this key demographic.[5]

Gender was also a factor in McCain's choice, which rested at least in part on the long-standing idea that female voters would necessarily gravitate toward a female candidate. The 2008 Democratic primaries had been a long and often bitter fight between Barack Obama and Hillary Clinton. Both candidacies carried the promise of historical significance; if elected, Hillary Clinton would be the first female president of the United States, Barack Obama the first African American. McCain's team worried that a campaign led by two white men might send the wrong message in this electoral climate.

They also hoped that a female vice presidential pick would help bring disaffected Clinton supporters to their side. During the primaries, Clinton had garnered a great deal of support from women, especially older white women who strongly emphasized the significance of being able to vote for a female candidate. These women were deeply disappointed when Clinton conceded the Democratic nomination to Obama in June 2008 and again when Obama named Joe Biden and not Clinton as his running mate that August.[6]

It was plausible that some Clinton supporters might transfer their loyalty to McCain. Both candidates were moderates, whose policy positions and voting records often converged. In 2008, both spoke positively about civil unions for same-sex couples but did not support federal legislation on gay marriage. In 2006, they co-led a congressional delegation to witness the effects of global warming in Alaska and spoke out about climate change. They both favored US military intervention abroad and voted in favor of the Iraq War in 2002.[7]

Clinton supporters who directed their disappointment at the Democratic Party establishment seemed especially apt to vote for McCain. Soon after Clinton's concession in the Democratic primaries, Maggie Fenerty of Philadelphia wrote to her local newspaper in frustration. For her, Clinton's treatment by the media and "the chauvinist Democratic Party leadership" served as painful reminders of the sexism that she had experienced in her own life.[8] Cynthia Ruccia of Ohio—who had twice run for Congress on a Democratic ticket—went even further. She launched a media campaign encouraging women to vote for McCain to protest the Democratic Party's treatment of Clinton. "Women who have been the backbone of the Democratic Party feel our party has betrayed us," she told reporters. "This was our time."[9] For women like Fenerty and Ruccia, the opportunity to vote for a female candidate superseded party identification, at least to some extent.

The McCain campaign had good reason to believe that adding a woman to the ticket could help attract the votes of Clinton supporters sour on the Democratic Party. But the choice of Palin—Clinton's near opposite in policy goals and political style—revealed a simplistic assumption that gender *alone* would be enough to sway women's political choices. This strategy proved ineffective, and for some, it was infuriating. Shortly after Palin's nomination, *New York Times* columnist Gail Collins expressed her exasperation at the "idea that women are going to race off to vote for any candidate with the same internal plumbing."[10] Iconic feminist activist and Clinton supporter Gloria Steinem echoed this critique, adding that Palin was antithetical to "pretty much everything Clinton's candidacy stood for." For disappointed Clinton supporters to "vote in protest for McCain/Palin, would be like saying, 'Somebody stole my shoes, so I'll amputate my legs,'" Steinem wrote.[11]

Aside from their gender, the two candidates had little in common. Palin's energetic conservative populism stood in sharp contrast to Clinton's reserved and methodical center-left approach, on issues from foreign policy to the proper role of government. Abortion and health care were focal issues for both women, who stood on opposites sides of debates over *Roe v. Wade*, embryonic stem cell research, and public health care. Whereas Hillary Clinton was restrained and experienced, Palin was charismatic and promised that her lack of federal government credentials would mean "no more politics as usual."[12]

Even in their approach to gender, the two candidates diverged. Clinton minimized the issue, insisting that voters should elect her for her qualifications and not because she was a woman. Taking women's support for granted, Clinton and her advisors assumed that their real challenge would be convincing men to vote for a female candidate. With that in mind, they decided on a strategy that downplayed "feminine" qualities like empathy and approachability in favor of more "masculine" traits like readiness and resolve. They modeled their campaign on three decades of common wisdom that female candidates needed to be tough to succeed, following the model of former British Prime Minister Margaret Thatcher, also known as the "Iron Lady."[13]

Sarah Palin leaned into a more feminine persona, in both her personal style and her choice to highlight her role as a mother of five children, including an infant son. Even when she asserted her toughness, she often did so through the maternal imagery of the "hockey mom" and "mama grizzly." Whereas conventional wisdom told women to wait until their children were grown to run for elected office (to avoid questions about balancing motherhood and public life), Palin connected her experience as a mother to her political role.

This fusion of motherhood and political engagement, known as "maternalism," has a long and complex history in the United States. After the American Revolution, the idea of "Republican Motherhood" helped justify women's exclusion from voting by explaining that their civic responsibility lay in raising patriotic and well-educated children.[14] In the century and a half that followed, while some women continued to insist that the vote would only distract women from their domestic duties, others began to argue that women's supposedly innate moral purity and maternal instincts would bring balance to a political system dominated by men's corruption and warmongering. In the twentieth century, women across the political spectrum used maternalist ideas to justify their activism on opposite sides of issues ranging from the fight against communism to school desegregation.[15] Maternalism is premised on gender essentialism, the idea that all women share the same natural traits and interests, related to motherhood. Ironically, its political usage over time has spanned such a wide range of political positions that its history only underscores women's political diversity.

In the second half of the twentieth century, many conservative women continued to rely on maternalist rhetoric, in local fights over school curricula and national battles about "family values." At the same time, this strategy began to fall out of favor among American feminists, who rejected it as too limiting in its definitions of women and women's interests. Palin's and Clinton's 2008 campaigns reflected this history. Clinton was endorsed by the feminist National Organization for Women, which has been a leading voice in bringing gender equality into the mainstream of American politics since its founding in 1966. Betty Friedan, a prominent early leader of the group, rose to national prominence with the publication of her 1963 book *The Feminine Mystique*, which argued that most women were unfulfilled by domestic and maternal roles alone. Sarah Palin was enthusiastically backed by Concerned Women for America, a conservative evangelical group founded in 1979 to oppose NOW and to fight the perception that "feminists . . . speak for all women in America."[16] Its founder, Beverly LaHaye, routinely relied on maternalism to frame her political vision and castigate the feminist movement as antifamily. By 2008, Concerned Women for America and other conservative women's groups had developed strong ties to the Republican Party through lobbying efforts and reliable get-out-the-vote campaigns. The National Organization for Women and other liberal feminist groups had forged similar connections with the Democratic Party.[17]

McCain's choice of Sarah Palin as his running mate rested in part on the idea that women would naturally hew to a female candidate. It also revealed an overly simplistic assumption that female candidates are more or less interchangeable. The stark differences between Palin and Clinton, in terms of policy priorities, electoral strategy, and rhetorical style, not only underscored women's present and historic political diversity but also highlighted the age-old folly of treating women voters as a unified bloc.

Sarah Palin's Contested Womanhood

Feminist critiques of Palin's nomination had the potential to start a conversation about women's political diversity. Instead, many of these critiques also presented uncomplicated assumptions about women's proper political allegiances, especially in assertions that all women should support feminist political agendas.

For many feminists, the idea that Clinton supporters might transfer their loyalty to Palin seemed preposterous for two reasons: first, the candidates were markedly different, and, second, the prospect that right-wing women had legitimate politics was unthinkable. These observers treated Palin as they had treated Phyllis Schlafly and other prominent conservative women in the past, dismissing them as ridiculous ironies—prominent women advocating against feminist priorities, while taking advantage of the platform that feminists had won for women in the political sphere. Their arguments collapsed "women's interests" and feminism into a single concept and defined antifeminist politics as antiwoman. In this way of thinking, antifeminist women become a paradox, a philosophical absurdity regardless of their existence in reality.

In fact, women have been at the heart of modern American conservatism for decades. In the first half of the twentieth century, they articulated a maternalist "housewife populism," arguing that women's familial roles and "inherent spirituality" made them natural conservatives.[18] In the years following the Second World War, they fought to keep Christian influences in public school curricula and sex education out. Women's enthusiastic support buoyed far-right candidate Barry Goldwater's presidential campaign in 1964 and helped to push the Republican Party rightward in the decades that followed. During the 1970s, conservative women opposed the decriminalization of abortion in *Roe v. Wade* and prevented the ratification of the feminist-backed Equal Rights Amendment. As the modern Religious Right emerged during this decade, men like Jerry Falwell and Pat Robertson may have been its most visible spokesmen, but women's groups like Concerned Women for America and Phyllis Schlafly's Eagle Forum shaped the movement and propelled its success.[19]

During the culture wars of the 1980s and 1990s, feminists largely dismissed conservative women as dupes who acted against their own best interests. In her foundational 1979 polemic, *Right-Wing Women*, Andrea Dworkin denigrated the notion of women's "natural" conservatism as nothing more than the product of centuries-old "gossip among men," given credence by "noxious male philosophers," scientists, and artists.[20] She acknowledged the existence of contemporary conservative women, including Phyllis Schlafly and Anita Bryant, but she rebuffed the possibility that these women acted out of their own agency and conviction. Instead, she argued that "the Right in the United States today is a social and political movement controlled almost totally by men but built largely on the fear and ignorance of women."[21]

During these same decades, the still-developing field of women's history—formed through the work of groundbreaking feminist scholars—understandably tended to focus on feminist pasts. This work was essential in establishing the profound significance of studying women's experiences, but its early focus on feminist and proto-feminist women contributed to a broad sense that antifeminist women were absent or at least unusual. By 2008, a rapidly growing body of scholarship on conservative women's histories had begun to develop; still, many in the popular press and general public accepted the normative assumption that "women's political history" was synonymous with "feminist history."

It is therefore unsurprising that most responses to Sarah Palin failed to recognize her as part of a broader history of deeply committed conservative women. Reacting to Palin's candidacy, Gloria Steinem credited the feminist movement alone with the fact that "even the anti-feminist right wing—the folks with a headlock on the Republican Party—are trying to appease the gender gap with a first-ever female vice president." Feminists certainly deserve some of the credit, but this analysis minimized the efforts of conservative women who had been active in the Republican Party's right wing for decades. Steinem accentuated her conflation of "women" with "feminists"—and her erasure of conservative women—in her claim that Palin "opposes everything most other women want and need."[22]

Palin attempted to quell these critiques by identifying with feminism in a limited way. When reporters asked her directly whether she considered herself a feminist, her responses varied. During the 2008 campaign, she told CBS's Katie Couric, "I'm a feminist who believes in equal rights," but equivocated with ABC's Brian Williams, saying: "I'm not going to label myself anything."[23] Two years later, she ignited a firestorm when she identified herself as part of "a new conservative feminist movement" that was pro-life, socially conservative, and premised on the notion that gender equality had already been won.[24] Feminists on the Left publicly disagreed about whether "conservative feminists" had a place in the movement; for many of the most prominent voices, the answer was an unequivocal "no."[25]

In 2008, some critics went further, not just excluding Palin from feminism but from womanhood itself. Feminist culture critic Cintra Wilson—in a column that began: "She may be a lady, but she ain't no woman"—called Palin an "opportunistic anti-female" and asserted that the "throat she's so hot to cut is that of *all* American women."[26] Wendy Doniger, a professor at the University of Chicago Divinity School, drew criticism from conservatives for her assertion that Palin's "greatest hypocrisy is in her pretense that she's a woman."[27] For these writers, McCain's error in choosing Palin had less to do with his failure to recognize women's political diversity and more to do with their own perception that women who cannot be counted as feminists do not really count as women. Even as they criticized McCain's campaign for its overly simplistic assumptions about women voters' willingness to vote for any female candidate, they perpetuated an understanding of women's political allegiances that erased the long and complex history of conservative women's activism.

Hillary Clinton and the Complexities of Feminist Solidarity

The rhetoric that Palin was not really a woman allowed critics to ridicule McCain's strategy, while maintaining their own understanding that women really ought to prioritize voting for someone "with the same internal plumbing," as long as she supported feminist political priorities. Many of Clinton's supporters expressed shock and betrayal when some women favored Obama over Clinton during the Democratic primaries.

Feminist author and former *Ms.* Magazine editor Robin Morgan reprised her famous 1970 essay "Goodbye to All That" to rebuke the women who did not support Clinton. "Goodbye to some young women eager to win male approval by showing they're not feminists (or at least not the kind who actually threaten the status quo)," she wrote. The essay conveyed broader critiques of young women as foolish, naïve, and unfeminist. "Goodbye to some women letting history pass by while wringing their hands, because Hillary isn't as 'likeable' as they've been told they must be," Morgan continued. "Goodbye to some young women . . . who can't identify with a woman candidate because she's not afraid of *eeueweeeu* yucky *power*."[28] For women like Morgan, who had fought in the trenches of feminist activism in the 1960s and 1970s, feminist solidarity required that women vote for this female, feminist candidate. Anything else represented a betrayal of the movement.

Washington Post reporter Anne Kornblut's book-length analysis of the 2008 campaign reflected the idea that Clinton's defeat had come at the hands of a generational divide between women on the Left, in which younger women were responsible for the apparent "death" of feminist solidarity. "Mothers and grandmothers who saw themselves in Clinton and formed the core of her support faced a confounding phenomenon," Kornblut wrote, "their daughters did not much care whether a woman won or lost." She argued that feminism had fallen victim to its own success, that because young women had grown up in a world shaped by feminist victories, they believed that "pretty much every battle of the sexes had already been waged and won" and therefore did not see the need to prioritize voting for a female candidate.[29]

Such analyses oversimplified a long history of intellectual diversity among feminists and failed to make room for the possibility that women who supported Obama were committed feminists with political priorities that diverged from those of Clinton supporters. For these women, the decision to support Obama was not a decision to abandon feminist solidarity at all. Obama, like Clinton and most other Democrats in 2008, shared similar feminist-backed policy priorities. For some women, the decision to support Obama over Clinton was an expression of feminist politics informed by intersectional analysis and profoundly wary of rhetoric about a unified sisterhood.

In the 1960s and 1970s, sisterly solidarity was a powerful rallying cry for many feminists. As historian Benita Roth has argued, this rhetoric emerged as a response to New Left activists who saw feminism as a diversion from fights against class and race oppression. These mostly male activists were raised to believe in biologically based gender difference and failed to consider the problem of discrimination against women. The framework of universal sisterhood helped feminists make the argument that "gender oppression was as fundamental and widespread" as other systemic imbalances of power.[30]

However, the politics of sisterhood tended to universalize the experiences of white, middle-class, cisgender women and to overlook other women, even as these women made essential contributions to the movement and demanded to be heard.[31] As their critiques gained traction, they fundamentally shaped ongoing conversations about the complexities of gender solidarity. The 2008 Democratic primary between Clinton and Obama reflected these tensions, but this was not simply a matter of a generational split among feminists. Intellectual diversity has always been a feature of the feminist movement. Narratives that emphasize generational divide oversimplify nuanced debates in a movement that has always contained multiplicities.[32]

Ideas about universal sisterhood also discouraged recognition of the ways in which women might oppress other women. For many women critical of Clinton, the candidate herself had failed at feminist solidarity when she defended her husband against sexual harassment and assault claims in the 1990s, publicly denouncing his accusers as liars and possible operatives in a "vast right-wing conspiracy."[33] By 2008, concerns about rape culture were central to feminist discourse, along with conventional wisdom that power imbalances could preclude consent and—above all—that feminists should default to believing women who report experiences of sexual violence and coercion.

The idea that women must vote for Clinton also replicated troubling patterns of tending to code "women"—unless marked by other qualifiers—as white and middle class. Black women were present in discussions about voter patterns in the 2008 election, but they were typically treated as implicitly separate from the category of "woman." "Women," it was assumed, would vote for Hillary Clinton. "Black women," another demographic category altogether, would probably vote for Barack Obama. By then, it had been nearly two decades since feminist legal scholar Kimberlé Crenshaw published the groundbreaking essay in which she coined the term "intersectionality" to critique precisely this mode of erasing black women from cultural conversations about gender and race. As a result of Crenshaw's work, the idea that identities like race and gender inseparably shape one another had become a maxim in feminist thought.[34] In practice, however, American cultural discourse still defaults to the understanding—to borrow from a foundational text in black women's studies—that "all the women are white, all the Blacks are men," and black women are too complicated to understand on their own terms.[35]

Highlighting these patterns, Patricia Hill Collins, author of *Black Feminist Thought,* described the 2008 campaign as "such a distressing, ugly period." She worried in particular that the surrounding rhetoric about race and gender might alienate young black women from feminism. In an article for the left-leaning *Nation* magazine, executive editor Betsy Reed asked Collins and other black feminists about their responses to the "demand that all women back [Clinton] out of gender solidarity, regardless of the broader politics of the campaign." Their reactions, she reported, "ran the gamut from astonishment to dismay to fury."[36]

In an article for the *Huffington Post* published in February 2008, Kimberlé Crenshaw and Eve Ensler criticized Clinton supporters for their increasingly truculent insistence that "voting for Clinton is the only sensible thing for women to do." Even as those in the Clinton camp denied "any intention to square off racism against sexism," Crenshaw and Ensler wrote, they "nonetheless remind us that the Black (man) got the vote before the (white) woman" while ignoring the fact that "real suffrage for African Americans wasn't realized until the 1960s."[37]

Though they did not name her directly, Crenshaw and Ensler penned this piece in response to a controversial op-ed by Gloria Steinem, which began by musing about a hypothetical black woman candidate but went on to treat race and gender as separable identities; "gender is probably the most restrictive force in American life," Steinem concluded.[38] For Crenshaw and Ensler, Steinem's remarks exemplified a strand of white feminism that had long "erased black women from political culture even as it purported to champion their interests."[39]

For as long as there has been a women's movement, there have been women who have opposed it or who have declared it irrelevant to them, for a wide variety of reasons. But even among women who have counted themselves as feminists, divergent priorities have always existed. For many of the feminists who put intersectional analysis at the center of their political priorities, Obama's progressive platform resonated more strongly than the appeal of voting for a centrist woman. Journalist Bonnie Erbé went so far as to assert that Obama's more progressive positions on health care, poverty, and abortion made him "more of a woman than Clinton."[40] In some sense, Erbé's argument was a reversal of other feminists' expulsion of Palin from the category of "woman." In another sense, it made exactly the same rhetorical move, collapsing "feminism" and "womanhood" so completely as to make them utterly synonymous.

Conclusion

Even well before gaining the right to vote, women occupied positions across the political spectrum, distinguished from one another in both fundamental and nuanced ways. On reflection, this may seem so obvious as to require no further explanation, yet our political discourse is still saturated with unexamined assumptions about what women's political involvement will—or *should*—mean.

These assumptions were especially pronounced in the 2008 presidential election, which featured the first female Republican vice presidential nominee and a strong female candidate in the Democratic presidential primaries. Fierce public debates over women's allegiances had the potential to highlight political diversity among women, both within and outside of the aegis of feminism. Yet, in the end, these debates stalled in ideas so entrenched that it was easier to rearticulate homogenized versions of feminism than to acknowledge the diversity of the movement. Even more striking, it was simpler for some to impugn Sarah Palin's identity as a woman than to wrestle with the notion that a woman might be a sincere conservative.

Of course, it is possible to argue that all women *should* be feminists—or even that all women should be conservative—but these are ultimately political arguments, and they must be recognized as such. When these ideas operate in our politics as embedded assumptions, they strip away the complexities of women's lived experiences and political histories. Women are a diverse constituency. Though they share one aspect of identity, even their experiences of womanhood are informed by myriad other factors, among them: race, religion, sexuality, economics, education, and region. Any attempt to characterize or predict women's political allegiances that does not take this diversity into account will fail. Any political conversation that ignores this reality will alienate broad constituencies of women.

Notes

1. Emma Bugbee, "Women Voters Figure Only as Mathematical Influence," *New York Tribune*, November 2, 1920, 4.

2. Emily Suzanne Johnson, *This Is Our Message: Women's Leadership in the New Christian Right* (New York: Oxford University, 2019), 121–145.

3. "Presidential Approval Ratings—George W. Bush," Gallup.com, accessed September 23, 2019, https://news.gallup.com/poll/116500/presidential-approval-ratings-george-bush.aspx.

4. David Barstow, "McCain Denounces Political Tactics of Christian Right," *New York Times*, February 29, 2000, A1; Carl Hulse, "Senators Block Initiative to Ban Same-Sex Unions: Amendment, Endorsed by Bush, Fails after Days of Debate," *New York Times*, July 15, 2004, A1; Michael Luo, "Evangelicals See Dilemmas in GOP Presidential Field: Leaders Haven't Won Over a Key Group," July 8, 2007, 15.

5. Bob Smietana, "McCain's VP Choice Thrills Conservatives," *The Tennessean* (Nashville), August 29, 2008.

6. David S. Broder, "Clinton Takes Women a Long Way," *Palm Beach Post*, June 13, 2008, A15; Ellen Goodman, "A Gender Talk We'd Like to Hear," *Boston Globe*, June 1, 2008, 10.

7. For a distillation of each candidate's positions, see the website maintained by the nonprofit, nonpartisan organization On the Issues: http://www.ontheissues.org/John_McCain.htm and http://www.ontheissues.org/Hillary_Clinton.htm, accessed May 13, 2017.

8. Maggie Fenerty, "Community Voices: Why She Lost," *Philadelphia Inquirer*, June 7, 2008, A08.

9. Thomas Fitzgerald, "Experts: Clinton Advanced Women's Cause, on Balance," *Philadelphia Inquirer*, June 8, 2008, A1, A6. The cornerstone of Ruccia's campaign was her website WomenForFairPolitics.com.

10. Gail Collins, "McCain's Baked Alaska," *New York Times*, August 30, 2008, A19.

11. Gloria Steinem, "Wrong Woman, Wrong Message," *Los Angeles Times*, September 8, 2008, accessed December 18, 2016, http://articles.latimes.com/2008/sep/04/news/OE-STEINEM4.

12. Carla Marinucci, "Palin: War against Russia an Option," *Atlanta Constitution*, September 12, 2008, A1.

13. Anne E. Kornblut, *Notes from the Cracked Ceiling: What It Will Take for a Woman to Win* (New York: Broadway Paperbacks, 2011), 16–17, 21.

14. Linda K. Kerber, "The Republican Mother: Women and the Enlightenment—an American Perspective," *American Quarterly* 28, no. 2 (Summer 1976), 187–205.

15. Ruth Feldstein, *Motherhood in Black and White: Race and Sex in American Liberalism, 1930–1965* (Ithaca, NY: Cornell University Press, 2000); Elizabeth Gillespie McRae, *Mothers of Massive Resistance: White Women and the Politics of White Supremacy* (New York: Oxford University Press, 2018); Michelle M. Nickerson, *Mothers of Conservatism: Women and the Postwar Right* (Princeton, NJ: Princeton University Press, 2012); Amy Swerdlow, *Women Strike for Peace: Traditional Motherhood and Radical Politics in the 1960s* (Chicago: University of Chicago Press, 1993).

16. Johnson, *This Is Our Message*, 1; *Do These Women Speak for You?* Washington, DC: Concerned Women for America, [1983?], pamphlet, RH WL Eph 1352.3, Wilcox Collection of Contemporary Political Movements, University of Kansas Special Collections, Lawrence.

17. Johnson, *This Is Our Message*, 78–81; Stacie Taranto, *Kitchen Table Politics: Conservative Women and Family Values in New York* (Philadelphia: University of Pennsylvania Press, 2017), 136.

18. Nickerson, *Mothers of Conservatism*, xxi.

19. Lisa McGirr, *Suburban Warriors: The Origins of the New American Right* (Princeton, NJ: Princeton University Press, 2001); Catherine Rymph,

Republican Women: Feminism and Conservatism from Suffrage through the Rise of the New Right (Chapel Hill: University of North Carolina Press, 2001).

20. Andrea Dworkin, *Right-Wing Women* (New York: Perigree Books, 1978), 13.

21. Dworkin, *Right-Wing Women*, 34.

22. Steinem, "Wrong Woman, Wrong Message."

23. Johnson, *This Is Our Message*, 136–138.

24. Sarah Palin, speech at Susan B. Anthony List's "Celebration of Life" Breakfast, Washington, DC, May 14, 2010, accessed at http://www.p2012.org /photos10/palin5140spt.html.

25. Johnson, *This Is Our Message*, 137–138.

26. Emphasis mine. Cintra Wilson, "Pissed about Palin," *Salon*, September 10, 2008, accessed December 20, 2016, http://www.salon.com/2008/09/10 /palin_feminism/.

27. Wendy Doniger, "All Beliefs Welcome, Unless They Are Forced on Others," *OnFaith.co*, September 9, 2008, accessed December 20, 2016, https:// www.onfaith.co/onfaith/2008/09/09/all-beliefs-welcome-unless-the/578.

28. Robin Morgan, "Goodbye to All That (#2)," *The Guardian*, February 14, 2008.

29. Kornblut, *Notes from the Cracked Ceiling*, 13–15.

30. Benita Roth, *Separate Roads to Feminism: Black, Chicana, and White Feminist Movements in America's Second Wave* (Cambridge, UK: Cambridge University Press, 2004), 188.

31. For example, Combahee River Collective, "A Black Feminist Statement (United States, 1977)," in *The Essential Feminist Reader*, ed. Estelle B. Freedman (New York: Random House, 2007), 326–330.

32. Leela Fernandes, "Unsettling 'Third Wave Feminism': Feminist Waves, Intersectionality, and Identity Politics in Retrospect," 98–99, and Leandra Zarnow, "From Sisterhood to Girlie Culture: Closing the Great Divide between Second and Third Wave Cultural Agendas," 273–274, both in *No Permanent Waves: Recasting Histories of US Feminism*, ed. Nancy Hewitt (New Brunswick, NJ: Rutgers University Press, 2010).

33. Brigid Schulte, "When the Heat Is Really On, Then Hillary Goes to Work," *Calgary Herald* (Canada), January 24, 1998, 4; Jennifer Hewitt, "Hillary Assails 'Vast Right-Wing Conspiracy," *Sydney Morning Herald* (Australia), January 29, 1998, 9.

34. Kimberlé Crenshaw, "Demarginalizing the Intersection of Race and Sex: A Black Feminist Critique of Antidiscrimination Doctrine, Feminist Theory and Antiracist Politics," *University of California Legal Forum*, special issue, *Feminism in the Law: Theory, Practice and Criticism* (1989): 139–168.

35. Gloria T. Hull, Patricia Bell-Scott, and Barbara Smith, eds., *All the Women are White, All the Blacks are Men, but Some of Us Are Brave: Black Women's Studies* (Old Westbury, NY: Feminist Press, 1982).

36. Betsy Reed, "Race to the Bottom: How Hillary Clinton's Campaign Played the Race Card—and Drove a Wedge into the Feminist Movement," *The Nation*, May 1, 2008, online edition; May 19, 2008, print edition, accessed January 30, 2019, https://www.thenation.com/article/race-bottom-0/.

37. Kimberlé Crenshaw and Eve Ensler, "Feminist Ultimatums: Not in Our Name," *Huffington Post*, February 5, 2008, updated May 25, 2011, accessed January 30, 2019, https://www.huffingtonpost.com/entry/feminist-ultimatums -not-i_b_85165.

38. Gloria Steinem, "American Women Are Never Front-Runners," *New York Times*, January 11, 2008, accessed April 30, 2019, https://www.nytimes .com/2008/01/11/opinion/11iht-edsteinem.1.9152446.html?rref=collection %2Ftimestopic%2FSteinem%2C%20Gloria.

39. Martha S. Jones, "Histories, Fictions, and Black Womanhood Bodies: Race and Gender in Twenty-First Century Politics," in *Toward an Intellectual History of Black Women*, ed. Mia Bay, Farrah J. Griffin, Martha S. Jones, and Barbara D. Savage (Chapel Hill: University of North Carolina Press, 2015).

40. Bonnie Erbé, "If Hillary Loses, Do Women Lose?," *US News and World Report*, February 13, 2008, accessed January 29, 2019, https://www.usnews .com/opinion/blogs/erbe/2008/02/13/if-hillary-loses-do-women-lose.

Susan B. Anthony's grave in Mount Hope Cemetery in Rochester, New York, covered in "I Voted Today!" stickers on the day after the 2016 election. Photograph courtesy of Daniel Penfield; courtesy Wikimedia Commons.

CHAPTER 17

Tribute Politics

*How Feminist History Became a
Reference Point in the 2016 Election*

NICOLE EATON

WHEN HILLARY CLINTON became the first female presidential candidate nominated by a major political party, the *New York Times* declared: "Hillary Clinton Makes History."[1] During the 2016 election, "making history" became part of a popular discourse that melded past and present to help build support for Clinton. Activities such as wearing white clothes to vote and placing "I Voted" stickers on suffragists' graves enabled Clinton's campaign and supporters to tap into a feminist usable past to create a sense of solidarity among voters. In creating a usable past, people in the present use history to address issues in the present. The production of historical narratives has been a vital tool for creating change in various social movements, including feminism. Clinton is not the first politician, nor even the first female candidate, to do so.[2] In 1972, Shirley Chisholm, the first African American woman to run for president, chose the gravesite of abolitionist and suffragist Sojourner Truth to inaugurate her campaign. During the 2016 election, Clinton laid claim to the mantle of suffragists as a conscious, political act.

The Clinton campaign framed the election narrative as a form of tribute politics. What made this form of a usable past unique was the widespread emphasis placed on gratitude to feminist foremothers. This was a narrative put forth by Clinton in her speeches and ads that was widely consumed and reimagined by supporters and by the media. In saying thank you, there is an implication of gratitude, respect, and admiration. Most important, giving tribute comes with a sense of moral, and in this case, political obligation that is both motivational and inspirational. It gave supporters a sense of ownership over the past, a consciousness of a shared membership in a movement. Her presidential nomination was not just a victory for Clinton but for all women. Tribute politics framed how Clinton's run was widely received.

The Clinton campaign's usable past attempted to transform something that seemed unimaginable—women and presidential power—as something not only possible but seemingly preordained. Since the passage of the Nineteenth Amendment, the presidency seemed the logical culmination to women's new role as voting citizens. In a 1920 cartoon, "The Sky Is Now Her Limit," artist Elmer Andrews Bushnell depicts a young woman carrying buckets on a yoke, gazing at a ladder rising into the sky, with the lower rungs marked as "Slavery," "House Drudgery," and "Shop Work." The highest rungs were labeled "Equal Suffrage," "Wage Equity," and the zenith was identified as "Presidency."[3] Yet the quest for a Madame President remained elusive—until Clinton. Unlike previous female presidential candidates, Clinton entered the race with front-runner status.[4] There was a widespread sense that it was time for American women to finally reach the top rung. As Democratic congresswoman Marcia Fudge said at the 2016 Democratic National Convention, "It is our time as women. It is our time."[5] Such appeals presented Clinton's campaign as an unfinished revolution.

Wanting to capitalize on her front-runner status without appearing as an "insider," Clinton also relied on a usable past to coalesce diverse political identities and build alliances under the gravitas of history. In an election cycle where outsider politicians such as Bernie Sanders and Donald Trump held great appeal, Clinton's "Making History" slogan presented Clinton as a fellow outsider who could rally other groups marginalized from political power to be "Stronger Together." Tribute politics reflected Clinton's longtime commitment to recognizing women's history as well as an important effort at promoting unity in the Democratic Party. The strength of this tribute politics rhetoric was the appeal it held for liberal feminists—a formulation that would, it was hoped, elide Clinton's background of promoting neoliberal economic policies.

However, ultimately, the tribute narrative was not enough to overcome her centrist past for key voters Clinton needed on the Left, especially white supporters of Bernie Sanders (including feminists interested in economic justice) and African Americans and people of color.

Critics offered counternarratives that reflected the challenges of organizing around identity politics. Before the election, it was widely predicted that America's growing diversity would help Democrats keep the White House. Ultimately, the triumph of Clinton's opponent, Republican nominee Donald Trump, suggests that the backlash against that diversity proved slightly more appealing to the electorate in key battleground states.[6] Conservative women dominated the narrative surrounding abortion in those states, one of the other central issues of the election. Clinton's tribute politics inspired countless activists during the 2016 election, and many created their own homages such as the #wearwhitetovote campaign. Yet, the celebratory tone of the "making history" rhetoric not only inspired a backlash on the Right but also failed to build a coalition that could sufficiently contend with historical and contemporary strains over race and class on the Left, including among feminists.

Tribute Politics

While Clinton addressed women's issues from the start of her campaign, once she officially clinched the Democratic nomination in June 2016, she began overtly emphasizing not only gender but also the historic nature of her run. On that historic night, Clinton unveiled a campaign video, entitled "History Made," that highlighted the history of women's activism to reinforce the notion that her campaign represented the apex of American feminism. The first part of the video featured images of suffragists and historical clips from politicians and activists, including Shirley Chisholm, Gloria Steinem, Rosa Parks, Dolores Huerta, and Sandra Day O'Connor, among others. In doing so, the video paid tribute to a matrilineal lineage of women who paved the way for Clinton's triumph. [7]

Significantly, the video narrated an intersectional story of women's protest that continues into the twenty-first century.[8] As one headline put it, "Hillary Clinton Declares Victory—for All Social Justice Activists."[9] Toward the end of the video, voice-overs and images highlighted contemporary activists protesting for racial justice, immigration reform, reproductive control, and LGBT rights. Sybrina Fulton, the mother of Trayvon Martin, was featured campaigning with Clinton for gun control, while teen voting rights advocate Madison Kimrey declared, "I am part of the new generation of suffragettes.[10] I will not stand silent."[11] These images of radical, modern-day protest put forth the notion that these activists were all striving for one goal that Clinton could help them realize.[12] The intent was to make Clinton's campaign appear revolutionary in order to build a diverse coalition around a variety of progressive causes.

The video concluded with activists intoning a theme of gratitude for the legacy of women's protest. A desire to "want to help give back" was reflected in the words of transgender African American activists Blossom Brown and Cherno Biko, who declared in unison: "I've met so many other transgender people, their voices haven't always been heard. But I told them, our time is coming. We're going to change the world together." Cecile Richards, president of Planned Parenthood and daughter of the late governor Ann Richards of Texas (also featured in the video), said of her mother, "If even in some tiny way, I get to carry on the work that she and a whole generation of women did to give us rights, that's huge." Through the montage, Clinton claimed her nomination as a feminist climax. As CNN framed it, the night celebrated, "The long journey from Seneca Falls to Hillary 2016."[13] Clinton symbolically took American women on her journey, lifting them with her as she climbed the ladder. Many supporters claimed a personal victory. One woman tweeted: "Waited my whole life for this!!! NJ's Alice Paul is proud!!! Thank you for making one of my dreams come true!"[14]

Clinton made the connection to the past even more personal by frequently referencing her mother, Dorothy Howell Rodham. Clinton informed her audience that night, "on the very day my mother was born in Chicago, Congress was passing the 19th Amendment to the Constitution. That amendment finally gave women the right to vote." As communications scholar Kiana Scott has observed, "Clinton presents her personal narrative as matrilineal."[15] Clinton continued, "And I really wish my mother could be here tonight. I wish she could see what a wonderful mother Chelsea has become, and could meet our beautiful granddaughter, Charlotte. And of course, I wish she could see her daughter become the Democratic Party's nominee for president of the United States."[16] In the speech, women are placed at the center of Clinton's family history and by extension at the center of American history. Focusing on maternal imagery humanized Clinton and made her more relatable. This was a far cry from her 2008 presidential bid when her rhetorical style was described as "impersonal," and her speeches rarely included personal examples.[17] This familial narrative was representative of an important campaign strategy around gender.

Gender Politics

Emphasizing her role in history was a dramatic shift from her first presidential bid in 2008. The specter of gender held an ambivalent place in Clinton's convoluted path to the nomination. Depending on the perspective, Clinton's gender was anything from a danger to an inspiration— the one thing it was not was irrelevant. Among Clinton advisors, there was no consensus on the best way for Clinton to handle running as a woman candidate. The 2008 campaign struggled with how much to emphasize that Clinton could make history as the first woman president. Instead, following the advice of strategist Mark Penn, the campaign highlighted Clinton's toughness. In a 2006 internal memo, Penn argued, "Most voters in essence see the president as the 'father' of the country. They do not want someone who would be the first mama, especially in this kind of world."[18] Embracing a gender frame in 2016 came about for various reasons. Trump forced gender as a major issue in the election by modeling toxic masculinity and accusing Clinton of "playing the women's card." Clinton responded by declaring that she's fighting for women's issues, so "deal me in."[19] The campaign's decision was also likely a response to perceived lessons from 2008.

This concern over perceptions of women's weakness in politics echoed earlier anxiety surrounding Geraldine Ferraro. In 1984, Ferraro, running as the Democratic Party's vice presidential nominee, became the first woman on a national ticket. She was chosen as the nominee only after Democratic women launched a campaign to get a woman selected. The National Organization for Women threatened a floor fight at the DNC if a woman was not chosen as the vice presidential candidate.[20] Some argued that part of Ferraro's appeal was that, unlike other women politicians such as Shirley Chisholm and Bella Abzug, men did not find Ferraro "shrill."[21] When Ferraro delivered her acceptance speech on July 19, 1984, she downplayed the historic nature of her nomination. The explicit theme of the address was immigration and the American Dream—gender was only implicit in her speech.[22] The need to look strong and downplay gender was perhaps well grounded, as discomfort with Ferraro's sex was common. The media watched for signs of weakness, especially wondering if she would cry. Once Ferraro was asked, "Do you think that in any way the Soviets might be tempted to try to take advantage of you simply because you are a woman?"[23] The satirical and sexist *The Official Geraldine Ferraro Coloring Book*, written under the penname "S.B. Anthony," asked Americans if they would vote Yes for Ferraro or No to "Send her back to the kitchen. The button I want her to press is the microwave."[24] Only 22 percent of women polled were enthusiastic about Ferraro on the ticket, in fact, nearly as many— 18 percent—regarded it as a "bad idea."[25]

In contrast, postmortems on Clinton's 2008 campaign nearly twenty-five years later, highlighted how downplaying gender contributed to Clinton's loss.[26] Ironically, the choice of conservative Sarah Palin as the vice presidential candidate on the Republican ticket helped push the boundaries of gender and politics. Even though she was not a feminist— she actively worked against many women's issues such as reproductive control and health care—Palin embraced her femininity. As Liesl Schillinger wrote in the *New York Times*, "Palin had entered the race as a woman, clutching her newborn in her arms, making it clear that she regarded her sex not as a deficit, but as an asset." This presentation stood in juxtaposition to Clinton who performed as if she were a male candidate.[27] As Schillinger noted, "the Clinton campaign persevered in stoic masculinity until it was left choking in its own gorilla dust."[28]

Clinton and her team came to realize that gender was not necessarily a liability, and in 2016, her campaign constructed an imagined feminist community. In Clinton's imagined feminist community, history worked to create a shared, political identity for women, united together in a common cause with a glorious history that implied a glorious future. Referencing history was a strategy Clinton used to convince voters that she was not part of the "establishment," by reminding the public that her election would be a radical shift for women and political power.[29] Clinton's usable past was a call for unity to engage supporters of Bernie Sanders as suggested by her tagline "Stronger Together." Her election narrative was heroic and inspirational but like similar examples of political storytelling, it lacked nuance and complexity. The constructed ideal flattened out historical and contemporary tensions between constituents and simplified the challenges of coalition building. In presenting a triumphant message, the images elided the struggles for recognition and equality within the women's movement and the Democratic Party.

While the narrative was intersectional, many questioned whether the vision correlated with reality and accused Clinton of only representing white, middle-class Americans. In the essay collection *False Choices: The Faux Feminism of Hillary Rodham Clinton* critics alleged that Clinton's feminism, despite the progressive rhetoric, was simply paying lip service and overlooked questions of economic justice. The Clintons had presided over the 1996 Welfare Reform Act, which studies claim ultimately increased the number of children living in poverty.[30] Because of this history, many supporters of Bernie Sanders never supported the Clinton campaign. The title of the opening essay by Kathleen Geier, "Hillary Clinton, Economic Populist: Are You Fucking Kidding Me?," set the tone for the collection.[31] Similarly, the prologue of the book was a play in one act. One character, Elizabeth, comments to her partner, Laura, "Oh come on. Can you really deny that having our first female president would be historic?" Laura responds: "No, I can't. But an opportunity for one is a pretty meager antidote to the jobs crisis."[32] Despite Clinton's status as feminist icon, many progressives believed that Clinton's policies represented "a kind of trickle-down feminism" that focused only on aiding elite women in hopes that breaking down barriers to equal opportunity would open doors for all women. However, according to journalist Laurie Penny, "Trickle-down feminism is as nonsensical a liberation strategy as trickle-down wealth redistribution. The problem with a glass ceiling is that nothing trickles down. While we all worry about the glass ceiling, there are millions of women standing in the basement—and the basement is flooding."[33]

Not fully addressing the long history of racial strife between women reflected the fault line of contemporary progressive politics. Many women of color supported Clinton over the alternative represented by Trump and his hypermasculine and racist platform. Trump was constructing his own election narrative, "Let's make America great again," premised on an imagined past, which according to Clinton meant "back to a time when opportunity and dignity were reserved for some, not all."[34] During the primaries, African American women were strong supporters of Clinton over Sanders, and women of color favored Clinton in the general election with 94 percent of black women and 68 percent of Latina women voting for Clinton.[35] However, often her candidacy was greeted without enthusiasm and more like the lesser of two evils. Some black women adopted a hashtag to express their ambivalence: #GirlIGuessImWithHer.[36] Because of Clinton's history of supporting neoliberal policies she failed to win support from Sanders's supporters and her failure to excite both male and female African Americans meant many Democratic voters did not turn out to vote for Clinton as they had for Barack Obama in 2008 and 2012, thereby contributing to Clinton's loss by the slimmest of margins in key battleground states, such as Pennsylvania, Wisconsin, and Michigan.

Fashion Politics

One of the most visible ways Clinton placed herself in the feminist tradition was through wearing her trademark pantsuit in the color white to honor the suffragists.[37] With this fashion choice, Clinton continued a tradition pioneered by previous trendsetting women politicians. National Organization for Women often asked members to wear white to its marches "to honor our foremothers."[38] Chisholm is pictured wearing white on her 1972 presidential campaign poster, and in 1984, when Ferraro accepted the vice presidential nomination, she wore a white suit.[39] Clinton made sure the aura of history surrounded her, as the *New York Times* reported, "That suit, quietly yet clearly, made reference to history, specifically the history of the women's movement."[40]

Clinton's association of fashion with politics had roots within the suffrage movement when women's clothing was used to convey a political message. Often women's fashion has functioned to curb women's influence in the public sphere. Yet, the use of fashion as a tool of feminist political expression has been long-standing.[41] In the 1850s, reformers, most famously, Amelia Bloomer, advocated for dress reform. The uproar over the bloomer costume, however, undermined the burgeoning movement, and reformers readopted more traditionally feminine clothes. The responses to "Turkish pantaloons" for women were almost as wide ranging as the amount of attention paid to Clinton's pantsuits.[42]

By the 1910s, when the final push for suffrage was underway, a new connection between women's clothing and women's rights emerged. Suffragists began holding parades and wore "marching costumes" to visually convey the ideals of the cause.[43] Leaders encouraged marchers to wear white clothing, a symbolically powerful color associated with purity and virtue, which they hoped would counter lingering doubts about the immorality of women entering politics. By wearing white, suffragists could also feel part of a community formed by the bonds of womanhood.[44] Clinton understood the influence of fashion in communicating political messages and how a look could shape a political campaign.[45]

Inspired by Clinton's signature white pantsuit, thousands of supporters embraced clothing to exhibit solidarity and garner public support. Fashion became a means "to express their commitment and connection to a story greater than their own."[46] The fashion search platform Lyst reported a 460 percent uplift in queries for pantsuits. Katherine Ormerod, Lyst's editorial director, related, "The interest in white pantsuits in particular has certainly confounded expectations—especially as we usually see a seasonal dip for white color ways across every category."[47] The white pantsuit became a signifier to identify as a pro-Clinton feminist and celebrate the historical significance of her campaign, which was too often getting obscured in a tense and bitter election.[48]

Through fashion, supporters created a literal and virtual pantsuit nation that promoted popular feminism. Social media platforms became powerful tools for organizing and helped galvanize Clinton supporters. Empowered by virtual sisterhood, thousands of women wore pantsuits to vote and then posted a photo to the "secret" Facebook group Pantsuit Nation, "the digital equivalent of slapping an 'I Voted' sticker on a lapel."[49] Libby Chamberlain, the founder of the invitation-only group, created it to support Clinton less than three weeks before the election. More than 3 million people joined, creating a cyber safe space for the feminist community and raising more than $216,000 for the Clinton campaign.[50]

Wearing white appears to have emerged organically from various supporters who claimed to have been inspired by Clinton's own tribute. Kathy Webb, a member of the Little Rock City Board in Arkansas, encouraged supporters to wear white to vote. Webb recalled how seeing Clinton in white reminded her of the "very emotional day" when Ferraro wore white to accept the nomination. The *Boston Globe* reported the phenomenon of wearing white developed as a grassroots initiative, citing several Clinton campaign aides had been unaware of the trend. The hashtag #WearWhiteToVote began trending as supporters honored suffragists by wearing white to the polls. The hashtag evolved when college instructor Michelle Gajda and her two children, inspired by Clinton's homage, dressed in white to vote. Gajda stated,

"I wanted to show my children that they are witnessing history." When people asked her children whether they were going to a wedding, Gajda explained the meaning and, hoping to encourage others, posted pictures on social media with the hashtag #WearWhiteToVote.[51]

The #WearWhiteToVote trend came under scrutiny due to the challenge of bridging racial divides. The outpouring of tribute politics offered an opportunity to revisit historical racial tensions unresolved in the women's movement. Author Luvvie Ajayi voiced a central concern of women of color over accolades for the suffrage movement when she tweeted, "I'm surely not wearing white tomorrow." According to Ajayi, suffragists were "the epitome of white feminism." Others chose not to dwell on the racism of white suffragists and celebrate the work of black suffragists who persevered for the cause despite prejudice. Journalist Britni Danielle responded to #WearWhiteToVote, "If anything, I'll wear red, black, and green, for the BLACK suffragists who were pushed out but worked anyway."[52] Perhaps ironically, in the 1910s, suffrage fashion allowed those women who were excluded from the mainstream movement due to race or class to dress like their white, middle-class counterparts and symbolically stake a claim for their involvement in the cause. By adopting the color white, black suffragists like Mary Church Terrell and Ida B. Wells could associate with moral purity (a category often denied to black women) and thus use fashion as a means of advancing both gender and racial equality.[53] Observing this tradition, contemporary feminists such as activist Denise Oliver-Velez, former Young Lords Party and Black Panther Party member, tweeted, "#WearWhite-ToVote I'm honoring Black Suffragists like Mary Church Terrell today and wearing white."[54]

Clinton had prepared to wear white right into the Oval Office. As she recalled, "I had hoped to thank the country wearing white—the color of the suffragettes—while standing on a stage cut into the shape of the United States under a vast glass ceiling."[55] Women elected to Congress in the 2018 midterms carried on this "suffragette white" homage. When Congresswoman Alexandria Ocasio-Cortez (D-NY) was sworn in on January 3, 2019, she tweeted, "I wore all-white today to honor the women who paved the path before me, and for all the women yet to come. From suffragettes to Shirley Chisholm, I wouldn't be here if it wasn't for the mothers of the movement." In February 2019, Democratic congresswomen then wore white to President Trump's State of the Union as a symbol of unity and visual challenge to his toxic masculinity.[56]

Historical Politics

The ultimate expression of tribute politics occurred on Election Day: November 8, 2016. Thousands of people descended upon Susan B. Anthony's gravesite in Mount Hope Cemetery in Rochester, New York, to leave "I Voted" stickers in support of Clinton. Representative of the countless virtual homages to suffragists, one woman tweeted: "Thank you #SusanBAnthony. I cannot even imagine a world in which I would not have the right to vote. Your legacy—women voting, running for office, and more!" Newscaster Kim Block tweeted: "I will vote for many reasons, grateful that this woman helped earn me the right to do so."[57] When Anthony began trending on social media 110 years after her death, the central theme voiced was one of gratitude.

Anthony had a long history as a malleable symbol for political issues, beginning during her unfailing campaign for suffrage and continuing after her death in 1906. The Nineteenth Amendment was dubbed the "Anthony Amendment." When the National Woman's Party unveiled the ERA in 1923, feminists made a pilgrimage to Anthony's gravesite. Anthony's popularity as feminist patron saint was solidified when, in the wake of her revival during women's liberation, her likeness was engraved on a dollar coin in 1979.

The afterlife of Anthony's image found renewed importance during the 2016 election when her gravesite became a feminist shrine.[58] The scene had been set weeks before when Rochester mayor Lovely Warren, the first female leader of her city and only the second African American to hold the office, placed a thank-you card beside Anthony's grave on the day after Clinton accepted the nomination. Warren, elected mayor 141 years to the day that Anthony cast an illegal ballot in 1872, wrote to her foremother, "We thought you might like to know that for the first time in history, a woman is running for President representing a major party. 144 years ago your illegal vote got you arrested. It took another 48 years for women to finally gain the right to vote. Thank you for paving the way."[59] Warren's note elevated the long-standing tradition of local women leaving "I Voted" stickers and flowers by Anthony's grave. The city of Rochester invited people to visit and sign the card with their own words of gratitude. As one woman posted on Facebook, Clinton was "building upon the foundation that Susan B. mortared. . . . I have no doubt that one day my granddaughters and great-granddaughters will stand in front of Hillary Clinton's headstone and sign a thank you note to her." She concluded: "I sat on the curb in front of Susan B. Anthony's gravestone today. While my daughter played, I openly cried tears of gratitude."[60]

Some people tried to recognize that the suffrage movement was more than one individual. A few questioned why pioneers such as Elizabeth Cady Stanton or Carrie Chapman Catt received little attention.[61] Amy Bragg, a Detroit community history blogger, began visiting local graves of suffragists and posting photographs under the hashtag #VisitASuffragist.[62] She created a Google Map of various graves across the state, as her efforts spread across the nation. The tribute project put into stark relief the question: "What if the whole fabric [of] the world didn't have men as the default setting in history?"[63] Many, like Bragg, desired a matrilineal legacy and hoped that the election would change how women were seen in the past and the present.

Other commentators questioned the use of Anthony as symbol. While Anthony is often represented as a universal icon for American women, differences among women over issues of racial and sexual politics suggest the limits of such symbolism. As the *New York Times* noted, with the exception of Warren, there were few African Americans present, even though Rochester's population is 40 percent African American, reflecting the racial tensions that have long divided the movement. One woman, with the handle name, "Angry Black Woman," tweeted: "To everyone stanning [*sic*] for Susan B. Anthony: let's be clear, she only wanted WHITE women to be able to vote. Have a nice day." Another woman, Lauren @highoffjesus tweeted: "I know we're all feeling great about voting & thanking our girl Susan B Anthony for getting us here but remember that she was great & all but she was a racist and only lobbied for white women to get the privilege to vote, not WOC [women of color]."[64]

As with the controversy over #WearWhiteToVote, one of the challenges of tribute politics is that it flattens out historical complexity and places a nineteenth-century issue in a twenty-first-century context. Historians actively debate Anthony's racial views, and the veracity of claims on either side is often a question of interpretation.[65] As Ann D. Gordon, editor of the papers of Elizabeth Cady Stanton and Susan B. Anthony argues, "The charge that Susan B. Anthony did not want black women to vote is simply wrong. There's lots of evidence to show otherwise."[66] When Congress passed the Fifteenth Amendment granting black men the right to vote in 1869 (introducing the word "male" into the Constitution for the first time), some reformers objected that women were left out of the expansion of rights. Anthony, an ardent abolitionist, favored universal suffrage to expand the franchise to all women as well as black men. Anthony held a vision whereas "a citizen's right to vote" was protected by the federal government without any discrimination on account of race, color, or sex.[67] Yet, Anthony and Stanton opposed black male suffrage if women were not to be included. Stanton and Anthony formed unfortunate alliances with racists (and Stanton, in particular, increasingly adopted racist imagery and language). Historian Andrea Moore Kerr has argued that many suffragists at the time found Stanton's and Anthony's refusal to support the Fifteenth Amendment "not only politically unwise, but morally repugnant."[68]

When the past is condensed down to tweets and Instagram photos, this level of nuance disappears from the historical reality that is far more complex. Dismissing Anthony and other white suffragists as racist obscures the real import of studying women's history. As both Kerr and Gordon have suggested, a larger cultural and political conversation needs to evolve around race and voting rights then and now in order to learn from the past. Understanding the mistakes of previous women's movements sheds light on the pervasive power of patriarchy and white supremacy and the challenges of coalition building under such constraints.

The focus on Anthony-centered political discourse on a white feminist narrative led women of color to call for attention to African American trailblazers. Many Twitter users encouraged people to "visit the graves of black women who led the fight for gender *and* racial equality like Sojourner Truth, Ida B. Wells, Shirley Chisholm, Fannie Lou Hamer and Dorothy Height."[69] One tweet reminded, "Thinking abt Sojourner Truth, Ida b Wells, Shirley Chisholm & all the other folks (past&present) who didn't have the privilege #ElectionDay."[70] Writer Mikki Kendall affirmed, "I vote because of the Black women who marched, fought, suffered & died so I could be here today. I vote because it honors their sacrifices."[71]

Anthony became a symbol for Trump supporters, too, who were 53 percent of white female voters.[72] This conservative appropriation of the suffrage lineage was rooted in the antiabortion movement of the 1990s, when antiabortion strategy shifted from emphasizing the fetus to a rhetoric that argued abortion harms women.[73] The right-wing PAC, the Susan B. Anthony List, founded to elect antiabortion women to counter EMILY's List support of pro-choice women, was named after the pioneer. One organization called Feminists for Life (FFL) argued they were following the path of true feminist history, what they called the "pro-woman, pro-life legacy."[74] FFL worked for the passage of the Violence Against Women Act and enhanced child support enforcement laws but differed from mainstream feminist groups in their opposition to abortion. They based their arguments on the notion that nineteenth-century pioneers were antiabortion. FFL cite an 1869 article in which Anthony denounces "child murder," labeling abortion "a most monstrous crime." What is not mentioned is that the treatise argues against an antiabortion law. Additionally, Anthony scholars claim she did not write the article.[75]

In an election where abortion was a central issue, the privileging of Anthony's memory was a partisan issue on both sides of the political spectrum. Despite describing himself as "very pro-choice" in the 1990s, in 2016, Trump sent a letter to "Pro-Life Leaders" with a promise for "Defunding Planned Parenthood" and making the 1976 Hyde Amendment "permanent law to protect taxpayers from having to pay for abortions." Conservative women rallied to Trump and worked to unite voters around abortion. The Anthony List and its partner super PAC, Women Speak Out, spearheaded an "unprecedented GOTV Effort" reportedly spending more than $18 million nationally, reaching an estimated 1.6 million voters with their campaign to turn out "inconsistent pro-life voters" and "persuadable Democrats, including Hispanics" over Clinton's support of funding late-term abortion.[76] Exit polls suggest that focusing on abortion was successful as Trump received an overwhelming 81 percent of white evangelical voters to Clinton's 16 percent. He captured a majority among white Catholics—60 percent to 37 percent as well as one in five Hispanic voters.[77] Clinton's branding of tribute politics faced fierce resistance from women who claimed that she did not speak for all women. Ultimately, conservative women's counternarrative surrounding abortion dominated in key swing states.

Conclusion

In the 2016 election, the Clinton campaign looked backward to the suffrage past in an attempt to move history forward. Clinton's fashioning of tribute politics inspired millions of voters as many liberal feminists were swept away with the emotional possibility of the first female president. Yet there were sizable limits to the "making history" strategy. To feel empowered by the rhetoric, voters had to see their identity reflected in the milestone. For those voters who did not believe they would benefit from Clinton's achievement, the celebratory tone rang hollow. Clinton's usable past ultimately did not successfully grapple with present-day political challenges to win over the white working-class and to mobilize the minority and youth vote.[78] It was an overly confident narrative that from the onset was premised on a glorious conclusion but failed to take into account real differences among women and the ingrained misogyny and racism of American political culture.

The widespread consumption of tribute politics in the 2016 election demands that we recognize history and collective memory as important tools for political organizing. It means acknowledging that women's history is a past imperfect and we must work to make a future that does not repeat those same mistakes. On January 21, 2017, activists around the world protested in the Women's March, an event that channeled the outrage felt over Clinton's defeat to become the largest single-day demonstration in American history. Many protesters were Clinton supporters—and their feelings of gratitude had shifted to anger. Now with the pink pussy hat as the focal symbol of solidarity and sisterhood, the strategy of tribute politics had turned into a politics of righteous fury. The challenge of popular feminism has been, and continued to be with Clinton's loss in 2016, centered on how to turn symbolic narratives into concrete political, economic, and social change.

Notes

1. "Hillary Clinton Makes History," *New York Times*, July 29, 2016.
2. Throughout Clinton's political career, she fought tirelessly both for women's rights and for women's history because she recognized the power of the past for social activism. As senator, Clinton introduced legislation to establish the Votes for Women History Trail Act as well as legislation to establish the Harriet Tubman National Historical Park.
3. Elmer Andrews Bushnell, "The Sky Is Now Her Limit," Library of Congress Prints and Photographs Division, accessed April 26, 2019, www.loc.gov/pictures/item/2002716769/.
4. Nichola D. Gutgold, *Almost Madam President: Why Hillary Clinton "Won" in 2008* (Lanham, MD: Lexington Books, 2009), 4.
5. Clare Foran, "Hillary Clinton's Feminist Triumph," *The Atlantic*, July 28, 2016.
6. John Sides, Michael Tesler, and Lynn Vavreck, *Identity Crisis: The 2016 Presidential Campaign and the Battle for the Meaning of America* (Princeton, NJ: Princeton University Press, 2018), 9.
7. Olivia B. Waxman, "These Are the Historical Figures in Hillary Clinton's Victory Video," *Time*, June 8, 2016.

8. Amee Latour, "Hillary Clinton's 'History Made' Victory Video Is Strikingly Intersectional (as It Should Be)," *Bustle*, June 7, 2016.

9. Charlie Spiering, "Hillary Clinton Declares Victory—for All Social Justice Activists," Breitbart, June 8, 2016.

10. The term *suffragette* originated in the 1910s with the British press, used to mock women experimenting with more radical protest tactics. Some British suffragists reclaimed the term to give it a positive connotation. However, American suffragists always saw the name "suffragette" as derogatory and refused to use it. The popularity of the phrasing "suffragette" in American collective memory arose from the satirical depiction of Mrs. Banks in Disney's 1964 film *Mary Poppins*. The phrasing "suffragist" is therefore more historically accurate when describing the American suffrage movement.

11. "History Made," campaign video, June 7, 2016, available online through the Iowa State University Archives of Women's Political Communication, accessed January 22, 2019, https://awpc.cattcenter.iastate.edu/2017/03/10/history-made-june-7-2016.

12. Spiering, "Hillary Clinton Declares Victory."

13. Rachel Smolkin, "The Long Journey from Seneca Falls to Hillary 2016," CNN.com, June 8, 2016, accessed January 10, 2018, https://www.cnn.com/2016/06/08/politics/hillary-clinton-historic-nomination/index.html.

14. Janice E (@J16Hughes), "History made," Twitter, July, 27, 2016, 11:25 a.m., https://twitter.com/J16Hughes/status/758367707817402368.

15. Kiana Scott, "Madame President: Hillary Clinton, Gender and the General Election," National Women's Political Caucus of Washington, accessed January 27, 2019, www.nwpcwa.org.

16. Hillary Rodham Clinton, "Victory Speech as Presumptive Democratic Nominee" Brooklyn, NY, June 7, 2016.

17. Description from Karlyn Kohrs Campbell, quoted in Gutgold, *Almost Madam President*, 6.

18. Ruth Marcus, "Hillary Clinton's Liberated Campaign," *Washington Post*, October 16, 2015.

19. Jaclyn Reiss, "Watch Hillary Clinton's New Ultra-Feminist Political Video," *Boston Globe*, June 7, 2016.

20. Douglas Martin, "She Ended the Men's Club of National Politics," *New York Times*, March 26, 2011.

21. Ronnie Eldridge, "In Praise of Shrillness," *New York Times*, August 3, 1984.

22. Geraldine A. Ferraro, "Inspiration from the Land Where Dreams Come True," July 19, 1984, Democratic National Convention, San Francisco, CA, available online through the Iowa State University Archives of Women's Political Communication, accessed January 22, 2019, https://awpc.cattcenter.iastate.edu/2017/03/21/inspiration-from-the-land-where-dreams-come-true-july-19-1984.

23. Alison Mitchell, "To Understand Clinton's Moment, Consider That It Came 32 Years after Ferraro's," *New York Times*, June 11, 2016.

24. S. B. Anthony "VINTAGE 1984 *The Official Geraldine Ferraro Coloring Book* poll BALLOT enclosed," eBay, accessed April 11, 2019, www.ebay.com/i /153425208971?chn=ps.

25. Tessa Stuart, "How Hillary Clinton Made Women's History," *Rolling Stone*, June 8, 2016.

26. See, for example, Gail Collins, *When Everything Changed: The Amazing Journey of American Women from 1960 to the Present* (New York: Little, Brown, 2009); Erika Falk, *Women for President: Media Bias in Nine Campaigns* (Urbana: University of Illinois Press, 2010); Gutgold, *Almost Madam President*; John Heilemann and Mark Halperin, *Game Change: Obama and the Clintons, McCain and Palin, and the Race of a Lifetime* (New York: Harper, 2010); Anne Kornblut, *Notes from the Cracked Ceiling: Hillary Clinton, Sarah Palin, and What It Will Take for a Woman to Win* (New York: Crown, 2009); Regina G. Lawrence and Melody Rose, *Hillary Clinton's Race for the White House: Gender Politics and the Media on the Campaign Trail* (Boulder, CO: Lynne Rienner, 2010); Rebecca Traister, *Big Girls Don't Cry: The Election That Changed Everything for American Women* (New York: Free Press, 2010).

27. Liesl Schillinger, "Sexual Politics," *New York Times*, September 16, 2010.

28. Schillinger, "Sexual Politics."

29. Alan Rappeport, "Gloria Steinem and Madeleine Albright Rebuke Young Women Backing Bernie Sanders," *New York Times*, February 7, 2016.

30. Jordan Weissmann, "The Failure of Welfare Reform," *Slate*, June 1, 2016.

31. Liza Featherstone, ed., *False Choices: The Faux Feminism of Hillary Rodham Clinton* (London: Verso Books, 2016). See also the review of the book by Amanda Erickson, "The Flawed Feminist Case against Hillary Clinton," *Washington Post*, July 28, 2016.

32. See Laura Flanders, "Clinton Contention," prologue to *False Choices*, in Featherstone.

33. Laurie Penny, "Don't Worry about the Glass Ceiling—the Basement Is Flooding, Says Laurie Penny," *New Statesman*, July 27, 2011.

34. Hillary Rodham Clinton, "Remarks at Planned Parenthood Action Fund," June 10, 2016, available online through the Iowa State University Archives of Women's Political Communication, accessed January 22, 2019, https://awpc.cattcenter.iastate.edu/2017/03/21/remarks-at-planned-parenthood-action-fund-jun-10-2016.

35. Barbara Burrell, *Women and Politics: A Quest for Political Equality in an Age of Economic Injustice* (New York: Routledge, 2018), 200. See also Phoebe Lett, "White Women Voted Trump. Now What?," *New York Times*, November 10, 2016.

36. Patrick Healy and Sheryl Gay Stolberg, "Historic Import of Hillary Clinton's Victory Is One More Source of Division," *New York Times*, June 8, 2016.

37. Victoria McGrane, "Suffragists Wore White 96 Years Ago. Now Clinton Voters Are Doing the Same," *Boston Globe*, November 2, 2016.

38. McGrane, "Suffragists Wore White."

39. Poster for presidential candidate Shirley Chisholm, 1972, object number 2014.167.3, Collection of the Smithsonian National Museum of African American History and Culture, gifted with pride from Ellen Brooks.

40. Vanessa Friedman, "Why Hillary Wore White," *New York Times*, July 29, 2016.

41. Einav Rabinovitch-Fox, "Dressing Up for a Campaign: Hillary Clinton, Suffragists, and the Politics of Fashion," in *Nasty Women and Bad Hombres: Gender and Race in the 2016 Presidential Election*, ed. Christine A. Kray, Tamar W. Carroll, and Hinda Mandell (Rochester, NY: University of Rochester Press, 2018), 137.

42. Lorraine Boissoneault, "Amelia Bloomer Didn't Mean to Start a Fashion Revolution, but Her Name Became Synonymous with Trousers," Smithsonian .com, May 24, 2018.

43. Rabinovitch-Fox, "Dressing Up," 137–143.

44. Margaret Finnegan, *Selling Suffrage: Consumer Culture & Votes for Women* (New York: Columbia University Press, 1999), 93.

45. Rabinovitch-Fox, "Dressing Up," 135–151.

46. Vanessa Friedman, "On Election Day, the Hillary Clinton White Suit Effect," *New York Times*, November 7, 2016.

47. Friedman, "On Election Day."

48. Victoria McGrane, "Suffragists Wore White 96 Years Ago. Now Clinton Voters Are Doing the Same," *Boston Globe*, November 2, 2016.

49. Annie Correal, "Pantsuit Nation, a 'Secret' Facebook Hub, Celebrates Clinton," *New York Times*, November 8, 2016.

50. Correal, "Pantsuit Nation."

51. McGrane, "Suffragists Wore White."

52. Sabrina Ford, "How Racism Split the Suffrage Movement," *Bust*, February 20, 2017.

53. Rabinovitch-Fox, "Dressing Up," 142.

54. Denise Oliver-Velez (@Deoliver47), "#WearWhiteToVote I'm honoring Black Suffragists," Twitter, November 8, 2016, 6:28 a.m., https://twitter.com /Deoliver47/status/795996480146444288.

55. Hillary Rodham Clinton, *What Happened* (New York: Simon & Schuster, 2017), 18.

56. Katie O'Malley, "State of the Union: Women to Deliver Powerful Feminist Message to Trump by Wearing White," *Independent*, January 31, 2019.

57. Hayley Miller, "Women Are Placing Their 'I Voted' Stickers on Susan B. Anthony's Grave," *Huffington Post*, November 6, 2016.

58. For more on Anthony as symbol, see Nicole Eaton, "Moving History Forward: American Women Activists, the Search for a Usable Past and the Creation of Public Memory" (PhD diss., Brown University, 2012); Ann D. Gordon, "Knowing Susan B. Anthony: The Stories We Tell of a Life," in *Susan B. Anthony and the Struggle for Equal Rights*, ed. Christine L. Ridarsky and Mary M. Huth (Rochester, NY: University of Rochester Press, 2012), 201–234.

59. A Mighty Girl, "In honor of this historic week for women in politics, Rochester Mayor Lovely Warren has set up a thank you letter next to the gravestone of Susan B. Anthony," Facebook, July 28, 2016, https://www.facebook.com/amightygirl/posts/in-honor-of-this-historic-week-for-women-in-politics-rochester-mayor-lovely-warr/1071749866194659/.

60. Kara Grasso Veeder, July 28, 2016, comment on A Mighty Girl, "In honor of this historic week for women in politics," https://www.facebook.com/amightygirl/posts/in-honor-of-this-historic-week-for-women-in-politics-rochester-mayor-lovely-warr/1071749866194659/.

61. Katie Rogers, "Four Prominent Suffragist Grave Sites in the Bronx Anticipating a Surge in Visitors This Election Day," *New York Times*, November 8, 2016.

62. Rebecca Onion, "Take the Long View of a Toxic Election with #VisitA-Suffragist," *Slate*, November 7, 2016.

63. Alysa Zavala-Offman, "This Woman Is Visiting the Graves of Michigan Suffragists—and Making It Easy for You to Do the Same," *Detroit Metro Times*, November 8, 2016.

64. Quoted in Hayley Miller, "Women Are Placing Their 'I Voted' Stickers on Susan B. Anthony's Grave," *Huffington Post*, November 6, 2016.

65. See for example, Jen McDaneld, "White Suffragist Dis/Entitlement: The Revolution and the Rhetoric of Racism," *Legacy: A Journal of American Women Writers* 30, no. 2 (2013): 243–250.

66. Tracy Schuhmacher, "Susan B. Anthony Was No Racist, Historian Says," *Democrat & Chronicle*, February 15, 2017.

67. Ann Gordon, "How to Celebrate a Complicated Win for Women," *New York Times*, August 27, 2018.

68. Andrea Moore Kerr, "White Women's Rights, Black Men's Wrongs, Free Love, Blackmail, and the Formation of the American Woman Suffrage Association," in *One Woman, One Vote: Rediscovering the Woman Suffrage Movement*, ed. Marjorie Spruill Wheeler (Troutdale, OR: NewSage Press, 1995), 77.

69. Zeba Blay, "These Black Women Also Deserve a Visit to Their Graves on Election Day: Susan B. Anthony Isn't the Only Woman Who Should Be Honored," *Huffington Post*, November 8, 2016.

70. Fatou G (@fgwaggeh), "Thinking abt Sojourner Truth, Ida b Wells, Shirley Chisholm," Twitter, November 8, 2016, 10:38 a.m., https://twitter.com /fgwaggeh/status/796059378902269952.

71. Mikki Kendall (@Karnythia), "I vote because of the Black women who marched," Twitter, November 8, 2016, 8:10 a.m., https://twitter.com/Karnythia /status/796022047512076288.

72. Phoebe Lett, "White Women Voted Trump. Now What?," *New York Times*, November 10, 2016.

73. Reva Siegel, "The Right's Reasons: Constitutional Conflict and the Spread of Woman-Protective Antiabortion Argument," *Duke Law Journal* 57 (2008): 1641–1692.

74. "Feminists for Life Celebrates Our Pro-woman, Pro-life Legacy," *American Feminist* 11, no. 1 (Spring 2004): 1.

75. Stacy Schiff, "Desperately Seeking Susan," *New York Times*, October 13, 2006, A27.

76. SBA List, "Mobilizing the Pro-life Vote in 2016 to Elect Donald Trump & Pro-life Senators," press release, November 8, 2016, accessed April 26, 2019, https://www.sba-list.org/newsroom/press-releases/mobilizing-pro-life-vote-2016 -elect-donald-trump-pro-life-senators-2. See also Tamar W. Carroll, Christine A. Kray, and Hinda Mandell, "Public Memory and Reproductive Justice in the Trump Era," *Nursing Clio*, November 6, 2018.

77. Katherine Stewart, "Eighty-One Percent of White Evangelicals Voted for Donald Trump. Why?" *The Nation*, November 17, 2016.

78. Molly Ball, "Why Hillary Clinton Lost," *The Atlantic*, November 15, 2016.

Adelina Otero-Warren, suffrage activist and superintendent of public schools in Santa Fe, New Mexico, from
1917 to 1929. George Grantham Bain Collection,
Library of Congress.

CHAPTER 18

Rooted in Community

The Scholarship of Chicana Political Leadership and Activism

MARISELA R. CHÁVEZ

IN 2018, voters in El Paso, Texas, elected Veronica Escobar to Congress to represent the Sixteenth District of the border city. During this historic midterm, women still achieved "firsts," a sign of the continued peripheral presence of women in electoral politics. As the first woman to hold this district seat, Escobar also became one of two Mexican American women to ever represent Texas in Congress. Yet, Escobar was not new to politics, having served as El Paso county commissioner and county judge. Her politics began as a student at University of Texas at El Paso. As she recalled, "I got civically engaged in my early twenties because there was a topic I was passionate about: immigrant rights. . . . I had to step up because I was speaking on behalf of marginalized groups." For many years since, she had "volunteered for campaigns of those who inspired me and those experiences connected me deeply to the community."[1]

Escobar's experience reveals an interconnected history traversing the space in between grassroots causes and party politics; it also shows how her politics, like so many that came before her, remained grounded in issues of labor, education, and immigration. Yet, little attention has been afforded to this long and varied history. Mexican American women's roles in shaping the US political landscape have, in the words of historian Vicki L. Ruiz, remained "in the shadows."[2] The centennial of the Nineteenth Amendment's ratification serves as a fitting moment to reassess what we know about the history of Chicana political leadership in its many forms, especially because of the broad and deep changes in the nation's population and electorate. As of 2018, Latinos/as represent the largest ethnic or racial group in the nation, standing at 58.9 million, or 18 percent of the nation's population.[3] Likewise, in electoral politics, the 2018 midterms brought the largest group of Latinas into office in US history—13 Latinas in Congress and 117 Latinas serving as state legislators across the nation.[4] This presence will have significant consequences going forward, but in thinking about "suffrage at 100," it is important to refocus attention on how Mexican American women have pushed for visibility in electoral politics well before the twenty-first century and have persistently helped bridge the gulf between community engagement and mainstream politics.

Chicanas rarely receive mention in mainstream politics, yet their community efforts to install streetlights, in union leadership, and as educational reformers across the nation have made an impact within families and communities. In fact, their invisibility is what ultimately led me to the historical profession as an undergraduate. Given my own experiences, I sought to explore women's participation in the Chicano/a movement. First, my goal was to obtain basic information of how women actually participated in the movement itself. This led to more complex questions about how women navigated a complex political ideology anchored in new notions of identity and belonging. With these questions regarding women's political agency, ideologies, and forms of political engagement, I join many other Chicana/Latina historians in an endeavor to both recover and to reconceptualize these histories.

The centennial of women's suffrage provides a fruitful opportunity to affirm that Chicana history calls for an expansion of what constitutes "politics." Recovering these stories will invariably lead to critique and reimagining of a suffrage narrative that underplays how women of color did not immediately nor consistently enjoy the right to vote.[5] Indeed, it is important to acknowledge and critique the ways in which the celebration of suffrage does not draw immediate attention to the women left out of this nation's collective conscience of suffragists and the suffrage cause. This chapter traces the developing scholarship of Chicana political leadership to make the case that this omission is inadequate.

With some exceptions, such as Soledad Chacón, elected New Mexico's secretary of state in 1923, Chicanas, like other women of color, were disenfranchised and excluded from traditional or mainstream politics. Yet, if we look beyond suffrage to labor, community organizing, civil rights, social movements, and feminist organizing, we see Chicanas engaging in political work and expressing their rightful political citizenship. While not comprehensive, what follows are select highlights of the intellectual work done since historian Cynthia E. Orozco's 1993 first review of Chicanas/Mexican American women's political history, "Beyond Machismo, La Familia, and Ladies Auxiliaries: A Historiography of Mexican-Origin Women's Participation in Voluntary Associations and Politics in the United States, 1870–1990."

Over twenty-five years have passed since Orozco's review, and as historian Miroslava Chávez-García notes, "Chicana history has come a long way in a relatively short time." And yet, "few [historians], however, have focused their pens (or word processors) on women in politics."[6] This holds true for other Latinas too. One consideration is related to the limited number of Chicana and Latina historians who have entered the academy. In 2012, only 0.6 percent of Latinos/as in the United States held doctoral degrees, and, of those degrees, women held half.[7] Historians make up only a portion of this group, which has consequences on the shape of Chicana and Latina history that has largely been a history of one's own.[8]

The works presented here—books, anthologies, and articles mostly by historians and some anthropologists, sociologists, and political scientists—begin to offer a fuller understanding of Chicanas' wide and varied presence in the US political landscape.[9] The materials included in this review are all historically grounded and centered specifically on ethnic Mexican women and their experiences in politics, with some exceptions, and published after 1990. I hope that this wider mapping of Chicanas' history making in the areas of politics will encourage more stories to be brought to light and, in turn, will change the ways in which we ultimately conceptualize women's political leadership as a whole, both in academia and in communities across the nation.

Suffrage, Post-Suffrage Organizing, and Political Citizenship

As is well known, the suffrage movement that led to the passage of the Nineteenth Amendment emerged out of the abolition movement, an effort where both whites and African Americans joined together to end slavery. As Rosalyn Terborg-Penn writes, "Often behind the scenes or ignored in the history of the woman suffrage and black suffrage movements, the African American female was significant in both. Passage of the Nineteenth Amendment, which enfranchised all American women, was due in part to the efforts of African American women."[10] For ethnic Mexican women, a united effort that propelled their engagement with suffrage did not exist. However, Mexican and Mexican American women actively advocated for their land rights, in support of revolutionary movements in Mexico, and local organizing around labor and social issues. While not suffragists per se, these women practiced a politics rooted in their communities, and their experiences merit inclusion in the spectrum of women's political activism in the United States.

Although they did not lobby for the vote as a bloc, Spanish-speaking women from wealthy, landowning families participated in the suffrage movement and entered mainstream politics. For example, Adelina Otero-Warren and María Concepción "Concha" Ortiz y Pino followed their family traditions of political officeholding. Elected when she was twenty-six years old, Ortiz y Pino served as a New Mexico legislator from 1936 to 1942. During the last years in office, she held the post of majority whip in the New Mexico House, a first for a woman in the state.[11]

Otero-Warren also achieved a first, as the "first Latina to run for Congress." As a member of the landed gentry in New Mexico, Otero-Warren would have probably considered herself a Hispana, a descendant of Spanish conquistadores. "Her life," as historian Elizabeth Salas notes, "demonstrates how quickly Hispanas adapted after they were thrown into the vortex of American life, three decades after the signing of the Treaty of Guadalupe Hidalgo and the Seneca Falls Convention in 1848."[12] Born María Adelina Isabel Emilia Otero in 1881, Otero-

Warren was both educated and divorced, having been married to US military officer Rawson D. Warren for only two years. In 1908, she joined the Congressional Union, a woman suffrage organization, and soon led an affiliated chapter in New Mexico. Losing her congressional campaign in 1922, she nonetheless worked in the state Republican Party, the New Mexico Federation of Women's Clubs, and between 1917 and 1929, as Santa Fe's superintendent of schools. Her example highlights how women of her era, class status, and racial/ethnic identity carved out a space for themselves within white-dominated women's organizations, including suffrage, and used these positions as a gateway into formal political structures and full citizenship.[13]

In this same era, ethnic Mexican women also engaged in a transnational politics, anchored in supporting revolutionary activities in Mexico and serving ethnic Mexican communities in the Unites States. The most recent work on this particular topic by historian Gabriela González focuses on Texas and situates these activities as "transborder human rights project[s]" rooted in both "the politics of respectability and the politics of radicalism." González analyzes respectability and radicalism through the experiences of women such as Carolina Malpica de Munguía, founder of the San Antonio charitable organization Círculo Cultural "Isabel, la Católica"; Jovita Idar Juárez, a precinct judge in San Antonio in the 1920s; anarchists such as Sara Estela Ramírez, a member of the Mexican political party el Partido Liberal Mexicano (PLM); among others.[14] These cases remind us that politics was multifaceted in this early period.

Traditional studies of Mexican American women in electoral politics are few and the most comprehensive recent ones are political science based, focusing on Texas. For example, José Ángel Gutiérrez takes a biographical approach in *Chicanas in Charge: Texas Women in the Public Arena*, highlighting women such as Olga Ramos Peña, one of the first ethnic Mexican women who participated in the women's Democratic Clubs in San Antonio in the midcentury and Alma Canales who ran for Texas lieutenant governor as a candidate of the Chicano third party La Raza Unida Party in 1972. In *Políticas: Latina Public Officials in Texas*, Sonia García, Valerie Martínez-Ebers, and Irasema Coronado survey the landscape of Chicana and Latina politicians and point out that "although Latinas have made gains in politics in recent years, there are still relatively few in office, and for the most part they are unrecognized as political actors."[15]

Given that both texts premise their analyses on previously ignored ethnic Mexican women in politics, the story of Olga Ramos Peña is an important contribution. As a member of the women's Democratic Clubs in San Antonio, Ramos Peña's political activism included recruiting other Mexicanas to join the Democratic Club, registering voters, joining Viva Kennedy Clubs organized to elect John F. Kennedy to the presidency in 1960, and running her husband's political campaigns for county commissioner.[16] Ramos Peña's political journey mirrors the activism of other ethnic Mexican women in California during this period, such as the more well-known Dolores Huerta, who joined the Community Service Organization (CSO) in Stockton, California, in the mid-1950s. In the CSO, Huerta worked for a time as the organization's de facto lobbyist in Sacramento before she emerged as a labor leader along with César Chávez and others with the United Farm Workers (UFW). As historian Margaret Rose has observed of women in the CSO, "Women used their roles in the home, family, and community to organize for social change."[17] Indeed, Rose further concludes that "political participation is typically viewed as being divided into two separate spheres, electoral and grassroots. . . . Latina leaders, however, frequently remain active or at least maintain connections in both spheres simultaneously."[18] Likewise, political scientist Diane-Michele Prindeville, among other scholars, encourages those studying Latinas in politics to close the distinct separation in the literature between electoral and grassroots activism, a false binary.[19]

First studies of Latinas in politics highlight the structural barriers that make it difficult for women to run, but we do not have a full sense of these racialized gender impediments. Missing still is a historical analysis of ethnic Mexican women in more traditional electoral party politics in the Democratic and Republican Parties. While there has been a great deal of scholarship on citizenship and immigrants' rights in various fields, publications that focus solely on women's activism and leadership have been limited. One monograph in the field of anthropology has addressed this topic by focusing on women in a grassroots immigrants' rights organization in San Francisco.[20] Recent attention to Chicanas' (and Latinas') political activism makes clear as well that citizenship must move beyond formal civic engagement to include cultural and social forms as well.

Labor, Civil Rights, and Reproductive Justice from the Early Twentieth Century to the *Movimientos*

Labor organizing represents an important thread of political history and has been well developed since the 1980s, but political historians need to integrate these histories to broaden the scope of what constitutes politics. Even in this area of robust scholarship, monographs that solely focus on ethnic Mexican women's labor and working-class culture since 1990 have been scarce. This scholarship has shown that Chicanas worked in large numbers outside of the home before and after World War II, provided essential rank-and-file leadership in unions, and served as professional organizers, especially in the canneries and in the fields of California and in the pecan industry of Texas. Historians such as Vicki L. Ruiz, Mario T. García, Zaragoza Vargas, and Gabriela González have spotlighted the work of Guatemalan-born Luisa Moreno and Tejana Emma Tenayuca, respectively.[21] Elizabeth Escobedo's work on ethnic Mexican women's experiences on the World War II home front highlights the relationship between wartime industry, labor, and union activism. Additionally, Fran Leeper Buss collaborated with María Elena Lucas to publish an edited oral history/biography on Lucas's life as a farmworker; there have also been numerous profiles and biographies of Dolores Huerta. Collectively, these histories have shown that women led movements first assumed to be male centered.[22] Surprisingly little work has followed Vicki L. Ruiz's 1987 book, *Cannery Women, Cannery Lives: Mexican Women, Unionization, and the California Food*

Processing Industry, 1930–1950. The only study that specifically explores labor organizing among ethnic Mexican women in the first half of the twentieth century published since then is Sonia Hernández's *Working Women into the Borderlands.* Yet, because Hernández's 2014 text considers transnational labor, the book devotes only two chapters on ethnic Mexican women within the boundaries of the United States.[23]

Much recovery work in Chicana civil rights history is yet to be done. For example, we would be hard pressed to learn about women such as Josefina Fierro de Bright, prominent member of the Sleepy Lagoon Defense Committee in the 1940s, or Emma Tenayuca, who as a labor organizer led the 1938 Pecan Shellers' Strike in Texas and later joined the Communist Party, as there are no monographs devoted to their lives. Instead, we find articles by historians Zaragoza Vargas and Mario T. García on Tenayuca and Fierro de Bright, respectively. Additionally, Tenayuca emerges as a "radical reformer" in the most recent work by Gabriela González.[24] Notably, *Latina Legacies: Identity, Biography, and Community,* edited by Vicki L. Ruiz and Virginia Sánchez Korrol, represents one of the few texts that provides a compendium of Latina histories via biographical chapters on figures such as Adelina Otero-Warren, Dolores Huerta, and Luisa Moreno, among others. The extensive *Latinas in the United States: A Historical Encyclopedia,* edited by historians Vicki L. Ruiz and Virginia Sánchez Korrol, stands as an excellent starting point for information on Latinas. While the scholarship on these women in labor and politics helps us ascertain a picture of early Latina women's civil rights struggles and activities as part of various groups, we still await biographies that will provide the much-needed depth that focusing on a single life might afford.

Likewise, we do not have a full history of women's engagement in ethnic and civil rights organizations established in the pre–World War II era. Scholarship of mixed-gender organizations, such as Cynthia Orozco's 2009, *No Mexicans, Women, or Dogs Allowed: The Rise of the Mexican American Civil Rights Movement,* provides the thread of women's activism in these groups, in this case the League of United Latin American Citizens (LULAC) established in Texas in 1929.[25] Another organization where we have limited information on women is El Congreso del Pueblo de Habla Española, founded in 1938. Women were active organizers in groups like these, recruiting members and running their operations in and around women's auxiliaries. Indeed, El Congreso was led by Josefina Fierro de Bright and Luisa Moreno. Seeing these groups as key political engines, we get a better sense of the multiple ideologies and identities of ethnic Mexican women and early iterations of a pan-ethnic Latina/o identity. While El Congreso, for example, saw itself as a pan-Latino organization that welcomed any Spanish-speaking person regardless of citizenship status, LULAC limited membership to US citizens.[26] Regardless of these distinct opinions, during this early period through the beginnings of the post–World War II era, women organized for their communities as communities. They did not, at this point, organize for themselves as women.

Chicanas' voluntary work and political activism in the 1950s is an especially rich area of scholarship ripe for development. The majority of work on Chicanas in this era covers women's involvement in groups such as CSO in Los Angeles or analyses of the blacklisted film *Salt of the Earth* (1954).[27] To understand how Chicanas shaped and were shaped by experiences of this era, our analysis needs to include broader studies of women's responses to Cold War politics. For example, very real consequences of political activism befell women labeled subversive or communist during this era. Josefina Fierro and Luisa Moreno both left the United States in 1948 and 1950, respectively, of their own accord rather than be subjected to deportation. By exploring and connecting experiences of women such as Fierro and Moreno and other activists of this era, we would move away from the notion of the 1950s as an apolitical decade, but as a period that provided a foundation for the ways in which women participated in the social movements of the 1960s and 1970s. These relationships have been a theme of my own publications where I have explored the roots of Chicana feminist organizations in Los Angeles to show the pre-movement foundations of these organizations.[28]

Finally, there exists a lack of published scholarship on reproductive justice and Chicanas, which emerged as an important issue during the

1960s and 1970s. The sole monograph on the topic that addressed Chicanas as its main focus was published in 2008 by sociologist Elena Gutiérrez. In *Fertile Matters: The Politics of Mexican-Origin Women's Reproduction,* Gutiérrez traces the sterilization abuse of Mexican women in Los Angeles and the subsequent lawsuit, *Madrigal v. Quilligan,* led by Gloria Molina, the first Chicana elected to the California State Assembly, and Antonia Hernández, who later directed the Mexican American Legal Defense and Education Fund (MALDEF). Additionally, the award-winning documentary *No Más Bebés* (No More Babies), produced by historian Virginia Espino and directed by filmmaker Renee Tajima-Peña, provides an important focus on the stories of the women forcibly sterilized, connecting their roles as plaintiffs in this lawsuit as activism in and of itself. These important contributions on reproductive justice makes clear the need for future scholarship on Chicana bodily rights as central to the wider history of women's health and the place of reproductive politics in electoral politics.[29]

Moving Scholarship and Activism into the Twenty-First Century

Early works written in the 1970s and 1980s share a common goal with recent scholarship that has been completed since: to show that women were indeed active participants in political struggles, defined "politics" on their own terms, and connected their personal lives to their political activism. Using the frameworks established, for example, by scholars such as Gloria Anzaldúa and Cherrie Moraga, focus in the 1990s turned to exploring theories of Chicana feminisms and alternative frameworks of leadership practiced by women. Alma García's *Chicana Feminist Thought: The Basic Historical Writings* collected Chicana writing from newspapers in the movement and showcased the breadth of women's political ideologies, providing an essential text that foregrounded the participation of women in the Chicano movement.[30] In the 2000s, Chicana scholars greatly expanded on García's anthology, highlighting the intellectual and political contributions of Chicanas previously overlooked in *movimiento* histories. From this work, we now know more about Chicanas' feminist ideas and practices, the role of the Catholic Church as a driver of political activism, and the transnational aspects of Chicana/Latina activism.[31] In this decade, the first anthology of a single Chicana's writing was also published, *Enriqueta Vasquez and the Chicano Movement: Writings from El Grito del Norte,* a joint project by Vásquez herself and scholars Lorena Oropeza and Dionne Espinoza.[32]

In the past ten years, this explosion of interest and attention to Chicana political history has continued. Maylei Blackwell authored the first monograph in 2011 on women in the Chicano movement, *Chicana Power! Contested Histories of Feminism in the Chicano Movement.* Blackwell focused on Las Hijas de Cuauhtémoc, established by Chicana students at California State University, Long Beach. Rather than provide a chronicle of the organization, she instead used its focus, causes, and actions to assert that the organization provided a "retrofitted memory," or an alternative conceptualization of the Chicano movement itself. Three additional studies expand understanding of Chicanas in the movement. From these works, we learn more of Elizabeth "Betita" Martinez, a longtime activist who edited the influential newspaper *El Grito del Norte* in New Mexico, and women from San Diego, California, involved in the movement.[33] *Chicana Movidas: New Narratives of Feminism in the Movement Era,* published in 2018, brings together *testimonios* of activists with scholars' assessments of their work in areas not previously considered such as queer women's experience.[34] The publication of *Chicana Movidas* marks an important shift in the scholarship on the Chicano/a movement that links grassroots and electoral politics in the late twentieth-century period, while also including contributions by activists themselves in the volume. These new narratives highlight the array of political activities that Chicanas have engaged in, ranging from Democratic Party organizing, to the Texas Political Women's Caucus, and their participation in international feminist arenas.

Drawing focus on this recent scholarship and future directions makes clear the long history of Chicanas doing political work in and around electoral politics. Veronica Escobar's path highlights a long-standing political tradition among Chicanas overall in which women have entered politics to change the conditions of their communities. This political work is important to recognize before and after women got the vote, for this community-driven advocacy happened inside and outside formal politics irrespective of Mexican Americans' access to suffrage. As we recover more political stories, the foundation laid by those before Veronica Escobar stepped into her role on Capitol Hill will become increasingly clear, and it will be easier to draw a line between politicians like her and those such as Nina Otero-Warren or Concha Ortiz y Pino. To trace out this lineage, we must continue to search for the vastly untold stories of Chicana political participation, affirm Chicana contributions to the political life of this nation, and challenge the standard narrative and arc of US politics to assert Chicanas' rightful place in the history of this nation.

Notes

1. Julianne Pepitone, "'This Is Our Moment': Veronica Escobar, Slated to Become Texas' First Latina Congresswoman," *NBCNews*, September 15, 2018, https://www.nbcnews.com/know-your-value/feature/our-moment-veronica -escobar-slated-become-texas-first-latina-congresswoman-ncna909806. Also see Emily Cochrane, "Texas Latina Emerges as House's Voice of Passion and Reason on the Border," *New York Times*, July 11, 2019, https://www.nytimes .com/2019/07/11/us/politics/veronica-escobar-border-debate.html?searchResult Position=2.

2. See Vicki L. Ruiz, *From Out of the Shadows: Mexican Women in Twentieth Century America* (New York: Oxford University Press, 2008).

3. "Hispanic Heritage Month 2018," United States Census Bureau, September 13, 2018, https://www.census.gov/newsroom/facts-for-features/2018 /hispanic-heritage-month.html.

4. "Women of Color in Elective Office 2019: Congress, Statewide, State Legislature, Mayors," Center for American Women and Politics, Eagleton Institute of Politics, Rutgers University, accessed May 12, 2019, https://cawp .rutgers.edu/women-color-elective-office-2019.

5. See Marisela R. Chávez, "'We Lived and Breathed and Worked the Movement': The Contradictions and Rewards of Chicana/Mexicana Activism in

el Centro de Acción Social Autónomo (CASA), Los Angeles, 1975–1978," in *Las Obreras: Chicana Politics of Work and Family*, *Aztlan: A Journal of Chicano Studies* 20, nos. 1–2 (1999); "Pilgrimage to the Motherland: California Chicanas and International Women's Year, Mexico City, 1975," in *Memories and Migrations: Mapping Boricua/Chicana Histories*, ed. Vicki L. Ruiz and John Chávez (Urbana: University of Illinois Press, 2008); "'We Have a Long, Beautiful History': Chicana Feminist Trajectories and Legacies," in *No Permanent Waves: Recasting U.S. Feminist History*, ed. Nancy Hewitt (New Brunswick, NJ: Rutgers University Press, 2010); and "Refocusing Chicana International Feminism: Photographs, Postmemory, and Political Trauma," in *Chicana Movidas: New Narratives of Women's Activism and Feminism in the Movement Era*, ed. Maria E. Cotera, Dionne Espinoza, and Maylei Blackwell (Austin: University of Texas Press, 2018).

6. Miroslava Chávez-García, "The Interdisciplinary Project of Chicana History: Looking Back, Moving Forward," *Pacific Historical Review* 82 (2013): 543, 562, https://doi.org/10.1525/phr.2013.82.4.542; Cynthia E. Orozco, "Beyond Machismo, La Familia, and Ladies Auxiliaries: A Historiography of Mexican-Origin Women's Participation in Voluntary Associations and Politics in the United States, 1870–1990," *Renato Rosaldo Lecture Series* 10, 1992–1993 (Tucson: University of Arizona, Mexican American Studies and Research Center, 1994), 37–78.

7. See Lindsay Pérez Huber, Maria C. Malagón, Brianna R. Ramirez, et al., *Still Falling through the Cracks: Revisiting the Latina/o Education Pipeline*, CSRC Research Report No. 19 (Los Angeles: UCLA Chicano Studies Research Center, November 2015), 3. Latino men with doctoral degrees constituted 0.3% of the Latino population as a whole. For whites, 2% and 1% of women and men, respectively, held doctoral degrees.

8. Chávez-García, "The Interdisciplinary Project of Chicana History."

9. When I first began to organize this piece, I considered solely using monographs. Upon my literature search, I realized that doing so would make this piece painfully short due to the limited publications that fit the parameters I had set out. Space limitations prevented inclusion of more interdisciplinary explorations, as well as the ways in which the arts and/or literature are political in and of themselves.

10. Rosalyn Terborg-Penn, "African American Women and the Vote: An Overview," in *African American Women and the Vote, 1837–1965*, ed. Anne D. Gordon and Bettye Collier-Thomas (Amherst: University of Massachusetts Press, 1997), 10.

11. See Vicki L. Ruiz, "Ortiz y Pino de Keven, María Concepción 'Concha,'" in *Latinas in the United States: A Historical Encyclopedia*, ed. Vicki L. Ruiz and Virginia Sánchez Korrol (Bloomington: Indiana University Press, 2006),

546–547; and Melanie Gustafson, Kristie Miller, and Elisabeth Israels Perry, *We Have Come to Stay: American Women and Political Parties, 1880–1960* (Albuquerque: University of New Mexico Press, 1999).

12. Charlotte Whaley, *Nina Otero-Warren of Santa Fe*, 1st ed. (Albuquerque: University of New Mexico Press, 1994); Elizabeth Salas, "Adelina Otero Warren: Rural Aristocrat and Modern Feminism," in *Latina Legacies: Identity, Biography, and Community*, Viewpoints on American Culture, ed. Vicki L. Ruiz and Virginia Sánchez Korrol (New York: Oxford University Press, 2005), 135.

13. See Ann M. Massmann, "Adelina 'Nina' Otero-Warren: A Spanish-American Cultural Broker," *Journal of the Southwest* 42, no. 4 (2000): 877–896, especially pp. 880–886; Elizabeth Salas, "Ethnicity, Gender, and Divorce: Issues in the 1922 Campaign by Adelina Otero-Warren for the U.S. House of Representatives," *New Mexico Historical Review* 70, no. 4 (October 1995): 367–382; and Whaley, *Nina Otero-Warren of Santa Fe*.

14. Gabriela González, *Redeeming la Raza: Transborder Modernity, Race, Respectability, and Rights* (New York: Oxford University Press, 2018), especially chaps. 3, 4, and 5. Also see Zaragosa Vargas, "Tejana Radical: Emma Tenayuca and the San Antonio Labor Movement during the Great Depression," *Pacific Historical Review* 66, no. 4 (1997): 553–580; and Mario T. García, *Mexican Americans: Leadership, Ideology & Identity, 1930–1960* (New Haven, CT: Yale University Press, 1989), chap. 6.

15. José Angel Gutiérrez, *Chicanas in Charge: Texas Women in the Public Arena* (Lanham, MD: AltaMira Press, 2007); Sonia R. García, Valerie Martínez-Ebers, and Irasema Coronado, *Políticas: Latina Public Officials in Texas*, 1st ed. (Austin: University of Texas Press, 2008), 5.

16. Gutiérrez, *Chicanas in Charge*, 21–25.

17. Margaret Rose, "Gender and Civic Activism in Mexican American Barrios in California: The Community Service Organization, 1947–1962," in *Not June Cleaver: Women and Gender in Postwar America, 1945–1960*, ed. Joanne Meyerowitz (Philadelphia: Temple University Press, 1994), 179, 183.

18. García et al., *Políticas*, 9–10.

19. Diane-Michele Prindeville, "A Comparative Study of Native American and Hispanic Women in Grassroots and Electoral Politics," *Frontiers: A Journal of Women Studies* 23, no. 1 (2002): 67–89, https://doi.org/10.1353/fro.2002.0011; Diane-Michele Prindeville, "Latina and American Women Leaders, Political Representation, and Environmental Policy," *Journal of Latino-Latin American Studies* 1, no. 1 (2003): 46–61; Prindeville, "Identity and the Politics of American Indian and Hispanic Women Leaders," *Gender & Society* 17, no. 4 (August 1, 2003): 591–608, https://doi.org/10.1177/0891243203254076. Also see Gutiérrez, *Chicanas in Charge*; and José Angel Gutiérrez, "Experiences of Chicana County Judges in Texas Politics: In Their Own Words," *Frontiers: A Journal of Women Studies* 20, no. 1 (1999): 181–191, https://doi.org/10.2307/3347001.

20. Kathleen M. Coll, *Remaking Citizenship: Latina Immigrants and New American Politics* (Stanford, CA: Stanford University Press, 2010).

21. Vicki L. Ruiz, "Class Acts: Latina Feminist Traditions, 1900–1930," *American Historical Review* 121, no. 1 (February 2016): 1–16, https://doi.org /10.1093/ahr/121.1.1; Ruiz, "Una Mujer Sin Fronteras," *Pacific Historical Review* 73, no. 1 (2004): 1–20, https://doi.org/10.1525/phr.2004.73.1.1; Ruiz, "Of Poetics and Politics: The Border Journeys of Luisa Moreno," in *Women's Labor in the Global Economy: Speaking in Multiple Voices*, ed. Sharon Harley (New Brunswick, NJ: Rutgers University Press, 2007), 28–45; Zaragosa Vargas, "Tejana Radical: Emma Tenayuca and the San Antonio Labor Movement during the Great Depression," *Pacific Historical Review* 66, no. 4 (1997): 553–80, https://doi.org/10.2307/3642237; Gabriela Gonzalez, "Carolina Munguia and Emma Tenayuca: The Politics of Benevolence and Radical Reform," *Frontiers; Lincoln* 24, nos. 2–3 (2003): 200–229.

22. María Elena Lucas, *Forged under the Sun Forjada bajo el sol: The Life of María Elena Lucas*, Women and Culture Series (Ann Arbor: University of Michigan Press, 1993); Mario T. García, *A Dolores Huerta Reader* (Albuquerque: University of New Mexico Press, 2008); Alicia Chávez, "Dolores Huerta and the United Farm Workers," in Ruiz and Sánchez Korrol, *Latina Legacies*, 240–254.

23. Vicki L. Ruiz, *Cannery Women, Cannery Lives: Mexican Women, Unionization, and the California Food Processing Industry, 1930–1950* (Albuquerque: University of New Mexico Press, 1987).

24. See Vargas, "Tejana Radical," 443–580; Mario T. García, *Mexican Americans: Leadership, Ideology & Identity, 1930–1960* (New Haven, CT: Yale University Press, 1989), chap. 6; and González, *Redeeming la Raza*.

25. Cynthia Orozco, *No Mexicans, Women, or Dogs Allowed: The Rise of the Mexican American Civil Rights Movement* (Austin: University of Texas Press).

26. Ruíz and Sánchez Korrol, *Latina Legacies*; Joanne J. Meyerowitz, *Not June Cleaver: Women and Gender in Postwar America, 1945–1960*, Critical Perspectives on the Past (Philadelphia: Temple University Press, 1994).

27. See Margaret Rose, "Gender and Civic Activism in Mexican American Barrios in California: The Community Service Organization, 1947–1962," in Meyerowitz, *Not June Cleaver*; Ruiz and Sánchez Korrol, *Latina Legacies*, chap. 13; and García, *Mexican Americans*, chaps. 7–8.

28. See Marisela R. Chávez, "We Have a Long, Beautiful History: Chicana Feminist Trajectories and Legacies," in *No Permanent Waves: Recasting Histories of U.S. Feminism*, ed. Nancy Hewitt (New Brunswick, NJ: Rutgers University Press, 2010).

29. Elena R. Gutiérrez, *Fertile Matters: The Politics of Mexican-Origin Women's Reproduction* (Austin: University of Texas Press, 2008); Virginia

Espino, "'Woman Sterilized as Gives Birth': Forced Sterilization and Chicana Resistance in the 1970s," *Las Obreras: Chicana Politics of Work and Family, Aztlan* 20, nos. 1–2 (1999). Also see *No Más Bebés: No More Babies*, directed by Renee Tajima-Pena, produced by Virginia Espino, documentary, June 14, 2015.

30. Alma M. García, *Chicana Feminist Thought: The Basic Historical Writings* (New York: Routledge, 1997); Irene Ledesma, "Texas Newspapers and Chicana Workers' Activism, 1919–1974," *Western Historical Quarterly* 26, no. 3 (1995): 309–331, https://doi.org/10.2307/970655; Teresa Córdova, "Grassroots Mobilization by Chicanas in the Environmental and Economic Justice Movement," *Voces: A Journal of Chicana/Latina Studies* 1, no. 1 (1997): 31–55; Dolores Delgado Bernal, "Grassroots Leadership Reconceptualized: Chicana Oral Histories and the 1968 East Los Angeles School Blowouts," *Frontiers: A Journal of Women Studies* 19, no. 2 (1998): 113, https://doi.org/10 .2307/3347162.

31. A. E. Gomez, "Feminism, Torture, and the Politics of Chicana/Third World Solidarity: An Interview with Olga Talamante," *Radical History Review* 2008, no. 101 (April 1, 2008): 160–178, https://doi.org/10.1215/01636545 -2007-043; Laura Gonzalez and Jane Bayes, "New Transnational Opportunities and Challenges for Women's Leadership: The Consejo Consultivo Del Instituto de Los Mexicanos En El Exterior (CC-IME)," *Signs: Journal of Women in Culture and Society* 34, no. 1 (September 2008): 37–41, https://doi.org/10.1086 /588434; Gabriela F. Arredondo, *Chicana Feminisms: A Critical Reader*, Post-Contemporary Interventions (Durham, NC: Duke University Press, 2003); Lara Medina, *Las Hermanas: Chicana/Latina Religious-Political Activism in the U.S. Catholic Church* (Philadelphia: Temple University Press, 2004).

32. Enriqueta Longeaux y Vásquez, *Enriqueta Vasquez and the Chicano Movement: Writings from El Grito Del Norte*, Hispanic Civil Rights Series (Houston, TX: Arte Público Press, 2006).

33. See Maylei Blackwell, *Chicana Power! Contested Histories of Feminism in the Chicano Movement* (Austin: University of Texas Press, 2011); Tony Platt, ed. *Elizabeth "Betita" Sutherland Martínez: A Life in Struggle*, special issue, *Social Justice* 39, nos. 2–3 (2013); and Rita Sanchez and Sonia Lopez, *Chicana Tributes: Activist Women of the Civil Rights Movement; Stories for the New Generation* (San Diego, CA: Montezuma, 2017).

34. Dionne Espinoza, María Eugenia Cotera, and Maylei Blackwell, *Chicana Movidas: New Narratives of Activism and Feminism in the Movement Era*, 1st ed. (Austin: University of Texas Press, 2018).

State Senator Zahra Karinshak, of Lawrenceville, Georgia (*seated left*) and State Senator Jennifer Auer Jordan of Atlanta, Georgia (*standing*). Elected for the first time in 2017, they fought to stop passage of a state law banning most abortions. Photograph by Keenan Rogers; courtesy Georgia State Senate Press Office.

CHAPTER 19

Pave It Blue

Georgia Women and Politics in the Trump Era

ELLEN G. RAFSHOON

ELEVEN DAYS AFTER the 2016 election, Kathleen Sherwood hosted a Saturday evening dinner at her ranch house in suburban Atlanta. The guests were a mix of Sherwood's friends, colleagues, and chiropractic patients who had voted for Hillary Clinton and had expected to elect the first woman president. While their children played outside in what remained of the late fall sun, the adults sat around her dining table and took turns expressing their angst at the prospect of a Donald Trump presidency in light of his unparalleled misogyny and paucity of government experience. Unsure about what the next step would be, they decided to meet regularly and have Sherwood moderate a Facebook page under the moniker "Common Path" to communicate about further actions.

Common Path was emblematic of the surge of liberal women's activism that emerged in pockets throughout the United States in 2017, including in formerly hostile territory. The historic women's marches held the day after Trump was sworn in as president set local records—Atlanta's demonstration was the largest protest since the 1968 funeral procession for the Rev. Dr. Martin Luther King Jr.[1] This mobilization quickly carried over to politics. EMILY's List, the Washington-based organization that elects pro-choice Democratic women, garnered 16,000 queries from prospective candidates after Clinton's defeat. One year earlier, only 920 were interested in getting assistance.[2] A sister organization, Georgia WIN List, endorsed a record thirty-six women in the 2018 midterms and had to turn away dozens of applicants for its yearlong leadership academy, a boot camp for aspiring politicians.[3] The investments in fresh talent paid off: 2018 was decreed the "Year of the Woman" because so many prevailed at the polls.

Women-driven political groups that banded together in the wake of Trump's surprising victory are best described as stand-ins for Democratic Party chapters that had dwindled in Georgia since the 1990s. After Gov. Roy Barnes lost his reelection in 2004, donations to the Democratic Party dried up, leading to deep staff cuts. As a result, many legislative seats were handed to Republicans as Democrats failed to muster candidates. Republicans consequently redrew districts to lock in incumbents, just as Democrats had done when they were in charge.[4] Moreover, in 2008 Georgia implemented the strictest voter identification law in the nation, which turned away urban nonwhites, the most likely Democratic voters.[5] In the months leading up to the 2018 midterms, secretary of state and gubernatorial hopeful Brian Kemp used more recent "use it or lose it" provisions to strip voting privileges from at least fifty thousand Georgians, prompting the *Atlanta Journal-Constitution* to proclaim it the "largest disenfranchisement" in US history.[6] In light of these obstacles, the 2018 triumphs for liberal Georgia women were all the more remarkable.

PaveItBlue, active in greater Atlanta, stands out among these new engines for women's electoral action outside of established party structures. Founded by a quartet of suburban women spanning two generations in age they reasoned that none of the issues they cared about would gain traction unless GOP leaders were ousted from office. Social media was a potent virtual connection point that expanded PIB's reach to thousands of others ready to join a "progressive brigade" for change.[7] Reflecting the demographics north of Atlanta, "Pavers" were wealthier and better educated than women elsewhere in the state. A native of Puerto Rico raising her biracial son in the quaint town of Roswell, Denise Ruiz was intimidated about joining the group. Yet she was attracted to PaveItBlue's women-only membership and focus on getting women elected. As she explained, "It's about the sisterhood."[8] Similar groups would spring up throughout the metro area: Indivisible, Jewish Democratic Women's Salon of Atlanta, Perimeter Progressives, Women's Energy Network, and a dynamic offshoot of PIB called "No Safe Seats." The leaders of these factions became power brokers during the 2018 midterms with the ability to sway their feisty minions to one or another candidate.

Drawing on oral interviews, this article traces the trajectory of women in the "blue wave" from living room and Facebook chats to canvassing and running for public office themselves. The first-time candidates were the most radically transformed, willing to embark on life-changing quests. This is the first essay to document their stories in Georgia, where more women were on the ballot in 2018 than in any other state.[9] No matter what office they sought, from city council to lieutenant governor, these candidates highlighted Trump's election as a compelling catalyst. As Deborah Gonzalez, an Athens entertainment lawyer who won a state legislative seat, noted of her decision to run, "I just felt that my values were not being represented. . . . I wasn't so much upset that Hillary had lost as much as I was upset that he had won."[10] Another victorious statehouse candidate, University of Georgia social work professor Shelley Hutchinson remarked: "It was just a punch in the gut because I told people there were not enough people in this country to endorse someone who's assaulting women and treats his own wife like trash and you know, grabbing pussies. I just never thought people would say, 'that's my guy.'"

These neophyte political aspirants had the enthusiastic backing of family and friends, which propelled them over the inevitable hurdles to come. Hutchinson, owner of several therapy centers, said colleagues persuaded her to "run for something" over lunch shortly after Trump's inauguration. Fired up after a member of the all-white Gwinnett County Board of Commissioners referred to civil rights icon, Representative John Lewis from Atlanta, as "a racist pig" on his Facebook page, her coworkers suggested that Hutchinson, who is African American, challenge him in the midterms. Hutchinson considered entering the commissioner's race but thought she'd have a better chance seeking a statehouse seat.[11] Her relatives provided crucial financial support after she announced her candidacy. "Even my father in law—God bless him—he gives every month—$107 because it's [House] District 107." During her teenaged children's summer break, they accompanied their mother on canvassing forays conducted in twilight hours to avoid the searing heat.[12] Although these novice candidates had mastered the "work-life" balance, they still found campaigning overwhelming at times. Even a candidate with no children of her own who ran for school board struggled. Angelia Pressley, a public relations professional, recalled through tears the guilt she felt at missing her sister's milestone birthday celebration due to a competing campaign event.[13]

The ninety-one women on the ballot for legislative, state, and federal offices in Georgia were a diverse lot: Latina, African American, Asian, gay, straight, transgender, Jewish, and Muslim. Women were nominees for both governor—lawyer, romance novelist, and House Minority Leader Stacey Abrams—and lieutenant governor—Sarah Riggs Amico, CEO of Jack Cooper Holdings. Most of my subjects were active in the costly Sixth District Special Election campaign that pitted documentary filmmaker Jon Ossoff against Karen Handel, a Republican former secretary of state and failed gubernatorial candidate. It was on the tree-lined streets of Atlanta's most desirable subdivisions that newly "woke" women knocked on doors by day and installed Ossoff signs under cover of night, joking at political mixers about working their "Oss offs." Despite Ossoff's loss, his devotees were not demoralized as some had feared. Instead, they built momentum in the months to come. Expert campaigners, in the midterms a year later they unseated Handel, who had embraced President Trump's policies, and replaced her with rookie Lucy McBath, a flight attendant for Atlanta-based Delta Airlines and a gun control advocate.[14] McBath's victory was emblematic of the Trump-era turnover throughout the Atlanta metropolitan region. "It wasn't a wave in the metro area, it was a tsunami," remarked Republican Fran Millar, who lost his state senate seat in 2018 to Sally Harrell, a former state representative and social worker.[15]

Mapping this new political territory highlights the motivations, aspirations, and changes in the day-to-day lives of these candidates and records in real time progressive women's efforts to alter Georgia's political landscape. Political scientists' conclusions about women running for office are largely confirmed. Compared to men with comparable levels of personal achievement, these women had previously underestimated their worthiness for leadership and needed extraordinary prompting to jump into a race.[16] But having made the decision to run, they received enviable grassroots support, and voters did not appear to see their gender as a liability. In fact, given the gender dynamics of the 2016 presidential race, in hindsight, being a woman was an advantage in 2018.[17]

To emphasize how starkly the political winds have shifted, it is instructive to look at Georgia's recent and moribund history of women in politics. In Georgia, the second-wave feminist movement only caught on around Atlanta, where chapters of the National Organization for Women and Planned Parenthood emerged in the 1960s and 1970s, as well as homegrown organizations such as the Lesbian Feminist Alliance and Georgians for an Equal Rights Amendment. During that era, women lawyers who had participated in desegregation battles turned to fighting sex discrimination. They scored Georgia's greatest feminist victory in convincing the Supreme Court to strike down the state's restrictive abortion law in *Doe v. Bolton*, the companion case to *Roe v. Wade*.[18] Yet, the legalization of abortion sparked a conservative backlash that deterred future progress on women's rights. As the Republican Party sought to build a firm footing in the South, it embraced "family values" over women's autonomy. Antipathy to the ERA in the 1970s on the basis of "home, family, and motherhood" was a way former Democrats could prove their bona fides as Republicans. The ERA never came to a floor vote in Georgia before the ultimate deadline approached in 1982; the state remains one of only thirteen to reject ratifying the amendment.[19]

Georgia has an abysmal record of electing women, with only four serving as state lawmakers from 1923 to 1963. After passage of the Civil Rights Act, Atlanta's Grace Towns Hamilton became the first African American woman elected to the General Assembly; she was also the only woman of color in any Deep South legislature.[20] With each passing decade, women's representation in the legislature doubled; nonetheless, it never reached more than 23 percent of the House and 16 percent of the Senate by the twenty-first century. Male leaders diluted their influence, assigning their female colleagues to fewer committees and curtailing their ability to sponsor legislation.[21] Until the 2018 midterms, when female representation in the statehouse hit a record 30 percent, it looked like progress in electing women had stalled.[22]

The context for a revived women's movement is the rapid demographic change Georgia has experienced since the 1996 Atlanta Olympics. The proportion of residents who are white and of European descent—more likely conservative GOP voters—is in decline.[23] The newcomers are immigrants from Latin America and East Asia as well as African Americans making a "reverse migration" as they seek to take advantage of favorable home prices and cultural ties.[24] Their political affiliation leans Democratic or is up for grabs as first-generation voters come of age. The suburbs surrounding Atlanta with highly educated populations and multinational employers have overwhelmingly benefited from these influxes. Nearly all the women I interviewed either did not grow up in Georgia or had left the state for higher education or to start their careers. Unsurprisingly, most made the defense of immigrants in the face of nativist policies pushed by President Trump and local GOP officials a mainstay of their campaigns.

Lindy Miller's story represents this political change. Miller woke up on the morning of November 9, 2016, at six o'clock in time to get dressed for work and get her three little boys ready for school. Before her feet hit the floor, she turned to her husband and announced, "I'm ready to run. I have to do something." A graduate of Harvard's Kennedy School of Government and CEO of a solar energy start-up, the ambitious thirty-nine-year-old knew she would seek electoral office someday. In 2013, she had completed the WIN List candidate academy, but before Clinton's defeat, she felt no sense of urgency. After her day-break epiphany, Miller thought otherwise. She set up a meeting to garner advice from Stacey Abrams, the most powerful female politician in Georgia, then mulling her own run for governor. Abrams pointed Miller to the Public Service Commission, charged with regulating utilities. No Democrat had occupied one of the five seats on the commission since 2000. Within days, Miller set about assembling a campaign team and amassing funds to travel across the state. Despite her passion for addressing climate change, this wasn't what propelled her candidacy, she explained. "This is not the America that my parents dreamed of when they moved here," she said, noting that her Jewish parents left South Africa for the Atlanta suburbs in the 1970s due to their opposition to apartheid. As a "global citizen," she was repulsed by Trump's repudiation of her most deeply felt values. "Trump represented division and divisiveness and us versus them."[25]

Miller's core campaign issue was addressing "inequality" of all kinds. She argued what was at stake in the race to become a utility regulator was "high bills holding back our communities." She also pledged to extend broadband internet service to rural areas with limited economic activity.[26] Though Miller and her Republican opponent were nearly tied on Election Day, she failed to prevail a month later in a runoff that is legally mandated if no candidate wins 50 percent of the vote. Power company interests donated $1 million to the Republican, and by then Democratic enthusiasm had waned.[27]

Over coffee at a Cracker Barrel, the kitschy southern eatery, attorney Zahra Karinshak remembered the night Clinton lost the presidential election as vividly as the other subjects of this chapter. Viewing the vote tallies on television alongside one of her daughters, the teen turned to her mom and proclaimed: "I've decided you've got to do something. You've got to run for office. You're a lawyer. You love people."[28] Her "apolitical" child's outburst "flipped a switch," said Karinshak. When she studied the returns later in the week, they showed her Gwinnett County district narrowly favored Clinton over Trump. It looked like an influx of immigrants and African Americans had transformed voting patterns.[29] Although for sixteen years not a single Democrat had sought to run for state senate in her district, the Republican incumbent decided he would run for governor next cycle and those circumstances augured well for an initial bid for office. Revolted by Trump's attacks on foreigners and especially veterans, Karinshak drew on her heritage as the daughter of an Iranian immigrant and her pathbreaking military background in her voter appeals. One of the first women to graduate from

the US Air Force Academy, Karinshak is married to a West Point graduate and the couple has seven siblings who are veterans. "Our overrid-
ing concern is for our country, it's not for anybody's purpose or agenda,"
she said.

In contrast to most first-time female candidates, Karinshak had recent political experience, serving as deputy counsel to Governor Roy
Barnes, the last Democrat to lead the state.[30] Barnes tasked Karinshak
with handling his risky scheme to remove Confederate symbolism from
the state flag. It was such an all-consuming and contentious effort—
Barnes prevailed in remaking the flag but at the cost of his reelection—
that Karinshak declared "I'm done with this."[31] Yet, like the other candidates surveyed in this chapter, Karinshak reassessed her forbearance
after Trump's victory. "I'd go to church . . . I'm in the courtroom. 'Zahra,
you need to run.' It's like the floodgates opened." Taking the military
mantra "be prepared" seriously, the Air Force veteran participated in
three candidate training "boot camps." Upon declaring her candidacy,
Karinshak recognized that her principal challenge was not her gender
but the feeble state Democratic Party. "We've been a red state for so
long, we have really not got an infrastructure that supports candidates,"
she said. Native political talent was slim so it took her a while to find
staff that had familiarity with getting out the vote locally. Once on
board, her aides leaned on grassroots activist groups like PaveItBlue and
social media to solicit voters.[32] With established media largely ignoring
local races, the only front-page story she garnered was in the *Korea
Times*. That Karinshak had visited the DMZ was a selling point to Korean Americans in her district.[33] Campaigning on her military record,
inclusivity, Medicaid expansion, and her experience prosecuting violent
criminals, Karinshak defeated her novice GOP opponent by eight points.

Although she worked in the Clinton White House and married into
a family with deep roots in Georgia politics, attorney Jen Jordan had
refrained from politicking for nearly two decades.[34] Instead, she concentrated on building her own law practice and raising her children.[35]
Behind the scenes, she advised women to run for office, but "after November [2016] things started to change from my perspective." When de-

ciding whether to run for an open state senate seat vacated by a long-term Republican, Jordan pondered how women might suffer now that the GOP controlled Georgia and the federal government. Her interactions with the all-male state Supreme Court in February 2017 reinforced her fears and prompted her candidacy.

At the time, Jordan was preparing oral arguments to defend a $3.7 million jury verdict she had won for a University of Georgia cheerleader sexually assaulted by a male dental technician while under anesthesia. The technician had taped the attack on his cell phone and was serving a lifetime prison sentence, but his employers claimed they were not responsible for his crimes. "I remember that when all of the justices came out, they were all men, and it really struck me that I was going to have a problem. . . . They're not going to get it," she recalled. During questioning by the panel, Jordan had a premonition that the verdict might be reversed. Two months later, she shared the bad news with her client.[36] She explained that conversation clinched her decision to run: "I was at a point where it wasn't enough anymore to work for people and to try to push their cases because . . . what mattered was if you were a policy maker. That's where the real power was, and the lack of women serving in office was obviously affecting what we value. If you're passing laws that affect just women, it's probably a good thing to actually talk to women."[37]

Aisha Yaqoob, a young Muslim rights lobbyist, and Karín López Sandiford, an information technology consultant and mother of four, were longshots when they ran for the statehouse in 2018. Trump won overwhelmingly in their districts. With the chances so slim for victory, why did they persist? Both women have immigrant backgrounds—Yaqoob's parents are Pakistanis, and Sandiford was born in Brazil—and felt their respective communities were threatened not only by a Trump administration but by xenophobic Georgia officials. After November 2016, they battled proposed state laws affecting Muslims and Hispanics. What was different after 2016 was that even the nonimmigrant community was in an uproar about these developments. Atlanta's Hartsfield-Jackson, the world's busiest airport, was the site of a vociferous demonstration after

Trump announced his "Muslim Ban." Yaqoob was among thousands of demonstrators chanting, "No KKK, no fascist USA! No Trump!"[38]

Shortly after the 2016 presidential election, Yaqoob was hired to be the executive director of Asian Americans Advancing Justice Atlanta. Her first week was a momentous one as her organization sought to halt passage of a bill introduced by southeastern Georgia representative Jason Spencer that would prevent Muslim women from driving if they donned "burqa" veils. Yaqoob, who wears a head scarf, lobbied assiduously, fearing that if the measure passed, more "crazy" bills would come along.[39] Her cause received an unexpected boost when comedian Sacha Baron Cohen duped the portly lawmaker into being filmed "mooning" and uttering racist slurs for his farcical *Who Is America?* program. The embarrassing video, which included a brief appearance by Yaqoob, became a national news item and garnered over 2 million YouTube views. Spencer recalled his bill and resigned his seat.[40]

Yaqoob's well-publicized policy triumph grabbed the attention of organizers of the 2017 Atlanta's March for Social Justice and Women. They tapped the lobbyist to be the event's finance director, and Yaqoob proved herself a dynamic fundraiser, attaining thousands in donations through an Amazon.com wish list. Energized by the extraordinary turnout at the protest, Yaqoob resumed work to stave off more xenophobic legislation. Working the halls of the capitol, knocking on lawmakers' doors, she thought, "If I'm just doing the work, I can actually just do this myself." To her surprise, that session her own representative, a longtime Republican incumbent, announced his retirement. After consulting with her family, she entered the Democratic primary for the seat, which she won.

Yaqoob used social media extensively in her general election campaign. "You can say the revolution has been snapchatted," she quipped. She promised to block anti-immigrant policies, reform police practices that disproportionally affected people of color, and support the county's upcoming referendum to extend rail service from Atlanta. But this University of Georgia graduate also devoted much of her efforts to convincing voters put off by her hijab that she was "a Southerner with strong ties in the community—just like them."[41] Yaqoob lost her race to Bonnie Rich, an attorney and one of the few novice female GOP candidates. She subsequently returned to her lobbying job defending immigrant rights.

Sandiford, the Brazilian-born engineer, described herself as "asleep" prior to 2016, but moved to step out of her "insulated suburban world" when she learned the General Assembly was mulling one law revising drivers' licenses to include citizenship status and another creating a database containing immigrants' arrest records.[42] Having never before done any political work, save voting including for Republicans, she joined PaveItBlue and participated in the Ossoff campaign. The group had members in her Cobb County neighborhood, where she assumed Trump support was universal. For the first time in her life, she put aside business and family matters to lobby in the statehouse, including visiting her own state representative—the one she would challenge a year later. It was a frustrating dialogue, she said, as the two argued over what he viewed as necessary from a public safety perspective, which, she insisted, violated immigrants' privacy rights. Attending a fundraiser for the Cobb County Democratic Party with her daughter later that year, one of the speakers asked the guests to rise from their seats if they were running for office in the 2018 midterms. "I just found myself standing up and saying, 'this is it!'" Sandiford's campaign was based on five pillars: education, expansion of Medicaid, quality of life, jobs, and gun reform, but she ended up tangling with her GOP opponent over who was the better Christian in their approach to political issues.[43] The blue wave never materialized in her race, and Sandiford lost by a twenty-four-point margin. Neither Sandiford nor Yaqoob could overcome the unfavorable math of their districts, designed to give the edge to Republicans.

The swearings-in of new legislators under the Georgia capitol's gilded dome on January 14, 2019, were altogether different than previous ceremonies. To mark the significance of the record number of women partaking, the female legislators donned pantsuits in brilliant white, breaking southern style rules for winter attire. The four-month session that followed provided ample evidence that gender does have a bearing on representation. The neophyte progressive women provided a jolt of energy to their incumbent sisters as they tackled several issues with direct applicability to women's lives. They challenged internal policies they perceived as sexist and garnered national attention for their impassioned opposition to a proposed law that would make most abortions a crime.[44]

At the start of the session, there appeared to be an effort at bipartisanship among women legislators, at least on a few issues germane to governance. The two Republican women in the state senate collaborated with the novice Democrats to protest inferior committee appointments. Renee Unterman, the longest-serving female Republican, had particular reason to complain. GOP power brokers stripped Unterman, a former nurse, of her chairmanship of the prominent Health and Human Services Committee. "Make no mistake, the Senate is playing high-stakes baseball. Ladies of the Senate . . . we're not even in the ballpark," she said. "We're outside looking over a fence, and we're trying to look into the ballfield to see who is playing."[45] Female senators also faulted their male counterparts for having voted unanimously to further insulate themselves from sexual harassment accusations. Later in the session, Senators Karinshak and Unterman stood side by side to announce they were reviving the push to ratify the ERA, something that had not been attempted in Georgia in a quarter century. "We need this amendment so that all women are treated the same as men no matter where they live in this great country," Karinshak announced at a press conference.[46]

Bipartisan cooperation between women legislators had its limits in the face of the single most partisan issue in Georgia: abortion rights. As the 2019 session drew to a close, "unapologetically pro-life" Republican Gov. Brian Kemp, echoing his party's position on the issue, demanded a ban on abortions after a fetal heartbeat is detected at six weeks.[47] Unterman, who would later declare her candidacy for US Congress, shepherded the bill to passage in the state senate, arguing that it was immoral to "throw away children who aren't perfect." In fighting what was termed the "heartbeat bill," the freshly minted progressive women lawmakers rallied the suburban female activists that put them in office. "Pavers," for example, showed up daily on the steps of the capitol dressed in red capes and white bonnets like characters from the dystopian Netflix series *Handmaid's Tale*, to signify state control over female reproduction.[48] Drawing on their litigation prowess, Jordan and Karinshak emerged as the Democrats' chief spokespeople denouncing the law, which promised jail time for abortion providers. In her floor speech, Karinshak noted the ban would be near impossible for Georgia to defend as similar ones had already been proven unconstitutional. In a thirteen-minute address that went "viral" on YouTube, Jordan stressed that women alone should make reproductive choices as she recounted the eight miscarriages she suffered to become a mother.[49]

Women and Democrats are still vastly outnumbered by conservative Republican men in the Georgia statehouse, leaving little doubt the abortion law would pass. Yet female legislators managed to draw national attention to their resistance and smooth the path for others like them in the future. In 2009, confronted with GOP opposition to his plan to stimulate the moribund economy, President Obama remarked, "Elections have consequences." Perhaps there is no better proof for Obama's dictum than what happened after he exited the presidency. In Georgia more so than the rest of the country, both the unconventional leadership of President Trump and the women-led movement to roll back its most noxious effects has brought about changes that appear to be more long-lasting than one election cycle.

Notes

The author wishes to acknowledge financial support from Georgia Gwinnett College and the invaluable research assistance of Michelle Samson, a 2019 graduate of the college.
    1. The King funeral on April 9, 1968, attracted one hundred fifty thousand people while the Atlanta March for Social Justice and Women logged sixty-three

thousand participants. Another six thousand to ten thousand Georgia women traveled to Washington and hundreds more marched in smaller Georgia cities. Maureen Downey, "It Was Important for Our Voices to Be Heard," *Atlanta Journal-Constitution*, January 23, 2017, A5.

2. Ruby Cramer, "EMILY's List Expands after 16,000 Women Reach Out about Running for Office," EMILY's List, accessed February 1, 2019, https://emilyslist.org/news/entry/emilys-list-expands-after-160000-women.

3. Melita Easters (chair of Georgia WIN List), interview by the author, Chamblee, GA, December 5, 2018.

4. Greg Bluestein, "Democrats Pick New Leader: Party Has Financial Shortfalls, Shortage of Candidates," *Atlanta Journal-Constitution*, September 1, 2013, B3.

5. Brentin Mock, "Where Voter Suppression Hits Hardest in Georgia," CityLab, October 18, 2018, https://www.citylab.com/equity/2018/10/where-voters-color-are-suppressed-hardest-georgia/573367/.

6. Alan Judd, "Efforts Put Voters at Risk of Disenfranchisement," *Atlanta Journal-Constitution*, October 27, 2018, https://www.ajc.com/news/state--regional-govt--politics/voter-purge-begs-question-what-the-matter-with-georgia/YAFvuk3Bu95kJIMaDiDFqJ/.

7. Founders were Lesley Bauer; her mother, Nancy Bauer; Jen Cox; and Sarah Clegg Crawford. Jen Cox, interview by the author, Marietta, GA, May 31, 2017; Jen Cox, Lesley Bauer, Sarah Crawford, and Nancy Bauer, "We Got Woke," May 23, 2017, in *A Blue Streak*, audio podcast, 50:55, https://paveitblue.org/a-blue-streak-podcast/.

8. Denise Ruiz, interview by the author, Roswell, GA, June 29, 2017.

9. Maine was tied with Georgia in the number of female candidates and accounted for half the females running nationally. Maria Saporta, "Record Number of Women Candidates for State Office," September 30, 2018, SaportaReport, https://saportareport.com/record-number-of-women-candidates-for-state-office-promoted-by-georgias-win-list/.

10. Deborah Gonzalez, interview by Michelle Samson, Atlanta, GA, June 15, 2018.

11. Commissioner Tommy Hunter was reprimanded by an ethics board for his social media slur. Tyler Estep, "A Year Later 'Racist Pig' Saga Still Reverberates," *Atlanta Journal-Constitution*, January 20, 2018, A1.

12. Shelley Hutchinson, interview by the author, Snelville, GA, June 6, 2018.

13. Angelia Pressley, interview by the author, Smyrna, GA, August 27, 2018. Pressley lost her race to a better-known male Democratic rival.

14. Jelani Cobb, "The Crucial Significance of Lucy McBath's Win in Georgia's Sixth Congressional District," *New Yorker*, November 17, 2018.

15. Diana Bagby, "Millar Will Miss 'Being in the Game' at State Capitol," *Brookhaven Reporter*, January 2019, 4.

16. Richard Fox and Jennifer Lawless, "Family Roles with Political Ambition: The New Normal for Women in Twenty-First Century U.S. Politics," *Journal of Politics* 76, no. 2 (2014): 398, 414.

17. Political scientist Susan J. Carroll, an expert on gender and political participation, explains that women are more reluctant to run for office than men and have a more difficult time raising money "but I think that what they don't worry about are the voters. There is good social science evidence that voters are not the main problem for women candidates even though there are voters out there who wouldn't vote for a women candidate, all things being equal." Susanna Diluta Waters, "Ask a Feminist: A Conversation with Susan J. Carroll on Gender and Politics," *Sign: Journal of Women in Culture and Society* 42, no. 3 (2017): 773.

18. Doe v. Bolton, 410 U.S. 179, 182–84 (1973).

19. Robin Morris, "Kathryn Dunaway: Grassroots Conservatism and the STOP ERA Campaign," in *Georgia Women: Their Lives and Times*, ed. Ann Chirhart and Betty Wood (Athens: University of Georgia Press, 2009), 236–259.

20. Lorraine N. Spritzer and Jean B. Bergmark, *New Georgia Encyclopedia*, s.v. "Grace Towns Hamilton (1907–1992)," accessed January 26, 2019, https://www.georgiaencyclopedia.org/articles/history-archaeology/grace-towns-hamilton-1907-1992.

21. Mary Eve Spirou, "The Challenges of Political Representation: Gender in a US State Legislature," *International Journal of Public Leadership*, 13 no. 1 (2017): 13–25.

22. In 2012, Georgia Republicans could pass constitutional amendments and override gubernatorial vetoes without a single Democratic vote. Jordan broke the "supermajority" after becoming a state senator representing the affluent Buckhead neighborhood in a 2017 special election.

23. Four of the five counties in the United States that registered the highest percentage swings in their white population share since 2000 were in Metro Atlanta. Jens Manuel Krogstad and Pew Research Organization, "Reflecting a Racial Shift, 78 Counties Turned Majority-Minority since 2000," accessed January 18, 2019, http://www.pewresearch.org/fact-tank/2015/04/08/reflecting-a-racial-shift-78-counties-turned-majority-minority-since-2000/.

24. One-quarter of a million black people moved to Atlanta and environs from 2000 to 2014. Henry Grabar, "Republicans Lost the Suburbs," *Slate*, accessed January 18, 2018, https://slate.com/business/2018/11/suburban-republicans-are-officially-a-thing-of-the-past.html.

25. Lindy Miller, interview by the author, Decatur, GA, August 17, 2018.

26. Jim Galloway, "Down Ballot Race Could Lead Way for Dems in November," *Atlanta Journal-Constitution*, May 30, 2018, B1.

27. Greg Bluestein, "Dems Lose Suburban Edge in Runoffs," *Atlanta Journal-Constitution*, December 6, 2018, B1.

28. Zahra Karinshak, interview by the author, Norcross, GA, June 5, 2018.

29. Tyler Estep, "The Power Shift Is in the Making," *Atlanta Journal-Constitution*, March 25, 2018, B1.

30. Karinshak worked under Sally Yates, the first woman to be US attorney for the Northern District of Georgia. Yates was fired from her position as acting attorney general by President Trump when she refused to enforce his 2017 executive order banning people from seven Muslim nations from traveling to the United States. Karinshak proudly touted her relationship with Yates when meeting with progressive women's groups.

31. Karinshak, interview.

32. Karinshak, interview.

33. "America Is an Immigrant Country: Interview with Zahra Karinshak," *Korea Times Atlanta*, accessed April 5, 2019, http://higoodday.com/mweb/?mid =news&act=dispOnpostContentView&doc_srl=592387.

34. Jordan's husband is Lawton Jordan, nephew of Hamilton Jordan, President Jimmy Carter's White House chief of staff.

35. Jen Jordan, interview by the author, Atlanta, GA, March 12, 2018.

36. "Ga. Justices Upend $3.7M Verdict over Dental Office Assault," February 28, 2017, Law360, https://www.law360.com/articles/896352/ga -justices-upend-3-7m-verdict-over-dental-office-assault.

37. Jordan, interview.

38. J. Scott Trubey and Rhonda Cook, "Thousands Protest Trump Immigra-tion Order," *Atlanta Journal-Constitution*, January 29, 2017, A1.

39. Aisha Yaqoob, interview by author, Duluth, GA, August 24, 2018.

40. Stories about the ban appeared on local television stations, on CNN, and in the *Washington Post*. The video can be seen at https://www.youtube.com /watch?v=4k4pMTsa1Kw.

41. Aisha Yaqoob, "What It's Like to Run as a Muslim Woman in the South," *HuffPost*, November 15, 2018, https://www.huffpost.com/entry/opinion-run -office-midterms-south-georgia-muslim-woman_n_5bce28fde4b0a8f17eef6909.

42. GOP State Rep. Alan Powell introduced the driver's license bill in the 2017 legislative session. Brian Kemp floated the database scheme when he was serving as Georgia secretary of state while running in the 2018 gubernatorial primary.

43. Karín López Sandiford, interview by the author, Roswell, GA, March 11, 2018.

44. Jim Galloway, "#Metoo Came to the Senate This Week," *Atlanta Journal-Constitution*, January 18, 2019, B1.

45. Curt Yeomans, "Renee Unterman Blasts Senate Colleagues for Treatment of Female Members," *Gwinnett Daily Post*, January 16, 2019, 1.

46. Galloway, "#Metoo."

47. "Kemp: I'll Sign, Fight for Pro-Life Legislation," Kemp for Governor, accessed April 29, 2019, https://www.kempforgovernor.com/posts/news/kemp -i%E2%80%99ll-sign-fight-pro-life-legislation.

48. M. T. Prabhu, "Vote on 'Heartbeat Bill' Could Mean Georgia Tests *Roe v. Wade*," *Atlanta Journal-Constitution*, March 9, 2019, A1.

49. State Sen. Jen Jordan's speeches can be viewed at https://www.youtube .com/channel/UCoGXaUyBXY6SSqOpHu647ug.

Sculptor Adelaide Johnson delivers her *Portrait Monument* depicting Elizabeth Cady Stanton, Susan B. Anthony, and Lucretia Mott to Congress (1921). Photograph by Harris & Ewing, Prints & Photographs Division, Library of Congress, Prints & Photographs Division, LC-H27-A-2445.

CHAPTER 20

Putting Women on a Pedestal

Monument Debates in the Era of the Suffrage Centennial

MONICA L. MERCADO

S INCE THE RATIFICATION of the Nineteenth Amendment in 1920, US women's groups and public commissions have made a case for honoring women with traditional public monuments—figurative sculptures of women in bronze and stone—and the desire to do so only grew as the centennial of women's suffrage approached. In July 2018, for example, the New York City Department of Parks and Recreation revealed plans for the first statue dedicated to "real women" in Central Park, responding to criticism that the country's most visited urban park, and one of the most famous parks in the world, was home to only three statues featuring female figures: the fictional Alice in Wonderland, Mother Goose, and Shakespeare's Juliet. "To be clear," journalist Chloe Angyal once wrote, of the twenty-two statues of historical figures in Central Park, "you can find a statue of a real-life dog, but no statues of real-life women."[1]

The 2018 announcement reflected years of work by members of the nonprofit Elizabeth Cady Stanton and Susan B. Anthony Statue Fund to pressure City Hall for a women's monument in Central Park.[2] After campaigning on social media, fundraising, and hosting public events, in 2016 the statue fund's leaders received conceptual approval for a statue of women's rights leaders Stanton and Anthony.[3] A public competition narrowed down ninety-one design proposals to four finalists, ultimately selecting sculptor Meredith Bergmann to pay tribute to the two suffrage leaders. Bergmann depicted Stanton and Anthony at work, their writing visible, in the artist's words, "as a long scroll of inscribed quotations, in chronological order, from women who worked with them and after them to fight for women's rights and the vote." The bronze scroll connected the women's writing desk to a ballot box. "I'm honored to have been chosen to make this monument to a movement that transformed our democracy so proudly from within, and without bloodshed, and that began with two women writing together," Bergmann announced. "It's a great subject for a sculpture."[4] The monument was slated to be dedicated in August 2020, marking the suffrage centennial.

Bergmann's proposed monument to "two women writing together," dramatically revised since she first won the design competition, serves as a highly visible example of the challenges and possibilities faced by projects that aspire to rewrite commemorative space. Carving out a place for women's history in Central Park, Bergmann and the Stanton and Anthony Statue Fund found their undertaking complicated by very public debates about the best way to mark a diverse and often divided women's rights movement. By contextualizing these debates in a longer history of US women's monuments, this chapter reveals the limits of efforts to transform public space with "monumental" figures and looks ahead to a range of urban projects that suggest figurative sculpture, with its tendency to represent ideas and movements through straightforward portraits of "great" Americans, may no longer be up to the task of commemorating complex histories.

One hundred years after the Nineteenth Amendment's ratification, questions of who is deserving of honor, and in what form, have shaped the public history of suffrage.[5] Recent counts of the approximately five thousand two hundred historical statues in the United States have shown that women represent less than 8 percent of monumental subjects.[6] As American women achieve new milestones in public life, it is perhaps no surprise that attempts to make their foremothers visible—by putting them, literally, on a pedestal—have accelerated in the 2010s, a decade when many other US monuments, particularly those dedicated to Confederate war heroes, came down.[7] But unlike temporary museum exhibitions, public programs, performances, protests, and parades, women's monument projects promise to permanently change the landscape. As their boosters seek support for new statues that will commemorate the American past, they also find themselves mediating present-day concerns about the role of women in contemporary political life and the visibility of women of color in movement politics.

Women's Rights, Women's Monuments

The statue fund's pursuit of a monument to Elizabeth Cady Stanton and Susan B. Anthony followed in the footsteps of earlier memorials that represented the US suffrage movement with two of its most prominent white leaders. This, historians argue, is not an accident. Stanton and Anthony were documentarians as well as activists, carefully crafting their story with a cast of co-editors in the multivolume *History of Woman Suffrage*, first published in 1881. The *History* highlighted white women's leadership in the national campaign for suffrage, marginalizing many local figures, and downplayed both women's role in fracturing the suffrage movement along lines of racial difference. As historian Lisa Tetrault contends, "the triumph of one particular story, over any other number of possible stories" was complete.[8]

Written into history during the Jim Crow era, that single suffrage story soon found its way into public art. In 1893, Adelaide Johnson's portrait busts of Elizabeth Cady Stanton, Susan B. Anthony, and Lucretia Mott went on display at the World's Columbian Exposition in Chicago. Their presence in the Court of Honor of the Woman's Building celebrated the ongoing movement and, in Anthony's words, offered proof that women artists and their women subjects could "stand equal to any man if not actually outrank any man" on exhibit.[9] Three weeks before Anthony's death in 1906, Johnson presented the Anthony bust to the Metropolitan Museum of Art.[10]

Adelaide Johnson's labors continued after the deaths of Anthony and Stanton. A substantial "portrait monument," featuring the Anthony, Stanton, and Mott busts, was commissioned by the National Woman's Party for the US Capitol and completed in 1921, six months after the ratification of the Nineteenth Amendment. Johnson's monument, sculpted from eight tons of Carrara marble, was not the first women's monument in the Capitol (that honor went to temperance crusader Frances Willard, installed in National Statuary Hall in 1905). But the occasion of the portrait monument's presentation to Congress—on what would have been Anthony's 101st birthday—brought more than seventy women's organizations together in celebration. The monument was moved to basement storage days later, where it remained for decades.[11]

The lack of women represented in the Capitol Rotunda was not an anomaly; it reflected a dearth of monuments to women nationwide. In 1985, while the portrait monument still languished in the Capitol basement, scholar Jean Bethke Elshtain proposed "to photograph and study statues of women on both public and private land." Elshtain and her daughter, photographer Heidi Lu Elshtain, wrote to historical societies and state preservation offices around the country, requesting information on sculptures of women. Their correspondents returned short lists of allegorical depictions, religious statuary, and "unnamed" forms.[12] "There is statuary here that includes women, but they represent philosophical ideals rather than actual historic figures," described a Pennsylvania Commission for Women staffer. "There is a paucity of statues of females," relayed another preservation officer.[13] Smithsonian curator Edith P. Mayo confirmed that no official or comprehensive data on statues of women on state or federal lands had ever been compiled and offered the Elshtains a short list of agencies "still funding women's projects" during the Reagan era.[14] Their proposed study was never funded.

The Elshtains' initial findings also suggest that the US women's movement of the 1960s and 1970s had little interest in monuments and memorials, even as feminists fought for the inclusion of women's history in academic settings and celebrated women's history with public demonstrations, such as the National Organization for Women's "Women's Strike for Equality," marking the fiftieth anniversary of the Nineteenth Amendment in 1970. By the amendment's seventy-fifth anniversary in 1995, however, a "Woman Suffrage Statue Campaign" emerged, determined to return Johnson's portrait monument to the Capitol Rotunda. "The Statue of Freedom, the Statue of Liberty, these are icons, not real women that girls and women can look up to," statue campaign leader Karen Staser told journalists in 1996, the year the portrait monument moved back upstairs as a permanent tribute to women's rights during a political moment that saw more women elected to Congress than in any previous decade.[15] Yet an anticipated moment of unity was mired in dissent: the National Congress of Black Women, led by C. DeLores Tucker, a longtime voting rights activist, lobbied unsuccessfully to have the likeness of another "real woman," abolitionist and women's rights leader Sojourner Truth, carved into the existing marble of Johnson's monument. Tucker built her case by claiming the history of suffrage as an intersectional one. "By excluding African-American women, the placement of a statue which only includes three white women suffragettes gives the inaccurate and racist message that the suffrage movement was a white woman's movement," Tucker wrote. "Suffrage was just as important to laboring women, poor women, and to black women as it was to white women." But the National Congress of Black Women's demands fell on deaf ears.[16] It would take two more decades before a bust of Sojourner Truth was unveiled in the US Capitol, the first sculpture to honor an African American woman in the building.[17]

In the years since the portrait monument's return to the Capitol Rotunda, new women's monuments have also emerged on the urban landscape, most notably sculptor Meredith Bergmann's first major commission, the Boston Women's Memorial, dedicated in 2003. The memorial features larger than life-size statues of three women with roots in the city: Abigail Adams, Phillis Wheatley, and Lucy Stone. Strikingly, Bergmann's design places the three figures *off* their pedestals, engaged in the acts of writing and thinking.[18] Bergmann's deployment of street-level figurative sculpture created a plaza that encourages visitors to interact with the monument. "Some swung their arms around Lucy's shoulder while posing for pictures. Others parked themselves alongside Phillis on her granite bench, or gazed into Abigail's stern, penetrating face," *Boston Globe* reporter Peter DeMarco observed. "Unlike many Boston statues," he noticed, "the three women's likenesses are eminently accessible."[19] And unlike most monuments, Bergmann's Boston memorial asserted that women were worthy of public honor. Fifteen years later, Bergmann found herself in the spotlight at the center of debates around a new women's monument, debates that question the inclusivity of traditional monumental forms.

"Breaking the Bronze Ceiling"

"We are going to break the bronze ceiling in Central Park to create the first statue of real women in its 164-year history!" proclaimed Pam Elam, president of the Stanton and Anthony Statue Fund, at the November 2017 rally to announce the site of New York City's first suffrage monument.[20] Elam, a lawyer with a graduate degree in women's history, had spent nearly a decade advocating for markers, memorials, and monuments to women in Manhattan. In 2015, the statue fund she founded with Coline Jenkins, Elizabeth Cady Stanton's great-great-granddaughter, began raising money for a permanent monument to Stanton and Anthony in Central Park.[21] Deploying the "bronze ceiling" metaphor just a year after Hillary Clinton's historic presidential campaign failed to break—in Clinton's own words—"that highest and hardest glass ceiling," Elam and Jenkins deliberately chose language linking contemporary electoral politics with their ongoing monument campaign.[22]

As their work unfolded, statue fund supporters also borrowed language demanding depictions of "real women" in monuments and memorials. While writer Allison Meier has argued that even allegorical depictions of women can be understood as depicting "real" women—their sculptors' models and muses—announcements of the Stanton and Anthony statue project consistently focused on the fact that only five statues in all of New York City depicted historical, "real women," compared to 145 statues of "real" men.[23] The statue fund's emphasis on the "real" recalls both Karen Staser's 1996 argument for returning Adelaide Johnson's portrait monument to the Capitol Rotunda as well as the "accessibility" of the female figures depicted in Bergmann's Boston Women's Memorial. For others, it also evoked the corporate success of Dove's campaign for "Real Beauty," launched by the personal care brand in 2004 and called one of the most successful ad campaigns of the early twenty-first century. For Dove, the "real" signified a more diverse range of women's bodies, coupled with a self-esteem message positioning the brand as "an agent of change to educate and inspire girls." The latter message—coupling education and inspiration—also marked the statue fund's public events, which often featured troops of local Girl Scouts. Children, these campaigns argued, especially benefit from "real" role models.[24]

Elam repeatedly shared this message with women's history groups and historic preservationists across New York. "The Stanton and Anthony Woman Suffrage Movement Monument will ensure that many of the forty-two million people who visit Central Park each year will become more aware of a history that fully and fairly includes the vast and varied roles women have played in it. Our statue project will honor all the women who fought for the vote," she declared in 2017.[25] But the statue fund's design competition instructed artists to center on just two women—Stanton and Anthony—a source of later debate. Meredith Bergmann's winning design for Central Park, selected by the statue fund and an appointed design jury, followed the rules and featured only Stanton and Anthony on the pedestal. A bronze scroll, "functional, legible, and assertive, reaching out to the viewer," added additional women's words to the monument, with a selection of twenty-two quotations representing feminist thought from 1848 to 1920 and ending with the text of the Nineteenth Amendment.[26]

As the timing of the suffrage centennial and Bergmann's statue fund commission intersected with national debates about the fate of Confederate monuments and urban statuary more generally, a number of journalists and historians responded to the Stanton and Anthony monument design in disbelief. The *New York Times* editorial board writer Brent Staples argued in a July 2018 op-ed that the "toxic legacy" of white suffragists "looms especially large."[27] In the *Washington Post*, historian Martha Jones expressed her frustration that the monument had not sought to raise the profile of a more diverse women's movement. "The monument to Stanton and Anthony commemorates figures who never managed to fully engage the world beyond their own pedestals," Jones wrote. "Too often, they advocated a narrow view of women's rights constrained by discredited ideas rooted in racism and class prejudice." To honor Stanton and Anthony in the twenty-first century, Jones suggested, sent "all the wrong messages."[28] Two years into the Trump presidency, Staples's and Jones's critiques shared space on newsstands with reports of Black Lives Matter protests and an emboldened and xenophobic white supremacist movement. Honoring Stanton and Anthony in this political moment appeared to many critics as glossing over the complicated legacy left by the suffrage movement's white leadership and, worse, erasing the contributions of women of color to US history.

In Chicago, Michelle Duster repeatedly called for "a more inclusive and expansive way of telling [suffrage] history." Duster—the great-granddaughter of African American activist Ida B. Wells—organized a successful crowd-funded campaign in support of a granite and bronze monument to Wells on Chicago's South Side, elevating black women as monumental subjects. Questioning the "limited version" of the suffrage movement represented by Bergmann's Central Park monument design, Duster's voice joined the chorus of voices critical of the statue fund as the suffrage centennial drew closer.[29] The sharpest of those voices, *New York Times* writer Ginia Bellafante, attracted new attention to Bergmann's designs when her analysis ran with the headline, "A Suffrage Monument Fails Black Women." For her piece, Bellafante spoke to Meredith Bergmann, who admitted her Central Park design was "very conservative." Bellafante spoke to feminist icon Gloria Steinem, who registered concern that "a statue of two white women [represent] the vote for all women." And Bellafante spoke to Pam Elam, who argued, "you can't ask one statue to meet all the desires of the people who have waited so long for recognition."[30]

Announcing Bergmann's Central Park design in the same year that the New York City Public Design Commission removed one highly contested statue from Central Park (of nineteenth-century surgeon J. Marion Sims, whose experiments were performed on the bodies of enslaved women), the other Stanton and Anthony fund leaders maintained a curious silence on matters of representation.[31] Bergmann, on the other hand, went back to the drawing board. In preparation for a New York City Public Design Commission review of the monument in March 2019, she removed the scroll of quotations, alleviating concerns that the other women's names were "literal footnotes in a history coauthored by Anthony and Stanton." The design commission's feedback, described by one reporter as "mixed but mostly supportive," included a strongly worded suggestion, not to the sculptor but to her patrons from Commissioner Mary Valverde (a sculptor herself). "Going forward, the Statue Fund needs a more inclusive approach," Valverde said. "I want the committee to be more diverse and the artists more diverse."[32]

While the Stanton and Anthony Statue Fund aimed to honor "all the women who fought for the vote" a century ago, Bergmann's designs and New York City officials were forced to respond to calls for more inclusive and intersectional commemorations. The politics of memory were especially charged in the wake of white supremacist defenses of Confederate monuments during the early Trump administration. After the violent 2017 rallies in Charlottesville, Virginia, organized by white nationalist leader Richard Spencer to protest the planned removal of a monument to Confederate general Robert E. Lee, New York City Mayor Bill de Blasio initiated a review of all public statues in the five boroughs. The review also extended his administration's support of new public monuments honoring women. "This is the day we finally start putting women where they belong," Deputy Mayor Alicia Glen declared, "on pedestals."[33]

Could more pedestals make room for a wider range of monumental subjects? Joined by New York's First Lady Chirlane McCray—a onetime member of the black feminist Combahee River Collective—Glen issued an open call for nominations of "women, groups of women, and women-led events that significantly impacted the history of New York City." This city-sponsored initiative, named She Built NYC, promised $10 million from the Department of Cultural Affairs for new monuments across the city and encouraged new public-private partnerships to raise additional funds toward "fostering greater representation of women in New York City's public realm." McCray urged an expansive notion of representation. "There are big gaps in our City's public art," she argued, "with few statues of women, trans and gender nonconforming people. The message that lack of representation sends is that these people have no value and did not make contributions to our city."[34] The first group of She Built NYC honorees, selected in early 2019 from more than two thousand nominations, ensured each of New York's five boroughs will soon be home to a monumental woman, beginning with artists Amanda Williams and Olalekan Jeyifous's *Our Destiny, Our Democracy*, a forty-foot tall abstract steel monument honoring Congresswoman Shirley Chisholm, planned for Brooklyn's Prospect Park.[35]

New York's monumental women campaigns received major national media attention leading up to the suffrage centennial, but they were not the only efforts to tackle the legacies of public statues that disproportionately honor American men. On the West Coast, a feminist quest for public space was written into urban policy. An October 2018 ordinance passed by San Francisco's Board of Supervisors created the Women's Recognition Public Art Fund to "accept gifts to pay for the design, construction, repair, maintenance, and improvement of public art depicting historically significant women on City property." The new ordinance also required "at least thirty percent of nonfictional figures depicted or commemorated in statues and other works of art on City-owned property, public building names, and street names" must be women. Catherine Stefani, a sponsor of the ordinance, explained women's underrepresentation in public space to the *San Francisco Examiner* in simple terms. "The accomplishments of great women deserve to be recognized alongside the accomplishments of great men."[36]

Conclusion: Revisions and Counter-Monuments in the Twenty-First Century City

Five years after they first founded the statue fund, Pam Elam and Coline Jenkins continued to pound the pavement, seeking support for Meredith Bergmann's "real women" monument to Elizabeth Cady Stanton and Susan B. Anthony.[37] But the woman designing their pedestal made room for one more. Compelled to respond to the critiques offered by scholars, journalists, and the New York City Public Design Commission, in August 2019, the statue fund announced Meredith Bergmann's third design, which added Sojourner Truth to the Central Park monument, sharing a work table with Stanton and Anthony. "Our goal has always been to honor the diverse women in history who fought for equality and justice and who dedicated their lives to fight for Women's Rights," read an updated statue fund press release, downplaying the organization's original goal of honoring Stanton and Anthony specifically.[38] In contrast, Meredith Bergmann's revised artist's statement, released online in September 2019, directly referenced the difficult task she faced, addressing historians and the public. "The historical record is complex, as are the people I'm portraying," Bergmann wrote. "We need to be true to our new understanding of the historical record which does not shrink from calling out injustice and oppression, or minimize the contributions of people of color or the harms done to people of color." Seeing Truth, Anthony, and Stanton, together on one pedestal, as "women of different races, different religious backgrounds and different economic status working together to change the world," Bergmann hoped, would inspire visitors to Central Park for years to come. Her allusions to "sisterhood, cooperation, and activism," brought to mind the Women's March and #MeToo movements of the same era, unambiguously linking past and present.[39] In October 2019, the design commission voted to approve Bergmann's new design.[40]

If Bergmann's September 2019 statement emphasized complex and diverse narratives, it also insisted on maintaining other conventions. "Recognizable bronze figures sit and stand on a granite pedestal with inscriptions," she described, so that the women's monument would "harmoniously coexist" with Central Park's existing statues.[41] But elsewhere, new public art projects and grassroots efforts to insert memorials to women in existing landscapes have questioned the very notion of traditional figurative sculpture in twenty-first-century American memorials. What some scholars have defined as the "counter-monument"—

first proposed by writers examining Holocaust commemorations that troubled notions of permanence and gave the public a role in making meaning—could also inspire suffrage commemoration projects to wrestle with absence and erasures instead of arguing for and adding more "great," "real" women.[42]

A group of projects that reimagine monumentality offer alternatives. Instead of putting women's forms on a pedestal, they create clusters of women's names on the landscape. In 2017, Philadelphia-based artist Sharon Hayes erected *If They Should Ask*, confronting what Hayes explained as "the persistent and aggressive exclusion of women from this form of public recognition." Hayes's temporary installation in Philadelphia's Rittenhouse Square, part of the public art and history project *Monument Lab*, consisted of nine concrete pedestals. "On this site there could be a statue to," the inscription on one pedestal begins, asking the visitor to contemplate the possibilities. The many names that follow, inscribed around the pedestals, invite the viewer to seek out more information (or contribute their own ideas to the website if theyshouldask.com). By taking away the women from the pedestals, Hayes demonstrated the inadequacy of proposed statues. Instead, the names on each of the nine pedestals—drawn from a series of community meetings—offered a range of recognizable women and little-known figures, from Alice Paul to the transwomen at the 1965 sit-in at Dewey's Café, one of the earliest demonstrations demanding the right of public accommodation for gays, lesbians, and gender-nonconforming Philadelphians.[43] Hayes's contribution to *Monument Lab*, and to the counter-monumental, required the public's active engagement with women's history.

Similarly, writer Rebecca Solnit's essay "City of Women" imagined a series of active encounters that would confront New Yorkers with women's history and repair public space with women's presence. "A horde of dead men with live identities haunt New York City and almost every city in the western world," she argued. "Their names are on the streets, the buildings, the parks, squares, colleges, businesses, and banks, and they are the figures on the monuments." Solnit's imagined project proposed new names for old places in order to put women's history into daily conversation.[44] But renaming projects are not simply experiments in imagination; Chicago's Congress Parkway was renamed Ida B. Wells Drive in February 2019, part of Michelle Duster's ongoing work. One month later, the New York City parks department renamed Manhattan's Hudson Yards Park for the late Congresswoman Bella Abzug—a "huge step," Commissioner Mitchell J. Silver declared, "towards etching the memory of influential women into our public identity."[45]

If women's historians are taught to read "against the grain," perhaps the greatest contribution to what Erica Doss has called "memorial mania" could be to imagine new forms, not only pushing back against "great" monumental subjects but also prevailing monumental norms. Each year since 2004, on the March 25 anniversary of the Triangle Shirtwaist Factory Fire, New Yorkers join Ruth Sergel's Chalk Project, a counter-monument honoring the 146 men and women who lost their lives in the disaster and its aftermath. Volunteers use sidewalk chalk to mark the names and age of death of Triangle Fire victims on the pavement. "Building after building, block after block," Sergel writes, "the human cost of the Triangle fire is marked across a city." Chalking, as Sergel imagines it, creates memory through the physical act of writing and the potential street interactions that result. "It is an intervention," she describes, "a transgressive act that suggests a different story seeping up from the pavement."[46] What kinds of transgressive acts could suffrage commemorations incorporate?

In their words and designs, Hayes, Solnit, and Sergel each suggest a skepticism about the suitability of traditional monuments for contemporary meaning making. As the suffrage centennial approaches, however, the reach of this skepticism remains limited. Outside of New York, private funders are organizing campaigns for new monuments to women that are likely to outlive the public celebrations marking the centennial of the Nineteenth Amendment. In 2016, the Tennessee Woman Suffrage Monument organization placed five statues in Nashville.[47] In Fairfax County, Virginia, the Turning Point Suffragist Memorial Association is raising money for a memorial near the site of the Occoquan

Workhouse, where suffragists were imprisoned for participating in the 1917 White House suffrage picket.[48] In Washington, DC, a bipartisan group of legislators offered H.R. 7309—a bill to authorize sculptor Jane DeDecker's *Every Word We Utter* monument (a finalist for the Central Park commission) to be built in the nation's capital.[49] And in April 2019, the Cambridge, Massachusetts, City Council organized a review committee to solicit designs for a monument to honor local suffrage leaders. "There were a lot of lessons learned about what happened in New York, and it is important to name the marginalization of black women in the suffrage movement," Cambridge City Councilor Sumbul Siddiqui told reporters. Putting women on a pedestal is no simple task. As local and national politics intersect with the politics of women's history and memory, future monument projects will continue to reckon with the Central Park suffrage statue in years to come.[50]

Notes

1. Chloe Angyal, "Not One Woman Gets Her Own Pedestal among Central Park's Statues," Reuters, September 5, 2014, http://blogs.reuters.com/great -debate/2014/09/05/real-women-belong-in-new-yorks-central-park. That "real life" dog is Balto, honored for leading a sled dog team carrying medicine to halt a diphtheria outbreak in Alaska in 1925.

2. The statue fund was founded in 2014. See Namita Luthra interview, WBAI 99.5 FM City Watch, August 4, 2019, https://www.youtube.com/watch?v =LquIRH80GWo&feature=youtu.be.

3. Chadwick Moore, "Fighting to Bring Women in History to Central Park," *New York Times*, New York edition, July 13, 2015, A15.

4. On the reveal of Bergmann's original design see Mikey Light and Joe Dziemianowicz, "Sculptor Chosen to Design the First Statues of Real Women in Central Park," *New York Daily News*, July 19, 2018, https://www.nydailynews .com/new-york/ny-metro-sculptor-chosen-real-women-central-park-20180719 -story.html; "Sculptor's Page," accessed March 15, 2019, https://web.archive.org /web/20190315164636/https://monumentalwomen.org/sculptors-page.

5. Monica L. Mercado, "The Politics of Women's History: Collecting for the Centennial of Women's Suffrage in New York State," *Collections: A Journal for Museum and Archives Professionals* 14, no. 3 (September 2018): 331–350.

6. Danny Lewis, "It's Way Too Hard to Find Statues of Notable Women in the U.S.," *Smithsonian Magazine*, February 29, 2016, https://www.smithsonian

mag.com/smart-news/its-way-too-hard-to-find-statues-of-notable-women-in-the
-us-180958237.

7. See "All Monuments Must Fall: A Syllabus," collected by Nicholas Mirzoeff and others in 2017, New York University Faculty Digital Archive, https://archive.nyu.edu/handle/2451/40071.

8. Lisa Tetrault, *The Myth of Seneca Falls: Memory and the Women's Suffrage Movement, 1848–1898* (Chapel Hill: University of North Carolina Press, 2014), 2–7.

9. Sandra Weber, *The Woman Suffrage Statue: A History of Adelaide Johnson's Portrait Monument to Lucretia Mott, Elizabeth Cady Stanton, and Susan B. Anthony at the United States Capitol* (Jefferson, NC: McFarland, 2016), 3, 34.

10. Weber, *Woman Suffrage Statue*, 47, 49.

11. Courtney Workman, "The Woman Movement: Memorial to Women's Rights Leaders and the Perceived Images of the Women's Movement," in *Myth, Memory, and the Making of the American Landscape*, ed. Paul A. Shackel (Gainesville: University Press of Florida, 2001), 48–52.

12. See, for example, R. Stuart Wallace to Jean Bethke Elshtain, August 29, 1985; Frank Kelly to Jean Bethke Elshtain, August 16, 1985; and Irwin Pickett to Heidi Lu Elshtain, July 25, 1985, folder 1, box 59, Jean Bethke Elshtain Papers, Special Collections Research Center, University of Chicago Library (hereafter SCRC).

13. See Evelyn Frantz to Heidi Lu Elshtain, August 7, 1985, and Wm. McKenzie Woodward to Jean Bethke Elshtain, September 16, 1985, folder 9, box 58, SCRC.

14. Edith P. Mayo to Jean Bethke Elshtain, folder 2, box 59, SCRC.

15. Workman, "Woman Movement," 53; James Brooke, "3 Suffragists (in Marble) to Move Up in the Capitol," *New York Times,* September 27, 1996, A18.

16. On the National Congress of Black Women, see Tetrault, *Myth of Seneca Falls,* 197–198. C. DeLores Tucker to Constance A. Morella (October 23, 1996) quoted in Kevin Merida, "A Campaign to Colorize the Capitol's Art," *Emerge* 8, no. 8 (June 1997): 24.

17. Robert L. Traynham, "Sojourner Truth Takes Her Place in the Capitol," *Philadelphia Tribune*, May 3, 2009, 7A.

18. See Meredith Bergmann, "The Boston Women's Memorial," *American Arts Quarterly*, 22, no. 3 (Summer 2005); Nick Capasso, "'Remember the Ladies': New Women's Memorials in Boston and Contemporary Commemorative Public Art," *Sculpture* 19, no. 5 (June 2000): 46–51.

19. Peter DeMarco, "Women Pioneers Take a Bow," *Boston Globe*, October 26, 2003.

20. Lisa L. Colangelo, "Central Park's Literary Walk to House Women's Suffrage Monument," *amNew York*, November 6, 2017; and Tequila Minsky,

"Monument to Suffrage Pioneers to Break Central Park 'Bronze Ceiling,'" *The Villager*, November 20, 2017.

21. See the Pam Elam Papers, University of Kentucky Archives, and Monumental Women, the website of The Elizabeth Cady Stanton and Susan B. Anthony Statue Fund, https://monumentalwomen.org.

22. Einav Rabinovitch-Fox, "Dressing Up for a Campaign: Hillary Clinton, Suffragists, and the Politics of Fashion," in *Nasty Women and Bad Hombres: Gender and Race in the 2016 U.S. Presidential Election*, ed. Christine A. Kray, Tamar W. Carroll, and Hinda Mandell (Rochester, NY: University of Rochester Press, 2018), 146.

23. The five "real" women are Joan of Arc, Eleanor Roosevelt, Gertrude Stein, Golda Meir, and Harriet Tubman. On allegorical sculptures of women in the city, see Allison Meier, "The Unsung Female Muses of New York's Public Sculpture," Hyperallergic, February 15, 2016, https://web.archive.org/web /20160216093028/https://hyperallergic.com/274340/the-unsung-female-muses -of-new-yorks-public-sculpture.

24. See Dara Persis Murray, "Branding 'Real' Social Change in Dove's Campaign for Real Beauty," *Feminist Media Studies* 13 (2013): 83–84; and Nina Bahadur, "Dove 'Real Beauty' Campaign Turns 10," *HuffPost Women*, January 21, 2014, https://web.archive.org/web/20190116133843/https://www .huffingtonpost.com/2014/01/21/dove-real-beauty-campaign-turns-10_n _4575940.html?ec_carp=2458179946827580952.

25. "Stanton and Anthony Statue Fund awarded $500,000 Challenge Grant from New York Life Insurance Company," March 2017, Friends of the Women's Rights National Historical Park, https://web.archive.org/web/20170326193213 /http://womensrightsfriends.org/news_archive.php.

26. For the original plans, with Bergmann's commentary, see "The Winning Design," https://web.archive.org/web/20190315164636 /https://monumentalwomen.org/sculptors-page.

27. Brent Staples, "The Racism behind Women's Suffrage," *New York Times*, July 29, 2018, SR8.

28. Martha S. Jones, "How New York's New Monument Whitewashes the Women's Rights Movement," *Washington Post,* March 22, 2019, https://www .washingtonpost.com/outlook/2019/03/22/how-new-yorks-new-monument -whitewashes-womens-rights-movement.

29. Michelle Duster, "The Women's Suffrage Movement Included More Than Two Women and So Should the Monuments," *Essence*, January 29, 2019, https://web.archive.org/web/20190129194158/https://www.essence.com/news /the-womens-suffrage-movement-included-more-than-two-women-and-so-should -the-monuments. On monuments to African American women, see Alexandria Russell, "Sites Seen and Unseen: Mapping African American Women's Public Memorialization" (PhD diss., University of South Carolina, 2018).

30. Online, the critique ran days earlier with an even more provocative headline, "Is a Planned Monument to Women's Rights Racist?" See Ginia Bellafante, "A Suffrage Monument Fails Black Women," *New York Times*, New York edition, January 20, 2019, MB3.

31. William Neuman, "On Politically Treacherous Ground, Panel Skirts Columbus and Roosevelt," *New York Times*, New York edition, January 13, 2018, A16; and William Neuman, "Sims Statue in Central Park to Be Moved," *New York Times*, New York edition, April 17, 2018, A23.

32. Zachary Small, "A Monument to Women's Suffrage Receives Unanimous Approval Despite Controversy," Hyperallergic, March 19, 2019, https://hyperallergic.com/490554/a-monument-to-womens-suffrage-receives-unanimous-approval-despite-controversy.

33. Erin Durkin, "NYC Launches Push for New Monuments Honoring Women," *New York Daily News*, June 20, 2018.

34. On She Built NYC see NYC.gov, June 20, 2018, https://web.archive.org/web/20180710043557/https://www1.nyc.gov/office-of-the-mayor/news/307-18/she-built-nyc-de-blasio-administration-advisory-panel-commission-public-artwork; and Ginia Bellafante, "These Women Deserve a Statue," *New York Times*, July 29, 2018, MB1.

35. For the top 327 nominations, see "She Built NYC Public Nominations," https://web.archive.org/web/20190311174523/https://women.nyc/wp-content/uploads/2019/03/Women-NYC-She-Built-Nominations.pdf. On the Brooklyn plan, see Jillian Steinhauer, "Chisholm Monument Finds Its Designers," *New York Times*, New York edition, April 24, 2019, C1.

36. "San Francisco Decrees 30 Percent of City's Public Art to Depict Historical Women," *Artforum*, October 9, 2018, https://www.artforum.com/news/san-francisco-decrees-30-percent-of-city-s-public-art-to-depict-historical-women-77037. For the text of the ordinance, see Enactment No. 243-18, October 26, 2018, City and County of San Francisco Board of Supervisors.

37. See, for example, Coline Jenkins and Pam Elam interview, *CBS Sunday Morning*, May 26, 2019, https://www.cbsnews.com/news/monumental-women-breaking-the-bronze-ceiling.

38. Zachary Small, "Controversial Monument to Women's Suffrage Redesigned to Include Sojourner Truth," Hyperallergic, August 13, 2019, https://hyperallergic.com/513303/controversial-monument-to-womens-suffrage-redesigned-to-include-sojourner-truth.

39. "Sculptor's Page," accessed September 29, 2019, https://web.archive.org/web/20190929170625/https://monumentalwomen.org/sculptors-page.

40. Notably, Mary Valverde, the sculptor on the Public Design Commission, along with two other members, abstained from the vote. "I got a lot of input from many different sources on this project, much of it conflicting, much of it contentious," Meredith Bergmann told reporters afterward. "I am confident now

that the monument will work." See Hakim Bishara, "Central Park Women's Suffrage Monument Approved after Months of Heated Debate," Hyperallergic, October 23, 2019, https://hyperallergic.com/524362/central-park-womens -suffrage-monument-approved.

41. "Sculptor's Page."

42. On counter-memorials and counter-monuments, see Erica Doss, *Memorial Mania: Public Feeling in America* (Chicago: University of Chicago Press, 2010), 356–376.

43. Paul M. Farber and Ken Lum, eds., *Monument Lab: Creative Speculations for Philadelphia* (Philadelphia: Temple University Press, 2019), 97, 102–103.

44. Rebecca Solnit, "City of Women," *New Yorker,* October 11, 2016, https://www.newyorker.com/books/page-turner/city-of-women.

45. Mary Mitchell, "Ida B. Wells Finally Gets a Top Honor with Street Name," *Chicago Sun Times*, February 11, 2019; Devin Gannon, "Hudson Yards Park Renamed in Honor of Activist and Former NY Congresswoman, Bella Abzug," 6sqft.com, March 5, 2019, https://www.6sqft.com/hudson-yards-park -renamed-in-honor-of-activist-and-former-ny-congresswoman-bella-abzug.

46. Ruth Sergel, *See You in the Streets: Art, Action, and Remembering the Triangle Shirtwaist Factory Fire* (Iowa City: University of Iowa Press, 2016), 22–23.

47. Jessica Bliss, "Alan LeQuire's Women Suffrage Monument Unveiled in Nashville's Centennial Park," *The Tennessean*, August 24, 2016.

48. "Why the Suffragist Memorial," Turning Point Suffragist Memorial website, https://web.archive.org/web/20180216103959/https://suffragist memorial.org/why-the-suffragist-memorial.

49. US Congress, House, *To authorize the Every Word We Utter Monument to establish a commemorative work in the District of Columbia and its environs*, December 13, 2018, 115th Cong., 2d session, https://www.congress.gov /115/bills/hr7309/BILLS-115hr7309ih.pdf.

50. Christopher Gavin, "Meet the Cambridge Mother-Daughter Pair Who Pushed for a Women's Suffrage Monument," Boston.com, April 23, 2019, https://www.boston.com/news/local-news/2019/04/23/cambridge-mother -daughter-womens-suffrage-monument.

Green New Deal, portrait of Congresswoman Alexandria Ocasio-Cortez (D-NY), as the second coming of President Franklin D. Roosevelt. Illustration by Rusty Zimmerman.

CHAPTER 21

Toward a New New Deal . . . and the Women Will Lead

EILEEN BORIS

A N ICONIC PHOTOGRAPH of Franklin Delano Roosevelt has the bespectacled president sitting in an open roadster with one hand on the wheel, a fedora perched on his head, and a lighted cigarette holder between his teeth.[1] This image has come to reflect a longing for the US version of the welfare state that Roosevelt and his administration forged out of the economic collapse of the Great Depression. Subsequent generations of progressives and liberals alike have hoped to extend the New Deal through bold programs against rising inequality without the racialized and gendered exclusions that haunt Roosevelt's legacy. Each new face has promised success. Following the 2008 presidential election, *Time* magazine portrayed Barack Obama as Roosevelt, projecting his arrival as the dawn of "The New New Deal."[2] A decade later, FDR morphed into AOC: Democratic congresswoman Alexandria Ocasio-Cortez, the youngest woman, at twenty-eight years old, ever elected to the US House of Representatives.

A self-proclaimed socialist, a former volunteer for Senator Bernie Sanders during his 2016 battle against Hillary Clinton, Ocasio-Cortez took on the Democratic Party establishment. In June of 2018, she beat a ten-term incumbent in the Democratic primary race for New York's Fourteenth Congressional District, which spans parts of Queens and the Bronx. The Puerto Rican Ocasio-Cortez won on the basis of her redistributive platform, grassroots organizing, and personal appeal in a rapidly gentrifying majority-minority district.[3] In positioning her as the second coming of Roosevelt, painter Rusty Zimmerman replaced FDR's cigarette holder with a sunflower symbolic of the "Green New Deal" that Ocasio-Cortez promoted to combat climate change (see p. 414). (see p. 414) As a congresswoman-elect, she visited protesters sitting in at the office of soon-to-be reelected Speaker Nancy Pelosi. These young women and men were demanding that the Speaker prioritize the problem of climate change during the 116th Congress.[4] Though challenging an older generation of women political insiders, like Clinton and Pelosi, Ocasio-Cortez wore white to her swearing-in ceremony, the same color that Clinton donned to accept the Democratic presidential nomination in 2016.[5] Ocasio-Cortez sought to honor "the women who paved the path before me, and for the women yet to come. . . . From suffragettes [suffragists] to Shirley Chisholm. . . ."[6]

That this woman for green was also a woman in white tells us much about the feminist revolution at the heart of the pushback from 2016 to 2019 against the persona and policies of Donald Trump. The businessman beat Clinton in the Electoral College to capture the presidency, despite losing the popular vote by nearly 3 million ballots. Feminists rejected the overtly misogynist Trump, his anti-black and anti-immigrant stances, and his pandering to those who would restrict reproductive rights. Millions of women and their supporters protested Trump's inaugural on January 21, 2017. This "Women's March" became the largest single protest event in US history. The assembled chanted slogans, such as "We are the popular vote," and wore pink "pussy hats" in defiance of a videotape from 2005 that emerged in the general election, in which Trump boasted about grabbing women's crotches without consent.[7] Speakers called on women to run for office.

Women's upsurge, however, was not just about Trump's behavior. It was about women left behind economically, put in their place by sexual harassment and weighed down by the burdens of history: what some commentators call "the afterlife of slavery," or the persistence of inequalities stemming from racial capitalism, an organization of society in which racial power determines multiple forms of exploitation.[8] The envisioned new order would be an intersectional one that addressed the myriad identities and structural forces that resulted in gross inequality. The women in the streets and many newly in Congress had absorbed the standpoint of black feminism, a theory of intersectionality developed in the cauldron of social movements and adopted as central to the field of women and gender studies. Since the 1970s, hundreds of colleges and universities, public and private, in every state and region, offered courses that put women's experiences and the social construction of gender at the center of analysis.[9] Students learned about the "matrix of oppression" that came from interlocking identities and structures of gender, race, class, sexuality, disability, and other social positions.[10]

Activists sought to translate theory into policy. They sought to fight for all whose American dream was becoming a nightmare of violence, discrimination, and lack of resources. They demanded health care for all, including reproductive wellness. They would reward care work, alleviate poverty, and provide affordable housing. They would create a sustainable world, reducing pollution and rolling back climate change through deployment of renewable energy and environmentally friendly infrastructure. Women of color, notably queer feminists among them, stood at the forefront of burgeoning social justice movements, including abolishing for-profit private prisons, establishing sanctuary cities for undocumented immigrants, organizing labor in the service and agricultural sectors, and opposing corporate grabs of indigenous lands and the curtailment of public services.[11]

Informing this analysis is a basic premise: the world of the New Deal is not our world, nostalgia and longings aside.[12] The New Deal confronted a different economy revolving around manufacturing. New Deal programs purposely excluded African American and Mexican laborers by leaving agricultural and domestic work out of the Social Security program, the Fair Labor Standards Act (FLSA), and other labor legislation. Policies facilitated the earnings of white men so this group again could support their families as breadwinners, earning a wage large enough to allow a wife and children to remain out of the labor force. Given employer pushback, the Democratic Party under FDR relied on the votes of southern segregationists, whose price for support was the exclusion of African Americans and other racial minorities from New Deal programs designed to provide job security and related benefits.[13]

During the last third of the twentieth century, the old smokestack economy had collapsed alongside the unions that the New Deal strengthened through the National Labor Relations (Wagner) Act. A new, bifurcated economy emerged, powered by the digital revolution and the largely unregulated growth of financial services. Work divided between professional and creative careers versus lesser-paid retail, hospitality, care, and janitorial posts. Men of color and women disproportionately occupied the low-waged end of the new service sector, with immigrants taking jobs shunned by those with other options. With some notable exceptions, these jobs lacked union representation. Indeed, the old categories of employer and employee seemed to fade as independent contracting in a new "gig economy" took hold.[14]

Once it appeared that a single (male) wage was enough for a family, but fewer households could get by without the labor force participation of all adult members by the 1970s. Women's earnings became essential for families, even if women disproportionately composed the nation's minimum wage workforce. The problem of the wage-earning mother and the question of who will do the work of care in an aging society emerged as pressing concerns.[15] Despite differences of race and class, women as a sex class increasingly spoke out, especially when it came to gender violence and harassment in the workplace and the ways that the sexual division of labor and normative assumptions about family and care impacted their career prospects and earning potential. This revolution pushed the issues of childcare, health care, elder care, education, and social protection—once brushed aside as women's issues—to the center of political life.

To understand women in politics as we enter the second century after the Nineteenth Amendment, we must turn to the grassroots movements that defined an emerging agenda. This chapter highlights the unfinished civil rights revolution preceding the entrance of progressive women into Congress. It introduces the activities of the National Domestic Workers Alliance (NDWA), We Belong Together, Black Lives Matter, #MeToo, and the Women's March. It concludes by looking at the agendas of officeholders first elected in 2018—highlighting Alexandria

Ocasio-Cortez and the other three women of color representatives who became known as "the Squad" for their bold defiance of President Trump's agenda: Minneapolis's Ilhan Omar (a Somali immigrant), Detroit's Rashida Tlaib (a Palestinian American), and Boston's Ayanna Pressley (an African American).[16] They questioned the status quo, while their counterparts in the Senate sought to enact the most acceptable proposals. This time the hope was for women to lead, combining the politics of presence from a surge of women winning elective office with platforms pushing the Democratic Party back to and beyond its New Deal incarnation.

New Terrains

The New Deal was predicated on an economic arrangement that became increasingly shaky: the family wage in which men earned money and women spent money. The Great Depression had disrupted the heterosexual family. With unemployment hitting heavy industry first, husbands and fathers often were the first ones laid off; the service sector and pink-collar jobs dominated by women declined only later. Faced with male unemployment, most New Dealers, women as well as men, sought to sustain the ideal of the male breadwinner: he who earned a family wage large enough to support a stay-at-home wife and children.[17]

Social Security (including unemployment and pensions) sought to insure families from hardship through the labor force participation of male breadwinners. Women obtained access to this safety net through marriage to a man who had worked in an occupation covered under the law. During a time when a majority of wives lacked sustained labor force participation, the terms of social insurance both subsidized female domesticity and provided real gains for some women. These women were predominantly white. Under Survivor's Insurance, widows with children under age eighteen received three-fourths of the pension of their late husband (unless they remarried or entered the workforce); the divorced or never married were relegated to the more arbitrary Aid to Dependent Children (ADC, later known as Aid to Families with

Dependent Children or AFDC), with benefits determined by the individual states. This system doubly disadvantaged the vast majority of African American, Mexican American, and immigrant women (especially Asians restricted from citizenship) whose husbands were not included in the social insurance system and whose own occupations were not eligible for these benefits.[18]

Despite real gains from the New Deal and subsequent Great Society legislation of the 1960s, legal and structural disadvantages persisted for women, immigrants, and men of color. The welfare policies of more conservative Reagan Republicans and Clinton Democrats pushed poor single mothers into the low-waged workforce by imposing time limits, work requirements, and intensified surveillance of personal life. In 1996, Clinton replaced AFDC with Temporary Assistance for Needy Families. The number of welfare recipients soon declined as greater poverty spread among those now excluded.[19] Already at the bottom, women and men of color were disproportionately impacted in the service sector. New forms of organizing soon emerged from those left behind, with women leading the way.

Male dominance at work slowly changed. The powerful unions that solidified after World War II were in basic industry, where men labored. But even the textile and garment industries, with largely female workforces, had male leadership. Women composed about a third of the labor force in 1950, concentrated in light manufacturing. Some sixty-five years later, that number reached 50 percent, with nearly 70 percent of mothers with children under age eighteen formally employed.[20] The unorganized home health aide replaced the unionized automobile assembler as the prototypical laborer. To meet the needs of an aging society, experts predicted a 50 percent growth rate in care jobs, only surpassed by alternative energy technicians and installers. Nonetheless, the wages of care remained paltry, under the poverty line for a family of four, with half of home care workers receiving some form of public assistance.[21] Access to pregnancy, family, and medical leave remained inadequate, limited by size of enterprise, relation to the person requiring care, length of employment, and geographical location.[22]

Among women wage earners, the struggles of domestic workers captured national and international attention. The Fair Labor Standards Act and the National Labor Relations Act also had excluded household workers. Not until 1974 did this predominantly female and mostly women of color (African American and immigrant) workforce come under the wage and hour law. The US Department of Labor then reclassified home health workers as elder companions and excluded them from overtime. Four decades later, the combined efforts of unionized care workers and ethnic-based domestic worker associations finally pushed the Obama administration to remove this restriction.[23] In 2015, 30 percent of 2 million home care workers belonged to unions, but these were concentrated in only a few Democratic-controlled states and subject to intense backlash by conservative legal foundations and Republican politicians.[24]

A decade after its 2007 founding, the NDWA had sixty affiliates in thirty-six cities and seventeen states, covering twenty thousand workers. Though not technically a union, it had become an affiliate of the AFL-CIO. By the end of 2019, campaigns for Domestic Worker Bills of Rights won wage, hour, break, contract, and other standards in nine states and two cities. NDWA assumed a predominant form among social justice organizations: a professional and paid staff that worked to empower and develop grassroots leadership and autonomous self-activity for a specific local in collaboration with other groups.[25] It provided a holistic vision, seen in its coalition actions. It generated a multiorganization alliance, "Caring Across the Generations," and joined with both other low-waged women workers and Hollywood celebrities to fight sexual harassment. In July 2018, with actress Jane Fonda, a long-time activist for progressive causes, and the Alianza Nacional de Campesinas, a grassroots group for women farmworkers, it lobbied Congress for expanded protections against assault in all workplaces, no matter how small, to reach workers who often labor in isolation.[26]

Domestic workers constituted only one component of the care work economy, the site of dramatic labor actions in the first decades of the twenty-first century. Organized professionals placed care at the forefront of their concerns. In Rhode Island, Massachusetts, California, Minnesota, Florida, Missouri, Kansas, Texas, and Nevada, nurses in 2018 protested unsafe conditions, inadequate staffing levels, and top-heavy administrations. Nearly two thousand struck at the University of Vermont Medical Center demanding that such nonprofits put patients first.[27] Teacher walkouts illuminated the extent to which the privatization of public tasks and lack of spending impacted schooling. In Chicago in 2012, West Virginia in 2018, Los Angeles in 2019, and again Chicago in 2019, strikes morphed into worker-community uprisings to enhance learning as well as raise teacher pay.[28] During the 2018 midterm elections, hundreds of teachers ran for office at the state level, continuing their fight for improved public schools and a better future for all children.[29] Unlike most domestic workers, these groups were public employees, who had gained the right to organize in the 1960s but faced decertification from conservative court rulings that undermined their legitimacy.[30]

The Expanding Social Movement Milieu

Women's entrance into electoral politics occurred in the context of widening social protest by grassroots organizations that sought to reshape the Democratic Party. As historian Lara Putnam and political scientist Theda Skocpol noted, local women rebuilt the party from below in the wake of Donald Trump's election. Around the country, they gathered in living rooms to educate themselves on key issues, write postcards to other states, and make calls. They canvassed for local candidates and packed congressional offices. Though not identified as leftists, "they organize vigils to protest family separation at the border, support youth who #marchforourlives against gun violence, and cheer candidates who demand health care for all." They call for a "stronger public safety net, higher public investment in education, health care, and support for individuals with disabilities."[31] A notable gender gap existed among white people, with the Republicans winning white men and an aging group of white women, but Democrats taking younger and middle-aged white women and increasingly younger white men.

But even before this Trump-era surge of activism, women of color were politicizing care to benefit recipients as well as workers. Although the Democratic Party had sought to rectify race and gender discrimination after 1960, neoliberal policies in the Clinton years vitiated a political legacy of economic redistribution. Mass incarceration and immigration restrictions threatened equal rights and social justice. The NDWA launched We Belong Together in 2013 with the motto "Women in support of common sense immigration reform." Arguing that immigration reform is a women's issue since most immigrants were women and children, this spinoff undertook dramatic actions, including rallies and civil disobedience.[32] In 2018, it joined other progressive groups traveling to the Mexican border and held sit-ins to protest the Trump administration's new policy of separating children from their families as they entered the country to ask for political asylum. Commenting on the hundreds of marches organized in June 2018 across the nation, NDWA political director Jess Morales Rocketto reflected, "I have literally never seen Americans show up for immigrants like this. We just kept hearing over and over again, if it was my child, I would want someone to do something." Days later, nearly six hundred women were arrested at the Senate office building.[33] NDWA organizer Alicia Garza, cofounder of Black Lives Matter, fused coalitional politics with a sharpened emphasis on racial justice when she admitted that the exclusionary history of white feminism "hasn't changed. . . . What has . . . is that I understand that the coalition that is going to save us has to be much bigger than what it is."[34]

Movements against violence reflected this quest for freedom, dignity, and justice. In 2013, Garza, along with Patrisse Cullors and Opal Tometi, formed Black Lives Matter in response to the acquittal of the murderer of Trayvon Martin, a teenager visiting a gated community who was gunned down returning from a convenience store. Under the hashtag #BlackLivesMatter, a movement exploded, fueled by all-too-public racialized police brutality. Placing women, queer, and trans people in leadership, this network of over forty chapters by 2019 rejected heteropatriarchal norms too often pervading liberation struggles.[35]

In another move against violence, black feminist Tarana Burke first coined "Me Too" in 2006 when she worked with survivors of sexual assault. Eleven years later, that phrase went viral as a Twitter hashtag when Alyssa Milano and other actresses charged powerful producers, actors, and scriptwriters with sexual harassment. Challenged by advocates for low-waged women workers, the entertainment industry established the Times Up Legal Defense Fund, administered by the National Women's Law Center, to aid those seeking legal restitution. The Supreme Court confirmation hearings of Brett Kavanaugh in fall 2018, a prelude to the midterm elections that year, fueled women's political anger when Republican lawmakers belittled and dismissed the accusations of university professor Christine Blasey Ford, who charged the nominee with attempted rape during their high school years.[36]

Defense of reproductive rights joined the fight against sexual violence as part of the umbrella platform of the March for Women's Lives. Co-organizer Linda Sarsour explained, "As women of color who came into this effort, we came in not only to mobilize and organize but also to educate, to argue that we can't talk about women's rights, about reproductive rights, about equal pay, without also talking about race and class."[37] Its agenda also covered Medicare for All, voting rights, decriminalization of sex work, and independent living for women with disabilities.[38] The march superseded the much lauded 2009 Tea Party protest, but suffered from charges of anti-Semitism. The facile equation of conflating opposition to Israeli state policies with anti-Semitism remained a potent divide deployed by Republicans—a tactic most visibly used in 2019 to undermine support for the first Muslim congresswoman, Ilhan Omar.[39]

Toward a New New Deal?

The midterm elections of 2018 ushered a record-breaking number of women of color into office. Some eighty-nine Democratic women, along with thirteen Republican ones, gained House seats; forty-three (forty-two of them Democrat) were women of color. Thirty-six were elected for the first time. With their Senate counterparts—seventeen Democrat, seven Republican—they represented the largest absolute number of women elected to Congress in a single cycle. Nine women captured governorships, and another record number went into state legislatures.[40] The women hoped to translate visions into practices that would renew democratic processes and substitute social justice for growing inequality. While not all were first-timers who embraced Left politics, most supported better health care, equal rights, reproductive health, and fair elections. Some wanted more incrementalist policies, and others sought to provoke fundamental change.

The agendas of progressive social movements gained expression in the programs of outspoken newly elected women of color. Omar came to Washington from the Minnesota legislature by way of the American Federation of State, County, and Municipal Employees. "Fighting alongside my union for fair wages, healthcare, and workplace protections allowed me to see firsthand what redistribution of power looks like," she told *Teen Vogue*, which placed her in the footsteps of Frances Perkins, Roosevelt's labor secretary. "The greatest lesson I learned from working within the movement and drawing on the experiences of my colleagues is how to harness power beyond the individual." The 2016 National Teacher of the Year, Jahana Hayes, a National Education Association and American Federation of School Administrators member, became Connecticut's first black woman representative. She ran to advocate for public education, speaking against Trump's border policies and attacks on unions.[41] Beating the incumbent in the Democratic primary, Boston City Councilwoman Ayanna Pressley also became her state's first black woman representative. A survivor herself, she pledged to fight sexual assault.[42] She vowed to abolish Immigration and Customs Enforcement and, with Ocasio-Cortez, Tlaib, and Omar, cut the budget of the entire Department of Homeland Security.[43]

Omar offered an especially aspirational platform. She highlighted planks on guaranteed free access to public education, Medicare for All, living wages and economic justice measures, Wall Street accountability, a just immigration system with paths to citizenship, environmental justice and a green economy, alternatives to incarceration, affordable housing, rights for the lesbian, gay, bisexual, trans, queer, intersex, and asexual community, peace and gun restrictions, improved public infrastructure, investment in arts and humanities, and clean elections.[44] Tlaib campaigned for a $15 minimum wage, union rights, protection of Social Security and Medicare/Medicaid, home ownership, ending "corporate welfare," equal pay, free college, and overturning Citizens United while restoring the Voting Rights Act.[45]

Not all newly elected congresswomen were radicals. Katie Hill, who ran as a bisexual white woman in California's Twenty-Fifth District, wanted to make government work. She criticized Trump's desired border wall with Mexico but was open to negotiations over greater border security.[46] Though the pragmatists, who had flipped Republican areas in 2018, might eschew major taxes on the wealthiest Americans, as advocated by Representative Ocasio-Cortez or Senator Elizabeth Warren, they joined the progressives in wanting to improve health care, end corruption, and clean up the environment. Like Illinois's Lauren Underwood, a black nurse, they would improve Obamacare before promoting Medicare for All.[47] These incrementalists would work with the leadership, even though some of them had told constituents that they would oppose reelecting Nancy Pelosi as House Speaker.

Social movement–driven politics, led by women, has remapped presidential discourse leading into the 2020 election. Since the 1992 "Year of the Woman," after outrage over sexual harassment during the Clarence Thomas confirmation hearing to the Supreme Court, the numbers of women running for office grew. The upcoming contest attracted a record number campaigning for president. Women presidential candidates sought to distinguish themselves early in the race, though they all embraced tenets of an agenda derived from the social movements. Commentators saw Senator Kirsten Gillibrand playing "the gender card": she ran "as a young mom" who positioned herself as the key defender against sexual harassment. Pundits associated Senator Kamala Harris with race. She was the co-sponsor of a federal Domestic Workers Bill of Rights with Seattle Representative Pramila Jayapal, who had close ties to NDWA, to improve conditions for women of color. Massachusetts Senator Elizabeth Warren stood for class, promoting an "Ultra-Millionaire Tax" and democratizing corporate governance. In contrast, Minnesota Senator Amy Klobuchar positioned herself as a moderate Midwesterner who could appeal to Trump voters from her region.[48]

After the surprise 2017 victory of Doug Jones to fill a vacant Senate seat in Alabama, some within the Democratic Party recognized that black women represented their most loyal constituency. Explained political strategist DeJuana Thompson, "when you've got rhetoric coming out about slashing critical resources to education and the programs that help sustain homes . . . black women are always going to show up for their communities." She underscored the larger point that black feminist activists had made over the past two decades: when black women act, "every other community is empowered."[49] An intersectional analysis enabled black women to link social and economic justice; their electoral turn came out of a long tradition to demand full citizenship and rights within the polity. They understood that disenfranchisement led to greater exploitation. The victory of Trump taught that lesson to others: stay home or vote for a third party and under the winner-take-all rules of US elections, you risk a nightmare. But even when a more liberal candidate wins, it takes an insider-outsider strategy, with social movements pushing those in office, to enact anything resembling one's agenda. Electoral politics had turned into a stage for social movement theater.

Just as the New Deal emerged out of the Great Depression, women of color–led intersectional politics responded to the economic and social crisis of the early twenty-first century, intensified by the economic collapse of 2008 and made even more urgent by the election of Donald J. Trump. While the New Deal directed programs to improve the conditions of male industrial workers and their families, twenty-first century women in Congress and their supporters in the streets sought a more inclusive New New Deal to address climate change, white supremacy, gender inequities, and economic inequality. Whether their freedom dreams were utopian or achievable lay in the future.

Notes

1. Photograph of Franklin D. Roosevelt, *Time* LightBox, April 1939, Warm Spring, GA, accessed January 21, 2019, http://timelightbox.tumblr.com/post /22385832160/warm-springs-ga-april-1939-cigarette-holder.

2. Peter Beinart, "The New New Deal," *Time*, November 24, 2008, accessed January 21, 2019, http://content.time.com/time/covers/0,16641,20081124,00 .html.

3. Vivian Wang, "Alexandria Ocasio-Cortez: A 28-Year-Old Democratic Giant Slayer," *New York Times*, June 27, 2018; Azi Paybarah, "Alexandria Ocasio-Cortez Will Push Washington. Will Washington Push Back?," *New York Times*, November 7, 2018.

4. Peter Rugh, "Gearing Up for a Green New Deal—Alexandria Ocasio-Cortez and the plan to change everything," *The Indypendent*, December 20, 2018, reprinted at https://portside.org/2018-12-20/gearing-green-new-deal -alexandria-ocasio-cortez-and-plan-change-everything.

5. Louise Bernikow, "With Hillary's Nomination, Lots of Interest in Suffrage Movement, but Did Media Get the Facts Right?," August 3, 2016, http://www .womensmediacenter.com/feature/entry/with-hillarys-nomination-lots-of-interest -in-suffrage-movement-but-did-medi.

6. Alexandria Ocasio-Cortez (@AOC), Twitter, January 3, 2019, in Lee Moran, "Alexandria Ocasio-Cortez Shuts Down GOP Haters with 8 Little Words," *HuffPost*, January 4, 2019, https://www.huffingtonpost.com/entry /alexandria-ocasio-cortez-gophaters_us_5c2f16d4e4b05c88b707ec87.

7. Erica Chenoweth and Jeremy Pressman, "This Is What We Learned by Counting the Women's March," *Washington Post*, February 7, 2017; Anemona Hartocollis and Yamiche Alcindor, "Women's March Highlights as Huge Crowds Protest Trump: 'We're Not Going Away,'" *New York Times*, January 21, 2017.

8. Saidiya Hartman, *Lose Your Mother: A Journey along the Atlantic Slave Route* (New York: Farrar, Straus and Giroux, 2007); Jodi Melamed, "Racial Capitalism," *Critical Ethnic Studies* 1, no. 1 (Spring 2015): 76–85.

9. The UCSB Feminist Studies Program sends mailings to more than seven hundred other departments alone. List from chair, April 2019.

10. Dorothy Sue Cobble, Linda Gordon, and Astrid Henry, *Feminism Unfinished: A Short, Surprising History of American Women's Movements* (New York: Norton, 2014), 161–165; Patricia Hill Collins, *Black Feminist Thought:*

Knowledge, Consciousness, and the Politics of Empowerment (Boston: Unwin Hyman, 1990), 221–238; Mackenzie Abernethy, "Intersectionality in the Women's March and the Classroom," *Choices Blog: History and Current Issues for the Classroom*, January 27, 2017, https://blogs.brown.edu/choices/2017/01/27/womens-march-in-the-classroom/.

11. Premilla Nadasen, "Black Feminism Will Save Us All," *In These Times*, September 11, 2018, http://inthesetimes.com/article/21429/black-feminism-intersectional-donald-trump-class-race.

12. The Living New Deal, accessed January 22, 2019, https://livingnewdeal.org/.

13. Eileen Boris, "Labor's Welfare State: Defining Workers, Constructing Citizens," in *The Cambridge History of Law in America*, vol. 3, ed. Michael Grossberg and Christopher Tomlins (New York: Cambridge University Press, 2008), 319–358.

14. David Weil, *The Fissured Workplace: Why Work Became So Bad for So Many and What Can Be Done to Improve It* (Cambridge, MA: Harvard University Press, 2014).

15. Kayla Patrick, Meika Berlan, and Morgan Harwood, "Low-Wage Jobs Held Primarily by Women Will Grow the Most over the Next Decade," National Women's Law Center Fact Sheet, August 2018, https://nwlc-ciw49tixgw5lbab.stackpathdns.com/wp-content/uploads/2016/04/Low-Wage-Jobs-Held-Primarily-by-Women-Will-Grow-the-Most-Over-the-Next-Decade-2018.pdf; Shawn Carter, "More Women are the Breadwinner at Home, but Most Still Say Men Treat Them Differently at Work," *CNBC News*, March 23, 2018, https://www.cnbc.com/2018/03/23/more-women-are-breadwinners-but-are-still-treated-differently-at-work.html.

16. Jeremy W. Peters, "Pelosi. Clinton. Obama. Now 'the Squad' Is the New Target for the Right," *New York Times*, July 27, 2019.

17. Susan Ware, *Beyond Suffrage: Women in the New Deal* (Cambridge, MA: Harvard University Press, 1981).

18. Boris, "Labor's Welfare State."

19. Felicia Kornbluh and Gwendolyn Mink, *Ensuring Poverty: Welfare Reform in Feminist Perspective* (Philadelphia: University of Pennsylvania Press, 2018).

20. Mitra Toossi and Teresa L. Morisi, "Women in the Workforce Before, During, and After the Great Recession," US Department of Labor, Bureau of Labor Statistics, July 2017, https://www.bls.gov/spotlight/2017/women-in-the-workforce-before-during-and-after-the-great-recession/pdf/women-in-the-workforce-before-during-and-after-the-great-recession.pdf.

21. Department of Labor, Bureau of Labor Statistics, "Fastest Growing Occupations, 2016–26," *Occupational Outlook Handbook*, https://www.bls.gov/ooh/fastest-growing.htm; PHI, *U.S. Home Care Workers: Key Facts* (Bronx,

NY: PHI), https://phinational.org/wp-content/uploads/legacy/phi-home-care
-workers-key-facts.pdf; Stephon Johnson, "Study: More Than 50 Percent of
Home Care Workers Are on Public Assistance," *New York Amsterdam News*,
September 14, 2017, http://amsterdamnews.com/news/2017/sep/14/study-more
-50-percent-home-care-workers-are-public/.

22. IMPAQ International and Institute for Women's Policy Research,
"Qualifying for Unpaid Leave: FMLA Eligibility among Working Mothers,"
issue brief, January 2017, https://iwpr.org/publications/qualifying-unpaid-leave
-fmla-eligibility-among-working-mothers/.

23. Eileen Boris and Jennifer Klein, *Caring for America: Home Health
Workers in the Shadow of the Welfare State* (New York: Oxford, 2015),
129–134, 227.

24. Leigh Anne Schriever, "The Home Health Care Industry's Organizing
Nightmare," Century Foundation, August 18, 2015, https://tcf.org/content
/commentary/the-home-health-care-industrys-organizing-nightmare/?agreed=1;
Boris and Klein, *Caring for America*, 226–231.

25. The states were New York, Hawai'i, California, Massachusetts, Connecticut, Illinois, Nevada, and New Mexico. Seattle and Philadelphia passed city
standards. Figures from NDWA website: https://www.www.domesticworkers
.org/about-us; AFL-CIO, "Our Unions and Allies," https://aflcio.org/about-us
/our-unions-and-allies; "Domestic Workers Ordinance," Office of Labor Standards,
Seattle, https://www.seattle.gov/laborstandards/ordinances/domestic-workers
-ordinance all.

26. "Jane Fonda teams up with domestic workers & farmworkers to fight
for women's rights at work," Press release, July 6, 2018, National Domestic
Workers Alliance, https://www.www.domesticworkers.org/release/jane-fonda
-teams-domestic-workers-farmworkers-fight-womens-rights-work.

27. Suzanne Gordon, "When Nurses Strike," *Jacobin*, July 17, 2018,
https://www.jacobinmag.com/2018/07/vermont-nurses-strike-safe-staffing
-ratios; Dan D'Ambrosio, "UVM Medical Center Nurses on Strike Have Plenty
of Company around the Country," *Burlington Free Press*, July 16, 2018,
https://www.burlingtonfreepress.com/story/news/2018/07/16/nurses-strikes
-nurses-feeling-overworked-across-country/783587002/; ABCActionNews.com,
"HCA Nurses Picket at Five Tampa Bay Area Hospitals over Staffing Concerns,"
July 12, 2018, https://www.facebook.com/tampabaynews/posts/nurses-on-strike
-nurses-say-the-hospital-needs-to-fix-staffing-and-scheduling-is
/10156685997880409/.

28. Robert Bruno and Steven K. Ashby, *A Fight for the Soul of Public
Education: The Story of the Chicago Teachers Strike* (Ithaca, NY: Cornell
University Press, 2016); Eric Blanc, *Red State Revolt: What the Teachers' Strike
Wave Means for Workers and Politics* (New York: Verso, 2019); Rachel M.
Cohen, "Coming Off LA Strike, a New Wave of Teacher Protests Takes Hold,"

The Intercept, January 29, 2019, https://theintercept.com/2019/01/29/la
-teachers-strike-virginia-colorado-california/; Mitch Smith and Monica Davey,
"Chicago Teachers' Strike, Longest in Decades, Ends," *New York Times*,
October 31, 2019.

29. Dave Jamieson and Travis Waldron, "More Than 500 Teachers and Other
Educators Are Running for Office This Year," *HuffPost*, September 11, 2018,
https://mail.google.com/mail/u/o/#label/Boris+writings%2FNew+New+Deal/FMf
cgxvzKbNqDKSCxdNQFQRMTKVKtgjq.

30. Joseph E. Hower, "Public Sector Unionism," *Oxford Research Encyclo-
pedias: American History*, http://oxfordre.com/americanhistory/view/10.1093
/acrefore/9780199329175.001.0001/acrefore-9780199329175-e-395; *Janus v.
AFSCME*, 585 U.S.___ (2018).

31. Lara Putnam and Theda Skocpol, "Women Are Rebuilding the Democratic Party from the Ground Up," *New Republic*, August 21, 2018, https://
newrepublic.com/article/150462/women-rebuilding-democratic-party-ground.

32. Candice Bernd, "'We Belong Together' Campaign Brings Feminism to the
Forefront of Immigration Reform," Truthout, October 8, 2013, https://truthout
.org/articles/we-belong-together-campaign-brings-feminism-to-the-forefront-of
-immigration-reform/.

33. Phil McCausland, Patricia Guadalupe, and Kalhan Rosenblatt, "Hun-
dreds of 'Families Belong Together' Rallies Held across the Country," *NBC
News*, June 30, 2018, https://www.nbcnews.com/news/us-news/thousands
-across-u-s-join-keep-families-together-march-protest-n888006; Marissa J. Lang,
"'We Will Not Obey': 575 Arrested as Hundreds of Women Rally in D.C.,"
Washington Post, June 28, 2018.

34. Quoted in Rebecca Traister, *Good and Mad: The Revolutionary Power
of Women's Anger* (New York: Simon & Schuster, 2018), 132.

35. "Herstory," Black Lives Matter, https://blacklivesmatter.com/about
/herstory/; "What We Believe," Black Lives Matter, https://blacklivesmatter.com
/about/what-we-believe/; Barbara Ransby, *Making All Black Lives Matter:
Reimagining Freedom in the Twentieth-First Century* (Berkeley: University of
California Press, 2018).

36. "#MeToo: A Timeline of Events," *Chicago Tribune*, January 23, 2019,
https://www.chicagotribune.com/lifestyles/ct-me-too-timeline-20171208
-htmlstory.html; Joanna Walters, "#MeToo a Revolution That Can't Be Stopped,
Says Time's Up Co-founder," *The Guardian*, October 21, 2018, https://www
.theguardian.com/world/2018/oct/21/metoo-revolution-times-up-roberta-kaplan.

37. Quoted in Rebecca Traister, "And You Thought Trump Voters Were
Mad," *The Cut*, September 17, 2018, https://www.thecut.com/2018/09/rebecca
-traister-good-and-mad-book-excerpt.html.

38. "Women's Agenda," accessed February 2, 2019, https://womensmarch
.com/agenda.

39. Chenoweth and Pressman, "This Is What We Learned"; Farah Stockman, "Women's March Roiled by Accusations of Anti-Semitism," *New York Times*, December 23, 2018; Sheryl Gay Stolberg, "Discord over Israel Reveals Democrats' Divide," *New York Times*, February 2, 2019.

40. CAWP, "Latest Numbers from the 2018 Midterms," *News & Notes*, November 28, 2018, at https://myemail.constantcontact.com/CAWP-News ---Notes--Results-Update.html?soid=1101446129151&aid=vHvVRYyuZtc.

41. Kim Kelly, "Midterms Labor Candidates are Shaking Up the Status Quo and Standing Up for Workers," *Teen Vogue*, September 18, 2018, https://www .teenvogue.com/story/midterms-labor-candidates; Courtney Connley, "Former National Teacher of the Year Jahana Hayes becomes Connecticut's First Black Woman Elected to Congress," CNBC, November 7, 2018, https://www.cnbc .com/2018/11/07/jahana-hayes-is-connecticuts-first-black-woman-elected-to -congress.html.

42. Katharine Seelye and Astead Herndon, "Ayanna Pressley Seeks Her Political Moment in a Changing Boston," *New York Times*, September 1, 2018.

43. Jake Johnson, "AOC, Pressley, Tlaib, and Omar to Shutdown Negotiators," *Common Dreams*, January 31, 2019, https://www.commondreams.org /news/2019/01/31/aoc-pressley-tlaib-and-omar-shutdown-negotiators-not -another-dollar-trumps-anti,.

44. "Vision," Ilhan for Congress, https://www.ilhanomar.com/vision; John Haltiwanger, "This Is the Platform That Launched Alexandria Ocasio-Cortez," *Business Insider*, January 4, 2019, https://www.businessinsider.com/alexandria -ocasio-cortez-platform-on-the-issues-2018-6.

45. "Priorities," Rashida for Congress, February 3, 2019, https://www .rashidaforcongress.com/priorities.

46. Katie Hill resigned in October 2019 after being slut-shamed by her ex-husband and accused of an inappropriate relationship with a staffer. Paul LeBlanc, Kyung Lah, and Haley Byrd, "Rep. Katie Hill Announces Resignation amid Allegations of Improper Relations with Staffers," CNN, October 28, 2019, https://www.cnn.com/2019/10/27/politics/katie-hill-announces-resignation/index .html.

47. Scott Morefield, "Democratic Rep. Katie Hill Says She Would Fund Border Barrier, Blames Impasse on 'Semantic,'" *Daily Caller*, January 12, 2019, https://dailycaller.com/2019/01/12/katie-hill-border-barrier-funding/; Ella Nilsen and Dylan Scott, "The Silent Majority of Democratic House Freshmen," *Vox*, January 27, 2019, https://www.vox.com/policy-and-politics/2019/1/23 /18183636/congress-2019-new-members-moderates.

48. Janet Hook, "Each on Her Own Path," *New York Times*, January 29, 2019; Bryce Covert, "The New Federal Domestic Workers Bill of Rights," *The Nation*, November 29, 2019, https://www.thenation.com/article/federal-domestic -workers-bill-of-rights-harris-jayapal-labor/; "Green New Deal," Gillibrand

2020, January 27, 2019; "Unhappy Rich People," Warren, January 27, 2019; "What We're Fighting For," Kamala Harris, January 28, 2019, emails in author's possession; Matt Stevens, "Amy Klobuchar," *New York Times*, November 30, 2019.

49. Chandelis R. Duster and Foluké Tuakli, "Why Black Women Voters Showed Up for Doug Jones," *NBC News*, December 13, 2017, https://www .nbcnews.com/news/nbcblk/why-black-women-showed-vote-doug-jones -n829411.

ACKNOWLEDGMENTS

This collaborative effort has been an act of the willing. We ambitiously issued a call for papers for this collection in summer 2018 with the expectation that our labors would be swift and our purpose focused—creating a collection timed for the suffrage centennial in August 2020. We are deeply appreciative of our contributors' commitment to our goal of reevaluating the place of women in politics since the ratification of the Nineteenth Amendment. It has been a whirlwind from start to finish, and each contributor rose to the occasion. The result is a collection that introduces the breadth of women's political history and its exciting future.

We want to thank our respective mentors, who paved the path forward as scholars, women's historians, and political historians through their work and example—Jane DeHart, Mari Jo Buhle, Eileen Boris, Robert Self, Laura Kalman, Leila Rupp, Nelson Lichtenstein, Estelle Freedman, and Daniel Horowitz. We are grateful to work in a wider web of historians whose scholarship and dialogue with us have also left an imprint on this collection in countless ways—Linda Kerber, Nancy MacLean, Nancy Cott, Nancy Hewitt, Joanne Meyerowitz, Dorothy Sue Cobble, Lisa Levenstein, Katherine Turk, Marjorie Spruill, Judy Tzu-Chun Wu, Katherine Marino, Natasha Zaretzky, Michelle Nickerson, and Susan Hartmann.

Our collection has been shepherded through to the finish line in capable hands at Johns Hopkins University Press. We are grateful to Laura B. Davulis for taking on this project, keeping us on task, and helping hone its direction. Her guidance has been invaluable, as has been the in-house support of Esther P. Rodriguez and publicity and production staff. We received incredibly helpful reviewer comments on our proposal and manuscript, which helped hone the shape and argument of this anthology.

We are also appreciative of the silent labors of the many archivists and librarians who have helped us and our coauthors develop research. We hope that the notes of this book offer a road map back to the archives that inspire historians to continue to expand our understanding of women in politics in the twentieth and twenty-first centuries.

Students have been willing guinea pigs to test out ideas that appear in the introduction and first chapter of this book. Stacie thanks her students across several classes in recent years at Ramapo College of New Jersey, especially Katie Barrales Cortes, who compiled the index for this book. Leandra benefited from engaging with students at University of Houston in her undergraduate and graduate classes but also in a class she taught at the Women's Institute of Houston in the final days of wrapping up this publication.

This book was a labor of love for us as we worked on other projects, personal, political, and professional. Stacie thanks her colleagues in the School of Humanities and Global Studies at Ramapo College of New Jersey for crucial funding that made work on this book possible. She remains forever grateful for the love and support of the Taranto, Mawn, and Balagat families, especially that of her mother, Terrie Taranto, and late father, Joe Taranto. She also wishes to thank her village of friends in and beyond Ridgewood, New Jersey. Above all, Stacie thanks her husband, Vincent Balagat, and two children, Gwen and Henry, for living with this book for two years and aiding its publication in various ways, big and small. Leandra thanks her family, the Zarnows, Sbardellatis, and Feuers, for their constant support and vibrant political debates, banter at times heated and always exciting that makes so clear how wide our democratic imagination stretches and how deeply we often agree to disagree. Leandra's husband, John, an outstanding political historian, always made sure to have the Sunday talk shows playing through the thick and thin of this project. Thank you for keeping me grounded and tuned in.

Editors

STACIE TARANTO is an associate professor of history at Ramapo College of New Jersey, where her teaching and research focus on post–1945 US political and women's history. She is the author of *Kitchen Table Politics: Conservative Women and Family Values in New York* (Politics and Culture in Modern America Series, University of Pennsylvania Press, 2017), which won the 2017 Arline Custer Memorial Award. Taranto's most recent scholarly articles have appeared in *Journal of Policy History* and the collections *Inventing the Silent Majority in Western Europe and the United States* (2017) and *Making Suburbia* (2015). Her popular writing and commentary have appeared in *Nursing Clio*, *The Atlantic*, and Made by History at the *Washington Post*.

LEANDRA ZARNOW is an associate professor in the Department of History and affiliated faculty in Women, Gender, and Sexuality Studies at University of Houston. She is a specialist in modern US women's political, legal, and intellectual history with additional interests in media and transnational studies. Her first book, *Battling Bella: The Protest Politics of Bella Abzug*, was published by Harvard University Press in 2019. Her work has appeared in *Law & Social Inquiry, Journal of Policy History, Feminist Formations,* and the collections *No Permanent Waves* and *Breaking the Waves*. She also discusses women in politics in the media, with past commentary and appearances in Axios.com, the *Houston Chronicle*, and Houston's NPR, Pacifica Radio, and PBS.

Contributors

MELISSA ESTES BLAIR is an associate professor of history at Auburn University and a member of the Executive Council of Auburn's Women's Studies Program. Before joining the Auburn faculty in 2015, she taught for six years at Warren Wilson College. Her first book, *Revolutionizing Expectations: Women's Organizations, Feminism, and American Politics, 1965–1980*, was published by University of Georgia Press in 2014. She has also written for Made by History at the *Washington Post*. She is a past chair of the Women, Gender, & Sexuality Committee of the Southern Historical Association, a member of the 2019 Darlene Clark Hine Prize Committee of the OAH, and currently serves on the Graduate Committee of the Southern Association of Women Historians.

EILEEN BORIS is the Hull Professor and Distinguished Professor of Feminist Studies, History, Black Studies, and Global Studies at University of California, Santa Barbara. Currently, Boris is serving as the president of the International Federation for Research in Women's History. She writes on the home as a workplace and racialized gender and the state. Her books include the prize-winning monographs *Home to Work: Motherhood and the Politics of Industrial Homework in the United States* (Cambridge University Press, 1994) and *Caring for America: Home Health Workers in the Shadow of the Welfare State*, co-authored with Jennifer Klein (Oxford University Press, 2012, 2015). She is the co-editor, with Rhacel Parreñas, of *Intimate Labors: Cultures, Technologies, and the Politics of Care* (Stanford University Press, 2010), and with Dorothea Hoehtker and Susan Zimmermann, *Women's ILO: Transnational Networks, Global Labor Standards, and Gender Equity* (Brill and ILO, 2018). Her writing has appeared in a variety of scholarly publications and the popular press.

MARISELA R. CHÁVEZ is an associate professor and chair in the Department of Chicana and Chicano Studies at California State University, Dominguez Hills. She teaches and researches Chicana/o history, politics, and identity; women of color feminisms; US social movements; and oral history. Her most recent article, "Refocusing Chicana International Feminism: Photographs, Postmemory, and Political Trauma," was published in *Chicana Movidas: New Narratives of Activism and Feminism in the Movement Era* (University of Texas Press, 2018). Her publications also include articles in the collections *Memories and Migrations* and *No Permanent Waves*. She is revising a manuscript that traces Chicana and Mexican American women's activism in Los Angeles from the late 1960s to 1980.

CLAIRE DELAHAYE is an associate professor of American Studies at Université Paris-Est Marne-la-Vallée. Her award-winning doctoral research scrutinized Woodrow Wilson and the struggle for woman suffrage from a national and transnational perspective. It was published as *Wilson contre les femmes* (Paris: Presses de la Sorbonne Nouvelle, 2012). Her current research project addresses historiography and memory of the woman suffrage struggle after the passage of the Nineteenth Amendment. She was a visiting fellow at the Kluge Center at the Library of Congress in spring 2018. Recent publications include "Suffragistes et suffragettes," co-written with Beatrice Bijon (Lyon: ENS Editions, 2017), "'A Tract in Fiction': Woman Suffrage Literature and the Struggle for the Vote," in *European Journal of American Studies*, and "Le lobbying des suffragistes au Congrès (1913–1920)," in *Politique Américaine*.

NICOLE EATON is an instructor in the History Department at Simmons College. She served as a visiting assistant professor in the Department of History at Brown University before holding an appointment as lecturer in history and literature at Harvard University from 2013 to 2016. She researches and teaches about US social movements, public history, and women's history. Her forthcoming book explores the relationship between women's rights and women's history by tracing how historical memory shaped the fight for gender equality from the 1840s to the present day.

LIETTE GIDLOW is the 2019–2020 Mellon-Schlesinger Fellow for the Long Nineteenth Amendment Project at Harvard University's Radcliffe Institute and an associate professor of history at Wayne State University in Detroit. She is the author of *The Big Vote* (Johns Hopkins University Press, 2004) and the editor of *Obama, Clinton, Palin* (University of Illinois Press, 2012). Her current book project, *The Nineteenth Amendment and the Politics of Race, 1920–1970*, explores connections between the woman suffrage amendment and the black freedom movements of the 1950s and 1960s.

HOLLY MIOWAK GUISE (IÑUPIAQ) is a University of California President's Postdoctoral Fellow at the University of California, Irvine. Her book manuscript World War II and the First Peoples of the Last Frontier, focuses on gender, Aleut internment, Native activism, and Indigenous military service in Alaska during the war. Her research methods bridge together archives, tribal archives, community-based research, and oral histories with Alaska Native elders and veterans. She has received funding for her research from the Ford Foundation Predoctoral Fellowship, the Cook Inlet Historical Society, the Western History Association's Walter Rundell Award, the American Philosophical Society, and various fellowships from Yale University. Her digital humanities project, worldwar2alaska.com, features oral histories. In autumn 2020, she joins the Department of History at the University of New Mexico as an assistant professor.

EMILY SUZANNE JOHNSON is an assistant professor of history at Ball State University, specializing in US histories of gender, sexuality, politics, and religion. She is the author of *This Is Our Message: Women's Leadership in the New Christian Right* (2019), which examines the roles prominent women played in building the modern religious right since its ascendancy in the 1970s. Her work has been published in academic forums, including *Religion and American Culture*, and in popular forums, including the *Washington Post*.

DEAN J. KOTLOWSKI is professor of history at Salisbury University. He is the author of *Nixon's Civil Rights: Politics, Principle, and Policy* (Harvard University Press, 2001) and *Paul V. McNutt and the Age of FDR* (Indiana University Press, 2015) and the editor of *The European Union: From Jean Monnet to the Euro* (Ohio University Press, 2000). He has published more than forty articles and book chapters on US political, diplomatic, and transnational history. He has been a visiting fellow at the Humanities Research Centre at the Australian National University (2017) and a Fulbright Scholar three times, in the Philippines (2008), Austria (2016), and Australia (2020).

MONICA L. MERCADO is an assistant professor of history at Colgate University, affiliated with Women's Studies and Museum Studies. Her research and teaching focus on US women's history, American religion, and the role of women's, gender, and sexuality studies in developing public history sites and curricula. She is currently writing a history of nineteenth-century Catholic girlhoods, with the support of the Women's Studies in Religion Program at Harvard Divinity School, the University of Notre Dame's Cushwa Center for the Study of American Catholicism, and the National Endowment for the Humanities. From 2014 to 2016, she directed the Albert M. Greenfield Digital Center for the History of Women's Education at Bryn Mawr College.

JOHANNA NEUMAN is a scholar in residence at American University. Her latest book, *And Yet They Persisted: How American Women Won the Right to Vote*, traces the history of women's suffrage over two centuries, from the 1770s to the 1970s, expanding the movement's timeline and restoring African American women to the suffrage narrative. Her first book on the topic, *Gilded Suffragists: The New York Socialites Who Fought for Women's Right to Vote*, documents the role of the celebrity endorsements in galvanizing social change. A former journalist, she covered the White House, State Department, and Congress for *USA Today* and the *Los Angeles Times*. During her career as a journalist, she received a Nieman Fellowship at Harvard University and served as president of the White House Correspondents' Association.

KATHLEEN BANKS NUTTER was, until 2019, the accessioning archivist for Special Collections, Smith College. Nutter has also taught at Smith and other area colleges and held an appointment as lecturer in the History Department at Stony Brook University from 2004 to 2011. She is the author of *The Necessity of Organization: Mary Kenney O. Sullivan and Trade Unionism for Women, 1892–1912* (Garland Publishing, 2000; Routledge, 2019) and several articles, including "'Militant Mothers': Boston, Busing and the Bicentennial," which appeared in the *Historical Journal of Massachusetts* (2010).

KATHERINE PARKIN is professor of history and the Jules Plangere Jr. Chair in American Social History at Monmouth University in New Jersey. She is the author of *Food Is Love: Food Advertising and Gender Roles in Modern America* (University of Pennsylvania Press, 2005) and *Women at the Wheel: A Century of Buying, Driving, and Fixing Cars* (University of Pennsylvania Press, 2017), each of which won the Emily Toth Award for best book in women's studies and popular culture. Her teaching and research interests include the history of women and gender, sexuality, and advertising and consumerism. She has been interviewed by the *Economist*, the *New York Times*, the *Washington Post*, NPR's Bob Edwards on Sirius-XM, and WHYY's Marty Moss-Coane in Philadelphia.

ELLEN G. RAFSHOON is an associate professor and cochair of the History Program at Georgia Gwinnett College in Lawrenceville. She teaches courses on the Cold War, America in the 1960s, and immigration. Her most recent publication, "Esther Taylor: Hadassah Lady Turned Birth Control Advocate," examined the founding of the southeast's first Planned Parenthood chapter. She is currently working on a book on women's political activism since the 2016 presidential election.

BIANCA ROWLETT is an assistant professor of history at the University of South Carolina Sumter. Her research interests include American diplomatic history, specifically Cold War foreign relations; Russian history; and modern European history. Her current projects focus on Reagan-era diplomacy. In addition to teaching American and Russian history courses, Rowlett is a board member and treasurer for the South Carolina Historical Association and was voted Professor of the Year by the student body each year since she joined the USC Sumter faculty in 2016.

SARAH B. ROWLEY is an assistant professor of history at DePauw University, where she teaches a wide range of courses interrogating relationships of power and the intersections of culture and politics in modern America. Specializing in gender and politics in the recent United States, her prior work centers on abortion politics in the 1960s–1980s. Her article on the religious pronatalist Quiverfull movement was published in *Feminist Formations*, while a forthcoming essay on former California Rep. Yvonne Burke will appear in an edited collection on black women and feminism. She is currently working on a book about gender and party politics in the 1970s–1980s, which is centered on feminist congresswomen.

ANA STEVENSON is a postdoctoral research fellow in the International Studies Group at the University of the Free State, South Africa. A historian of feminism, her research examines women and transnational social movements in the United States, Australia, and South Africa from the nineteenth century to the present. In 2019, she was awarded the W. Turrentine Jackson (Article) Prize by the Pacific Coast Branch of the American Historical Association and the Covert Award in Mass Communication History by the History Division of the Association for Education in Journalism and Mass Communication. Her co-edited collection, *Gender Violence in Australia: Historical Perspectives* (Monash University Publishing, 2019), has recently been published and *The Woman as Slave in Nineteenth-Century American Social Movements* (Palgrave Macmillan, 2019) will appear with Palgrave Studies in the History of Social Movements.

BARBARA WINSLOW is a professor emerita at Brooklyn College/City University of New York. She is the founder and director emerita of the Shirley Chisholm Project of Brooklyn Women's Activism, 1945 to the present. She has written *Shirley Chisholm: Catalyst for Change* (Westview Press, 2013) and *Sylvia Pankhurst: Sexual Politics and Political Activism* (St. Martin's Press, 1996; reprinted Verso, 2021). She co-edited with Julie Gallagher, *Reshaping Women's*

Histories: Voices of Nontraditional Women Historians (University of Illinois Press, 2018), and with Carol Berkin and Margaret Crocco, *Clio in the Classroom: A Guide to Teaching US History* (Oxford University Press, 2009). Her articles have appeared in the *Journal of Women's History* and *Radical History Review*.

JUDY TZU-CHUN WU is a professor in the Department of Asian American Studies and director of the Humanities Center at the University of California, Irvine. She previously taught for seventeen years at The Ohio State University. She authored *Dr. Mom Chung of the Fair-Haired Bastards: The Life of a Wartime Celebrity* (University of California Press, 2005) and *Radicals on the Road: Internationalism, Orientalism, and Feminism during the Vietnam Era* (Cornell University Press, 2013). Her current book project, a collaboration with political scientist Gwendolyn Mink, explores the political career of Patsy Takemoto Mink, the first woman of color US congressional representative and the cosponsor of Title IX. She also is working on a book that focuses on Asian American and Pacific Islander women who participated in the 1977 National Women's Conference. Wu co-edited *Women's America: Refocusing the Past*, 8th ed. (Oxford University Press, 2015), *Gendering the Trans-Pacific World* (Brill, 2017), and *Frontiers: A Journal of Women's Studies* (2012–2017). She also co-edits *Women and Social Movements in the United States, 1600–2000* (Alexander Street Press) and *Amerasia Journal*.

NANCY BECK YOUNG is a professor of history at the University of Houston, where she has taught since 2007. Previously she taught at McKendree College in Lebanon, Illinois. The University Press of Kansas published her most recent book, *Two Suns of the Southwest: Lyndon Johnson, Barry Goldwater, and the 1964 Battle between Liberalism and Conservatism*, in 2019. Young is the author of several other books, most recently *Why We Fight: Congress and the Politics of World War II* (University Press of Kansas, 2013), which won the Guittard Book Prize. She is researching two more book manuscripts: one a biography of John Nance Garner, who burned all his papers, and another on the idea of the First Lady. She has also won multiple teaching awards and is a regular contributor and commentator for various media outlets, including the *Washington Post*, NPR, and the *New York Times*.

Catholic(s), 22, 38, 137, 224, 350, 369, 440
Catholic Church, 369
Catt, Carrie Chapman, 18–20, 347
Center for American Women and Politics, 43
Central America, 297, 304–5, 311; and "Dictatorships and Double Standards," 299; and Kirkpatrick Doctrine, 297, 303–4; and Jimmy Carter's policies toward, 304–5, 311; and Ronald Reagan's policies toward, 297, 304–5; and "U.S. Security in Latin America," 304–5. *See also* Latin America
Central Park, 69, 395–96, 400–402, 405, 408
Chacón, Soledad, 361
Champion of the Great American Family (1989), 37
Chapa, Evey, 35
Chappell, Marissa, 40
Chávez-García, Miroslava, 361
Chela, Sandoval, 259
Chicago, 17, 28, 83, 90–91, 93, 97–99, 101–2, 104–5, 166, 194, 251, 286–87, 325, 339, 397, 402, 407, 422
Chicana, Chicanas, 35, 360–61, 363, 365–70
Chicana civil rights history, 366
childcare, 26, 155, 252, 260, 277
Childs, Lydia Maria, 17
Chinese Exclusion Act (1882), 22
Chisholm, Shirley, 8, 33, 202–5, 212, 215, 236–37, 239–41, 243, 245–47, 249, 251, 253–54, 265, 280, 283, 288–90, 335, 337, 340, 346, 349, 404, 416, 441
Church, Mary Terrell, 17, 68, 81, 83, 103, 237, 345
Círculo Cultural "Isabel, la Católica," 363
cisgender, 327
citizenship, 4, 11, 13–16, 19, 22–24, 26, 29, 31, 44, 46, 86, 149–50, 237–38, 267, 278, 362–63, 365, 367, 387, 420, 426–27
citizenship school(s), 31
Citizens' Review Committee, 37

civic housekeeping, 15
Civil Rights Law of 1964, 31, 265; and Title VII, 31–32, 265
Civil War, 16, 103, 240, 305
Clark, Septima, 31
Clinton, Hillary Rodham, 3, 40, 42–43, 93, 97, 215, 252–53, 298, 316–20, 22–23, 325–29, 335–47, 350–51, 377, 382–84, 400, 415–16, 420, 423, 439
Clinton, William J. (Bill), 40, 42–43
clubwomen, 81, 83
Cobb County, Georgia, 387
Cold War, 23, 27–29, 187–88, 194, 267, 299, 303, 367, 441
Collier, Lillian, 164, 170
Collins, Patricia Hill, 328
Colorado, 37, 65, 182, 170
Colored Women's Republican Clubs, 103
commemoration, 8, 59–64, 66–67, 69, 212, 262, 268, 403, 406–7
communism (communist), 19, 21, 24, 28, 189, 299, 302–5, 321, 366–67
Communist Party (US), 24, 366
Communist Party Woman's Charter, 24
Community Service Organization (CSO), 364, 367
Comprehensive Child Development Act (1971), 33
Concerned Women for America, 322–23
Confederate monuments, 61, 396, 403
Congreso del Pueblo de Habla Española (Congress of Spanish-Speaking Peoples), 367
Congress (US), 10, 22, 33, 63, 113–13, 117, 156, 164, 220–21, 236, 240, 253, 262, 274, 288, 358, 394; and political party, 1, 26, 183, 189, 245, 251–52, 319; and pressure on, 18–19, 21, 34, 59, 62, 83, 205, 248–49, 259, 265, 276–77, 421; and progress, 2–4, 7, 11, 20, 32, 36, 41–43, 68, 92, 203, 207, 215, 337, 339; and representation, 275, 278, 289, 291, 359–60, 362, 398–99, 418, 425; and stance, 23, 31, 65, 102–3, 115, 230, 247, 280–81, 299, 303, 345, 348, 416, 428. *See also* House of Representatives; Senate (US)

feminist historians, 61, 209, 213–15; and Ellen Carol DuBois, 209, 214; and Gerda Lerner, 210, 212–13; and Kathryn Kish Sklar, 214

feminist movement(s), 3, 7, 10–11, 167, 249, 259, 326–27, 367, 381, 398

Fenwick, Millicent, 264

Ferguson, James E., 167

Ferraro, Geraldine, 39, 200, 207, 215, 340

Fierro de Bright, Josefina, 366–67

Fifteenth Amendment, 16, 76, 103, 238, 348

Files, Rae, 170

financial survival, 119

Flappers, 22

Flower, Lucy, 102

fluoridation, 28

Food and Drug Administration, 135

Ford, Christine Blasey, 424

Ford, Gerald R., 35, 257, 263–64

Ford, Henry, 97

Fox, Richard L., 44

Franklin County (NC), 45

Friedan, Betty, 202, 206, 249, 322

Furies Collective, 35

Gabbard, Tulsi, 44

Gallup Polls, 41

Garcia, Alma, 368

Garcia, Mario T., 365–66

Garcia, Sonia, 364

Garza, Alicia, 423

Gasque, Elizabeth Hawley, 113

gay, 319, 380, 406, 426. *See also* LGBT(I) people; queer; and same-sex (relationships)

gender, 26, 43, 94, 111, 183, 221, 247, 251, 276, 337, 339–41, 417, 426, 437–42; and inequality/equality, 2, 12, 20, 40, 42, 133, 167, 175, 177, 237, 282, 298–99, 322, 325, 327, 384, 388, 428; and race/class, 24, 31, 115, 188, 229–30, 232, 238–39, 242, 245, 259, 265, 328–29, 345, 349, 364, 418, 423; and roles, 18, 22, 25, 27, 34, 44, 95–96, 118, 134, 137, 194, 246, 277–78, 280, 287, 289–92, 308, 310,

321; and voting, 15, 19, 21, 39, 105, 203, 207, 317, 319–20, 324, 381, 422

gender essentialism, 421

Georgia, 44–45, 77–78, 113, 241, 280, 376–82, 384–89

Georgia State Assembly, 44

Georgia WIN List, 377, 382

gig economy, 418

Gilbert, Patricia, 30

Gillibrand, Kirsten, 44

Goldwater, Barry M., 30, 442

González, Gabriela, 363, 365–66

Great Depression, 23–24, 93, 101–2, 168, 298, 415, 419, 427

Great Migration, 238

Green New Deal, 414–15

Griffiths, Martha, 32, 276

Gruening, Governor Ernest, 147–48, 150–51

Gulf War, 41

Gutiérrez, Elena R., 368

Gutiérrez, José Angel, 363

Gwinnett County, Georgia, 379, 383

Hale, Effie Humphrey, 103

Hallingstad, Amy, 156–57

Hamer, Fannie Lou, 31–32, 251, 349

Hamilton, Grace Towns, 381

Handel, Karen, 380

Hanna, Mark, 91, 94, 100

Harding, Warren G., 19

Harper, Minnie Buckingham, 115

Harrel, Sally, Democrat Georgia State representative, 380

Harris, Kamala, 44, 427

Hawai'i (Hawai'i an), 11, 249, 257, 259, 263, 266–69; and Japanese American, 11, 257, 263, 267; and martial law, 268; and Native Hawaiian, 269; and settler colonialism, 269; and state-hood, 269

Hayes, Jahana, 425

Health, Education and Welfare, Department of, 129, 139, 140

Health and Human Services, Department of, 127, 140

health care, 1, 28, 133, 153–54, 320, 329, 340, 417–18, 422, 425–26, 438

CPSIA information can be obtained
at www.ICGtesting.com
Printed in the USA
LVHW041731121120
671534LV00004B/938

9 781421 438689